WORKSHOPS IN COMPUTING
Series edited by C. J. van Rijsbergen

Gillian Lovegrove and Barbara Segal (Eds.)

 # Women into Computing:
Selected Papers 1988–1990

BCS

Springer-Verlag London Ltd.

Gillian Lovegrove, MA, PhD, MBCS
Department of Electronics and Computer Science
University of Southampton
Southampton, SO9 5NH

Barbara Segal, BSc
Department of Computer Science
University College London
Gower Street, London, WC1

ISBN 978-3-540-19648-8

British Library Cataloguing in Publication Data
Women into computing: selected papers, 1988–1990 –   (Workshops in computing)
  1. Great Britain computer industries & services. Women personnel
  2. Great Britain. Education. Curriculum subjects. Computer systems.
  I. Lovegrove, Gillian *1942–*   II. Segal, Barbara *1944–*   III. British
  Computer Society   IV. Series
004.07041
ISBN 978-3-540-19648-8   ISBN 978-1-4471-3875-4 (eBook)
DOI 10.1007/978-1-4471-3875-4

Library of Congress Cataloging-in-Publication Data
Women into computing: selected papers, 1988–1990/Gillian Lovegrove and
Barbara Segal. eds.
  p. cm. – (Workshops in computing)
"Published in collaboration with the British Computer Society." Includes
bibliographical references and index.
ISBN 978-3-540-19648-8
  1. Women electronic data processing personnel–Congresses.
2. Women electronic data processing personnel–Training of–Congresses.
I. Lovegrove, Gillian, 1942–   . II. Segal, Barbara. 1944–   . III. British
Computer Society.   IV. Series.
HD6073.D37W66 1991   90-22308
331.4'81004–dc20   CIP

2128/3830–543210   Printed on acid-free paper

Preface

This book contains the majority of the papers presented at the 1990 Women into Computing Conference, together with selected papers from the 1989 and 1988 Conferences. In 1988, the main theme running through the Conference was that of dismay at the low number of women taking computing courses or following computing careers. The 1989 Conference was concerned solely with workshops for schoolgirls and the 1990 Conference concentrated on strategies rather than an assessment of the situation.

As editors, we set as our task to make a selection of papers presenting the overall picture in 1990. We found that many of the issues discussed in 1988 are still a cause for concern in 1990, but that strategies to improve the situation are many and varied.

Section I contains speeches from the invited speakers and needs little introduction. Section II contains papers covering some attitudes and issues of concern, ranging from the specific (Gill Russell on child care and Laurie Keller on hacker mentality) through to broader aspects of gender inequality (the papers of Flis Henwood, Margaret Bruce and Alison Adam, and Lyn Bryant). Susan Jones takes a look at the reasons why we should want to see more women in computing, whilst Gillian Lovegrove and Wendy Hall present a more general paper on school and higher education.

Section III concerns school education. Some of the papers here reflect statistical surveys (Philippa Buckley and Barbara Smith on GCSE choices, Judy Donnelly on the computer education of A-level students, Helen Watt on computing experience both at home and school, and Peter Glissov on various attitudinal factors), whereas those of Audrey Milner, Elaine Coleman and Janet Spavold are based on general observations in the classroom. Linda Anderson presents a case study of a single female pupil and Irene Pacitti describes some cooperative schools/industry projects in the Govan district of Glasgow.

The section on Higher and Further Education starts with two papers reporting students' attitude surveys (Alan Durndell and also Konrad Morgan and his colleagues). The paper of Karen Shipp and Diane Sutton and also that of Gill Kirkup and her colleagues discuss Open University initiatives to make computing courses attractive to women students. Jagdev Bansal discusses practical issues affecting women who would like to take computing courses at Birmingham Polytechnic.

The paper by Nicky Gunson and Peter Fielder and that by Anne Leeming arise from a critical look at management practices. Kathy Buckner puts forward the argument that success on an IT course does not relate to a maths background. Janet Johnson and Dave Arnold describe initiatives for the recruitment of women undergraduates, whilst Carol Whitesmith makes some interesting comments on industrial placements and subsequent job offers (or the lack of them).

With the exception of the paper by Philip Virgo and colleagues, which is concerned with the WIT Campaign, all the papers in Section V describe specific courses for women returners. It is encouraging to see that such courses exist over a wide geographical area and are designed for women from a range of educational backgrounds.

The careers section starts with a description of the UK Federation of Business and Professional Women by Christine Arrowsmith and continues with a description of career paths in the artificial intelligence domain, followed by a paper by Valeria Edgar-Nevill on the general area of careers in IT management.

WiC, with its roots in higher education, has placed a priority on organising events intended to encourage schoolgirls to consider computing as a possible area of study or employment. The papers in Section VII, with three exceptions, describe workshops for schoolgirls over the country. Each workshop has it own characteristics, with some directed towards a younger age-group, some residential, some large and some small. Helen Watt provides a useful prescription for organising a successful workshop, whilst Karen Shipp describes a workshop aimed at exploring women's prejudices about computing. The paper by Carole Goble and Caroline Moss describes the activity of the Greater Manchester WiC group.

Section VIII begins with accounts by Gillian Lovegrove and Dalene McShane of activities and initiatives in Europe concerned with technology and gender equality. The papers from Lorna Uden and Alan Durndell both describe societies where there appears to be no problem in attracting women to technical occupations and discuss some of the factors involved. The section ends with an account by Colin Beardon of measures taken at a university in New Zealand to increase the numbers of under-represented groups in computing courses.

The topics discussed in these papers illustrate that the authors are predominantly from education. The organisation called Women into Computing (WiC) exists to coordinate and promote activities mainly in the educational sector designed to make women aware of the opportunities for worthwhile and fulfilling careers in computing. Other national efforts have similar aims: WISE (Women into Science and Engineering) was launched in 1984 by the Equal Opportunities Commission and Engineering Council and its aim was to encourage more women to take up careers in science and engineering and to encourage industry to consider positively the employment of women, particularly at higher professional and technical levels of employment (see the paper by Baroness Platt in Section I). The Women into Information Technology Campaign (WIT), launched in 1988, parallels that of WISE but concentrates specifically on the IT sector (see the paper by Philip Virgo in Section V). WIT's Council of Directors is made up solely of representatives from major technical UK firms and professional organisations. WITEC is the COMETT Programme for Women into Technology in the European Community University Enterprise Training Partnership and was established in 1988 as a European network of partners working for the motivation, development and support of women in science, technology and enterprise (see the paper by Dalene McShane in Section VIII).

We take pride in the fact that this book represents the work of many women and men in computing besides that of the authors of the papers. We are grateful to Daf Tregear and Peggy Newton for their work on the 1988 papers and for the bibliography (see Appendix A). Gill Kirkup and members of the Open University, Jennifer Stapleton at Reading University, Hilary Buxton at Queen Mary College, Carol Whitesmith and Lisa Payne at Coventry Polytechnic were very helpful with their comments on the papers. Robin Ward also gave generously of her time in proof-reading.

It is hard to single out certain universities and polytechnics when so many contribute to WiC activities, but as regards this book, we are especially grateful to University College London and Southampton University for allowing us generous support including our time, advice from LaTeX experts (Sebastian Rahtz and Les Carr) and secretarial help (Marie Turner, Julie Clarke and above all, Kiran Mistry).

September 1990   Gillian Lovegrove
                              Department of Electronics and Computer Science
                                              University of Southampton

                                                              Barbara Segal
                                      Department of Computer Science
                                              University College London

Contents

Section V: Women Returners

Section VI: Careers

Section VII: WiC Activities

Section VIII: International and Cultural

1

Women into Computing: The need for Positive Action Now

Joanna Foster[1]

According to all the forecasts, the 1990's will be a time of rapid social, demographic and economic change. The employment market of the 1990s is likely to be characterised by severe skills shortages, particularly in the areas of science, technology and information technology. Labour market forecasts have indicated that to meet the projected increase in labour demand generally employers must be more effective about recruiting, training and retaining the skills of more women. And in computing and information technology the extent of the problem of skills shortages and pressing need to develop and use the skills of women works is made obvious by such activities as the WIT campaign, backed by the DTI and a large number of major UK IT employers.

The NCC Report "The IT Skill Crisis: the way ahead", estimates that given current wastage rates from industry and the fact that over half the professional level intake are graduates, a 40% increase in the recruitment of graduate trainees is required to maintain current policies and plans. At the same time, the number of school and college leavers entering the labour force is now falling sharply as a result of the declining birth rate over the past couple of decades. A further drop of 25% in the number of school leavers is predicted over the next 5 years.

So girls and women are excellently placed to benefit from the extensive employment opportunities in computing and IT over the next decade - and most importantly, to lay down their own terms. Attracting women into computing and IT cannot be seen as a short-term stop-gap measure which can be abandoned when the recruitment targets of major employers have been met. Nor can employers hope to attract girls and women into company cultures designed to meet the career patterns and aspirations of men. A fundamental shift in attitude and practice is necessary amongst those employers who are so desperate for skilled workers that they will take anyone - even women! The quote from one of the organisers of the WIT Campaign shows exactly what we are up against!

Women will be attracted into computing and IT when it is made clear to them by industry and government that they are crucial and sought after, that this traditionally male dominated area of learning and work (computers have been in schools ten years and in industry from 1946; how quickly men establish traditional ownership!) - is eminently suitable for women, is rewarding, satisfying and is designed to accommodate

[1] Equal Opportunities Commission, Overseas House, Quay Street, Manchester M3 3HN

women's as well as men's life patterns. This means that a tremendous shift in image is required. The traditional male ethos must be replaced by one which is women and family friendly in all its aspects. And this applies not only in the computing industry itself, but also in computing departments in further education (FE) and higher education (HE) and in schools.

The size of the task should not be under-estimated. It is clear from recent statistics that not only do women not choose to study computing and IT but that their disillusionment with this type of learning and work has actually grown over the past decade. The proportions of girls taking computer qualifications of all types from GCSE to degree level is falling. Generally, the higher the qualification level, the more rapid the fall. For instance, in 1981 28.5% of students who passed in computer examinations at "O" level were girls. In 1985 the figure had fallen to 26.8%. In 1978, 22% of students studying for "A" level computer qualifications were girls. But by 1985 this had fallen to 17.7%. In 1981 the number of women accepted by universities for computer science courses was 22.3%, but as the trend indicates, by 1986 the figure has fallen to 13.9%.

Why, when the numbers of girls in other male-oriented subjects are rising gradually, does computing show a slump? Research indicates that the *way* IT was introduced into school is the major cause of girls "turning off". You will probably recall that in the early 80's the government introduced programmes designed to place computers in all schools and to train teachers in their uses. The "Micros in Schools" scheme enabled a school via the LEA to purchase a subsidised micro-computer; the Micro-electronics in Education Programmes enabled a school to nominate teachers for in-service training in programs and usage. This resulted in a situation where computers were generally placed in maths departments and were understood and used primarily by male teachers using male-friendly programs and games which boys responded to eagerly. Any attempts to make this type of learning attractive to girls has, therefore, had the negative image of the male/maths association to overcome first.

The delivery and image of computing and IT in schools continues to be an area of vital importance in determining girls' attitudes to computing as a subject and as a subsequent career and as such should be a major target of any attempt to increase participation rates of girls and women at FE/HE level and in industry.

School based education is the primary source of skilled people - and the best opportunity for the individual to acquire sound skills. Upskilling and retraining of women can increase the pool of potential IT labour but if the initial system of delivery of IT learning in the classroom is wrong, and this is not rectified, then the problem will continue. In fact, it is likely to get worse because girls now in the education system will be "turned off" information technology and computing and are therefore less likely to retrain at a later stage in their careers, whereas current "retrainees" will not have experienced IT in their schooling and may be more receptive to its opportunities as a result.

So what can be done to make computer education in schools more girl-friendly? One of the simplest devices is a purely technical one - don't give girls the chance to reject computing and IT before they realise the dire consequences of their decision for subsequent career opportunities.

Delaying subjects choices is a strategy for improving uptake amongst girls which, coupled with good teaching, is likely to have a very positive effect.

The approach to IT for the National Curriculum advocated by the Design and Technology Working Group ensures that all pupils will have acquired "a firm basis of knowledge, skills, understanding and values in IT capability". It continues, "In the fourth key stage we anticipate that many pupils will wish to develop their IT capability ... on this basis we recommend that pupils should be able to take a GCSE in Information Systems".

This approach would appear to be beneficial to girls who would acquire IT learning up to the age of 16 with access to an appropriate GCSE.

However, the Government has vetoed proposals from the working group to boost computers in schools because it is not prepared to meet the cost. In addition, the Government has decided to cut spending on computer education by £5 million despite the launch in 1988 of a 5 year initiative "IT in schools" and the appointment of 650 advisory teachers, amid speculation that the National Curriculum would have massive resource implications which would be met.

This is particularly worrying in the light of the recent report "Information technology from 5-16, April 1989", which found that schools are unable to meet pupils' demands for computing courses and girls are falling behind boys in using computers in the classroom. "The number of pupils opting for examinable courses in computing is usually greater than the school can provide for."

So many schools are physically unable to meet the demand for computing courses at the present time and indications so far are that the National Curriculum will not alter this situation. Attempts to increase take-up of computing courses by girls may fail because schools are unable to support in principle or practice an increased pool of exam candidates. This situation must be challenged. WiC should:

1. make strong representations to Government on the the damage to girls' opportunities in IT (and therefore the pool of skilled IT labour),

   - by restricting spending on computers in schools and thus
   - failing to support the approach to IT advocated by the National Curriculum working party;

2. identify this problem to employers and the WIT working parties. It is likely that a physical increase in the numbers of computers in schools (sponsored by employers if necessary) will do more good in increasing interest and subsequent uptake at HE level than just talking to girls about IT as a career, which may raise expectations which the school is unable to meet.

Another Strategy for making more girl-friendly in schools is the introduction of single-sex groupings.

One of the main problems for girls and IT is their failure to acquire time on computers which are dominated by boys. Some schools have sought to rectify this by running girls only computer clubs. However, it would seem sensible to advocate single-sex teaching groups within curriculum time which would ensure that girls not only get the opportunity to use the computers but could also benefit from software geared to their needs and interests and a woman teacher as role model. The single-sex group proposition could be extended to courses in colleges, universities etc and for retraining and upskilling courses.

The importance of *role models* in influencing the subject choices and career choices which girls make at school should not be underestimated. It would be interesting to examine to what extent the male image of IT is borne out in reality; to identify who teaches IT in schools, colleges, universities; who talks about IT and its applications in industry to school-children; who are the role models within industry for career progression for women? I suspect that the picture would be very bleak.

IT is an extremely male-oriented industry and strategies to encourage girls have to take on board the importance of women role models in all sectors in influencing girls' attitudes to IT. Any initiative which fails to recognise and address this issue is unlikely to succeed in breaking down stereotyping in IT which has been attributed directly to the masculine image of technology in the classroom. Role models from industry talking about careers in IT – in a school where computers are based in the male domain of the maths department – are unlikely to make any significant impact.

Women from industry should actually go into schools to do some IT teaching/project work. Perhaps secondment for one term funded by industry is an idea which could be explored further.

Initial teacher-training establishments should be encouraged to address under-representation of women IT teachers in school and at FE and HE level, and to include IT modules on their courses for all student teachers.

The elimination of gender bias from teaching programmes and materials is vital. Girls must have equal ownership of IT/computing in the classroom if they are to be able to relate to the message "careers in IT" in any meaningful way. The Equal Opportunities Commission (EOC) has taken an active role in encouraging girls to study IT in schools the last ten years and has funded guidelines for good practice which are helpful tools in the task of making computing and IT girl-friendly. [2]

School-based education, successfully delivered, can lay the foundation for a career choice of computing and IT. However, it is essential that FE/HE support and build on these foundations by changing their image and practices. Girls may study and enjoy IT at school, but will only choose computing at FE/HE level when the prospect is sufficiently attractive. Further Education/Higher Education needs to identify its target groups – school leavers and women returners/mature entrants and to develop strategies which will satisfy their special needs. This will undoubtedly necessitate a review

---

[2] 1983 *Information Technology in Schools* – Guidelines of good practice for teachers of IT – was published. This work was produced by the London Borough of Croydon with EOC funding. 1986 *Investigation of gender differences in the take-up of computer studies in secondary schools* Lorraine Culley, Nottingham, EOC funded.
Dec 1986 *Equal Opportunities and Computer Education in the Primary School* – Guidelines of good practice for teachers – report of project funded by the EOC, DTI and Sheffield LEA. One copy sent to every primary school.

and revision of policy and practice – which is currently based on the assumption of male students, taught by male lecturers to provide male employees for male dominated industries.

Computing and IT has a negative image for the majority of girls and women. This is clear from the fall in participation rates. This image must be improved. Girls and women making choices about careers need to understand what computing courses are all about, what they can offer. So FE/HE must take a critical look at their presentation, starting with the prospectus and course descriptions, and photographs should be checked. Does the description explain the relevance of the course to work choices? Does it refer to project work and team work – methods of learning which are known to appeal to girls and women?

When courses are advertised in local schools a statement should be included saying girls are welcome to apply, and descriptions of women undergraduates and their work can be given. To attract mature students, recruitment material should be prepared which identifies ways in which the provision on offer can overcome their perceived "barriers to access". So, flexible timing of courses, crèche facilities, women lecturers and tutors, availability of grants, counselling, taster courses must all be highlighted. Higher Education should not be guilty of selling its wares to a narrowly defined market of grammar and independent schools; all adjacent schools should be visited and circulated with material and local events for women should be targeted and brochures left in public places like doctors' surgeries and supermarkets.

Colleges should offer girls/women-only open days which could include the opportunity for hands on experience and discussion with women lecturers. School - FE/HE links can be strengthened by inviting groups of girls to visit and work on main-frames, perhaps doing project work for GCSE.

Under S.47 of the Sex Discrimination Act, (1975) FE/HE can run single-sex courses to encourage girls and women onto non-traditional types of employment. This approach has been adopted very successfully by the EITB to encourage school-girls into engineering, and similar taster courses in computing are producing very positive recruitment results, particularly in Scotland. Funding for such courses in computing is subject to support from industry and therefore, not guaranteed on a long-term basis. Representations could be made to government to establish a fund for this purpose.

Further Education/Higher Education should widen access and revise their admissions policy. What "A" levels are required by HE? Are they essential? Admissions tutors should look for a wider range of qualifications and include more arts subjects. Why are female applicants rejected? Is there a common denominator? Certain entry qualifications can be modified or waived for mature students and women returners. If necessary, a modified course running under S.47 can be run for women only, eg a pre-degree course or refresher course for women who may have graduated 10-15 years ago.

The concept of girl-friendly schooling is now widely understood and is being developed in schools. However, the same concept does not yet appear to have caught on at FE/HE level, - except amongst WiC members! The sorts of issues to be considered include teaching styles and presentation, seminar and tutorial organisation – making sure girls fully participate, they tend to be the quiet ones – use of project work and teamwork to create a supportive environment for students who may lack confidence.

Employers are the final link in the chain. Employers can help to attract girls and women into computing and IT by sponsoring, financially and physically, positive action in schools at FE/HE level. However, employers must not be lulled into thinking that they can "buy" themselves out of skills shortages by providing cash for external quick-fix recruitment solutions. Retention of staff and securing long-term supply is crucial, and women will not stay in a working environment which cannot accommodate their dual needs of job satisfaction and family responsibilities. Employers need to ask why they are failing to attract women into computing, to take a long hard look at their own image and practices and to adopt an equal opportunity strategy which tackles problem areas head on and in a positive way. The following issues should be considered:

- the image the company presents to the outside world – it should be linked with the local community, it should open its doors for visits from outside groups, it should encourage work-shadowing schemes, and send women ambassadors into schools;

- recruitment and advertising material should address and feature women and men and should invite applications from women specifically (S48 makes positive action in recruitment advertising lawful. However, selection must be done on merit alone). – Recruitment and selection methods – companies should extend the pool of potential employees from newly qualified graduates to include women from non-technical areas such as arts and languages and mature entrants;

- career development for women – job descriptions for promoted posts should not simply reflect the job as performed by the previous (male) post-holder, but should identify skills and responsibilities in a non-gender biased way;

- training – to enhance promotion opportunities for all staff and to ensure that special needs of women who may have entered the company via a non-traditional route are met. Employers can provide special training and upskilling for existing employees who show aptitude, eg secretaries and women with higher qualifications who work in low-skilled jobs (due to discrimination or no opportunities for women to be promoted due to job segregation).

Flexible working conditions – part-time work, job-sharing, flexible hours – should be introduced, as well as career break schemes to accommodate domestic responsibilities and enhance career progression for women and men.

The need for co-operation between education and industry to encourage girls and women into IT, is undisputed; however, the way that co-operation is translated into practical action is vital to fulfilling the objectives. Ad hoc measures to meet skills shortages may have short-term impact in increasing recruitment, but are unlikely to reverse the negative trend in the long-term or to open up in any meaningful way opportunities for women in IT. School, universities and industry must adopt strategies which tackle the reasons for under-representation of girls and women directly and on a long-term basis.

Good equal opportunity policy and practice must become a permanent fixture in the teaching of computing and IT, and in the computing industry. Investment in getting structures right now will reap massive rewards for the economy of the country, striving to compete in the wider European market and for some women themselves who are now rightly demanding careers on their own terms and who have a right to the rewards a career in computing can bring.

2

Beyond the Great Divide

Mrs Steve Shirley, OBE[1]

Let[2] me start by asking the question: Why in 1988 do we have to run a conference on this theme?

After all, didn't sex discrimination and equal opportunities cease to be an issue once the 1975 Act came into force? The battle is won, say the media pundits, surely we don't need any more of these sex specific conferences and seminars?

The fact is, the legal battle may be almost won, but there is still a great psychological war to sort out. For reasons of training and school encouragement – even of colour coding at birth (you know, blue for a boy and therefore mechanical things, pink for a girl and therefore dolls) – far too few women are grasping the enormous opportunities that exist in some of the most exciting employment fields available to them – and computing is one area I put right at the top of the list.

The fundamental problem, as you all know, is that although most companies employ more and more women, (it's rapidly hitting the half-way mark) the curves look like a large over-ripe pear – all the women lumped in the lower part of the company hierarchy and very few rising to the top. When we look at technical and management positions, fewer than 10% of senior jobs are held by our half of the population. The spread is better in some service industry sectors such as advertising and marketing, but as soon as we look at any job where there is the slightest whiff of technical skill needed, the position deteriorates rapidly.

If we examine the computing industry and look at the figures there, the pear becomes really soggy. A survey last year showed that only 2% of managers in the computing industry were women, and only 18% of programmers were women. Yet down at the bottom in the less skilled, less sophisticated areas of data input, 95% of the work was carried out by women. This just isn't good enough.

Here we have a situation where the most aggressive, the most dynamic, the most all-pervading force that will dominate business in the 21st century, is being denied to half the population. Strangely, this is apparently through women's choice, or so we are often told. Much more likely it is because teachers in schools, parents at home – especially grandparents, they are the worst offenders because they are deeply rooted in the social values of the 1920's and 30's – all these people around us are shaping attitudes and directing girls in schools away from the opportunities open to them. I need hardly tell this audience with so many educators in it, that women are very

---

[1] F I Group plc, Hemel Hempstead HP2 7EZ
[2] This paper is from the 1988 conference

impressionable during the teenage period and seem to be less ready to defy convention than boys – (although the punk revolution may have been the first signs of a change here!). It is during this teenage period of uncertainty in a girl's life, that the older generations within the family can have a bad effect and turn their offspring away from technically-oriented careers because "they are for the boys".

Schools are not altogether blameless either – how many times have I seen form mistresses and careers managers suggesting that the girl interested in medicine should take up nursing (a boy would automatically think of becoming a doctor) or an interest in food and marketing being directed towards home economics instead of a degree in biochemistry or business school. I was at a school recently which not only had a careers master for the boys and a careers mistress for the girls – neither of whom attempted to specialise – but were surprised that I was upset about it!

Research carried out on why women don't enter computing highlights a lack of career-break opportunities to have babies, lack of crèches in companies, too few flexi-time working hours and many other short-term problems. This is all rubbish!

It is an excuse, an apologia, for the barriers that have been created by a society and have been erected within our career guidance structure – that is why the presence of so many teachers here today is so vital because together we must find ways to get Women into Computing.

First of all, let's clear away some of the fundamental misconceptions that exist about the working mother. The American child psychiatrist Dr. Sanger, who founded the Early Care Centre in New York, has published the results of a 10-year study. Far from working mothers being the cause of childhood problems, the children of mothers who work were seen to develop better than other children and the fact of work and what it did for the mother's intellectual and emotional attitudes, actually enhance her child's development.

The evidence shows that, although there may be some slowing of language skills if the child does not spend time in adult company all day, there is a compensating development in inter-active social skills and growth in confidence. In a nutshell, Sanger says – and the great child psychologist Piaget supports this – a mother's task surely is to launch her offspring into the wide world with sufficient confidence and skills to make a success of their life.

The information society is a devourer of skills. Unlike the first industrial revolution, it does not require brute strength to work in computing, but rather flexibility, creativity, deftness.

The speed of change acts in women's favour as regards any career gap. For when employers know that everyone has to be retrained year after year then it matters *less* if someone has been out of the workforce for whatever reason . . . like having a baby.

So, Ladies, banish all those guilt feelings and rationalise your attitudes towards work and management. Do you want to reach a senior position in computing – is the Boardroom your ultimate goal? Directorships are jobs like any other jobs and the skill must be learnt, the effort made and the sacrifices weighed against personal gains.

Knowledge, skills, commitment, honour – all old-fashioned words? And, of course, courtesy and quality – that has little to do with gender. So I'd advise women not to always think about being a woman, but think about the business in hand and about your colleagues. It does seem that the current emphasis on assertiveness and on self-presentation is dangerous in shifting the emphasis from the right preoccupation on actually conveying what you are trying to convey, to a misguided preoccupation with yourself saying it. If you look at yourself all the time, you will blame others for not understanding you. If you think about them, you will sharpen your ability to say things in a way which reaches them. That is true for both men and women.

I do not deny the importance of points of presentation – dress for example – of course they are important, but in business I see them as within the context of courtesy and as affecting others' expectations.

The real problem when it comes to motivation, is one of role models. There are very few women with the appropriate track record in management, with related disciplines or an understanding of public affairs gained from experience in societies and institutions to get them to the top. The perception of women tends to assign them to other roles. These perceptions unfortunately are held by women as well as men. The biological fact that women bear children and the expectation that women rear children has inevitably affected our careers quite differently to those of men. Indeed there were more women in senior positions in our computing industry 30 years ago when some career women were prepared to give up marriage altogether. Since that time we have tried to accommodate both sets of pressures: career and family, and the job market has not adjusted to the fact.

In 1959 when I made it clear that I was going to go on working after marriage, the widespread, almost universal reaction from family and friends was "Oh, I thought Derek had a good job", as if the only reason a married woman would work was for the money. Nowadays, in most social circles, a girl would be considered lazy if she did not contribute to the family finances after she was married. In my youth, to continue working once there were children was considered outrageous – the emphasis on bonding with the family and the horror stories of unloved children turning to drugs and delinquency was an incredibly powerful threat which haunted my generation.

As I said earlier, research is showing such views to be outdated and we must be prepared to go onto platforms and appear in the press saying so. We must not be afraid in business to argue our case – there are far too many women who can't see a parapet without ducking behind it. You don't build an empire, however well-timed in the market, by sweet smiles alone – I can say that from experience. I'm using outmoded metaphors. So it is that society reinforces itself.

Looking round this audience, can I remind you that the need to get women into computing is not only for women but for humanity. Technology can so easily dehumanise. Military technologies ... just look at some of the games ... are measured in terms of *firepower* and *megadeaths*. If today's information technology revolution is not to repeat the mistakes and misery of the industrial revolution, girls have got to stop seeing computing as alien, dangerous and complicated.

Society needs women's understanding and women's contribution. As a woman who got into computing very early in its history – and while I think this may be something you may wish to ask me about in question time, let me share with you some more current experiences within the computing industry.

When I first found myself negotiating with unions, I was totally unprepared for the brutality of the language used and apparently intransigent positions. Then it was my belief that I was a skilled negotiator because meetings finished in much better mood than they started. Later still, I realised the first layer of truth - the officials needed to go out of the meeting and tell their colleagues "I told the silly woman XXXX" and began to respect them as people of honour.

One of the most powerful words in management is "We". It links the different coloured collars, it links the different coloured skins; at worst it triggers the question of "Who is we?" and that of itself is the start of understanding. Yet it is amazingly difficult to divest that egoistic "I". Many a letter has had to be re-written because too many paragraphs start with "I this ... " "I that ... ".

What is stopping women getting into computing? Often it is *us*. We are our own worst enemies. If we want to get into the game, we have to learn the rules. The importance of body language – male body language because that is the sex of most computing environments – cannot be over- emphasised. The outward symbols of business matter – they matter a lot. What message do I get when recruiting a computer consultant when an obviously competent woman attends the interview in a décolleté dress? Do I choose to see her representing my company to its customers in the City? Or do I choose the sober-suited man who clones my target audience? If I like to have a range of clothes in different colours and fashionable styles, then I must compete in price and cut with the classic suit my husband has for best – because that is what the competing salesmen will wear. All of us are in sales. We sell ideas, we sell our concepts. We sell ourselves. I am conscious that the inability to place me in a class, whereabouts in the country do I come from, acts in my favour. And I will build and capitalise on those strengths.

Companies that conform to the individual attract and keep the best. ICI is starting to consider couples where neither have the "lead operation". Previously, ICI expected people to move where sent, the exceptions being health or elderly parents or children's schooling, never a spouse. Harvey Jones consistently refers to managers as males with female spouses though he throws in the occasional "he or she". As a small attempt I try to use the non-sexist terms, for example, "each manager should submit his claim form by ... " can be replaced by the plural "managers should submit their claim forms by ... ". It takes a bit of effort but I do find it worthwhile. Language plays an important part in easing the processes of change – often by linking new concepts to familiar ones.

Chairmen (there are few women chairing major public companies, though Woolworths has its woman CE) find it hard to invite giggly women – no matter how innovative – to join their Boards. Even when attending social functions, women in industry – even a young industry like computing – are expected to look the part, not the sex symbol, and if this is the price a woman does not want to pay, she has to recognise it.

Committees in particular have local ways of working and the newcomer of either sex needs to observe and understand the way the chair operates. Points need to be made clearly, unemotionally (or you pretend to lose your temper, that's one weapon though not to be used overmuch). Actually to lose your temper or perhaps worse, break into tears, is not on. Monthly health problems are just that – health problems – and have no place in computing. Neither do flirtations nor relationships with other people at work. If such a relationship is going to get in the way, then one or other has to get out – and before the gossip starts and before the organisation is endangered.

Let me focus onto the particular career path we are discussing today. The world of computing, because of the nature of its technology and the work itself, is probably one of the most suitable – and exciting – jobs for any woman to enter.

Forget then all that rubbish about career paths being broken and lack of crèche facilities – computing is one of the few jobs where working from home is as easy and as well-paid as working in a traditional office, so long as you are well-trained.

For those of you who are not up-to-date, my company the F I Group employs (on a consultancy, part-time and full-time basis) over 1,000 highly-qualified, highly-trained women working on a networked basis all over the country, providing some of the most sophisticated computing systems in use today. We handle massive defence contracts, systems for banks and City institutions and work on a partnership basis with all the great computer companies like IBM, DEC and UNISYS. Because of the way computing systems can be linked up, programmers can call in help from each other; they can work at any time of the day or night; and, in the process, give a service to our clients that is more efficient and frequently more sophisticated than can be offered by our competitors. We are a 92% female organisation, and I'm pleased to see Microsyster here too.

We are able to draw upon some of the most experienced systems analysts available today, executives who would be lost to the business community if they were forced to travel into the traditional office centres on a regular 9-5 schedule.

Another thing. The demographics of the 1990's and 21st century are such that there will be a major shortage of young people coming out of our universities, just at the time when the demand for computer-trained managers is rising to a peak.

You, or your pupils and students, are moving into a sellers market. This means that the pressure on companies to offer jobs that suit the employee (not the employer) is going to get heavier. In computing most successful companies have a labour turnover between 5-15% although the average is around 20%. It is forecast that in London and the South East this will rise to 40% per annum. What an opportunity that is.

The demand to accept home-working, more flexible hours and the use of the external consultant is growing all the time. This growth you'll be pleased to hear, applies to salaries too. If I had to make a prediction, I'd say that of all the jobs open to men or women in the next decade, the computing industry offers the fastest promotion prospects, one of the best salary scales and (as far as women are concerned) the most flexible opportunities for working unusual hours, or working from home during the child-rearing period. We couldn't have structured a better profession or skill that meets women's dual needs of career and home, if we had tried.

I don't need to go into detail of opportunities, speakers from IBM and various software companies will be filling in on this type of detail later. Just take it from me that this is one of the great growth opportunities for women of this decade. I should know. I've devoted my life – to date – to the computing industry, I've built one of the major software and systems houses. And made my pittance into the bargain! Everyone in this room can do the same if they really want to.

Let me finish this Introduction. Over the next two days we must examine where the psychological blocks exist. We are here in Lancaster not just to talk but to find practical ways for women returning to the workforce after a gap, and our bright young women just entering the world of work, to grasp the computing opportunities available. We are here in Lancaster for one purpose: to work out how to get more Women into Computing. We have responsibility to this generation and we must not fail them.

3

Computing in Schools: the Same Old Story

Robin Ward[1]

Why do we have conferences on "Women into Computing"? Why are articles, papers, books, etc written on the subject of computers and women? The fact that it is still thought necessary to raise people's awareness of the situation is a sad comment on the efforts of so many people in the past.

Two years ago, in July 1988, I addressed the first WiC conference at the University of Lancaster. There were many delegates dedicated to widening horizons, destroying stereotypes and encouraging members of the female sex to consider jobs or careers in computing.

I spoke at some length about the project **Girls and Information Technology** which I had just completed for Croydon and the Equal Opportunities Commission. I bemoaned the fact that not a great deal of headway had been made since WISE year (Women into Science and Engineering) in 1984.

I wrote a report which contained many suggestions for teachers, schools and LEAs. With many other like-minded people, I contributed articles and chapters in books, visited schools and other educational establishments, talked at meetings and conferences, and felt that the word was being spread! All it would take was for people to be made aware of the situation!

I am not sure how many people attending the 1990 WiC Conference were present at the launch conference in 1988 or, indeed, attend other conferences on the same subject. I could hazard a guess that there are quite a number. During the two years I spent on the **Girls in IT Project**, I travelled to quite a few conferences, exhibitions and seminars around the country. It was a wonderful opportunity to see friends, discuss what we had been doing since the last conference, exhibition, seminar, etc. The word was spreading all right – but to those who were already committed!

How easy it is to appear wise; how exhilarating it is to be applauded for stating the obvious to an audience who already agrees, in principle, with what you are saying. I assume that you are here because you are in favour of equal opportunities in its widest sense. You are interested in encouraging girls and women into careers in computing.

I quote from the WiC leaflet for the First National Conference:

> "Women into Computing (WiC) is a national organisation committed to encouraging women into computing undergraduate courses and careers.

---

[1] Davidson Centre, Davidson Road, Croydon CR0 6DD

Currently less than 10% of computing undergraduates are women. Yet the language and reasoning abilities needed for computing can be found equally in both men and women. By failing to attract women, the computer industry is losing out on valuable talent and, by failing to enter computer courses, women are losing out on interesting well-paid jobs which remain unfilled."

These facts remain true. Indeed, the situation appears to be getting worse in some areas. We cannot expect to bring about important changes overnight. I can remember saying those words in 1984 – but six years have passed with very little change at all except that, at least in Croydon, fewer girls than ever are opting for Computer Studies in school.

How many of you have spoken the words "equal opportunities" to teachers, heads, lecturers and others in education; to people in industry and commerce; to those responsible for careers and other areas of influence; and found that suddenly there was a polite smile, glazed eyes and a wondering attention. **These** are the people who **should** attend the meetings, lectures, conference, etc – but never do.

Policy statements are drafted by departments, schools, local authorities, government bodies – all including the proud words, Equal Opportunities. What to they **really** mean in terms of the girls in school? How are our girls being encouraged to look outside traditional areas?

It annoys me to read articles in newspapers, pamphlets, magazines, etc saying the same things, making the same comments and suggestions which I and many others made in articles, books, reports etc many years ago! People appear to agree with the sentiments expressed but nothing seems to change!

As the years have gone by, I have noticed that fewer and fewer girls in secondary schools have been choosing Computer Studies as a subject. There are reasons for this but many of the reasons are the same ones which have been pointed out so many times before.

- Most Computer Studies teachers are still maths teachers (often male) – role models are considered important, especially for girls.

- The Computer Studies "image" of hard technology has not changed. The syllabi of many courses have improved but it is hard to persuade girls that this is so - the "environment" of the CS classroom remains.

- The introduction of **IT** and **BIS** has turned girls away from Computer Studies - they feel safer as the image is a softer one. Traditionally, Business Studies was a subject enjoyed by girls as it helped prepare them for the secretarial work they wanted. Even with the ability, too many girls lacked the confidence to look outside the traditional stereotyped roles. IT was introduced as a new subject designed to interest girls as well as boys. These courses are often taught by women, many of whom have retrained from girl-friendly areas such as History, English, PE, Business Studies, etc. Option choices are poorly placed – eg Computer Studies or French; Computer Studies or History; CS or Information

Technology; CS or Business and Information Studies – which caused problems for girls. Since the subjects they were interested in were placed opposite CS, then it hardened the idea that CS must be for boys. (This, of course will no longer apply with the introduction of National Curriculum – which makes the study of Computer Science as a subject even more difficult! Where does it fit in? Is this good or bad? Do we really need it at secondary level?)

- Teaching is still geared towards boys in many classrooms – girls are often ignored or made to feel inferior. Even in the best regulated classes, boys demand – and get – the lion's share of the teacher's attention.

- Girls too often fail to trust themselves or their abilities. They stand back and try to work things out; unwilling to risk ridicule from their more adventurous male classmates. This trait often continues through life.

- Computer Studies classes are anywhere from 60 - 100% boys. (Do the numbers really matter or is it the underlying reason for the numbers which is dangerous? Do these proportions mean that girls still see computers as for boys only, except where they are used in a cross-curricular way?)

- Stereotypes are too often accepted as the 'norm' – society has not moved very far away from the idea of man at the helm; women as the helper. The media still helps to perpetuate this myth. In those advertisements where the woman appears as a person in authority, it is often seen as a false or contrived situation.

- Careers information is lacking or insufficient. This service will become increasingly more important as the numbers of school leavers decrease and specific areas of skill are required.

The last point is extremely important. Out of all the suggestions made over the years, this one has been the least supported. One of the main complaints which arose time and time again as I interviewed girls and their parents was the fact that career choices had to be made from ignorance. Many parents, keen to help their daughters, made suggestions of possible paths to follow. They admitted that these suggestions were based on their own experience and background.

Even when the fathers were in engineering or other technological careers, they had no thought of their daughters following in their footsteps.

A number of girls who had enjoyed the Computer Studies course admitted that they were not intending to go on with the subject and were not considering a career in engineering or computing. The principal reason was that the wide variety of interesting careers which were open to them had not been discussed or even mentioned, at home or at school.

I made a strong recommendation that careers information should be given to pupils as early as possible, certainly no later than the second year of secondary education. It was not intended to guide individuals into specific careers; rather that general information should be made available on as many different types of jobs and careers as possible, making it very clear that few jobs required one sex or the other!

It would be helpful if a bank of people in non-traditional roles could be made available to schools for visists, advice, work experience, etc. It is not always necessary to have experts or people in high positions, as this tends to discourage pupils of lower ability or those with little self-confidence. Often a school will find that it has some very useful parents who would be pleased to be part of such a scheme.

In the **Adult and Youth Training News, Issue 1** (published by the Employment Department Information Division), I read a report of an interview with Cay Stratton. She is an American who has been recruited by the British Government as adviser to the Secretary of State for Employment on training matters. She has a great deal of experience in Employment Training and Economic Development and is advising on the formation of the new TECs (Training and Enterprise Councils), a flexible and locally responsive approach to training.

Cay suggested that schools and TECs should work together and stated that some TECs have shown an interest in giving careers information to primary schools. She stressed the importance of giving young people knowledge of a widening range of careers because

> "traditionally career guidance has not always opened enough doors. Girls tend to switch off from maths and science subjects at around 14 - 15 years old never to return. This actually means losing half the client group of potential computer technicians and engineers - two areas with acute skills shortages".

Why do so many talk about it and so few do anything about it?

When I was teaching in a secondary school in Croydon some years ago, there was a lesson called "Careers" on the timetable of many fifth year pupils. Any information given at that time was too late. Options had been chosen; avenues closed. This referred mainly to areas where a specific science was compulsory. Computing skills could, however, be gained in further education. The problem was to inform students of how, where, why, etc.

Careers departments in many schools were slow to include new careers. In the early 80s, I visited a number of schools and found little or no reference to computers so that, even if a student had the aptitude, it would have been difficult to obtain the right advice. Many girls had already settled on their plans for the future, based on what they, their teachers and their parents knew from their own experience.

As more and more computers began filter into the schools, more and more pupils began to gain some competence in using them. It was a struggle for many girls in Computer Studies classes but, as Information Technology and Business and Information Studies became part of the curriculum, girls began to find that computers were tools which they could manipulate just like any others. Those girls who managed to sit the Computer Studies exam often got higher marks than the boys.

Competence brings confidence. Many of the fourth year boys who come to me for work experience using computers have computers at home and are very keen on finding out how my computers work.

The girls, few of whom have access to computers at home, often confide that computers are wonderful! and exciting! One very eager girl informed me the other day that she was going to make a career programming computers. Since this was most unusual, I questioned her further. She told me that there was nothing she would rather do after she left school than sit at a computer keyboard all day and type in information!

The National Curriculum will ensure that all pupils have technological experience. They will have the used computers in a variety of ways over a period of years and should have accepted them as useful tools in many different situations. It may be difficult to include Computer Studies in very crowded curriculum but this need not be a great problem. With the correct information, careers in computing will still be open.

Pupils, girls **or** boys, who have enjoyed their experiences with computers and feel they would like to learn more, can still opt for courses leading to careers in computing. They do, however, need the correct information!

I contacted the careers/industry liaison officer for Croydon the other day and asked if any of our schools gave career guidance or advice in the first three years of secondary school. The answer was no.

I asked her, and some schools, how careers information was introduced. There are a number of different methods but there is a common thread – pupils are first asked about their likes/dislikes/preferences, etc – in other words they are questioned on what they know. Advice on possible careers is then given based on this data.

This means that if a pupil has not shown any interest in a career in computing, one will not suggested. Too many students, generally girls, might not have thought of it themselves but would have welcomed it as a possibility.

We talk about issues and strategies; we talk about encouraging girls to enter non-traditional careers; we **talk** about lots of things. Isn't it about time we **did** something? Take the message outside of our own committed groups. Make appointments to see heads and governors in schools in your area. Ask them what provision has been made in their school to promote interesting, well-paid and badly needed jobs and careers in the computing industry.

With the introduction of **LMS** (Local Management of Schools), heads will be anxious to find as many ways as possible to persuade pupils to choose their schools. This could be the perfect opportunity to give them the idea of introducing an important new initiative. Very little curricular time could be spent on getting spectacular results – worth a try.

Regularly, newsletters feature equal opportunities for women - the **TVEI FORUM** from Hampshire recently quoted from its submission to the Training Agency. All the points they listed are important; all the point are relevant; ... all the points have been made before. No mention is made of providing information which will open doors to real equality of opportunities in the life after school.

Regularly, newspaper articles appear on the subject of women and computing/IT. On Thursday, 5 July, **JOBSCENE** in The Times stated that women are being recommended as being a better investment than their male counterparts, according to a report published by the British Computer Society.

The article was full of statistics – all showing women as a distinct minority in areas of technology and with a very low percentage of senior positions. It is all very well to educate the girls – it is also imperative to educate the boys! Those graduates of all-boys schools too often perpetuate the stereotypes the mixed schools are desperately trying to eradicate!

The **Institute of Manpower Studies** points out that there is a growing recognition that women are a vital skills resource. In its report **Good Practices in the Employment of Women Returners,** it also states that women have more "holistic attributes, for example, higher educational attainments, ability to work in teams and supportive attitudes towards colleagues".

What happens to those girls who persevere with non-traditional subjects? When they enter non-traditional areas of employment, will they be given the support they need? Will they be able to expect to advance at a similar rate to their male colleagues? These are important points to consider.

Is it not about time to help girls and women to help themselves; to let them know about their opportunities when they are young enough to choose from an informed base and to invest in the future wisely.

4

Getting Women into Computing

John MacGregor[1]

Computers have made vast changes to all aspects of our lives – home, work, education and leisure. Yet there is still an unequal participation of women in the world of computing. At face value this is surprising; there is nothing in the nature of computing which makes the industry intrinsically less suitable for women than for men. Indeed, some women may find that the possibility of flexible working hours and the opportunity to work at home make computing particularly attractive. The roots of the problem seem to lie in the home and school environment, particularly in the tendency of parents and, significantly, pupils themselves to believe that computing is "a boys' subject".

These attitudes can and must be changed. For its part, the Government is taking positive action to increase awareness among girls and women about the opportunities which exist in the field of computing.

In schools, the most important and far reaching measure we have taken is the introduction of the National Curriculum. Technology – including IT – will be taught to all girls as well as boys between the ages of 5 and 16. There will be few pupils, by the age of 16, who have not had significant hands-on computing experience including, in most cases, experience of computer modelling, software selection and retrieval and interpretation of data.

It is not just in technology that IT will come into its own. We expect that in virtually all subjects, pupils will use IT as a tool in the learning process. The attainment targets for the core subjects of Mathematics, Science and English all feature aspects of IT and the reports of the History and Geography Working Groups indicate a wide range of uses of IT in these subjects. Improved careers guidance will reinforce this and enable pupils to gain a clear idea of the options open to them. Thus, girls and boys will be able to base their future choices on experience and informed judgements, rather than a stereotyped image of an unfamiliar subject.

The benefits of the National Curriculum will take time to filter through the education system. In the meantime, we are continuing with other measures aimed at encouraging more women to take up computing. For instance

- in the four years from April 1988, providing central government grant supporting local authority spending totalling £105 million to increase the number of

[1] House of Commons, Westminster

microcomputers into schools and train classroom teachers in the use of IT.

- through the TVEI Extension Programme, on which the Government is spending £900 million over the 10 years to 1997, encouraging the use of IT in schools and requiring local authorities to develop strategies to combat sex-stereotyping in teaching materials and practice, and in the choice of subjects and future careers.

- sponsoring one of the WISE buses which have been doing a highly successful job over the last few years, giving thousands of girls hands-on experience of the latest equipment, and insight into the nature of careers in science and technology-based industries.

In further and higher education, too, we have been actively encouraging a widening of colleges' access arrangements with a particular view to enabling women who have the necessary ability and aptitude to undertake degree level studies in mathematics, sciences, IT and computing. Between 1979 and 1989 the number of access courses rose twenty-five-fold. 16,000 places are now available on such courses, a growing proportion of which are science or technology based.

Over the last ten years there has been a tremendous growth in links between schools and colleges and industry. Such links underline the relevance of school/college to the world of work and help to inform young people about career opportunities, through work experience and work shadowing, and contacts with adults other than teachers. I warmly applaud such activities. As tangible evidence of our support, Training and Enterprise Councils have been established which, among other things, will promote much closer liaison between local businesses and the providers of education. We are also putting several million pounds into supporting local Education Business Partnerships.

Outside the sphere of Government action, one of the most encouraging features of recent years has been the rapid growth of voluntary organisations and programmes - like WiC - aimed at attracting more women into computing. Schools, colleges, universities, industry and local authorities are, like the Government, devoting significant time, effort and resources to this issue.

There are grounds for optimism - the position is improving. But we should not be complacent. There is a long way to go. Current efforts must be maintained, indeed surpassed, if we are to enable women to realise fully their potential in this vital field.

5

Attracting Women Returners in Computing

Baroness Platt of Writtle[1]

The numbers of women undergraduates in computing are falling, although in the main those women come direct from schools, where they experience computing. Mature women returners in the main have not the advantage of that familiarity, so you might say we have a hopeless task. I am an engineer and don't believe any task is hopeless. One has to face the problem squarely, look for the hopeful and practical lines of action, learn where possible of successful schemes, put them into action, and then develop and improve them as the years proceed.

There is no doubt of the necessity of encouraging more women returners into computing. Every report one reads today is of skills shortages, especially in technological fields, which of course must include computing. At the same time the number of 18 year olds is falling dramatically: from 900,000 in 1981 to 600,000 in 1995 .

To overcome these skills shortages was one of the long term aims of the WISE campaign set up by the EOC and the Engineering Council in 1984. The Equal Opportunities Commission stated that literally half the talents of the nation are not fully utilised. The Engineering Council right from the start, when I was the only woman member, determined to encourage more girls and women into our profession. This year the British Computer Society became a Chartered Engineering Institution. Qualified members can become Chartered Engineers or Incorporated Engineers. WISE has been a successful campaign with the number of first year undergraduates now nearly 12%.

Although the young entrants are reducing, the total working population will increase steadily until the year 2012, due to the bulge of 18 year olds in the 1960's. Often they had no chance of leaving with good qualifications, which emphasises the importance of attracting returners into computing.

The NEDO report, "Switch on to Skills", produced last year, gives various ideas for practical solutions to the problem for companies to put into action. Their main emphasis is on the need for significant improvement in the utilisation of existing staff, particularly women, and they emphasise the need for good equal opportunities policies for women and the disabled, and other under-represented groups in technological fields of work.

Not surprisingly, a number of their recommendations concentrate on recruiting girls

---

[1] House of Lords, Westminster

into science and technology and also retraining mature in-house staff who will often be women. Attracting girls and women is shown to be vitally important so that in the future they are strongly motivated to become engineers, whether chartered or incorporated, or to gather skills in the IT and electronics fields.

As the report emphasises, aptitude and motivation are more vital ingredients for successful retraining than previous qualifications. That brings in whole new groups of people. How can we switch on the technological and computing skills of the female half of the population? As the report underlines, these sorts of strategies need to be of a long term nature if they are to succeed. They need to start with careful analyses of the problems, and planning practical solutions, and then over a number of years developing the resultant programmes, learning by experience and adapting them to grow on successful projects. NEDO suggest that it is better to develop and adapt a project which achieves 75% of its objectives, rather than scrapping it in favour of an entirely new scheme, which may be no more successful but is certainly more expensive. So a well planned, evaluated and developed evolution and strategy is far more successful in their view than short-term flash-in-the pan schemes, here today and gone tomorrow.

There are many mature women within the workforce today not fulfilling their capabilities and willing to retrain to attain promotion and responsibility, who did not have the opportunity when they were young. The real problem is lack of confidence. They will say they are only a house-wife, an untrue statement. They have gained scarce skills in practice ... time management, budgetary control, critical path analysis, industrial relations. The only trouble is, they don't know the up-to-date jargon. Enlightened employers will seek them out and enable both men and women to use their skills and talents to the full, to their own and their employer's advantage. As David Lisle of the M.S.C. said

> "Many women in their late twenties and onward regret the fact that they entered into a job at 16, 18 and 21 without giving sufficient thought to the career development offered. They now find themselves in an undemanding job with little or no chance of advancement over the remaining 20 or 30 years of their working lives. What a waste of potential this is – and what an indictment of employers if they then find that they cannot fill their needs for high quality staff."

I was asked to chair a WISE syndicate at a CBI conference in response to the first Butcher Committee on the shortage of IT skills. All day the message was, work away in the school to change attitudes, but that is the long-term solution. The short-term solution is in retraining the existing workforce. The House of Lords select committee on Education and Training for the New Technologies, of which I was a member, emphasised the importance of support for a continuing WISE campaign in schools and colleges as an important long term solution to the problem of skills shortages. However as their report says,

> "The short term needs of industry can only be met by increasing further the amount of retraining and conversion courses. In particular there

should be more courses designed to meet the need of women re-entering
employment.

There should be a large scale increase in provision of continuing education and employers' updating and retraining programmes, which have an
importance approaching that of initial education. Individuals will have to
.recognise the importance of self-improvement in returning."

Those recommendations are heartly endorsed in a new report "Women into Information Technology" organised through ITSA and backed by employers experiencing
skills shortages in the IT field. It is well worth reading for the practical solutions it
puts forward.

When employers spend thousands of pounds in investing in new and more productive high tech machinery, they must also invest in the retraining of the workforce so
that the operation of the machinery will be properly understood and it will achieve
its maximum benefit. Human resource development at all levels is just as important
as technological development. The NEDO report I referred to earlier concentrates
largely on the importance of training to combat skill shortages. One of the largest employers quoted was British Telecom. While 30% of BT's employees are female, the
vast majority of technical staff are male. Prior to 1976 no women were employed in
technical grades. They have a very wide-ranging programme of sponsorship of both
recruits and existing staff in HE and FE, but they began to see this supply might tail
off in the future. As the report says:-

"Coincidentally, concern over equal opportunities issues within the business, arising in part from the WISE programme in 1984, led to a mid-80's
review of policies and practices of the employment and development of
women within BT."

The review included analysis of employment statistics and comparisons with other
large organisations. Discussions were also held with senior managers throughout the
business on their perception of the need for engineers in the future. As a result of the
review, options to increase the number of women engineers were put forward in a
July 1986 paper. One of the suggestions was the development of a female employee
only programme which would prepare them for higher education in engineering and
related subjects.

It was reasoned that because of social conditioning and educational disadvantages
in scientific subjects, women with latent technical aptitude were less likely than their
male counterparts to have had the opportunity or encouragement to pursue an engineering career. Some form of catching-up provision was desirable for women who
were now seen as a hitherto untapped source of potential technologies. It was decided
to have as few restrictions on access as possible; motivation, application, and aptitude were seen as the key criteria. The new programme would be open to all women
employees at first level management and below. Minimum qualification requirements
were set at "O" levels in English and Mathematics at Grades A-C (or CSE Level 1).
There would be no age limit.

Eighteen women began the course in autumn 1987. Drawn from all parts of the United Kingdom and from a variety of posts within the organisation, their ages ranged from 19 to 33. The range of previous qualifications was wide. One student had three "O" levels while three had degrees in non-technical subjects. Most had five or more "O" levels and either one to three "A" levels or BTEC/SCOTVEC qualifications. The unifying factor was the absence of a technical background. As BT says "It is early days to assess the success of the course which will be realistically evaluated over the years". All the women have provisional university places mostly in electronic engineering with some in IT or maths. BT plans to run more of these courses in the future.

Over a number of years the BBC with European Community help has run successful induction courses at a lower level to encourage secretaries and clerical workers into technical fields of work. They deserve more imitation in other companies.

The HITECC Courses in Polytechnics are proving a very successful means of access for mature women over the age of 25, and girls with what I would call unwise "A" levels so that they can contemplate a career in engineering, which of course includes computing.

EITB have run short HILIGHT courses to enable women to take a free dip into the subjects which have contributed substantially to that success, and encourage them to take up the one year access course which will enable them later to reach degree standard in engineering. The courses are open to both sexes but are especially effective in sparking off the female sex into engineering.

The Engineering Council, as part of the WISE campaign, has published informative pamphlets to encourage girls and women into various fields of engineering including computing. They list a number of courses taking place all over the country to attract mature students back into these fields of work and are well worth publicising.

Kings College London have published a very good booklet "Girls into Technology" with a chapter on women taking part in a HITECC course at the Polytechnic of North London. Some of the quotes are vividly indicative of the sort of discouragement they met during their earlier education.

"It's fashionable not to like maths when you're at secondary school - they think you're weird if you like maths, especially if you are a girl."

"I came to associate maths with fear and panic."

"My mother thinks I've totally flipped to do this course and am going to be a motor mechanic or something. If I'd said I was doing an evening course in philosophy she'd have said, 'Oh how wonderful' ".

"My father-in-law, a chemist, thinks it's absolutely hilarious to do this course. I'm married, got a husband, a family, and do I need to do this?"

However, despite all the discouragement, they did the HITECC maths, positively enjoyed it and succeeded. A perfect example of the sort of second chance technology course for mature students which local colleges and polytechnics could run so well, being so easily accessible to many potential recruits who could continue to live at home and with sympathetic hours fit it in with their family lives, ready to return to work later on with confidence restored in their ability to master non-traditional subjects for women like computing.

West Cheshire College Engineering Department recruited 18 women all over 25 onto a course in mechanical electric and electronic technology. To the delight and pride of their course tutors at the end of their course all gained 1st class BTEC certificates including 31 distinctions and 103 merit passes.

At a lower level, again with European Community money, and also M.S.C. and County Council financial assistance, the South Glamorgan Women's Workshop was set up. A hundred women were recruited on a part time basis. The centre was near the bus and railway station in a converted warehouse, where a crèche was also provided. It proved most successful in teaching electronics and use of computers. Six months after the course, 63% of previously unskilled women had a paid job, in an area of high unemployment. Three of the women received publicity in The Times due to the success of their software consultancy. Between them they had nine dependent children, two under school age.

The OU Women in Technology Course has been particularly successful over a number of years and is probably the only way of involving married women returners, who are qualified engineers, on a national basis. The combination of distance learning and summer school is uniquely successful in bringing together women from a wide geographic spread of home addresses. Similar initiatives are possible on local radio, with tutorials arranged at colleges of further education, perhaps in conjunction with the Open College, so that the personal touch is not lost. "Educating Rita" told a very true story.

This is perhaps the place to emphasise Sections 47 and 48 or the Sex-Discrimination Act – where there have been few or none of one sex involved in a particular field of work over the last year – which obviously can apply particularly to computing, engineering and management for women – an employer or institution can advertise specially or run special training courses for them to give them encouragement to enter that field of work. These sort of initiatives are of great value. After that, when it comes to appointments Equal Opportunities for men and women rule the field. You cannot operate positive discrimination in the UK when you appoint. It is against the law. You must appoint the best person for the job.

I have talked about various good initiatives both by companies to persuade the non technical mature women into technical fields of work like computing, and also of colleges running courses to put those policies into effect.

Then one comes to the mature women themselves. How does one attract them? Too often they are frightened of technology in the first place and local short introductory courses like that in South Glamorgan and the Open College "Computing for the Terrified" are a very good introductory mechanism when women can work together, laugh together, and get over their fears. They need to see that their professional computer skills open the door to satisfying, well-paid careers which can very well fit in with family life. They need to see too that in the future those sort of skills can be combined with whatever particular interest the woman holds, to develop her career in a variety of ways.

I saw an industrial in-house magazine recently illustrating the control board for a system of theatre lighting. In the past too easily you could categorise drama as an art and in no way connected with technologies. How realistic would a performance be today without specialist lighting for dramatic effect, quick spotlights, colour change and microphones with computerised control? Whether it be tourism, air travel, or running a theatre or hotel, an art gallery, a school, an orchestra, a hospital, a bank, a departmental store or a factory, the computers will form the foundation of efficient and economical administration. Women equipped with computer skills and prepared to develop them with future short courses can look forward to a worth while career in the subject of their choice or the specialities they later develop.

Early on in the WISE campaign, as stimulating and expert young women technicians and chartered engineers came to speak at careers conventions and other events, it became evident that they themselves were anxious about their future careers in the industry. They had embarked on an engineering career and obtained promotion and were normally married. What was to happen to their hard-won expertise and promotion if they embarked on raising a family? They could so easily lose touch and become out of date, if they gave up work to bring up a family. It costs at least £20,000 to educate and train an Incorporated or Chartered engineer, so added to the anxiety of the women concerned in the loss of her skills, talents and in-house expertise is the sheer commercial loss of investment to her employer. The Engineering Council set up their career break working party under the Chairmanship of John Shrigley of GEC Marconi to look at different ways of preventing this unacceptable loss taking place.

The High Street banks had already pioneered schemes for bridging the career break, facilitating re-entry after a period of years of part-time work, from a minimum of a fortnight a year upwards, whilst the Bank kept the women in touch with new technological and other developments within the bank and offered them comparable work on their return after a properly negotiated period of absence.

The Engineering Council did not wish to be prescriptive, and presented a cafeteria of options to be selected by employers and their employees who need a career break to suit their individual and mutual convenience. The most important pre-requisite at the time the employee requests maternity leave is for her line manager to arrange a counselling interview and map out how the employee sees her future career. She may wish to come back to full or part time work soon after the birth of the baby, or may want a longer break. She will almost certainly be envisaging a return to something like twenty years of full time work later on. It is important to employer and employee that her expertise is not allowed to become out of date. Working arrangements such as job-sharing, flexi-time, availability of part time work, child care arrangements, off-site working such as ICL, IBM and F International have pioneered through the use of home-based computer terminals are all possible alternatives. You may be able to suggest better examples of your own. The most important qualities to be displayed during this counselling interview are those of flexibility, co-operation and imagination. With those qualities in action on both sides most difficulties can be overcome in a sensible manner, to the mutual benefit of both parties.

A good example is quoted in the NEDO Report "A Challenge for the 1990's", which refers to a pharmaceutical manufacturer who had recently adopted shift patterns to recruit more married women returners. They said, "It was like finding a hidden reserve of people. Our longstanding recruitment problems became much easier to manage and any old excuses for not employing returners – the hassle, the turnover, the kids – became pretty thin. It's an embarrassment that we've taken this long to adapt ourselves."

The Engineering Council's Career Break Working Party report shows that professional young women tend to postpone having their families until their late 20's, or early 30's, when they return to work after a short gap for the bringing up of their children. Already the National Health Service, the Board of Inland Revenue and others in the private sector are realising they cannot afford to lose their investment in the initial education and training of professional women employees, and are taking initiatives in putting innovative schemes into action. As Sir Francis Tombs says in his foreword to the Career Break Working Party Report,

> "It is the aim of the Engineering Council to encourage the pace-setters in our manufacturing process and construction industries to give a lead which others will follow."

Those employers who have developed successful career break schemes, such as the High Street Banks, have found they are helping them to become more competent and competitive, and give them a "cutting edge in the attraction and retention of the most able staff in a highly competitive market place". Intelligent and highly motivated professional young women know they want to combine a successful lifetime career with responsible family life, and will choose the employer with forward looking and imaginative career break schemes. Those schemes are not a luxury; they are a cost effective means of retaining investment in the most important resources of all, human resources.

Employers like Marconi, the Electricity Council, British Gas, Esso, British Telecom, the BBC, Unilever, Inland Revenue have put successful schemes into action. In days gone by employers may have said "Can I afford such a scheme?". Today enlightened employers are saying "We cannot afford not to do so".

I hope I have provided the sort of ideas you want both to attract women returners into computing and technology, and then with flexible working arrangements to keep their precious skills to their own benefit and that of the company and the United Kingdom. Things are changing and we must keep persevering and keep optimistic.

6

Employer – Education Cooperation

Jean Irvine[1]

Getting education and employer cooperation right is crucial across the whole of the UK economy particularly in counteracting skills shortages such as that faced by the IT industry by ensuring that our education system meets the needs of society not only today but in the future.

Good cooperation involves both parties working together for mutual benefit.

Working together over a period of time ensures development of mutual understanding of the needs of the two sectors and their strengths and weaknesses. Our society is changing rapidly and IT is one of the key drivers of that change. Fast changing markets and products, increasing globalisation and the prevalence of information and communication characterise modern industry and impact upon every aspect of our lives.

To survive and expand, employers need to increase their flexibility and speed of response by changing organisational structures, increasing flexibility in working patterns and beginning to tackle childcare. The concept of continuing reskilling and training is also gaining prominence.

We are no longer looking to education solely for school leavers or graduates, but as partners in providing a life time learning process. Achieving this demands a long term partnership between employer organisations and educational institutions to provide the right framework for cooperation, as well as generate short term benefits. This partnership will help break down some of the barriers of communications and understanding that have hindered some attempts at cooperation to date.

We employers need to be better at communicating our needs and in helping breakdown stereotypes. Education needs to be flexible in meeting the changing needs of employers. Otherwise the wrong course may be developed, people taught outdated skills, and students find it difficult to identify career opportunities correctly or get work; a very frustrating and wasteful outcome.

Cooperation can also be hindered by very mundane things; understanding the budget cycle, who holds the purse strings for sponsorship, who is the right coordinator. I have to confess that IT in education can seem like a maze to people in industry. So many initiatives have been started by different governments' departments and others, all appropriately acronymed! but with little public knowledge of how they relate. Does anyone really have a handle on the whole picture? Does it meet our needs? I am sure to those of you in education, employing organisations look also disconcertingly

---

[1] Concept 2000, 250 Farnborough Road, Hampshire GU14 7LU

like a maze. Working together as the *first* precondition of good cooperation requires both people in education and employers to get to know each other. It cannot be done from a distance and it is not a matter solely of money. It is the right people driving cooperative initiatives that bring with it the *second* precondition of cooperation, mutual benefit.

Employers undoubtedly have a responsibility to the community to help create wealth and provide varied, enriching work opportunities. But this has to be seen *not* as charity but *good business sense*. If businesses cannot compete and be profitable, they die and cannot serve the community. So a key dimension to ensuring mutual benefit to both education and employers is to develop a partnership that recognises the crucial importance of a well educated workforce – for a competitive UK industry, in which individuals work, and other interests are well balanced. In this respect England in particular is lagging behind other parts of the UK, behind many of our European and Far East competitors. In a fast changing industry like IT, this is disastrous.

In this context education needs to be seen as a process that develops the whole person with flexibility of attitude as well as specific technical skills, and one that focuses not just on the few academically gifted, but on tapping the resource that exists in returners, people who left school without going to further education but who have gained industrial experience. Let's not add ageism to sexism in IT!

This makes sense not just because of the demographic trends but also to broaden the base of our industrial growth and skills, in an ever changing world.

The educational sector can benefit enormously by cooperation with employers, not just through financial sponsorship but through gaining recognition of its central and growing role in our future industrial competitiveness. But it must also recognise employers' needs in the content of courses and development of the curriculum. To achieve that demands much closer contact than there may have been to date, eg people from industry spending time in schools and colleges, and teachers/lecturers spending time in industry. This comes back to the concept of cooperating in the form of a long term partnership. A partnership which has, in my view, 5 key features.

First-relevance to the social and industrial context of the specific community in which it is located.

Second-timeliness. I recognise the long life cycle of the education process but industry is increasingly being forced by competition to increase its speed of response. Education and training provision needs to become shorter, more modular and capable of change.

Third-focus. As a senior IT employer I get a lot of requests for sponsorship. Achieving national coverage for sponsorship is very difficult. In looking at them, I look for a return in terms of possible recruitment, broadening our access to skills etc. A positive response is more likely to be given a *local* educational institution with whom we have some contact. This is also relevant to the increasing need for educational institutions to have to compete in the market place for funds and sponsorship. Increasingly you need to differentiate your educational products from others in the market place to secure funds. In my view this market-related competition is becoming damaging to the education sector in the same way as it has done to the IT industry.

Faced with skill shortages the IT industry responded with competing pay spirals and a reluctance to train because trained staff were highly marketable. Breaking into this vicious circle was one of the key strands of the WIT campaign, that I will talk about later.

It is essential that educational institutions *cooperate* and *together* approach industry for sponsorship. Looking, for example, at the large number of workshops at this event on apparently identical topics, or observing the number of colleges apparently developing similar returner courses, leaves industry with a bewildering choice as to whom to sponsor.

Is there scope therefore for more collaborative development of courses and core research? This is why groups such as Women into Computing (WiC) have such an important role to play in bringing people together to share experience and ideas.

This brings me on to the *fourth area* – geography. Undoubtedly partnerships between *local* education and *local* industry work best. This is seen not only in different events but also in the drive to establish TECs. This provides opportunities to enhance local delivery of courses with continuing involvement in the form of support, work experience and job opportunity. It also provides an opportunity for educational institutions to tailor *specific* courses etc to meet *local* employment needs.

The *final* area is the need for the right individuals in both sectors to drive joint initiatives forward – a catalyst, full of enthusiasm, can work wonders!

I'd now like briefly to describe some successful cooperative initiatives demonstrating these features, that IT in the Post Office are involved in.

First is the WIT campaign, clearly focused upon reversing the down-turn in women entering IT through breaking down the barriers of understanding about IT careers, broadening the entry into the IT profession and tackling the issues that prevent flexible working and career advancement within IT. This is a joint industry, government and education compaign expected to cost £4M over the next three years, comprising a number of national working parties supplemented by a regional network to ensure local relevant implementation. A key feature of the campaign is to focus upon specific topics and provide practical not theoretical results. The provision of information services underpins all WIT activities to share experience and avoid duplication of effort.

A *second* example is the funding by my organisation of an *IT centre in a local secondary school*. In addition to equipment, we have provided training, support and work experience. IT is now being used there across the curriculum and the school has become an IT focus for the local education authority. We see initiative as a long term partnership.

A *related initiative* also near our Hampshire centre is an *Industrial Consultancy Group* coordinated by an industrial fellow, sponsored by a local company. This brings together over 30 local employers and 8 secondary schools through a variety of ways, including summer schools, competitions, an affiliate and champions scheme to help school children identify and follow through career opportunities, work experience and, for teachers, work shadowing plus sponsorship courses intended for returners in local FE colleges.

We are also participating as a local employer in a national DTI-funded scheme called *Electronics Now*, which is aimed at breaking down the barriers of understanding between schools, school-children and industry, about opportunities in electronics and IT. Combining sponsorship of videos with local events has involved to date nearly 90 events involving 8000 school children.

Local sponsorship of material, for example, for returners' courses at a local college, has been supplemented by our staff providing specialist subject teaching, and us providing work experience. It is clear from the job opportunities found by people attending such courses that they are very successful.

I am telling you about these to highlight the fact that we have found that successful education and industry initiatives depend upon local partnerships. They also depend upon the "people" aspects of cooperation, to ensure that they are relevant to the needs of both parties and to the local community.

It is often not money but time investment as part of a long term partnership – it is often easier to get employers to fund time than money, particularly part way through a financial year.

So in summary, the *key* is for industry and education to *get together* and for institutions on both sides to *cooperate* and *not to compete*, particularly on a local basis. For as John Ruskin wrote

> "Government and cooperation are in all things the laws of life, anarchy and competition the laws of death."

The successful economic and academic life of the UK depends on it and on IT!

7

Where Are the Girls Now?

Gillian Lovegrove,
Wendy Hall[1]

7.1 Introduction

Government initiatives in the late 1980's to increase the number of places for computer science students in UK universities at this time of economic stringency is continuing evidence of the current and predicted shortage of computer scientists in industry and commerce. The demand for computer science graduates is still such that many of them are in a position to pick and choose between jobs offers from the most prestigious software houses and industry, despite increasing economic stringency. There has been much press coverage of Government reports stressing the increasing need for such graduates so that students applying for computer science degree courses are still assured of excellent employment prospects when they graduate. The Butcher Report [Butcher 85] highlighted the IT skills shortages and stresses the fact that IT companies cannot afford to ignore the intellectual resources offered by women at a time of growing skill shortages and declining school and university populations: this is still relevant.

Despite national, WISE, WiC and WIT efforts, the percentage of computer science students at universities in the UK who are female is currently less than 15%. In our original paper [Lovegrove 87] we presented an analysis of the situation and suggested some possible remedies. This paper is an updated version of the original and takes a look at the latest figures.

7.2 Worrying Trends

At the authors' own university, Southampton, the number of female applicants to computing degree courses declined steadily over the early 1980's, until in September 1985 the unenviable record was achieved of no girls in the first year intake for either the single honours Computer Science or the Mathematics with Computer Science degrees. From 1985 to 1989, the figures remained low. In a department where 25% of the Computer Science academic teaching staff are female and which in the past has recruited

[1] **Dept of Electronics and Computer Science, University of Southampton, Southampton SO9 5NH**

relatively high numbers of female students, this is a matter for some concern.

Southampton University is perhaps a special case, and one which will be discussed later in this paper, but the national statistics reflect the same state of affairs. UCCA records show that of the total number of students accepting places on computer science degree courses, the percentage of women fell from 25% in 1978 to 10% in 1987. There is an improvement in the figures in 1988 and 1989; the details of these figures are shown in Table 7.1 and in graphical form in Figure 7.1.

Table 7.1 UCCA Statistics for Female and Male Entrants: University courses in Computer Science.

Year	Men	Women	Total	%
1978	737	233	970	24
1979	966	299	1265	24
1980	1240	379	1619	23
1981	1306	374	1680	22
1982	1254	344	1598	22
1983	1309	295	1604	18
1984	1537	283	1820	15
1985	1318	149	1467	10
1986	1289	166	1455	11
1987	1560	170	1730	10
1988	1843	228	2071	11
1989	1853	277	2130	13

Figure 7.1 Entry to Computer Science Courses at UK Universities

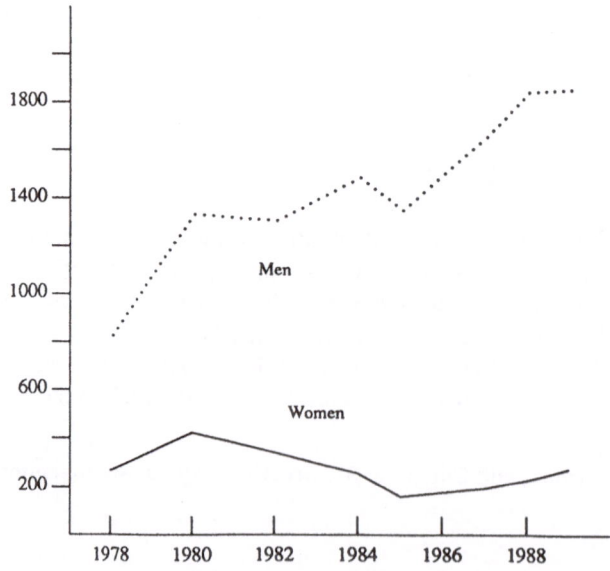

The UCCA method of classification of Computer Science changed in 1985 and the subject was re-classified as Computer Studies, so that comparisons between the years before and after 1985 are not strictly accurate, but the fluctuations in both absolute and percentage terms are still clear to see. First we will consider what caused the nose-dive in the number of girls studying Computer Science at university level in the mid 1980's.

It could be argued that computing science is regarded by many as either a "hard" science or an offshoot of mathematics and as such would naturally fail to attract girls. Indeed, at many universities and polytechnics a standard requirement for entry to a computer science degree course is A-level Mathematics and certainly at Southampton the majority of applicants are taking Mathematics and Science subjects at A-level.

This, however, only serves to increase concern since, UCCA records show that of the total number of students accepting places on mathematics degree courses, the percentage of women has stayed relatively constant at 31-33% between 1978 and 1989. For physics, during the same period, the percentage of women students rose from 12% to 16% and for chemistry from 21% to 33%. Even for that traditional male bastion of engineering subjects, the work undertaken by the Women into Science and Engineering (WISE) group over the last few years seems to have paid dividends, since the figures for the percentage of women students on engineering courses at Universities have steadily increased from 4% in 1978 to 13% in 1989. The details of all these figures are given in Table 7.2.

Table 7.2 UCCA Statistics for Female Students as a Percentage of Entrants: University Courses in Mathematics, Chemistry, Physics and Engineering.

Year	Mathematics	Physics	Chemistry	Engineering
1978	31	12	21	4
1979	31	15	23	5
1980	31	13	26	5
1981	32	15	26	7
1982	34	14	27	8
1983	33	15	28	8
1984	32	14	30	8
1985	32	17	30	11
1986	32	17	30	11
1987	31	16	34	11
1988	33	16	32	12
1989	33	16	33	13

Clearly, whilst the drive to attract more girls to the traditional mathematics and science subjects is having some effect, girls are being increasingly discouraged from reading computer science.

These figures are for home students only. It is an interesting comparison to look at the UCCA statistics for the number of women overseas students as a percentage of the total number of overseas students taking computer science degrees in the UK. Whilst the percentage is much higher overall, the trend is still the same. It dropped from 38% in 1978 to a low of 26% in 1984. So this phenomenon is not restricted to British students alone, but the percentages are by no means as worryingly low.

At school, girls seem quite keen to study Computer Studies at O or GCSE level. Every year up to 1986, approximately 30% of the candidates for this subject were female. However, the number of candidates for A-level Computer Science has fallen sharply since 1985 when it was already only 18%. This was to be expected given the downward trend in university applications for Computer Science courses at this time. It will be interesting to see what effect the introduction of GCSE's and the technology element of the National Curriculum has on these figures.

If girls are not motivated in school to take computer science options (or even worse are actually discouraged) then they will be unlikely to choose a career in computing. Before we consider what new positive action can be taken to improve the situation, it is important to examine the possible reasons why so few girls show any interest in computing and computers.

7.3 The Causes: Some Observations

There is no doubt that sex stereotyping exists pre-school and outside school. Evidence to justify this has been found in many of the surveys relating to girls and science [Smail 84, Culley 86]. The GIST survey [Kelly 84] found that boys and girls who endorsed sex stereotypes were least keen to learn about the science associated with the opposite sex. The fact that girls are negatively influenced by cultural factors is also observed by Haggis [Haggis 86]. On the whole girls are found to be more passive and conforming and also unwilling to make mistakes in front of boys. This latter observation is one of great importance, we believe, and is also apparent amongst university undergraduates. In general, girls are reluctant to sit down and experiment at a terminal, especially for the first time. Boys in comparison are keen to show their mastery over the new technology and are less afraid of the consequences if they take some incorrect action. The observation that boys are more likely to dominate lessons and clubs in schools is made in a number of studies including [Else 85, Haggis 86, Culley 86]. The demanding male student is more likely to command attention and get responses. Girls are generally more likely to learn by example rather than by experiment, reading from a set of instructions or following the instructions from a teacher. In mixed laboratory classes it is common for the boys to take a more aggressive approach than girls to the selection of seating and equipment, which leads to the girls missing out when there are limited resources or different qualities of equipment (as described in [Kelly 84]).

As the authors of the London Borough of Croydon Report [Croydon 83] point out, children are more likely to develop their interest in information technology at home than they are at school. However, parental aspirations are also sex-stereotyped. There is a tendency for the home micro to be bought for the boy of the family. A survey carried out by the MEP Primary Project [Straker 85] in 1985 showed that twice as many boys as girls have access to a microcomputer at home. Another survey has revealed that in all households owning microcomputers, boys are thirteen times more likely than girls to be using them. Moreover, only 4% of micros are used by the mother in the home [EOC 85a]. The feeling that computers are only for boys is reinforced if girls cannot find software that is of interest.

There is evidence as described by McLeod and Hughes [McLeod 84] that children aged 6 to 10 have uniformly positive attitudes towards computers. However strong evidence of sex-stereotyping was found amongst children of both sexes when asked whether they saw computers as the province of boys or girls. It seems that by the age of seven many children were already associating computers with boys and predicting that they will perform better with them. There is little doubt that media and software producers help to make computing appear a male domain [Smail 84, Haggis 86]. Advertisements for computers are noticeably sex stereotyped. Software firms produce largely aggressive and macho games from which women are often totally absent or cast in a passive helpless role. Space fantasy images are more appealing to boys.

It is an interesting observation that the figures for computer science students at universities begin to drop sharply in the early 1980's – just as microcomputers began to make its presence felt and computing facilities became more available to British school children. The younger girls' assumption that computing is not for them [Else 85] is one which will be difficult to unpick later, at a time when career choice is being considered.

One of the main findings of the Croydon Report was that the content of computing courses is often seen as irrelevant to the careers that girls are encouraged to choose and so they are less likely to be guided by teachers to take such courses. In addition to this, timetable constraints often result in the option subjects traditionally popular with girls (languages, home economics, etc) being timetabled against computing options. The demand for school leavers and graduates with a high level of IT skills far outweighs supply. Although there is a popular belief that arts O-levels, GCSE's, A-levels and degrees will do just as well as an entry point to a career in computing, careers teachers who advise girls in this way are widening the gender gap and allowing the girls to fall even further behind their male counterparts in terms of familiarity with computer technology and the lucrative careers that follow from this.

One final point to be made here is the lack of adequately trained IT teachers. In the primary schools the majority of teachers are women and yet the majority of primary teachers attending microcomputer courses are men [EOC 85a] and it is usually an enthusiastic male teacher who organises and promotes the use of computers in the school. Many women primary school teachers are intimidated by the new technology and this can affect the attitudes of the children in their classes. In secondary schools, the lack of IT specialists means that teaching in this field is often half-hearted or non-existent. The competition to get onto the courses run by the one or two teachers in the school who know and are enthusiastic about their subject, may be fierce and, for all the reasons mentioned above, girls will not push for these places. And so the circle goes on.

7.4 What can schools do?

The most important point here is that continuing, if not increased efforts should be made to make teachers aware that the problem exists and to direct them in how to deal with it. Implicit in this is the need for much more in-service training at all levels. By this we mean, training more IT specialists, increasing the number of women who feel confident and competent with modern technology in the classroom and including in these courses an appreciation of the issues raised in this paper. Providing the money for these courses and allowing teachers to go on them is of course a political issue [Evans 87] but it is well-recognised that the country needs more women in science and engineering and this is one way of achieving this object.

The Croydon Report [EOC 85a] emphasises the need for courseware to be designed in such a way that it is interesting to girls. This means choosing examples carefully to avoid subjects that are very male oriented. With imagination and a little forethought this is not too difficult a task. Even with this kind of courseware, it will still be necessary for teachers to be sympathetic to the fact that girls are frequently reluctant to learn about computers and the teachers may need to positively discriminate towards the girls to overcome this. Some secondary schools have found that girls respond better to computing as a subject when they are taught in single sex groups. Schools are also experimenting by setting up single sex computer clubs which seem to be successful in engaging the interest of girls in computers since the element of male competition is removed. Research in primary schools shows that, where teachers are aware of the gender implications as regards technology, mixed groups provide the best learning environment for all concerned [Milner 90]. More work needs to be done to find out whether this can be extended to secondary schools.

It is easier to make computers an ordinary classroom resource in primary schools than in secondary schools. Languages like Logo and Prolog encourage the use of computers in an imaginative way. The turtle graphics of Logo is appealing to both boys and girls and research has shown that this motivates children into greater use of computing facilities. Desktop publishing is providing expression for creativity, with the production of school newspapers as an excellent incentive. However, it is very important that this kind of use is extended to secondary schools. Unfortunately, due to lack of resources, there is a tendency in secondary schools to centralise computing facilities, which detracts from their casual use in everyday teaching across the curriculum. This is undesirable. Computers should be available for casual but integrated use across the curriculum, much as other resources eg a library of colourful books. The National Curriculum currently requires the teaching of IT and this policy is excellent, but it is crucial that it is made to happen in such a way that both male and female pupils find the experience pleasantly integrated.

Current thinking about a National Curriculum for studies after GCSE level may well mean that Computer Science vanishes as a subject to be taught in schools. If this results in applicants for Computer Science degrees choosing the subject because of their experience with the technology gained across the curriculum, then this is potentially healthier than the current situation. Computer Science at degree level is a much broader subject; it is important to take further steps to correct possibly narrow or incorrect view of Computer Science held by young men and women in schools.

In a questionnaire study, Newton [Newton 88] found that girls' experiences in dealing with males over computers clearly influenced their comments about why girls don't go into computing as a career. Schools can actively encourage girls to consider a career in computing by wherever possible making it easy for them to choose IT/computing options. At the very least, this will enable them to gain familiarity with the technology, which they will increasingly need whatever career they eventually choose. Careers teachers should be made more aware of the opportunities for girls in computing and related industries and should provide positive career counselling in this direction.

The current initiatives to create links between companies and education are potentially to the advantage of all. Examples of such schemes are cited in Jean Irvine's address [Irvine 90] to the WiC Conference in 1990, and Irene Pacitti's paper [Pacitti 90]. Another good example is in Hampshire, where IBM has fostered links with schools. The work of the WIT Campaign [Virgo 90] has and will help such ventures to prosper.

7.5   What can universities and polytechnics do?

Although decisions about choice of subjects have already been made long before UCCA forms are filled in, there are ways in which the universities can help to promote computing as a suitable subject for girls to study. Entry requirements to computer science degree courses should be as flexible as possible to include young women without a purely scientific background. However, for many university computing courses, applicants still require a mathematics qualification. It is possible to have completely open entry requirements for computing courses, especially at polytechnics, though these are often more business studies oriented: eg Thames Polytechnic have operated this policy for some time and whilst the number of girls on their courses is not increasing, it is above the national average [Morton 86a].

Computer Science, in common with other subjects studied at universities, changes its nature as the course develops over the three year period of study. Typically the first year includes courses on programming and supportive mathematics and electronics, whilst the third year includes applications courses, a project and possibly courses of a more reflective nature. Although expertise in programming is necessary for many courses, it is not the only ability required by a good computer science undergraduate. Qualities of good communication and organisation are also important and frequently women have these qualities more than men. However, there is a commonly held opinion in school children, parents, teachers and careers advisors that a computer science degree is all about programming. To counteract this, universities should publicise the nature of their computer science degree course by holding open days for schools aimed not only at sixth formers but also younger pupils before they choose their options. At such open days the many varied career opportunities can be displayed. All of this should consciously be aimed at the girls as well as the boys. Similarly prospectuses should be carefully worded to illustrate the more rounded nature of a computer science degree. It is encouraging if the prospectus includes "words of welcome" to women as well as men and if the photographs include women.

At the UCCA interviews, young women should be addressed by role models in the department at some point, making the applicants feel they are special and welcome. It is, of course, important not to overdo it, since the majority of young women are more than happy to enter a predominantly male environment, but by and large do not wish to find that they might be on their own.

Some universities and polytechnics have a positive discrimination policy towards women by offering them entry requirements one or two points (sometimes more) below the standard offer. For the most part, this is informal and not well publicised. The justification for this is

- it is not yet proven that A-level results correlate with degree results in computer science;

- young women are likely to have had worse teaching in science subjects at school;

- it is important to have a "critical mass" of about five female students for mutual encouragement and support.

It is too early to validate or invalidate positive discrimination policies like this, as for the most part such policies have only been put into effect recently. It is to be hoped that such policies have been put into effect not solely nor principally on the grounds that student quotas were down. Universities and polytechnics are normally flexible when it comes to offers to individuals with known problems at home or school and each case is considered on its own merit. If the admissions policy in the departments concerned is that each woman applicant is considered as potentially a special case (which indeed she is), then this would improve the situation.

Having attracted girls onto courses, the utmost care should be taken to retain them. As the girls are likely to be in a minority, some may feel overwhelmed by the all-male atmosphere. University lecturers are not renowned for their teaching ability and computer science lecturers are no exception: indeed they are more likely to be under pressure to spend more time on research and less on teaching (despite the fact that the subject changes more rapidly than average causing more frequent course revision). We would ask lecturers to discriminate positively towards women in their lectures by, amongst other things, being more aware of the difference in learning attitudes between male and female students.

Efforts should be made to put girls in the same tutorial group and to ensure that their personal tutors are aware that they may need to be more than usually supportive. Ideally extra tutorial support should be available for girls, but in view of the current shortage of teaching resources this may not be possible. It may also be necessary to examine the conditions under which the students work at terminals. For example, are they expected to work late at night and walk back alone to halls of residence?

7.6 What has changed since 1987?

The data for this paper was first collected in 1987 [Lovegrove 87]. When we ask the question what has changed since then, unfortunately the answer has to be, in real terms, very little. The numbers of girls entering computer science courses at university has risen slightly (see Table 7.1), which has to be encouraging because the downward trend does appear to have been halted. However, the reasons why girls turned away from computing in such large numbers have not yet been fully analysed, so we still have no firm guidelines as to how the situation can be best corrected.

7.6.1 IS SOUTHAMPTON A SPECIAL CASE?

Table 7.3 shows the trend for Southampton in contrast with the national trend, over the years for which the single honours degree has been given. It seems that despite an active WiC group in the Department and an active Women's Engineering Society in the Faculty, the numbers for women remain appallingly low. The degree content has not changed in character – indeed, the electronics component has diminished slightly. The Department has no positive discrimination policy for recruitment, but even if it had, there would be little effect, because the root problem is in the extremely low numbers of female UCCA applicants in the first instance; the conversion rate from applicants to registering students is about the same for males and females.

Table 7.3 Statistics for Female and Male Entrants to Southampton University degree in Computer Science.

Year	Men	Women	Total	%	National Percentage
1982	6	2	8	25	22
1983	10	1	11	9	18
1984	14	0	14	0	15
1985	14	0	14	0	10
1986	14	2	16	12	11
1987	30	1	31	0.3	10
1988	30	1	31	0.3	11
1989	39	0	39	0	13
1990	50	4	54	7	unknown

In 1986, the Department of Computer Studies in the Mathematics Faculty amalgamated with the Department of Electronics in the Engineering Faculty to become the Department of Electronics and Computer Science. Numbers of females embarking on engineering degrees are on the increase in the University, but in general the numbers on the Electronics degrees are still very low. Although the Computer Science degree has only a small compulsory electronics component in it, the siting of Computer Science within the joint Department would appear to be a deterrent to young women.

7.6.2 NATIONAL CHANGES SINCE 1987

In some ways the national situation has changed quite considerably. There has been a tremendous increase in awareness of the situation across government, industry and academia. When we published our first paper in 1987, we felt as if we were the only people who had noticed the problem. This is certainly not the case today. There have been a number of national conferences and seminars organised on the topic by various groups, and the activities of the WISE, WiC and WIT organisations must surely start to have an effect soon if only because of the sheer effort that is being put into them.

Research about the use of computers in schools has pointed to ways in which computers can be used in the classroom without alienating half of the student population. As these research guidelines are put into practice in schools, we can hope for further improvements in the situation. Universities are keenly trying to recruit more female undergraduate students for the practical reason that they need to recruit more students generally, and this means they are prepared to put resources into WiC workshops and publicity campaigns. The short-fall in the number of school leavers has meant that employers are increasingly trying to attract women into the IT industry, and so they are prepared to back campaigns like WIT and WiC as a means to achieving this end.

Despite all this, how much have attitudes really changed? Computing is still generally thought of as a rather "macho" subject that has a lot to do with video games, number crunching and the defence industry. Numerous examples of sexist advertising within the computing industry can still be found in the computing magazines and there are still very few role models within the industry to help change girls attitudes about the nature of careers in computing. We still have a long way to go.

7.7 Summary

There is little doubt that this country cannot afford to waste the resource offered by women in computing. The Equal Opportunities Commission has had discussions with many new technology employers and the point has been made regularly that the companies would welcome more job applications from girls and women. Several companies have pointed out that they alone could have employed all the electronics graduates leaving the UK universities in the last few years, and that girls represent the largest untapped resource of potential skill at technician and technologist levels as well as at professional level. Such comments are particularly relevant in view of the demographic trends which indicate a significant down-turn over the next ten years in the number of school leavers [EOC 85a].

In addition, to quote from the Butcher Report [Butcher 85]

> The very flexibility of IT, and the fact that IT systems make it possible to work from home as well as the office or factory, means that it is particularly well suited as a career for women at all levels.

The future information society will require skills such as knowledge engineering, systems analysis, linguistics, logic, organisation and communication. Women have just as much to offer in these areas as men, if not more. Recent figures are encouraging. It is up to us to continue efforts to provide an environment in which women will find personal fulfilment and a successful career in computing.

7.8 REFERENCES

[Butcher 85] Butcher Committee Final Report, *Information Technology Skills Shortages*, DTI, 1985.

[Croydon 83] *Information Technology in Schools*, EOC/London Borough of Croydon, EOC 1983.

[Culley 86] Culley L, *Gender Differences and Computing*, Department of Education, University of Loughborough, 1986.

[Else 85] Else L, "Wise girls will find the going is tough", *Computing*, 9 May 1985.

[EOC 85a] *Infotech and Gender: an Overview*, EOC, 1985.

[Evans 87] Evans A, and Hall W, "Programming Inequality", *Times Educational Supplement*, 2 October 1987.

[Haggis 86] Haggis K, *Computers – Toys for the Boys?*, University of Newcastle, Diploma in Advanced Educational Studies, Special Study 1986.

[Irvine 90] Irvine J, "Employer - Education Cooperation", in the *WiC 1990 Proceedings* and in this volume.

[Kelly 84] Kelly A, Whyte J and Smail B, *Girls into Science and Technology – Final Report*, University of Manchester 1984.

[Lovegrove 87] Lovegrove G L and Hall W, "Where have all the girls gone?", *University of Computing*, 9, 1987.

[McLeod 84] McLeod H and Hughes M, "Childrens Ideas about Computers", presented to a BPS Conference: *IT, AI and Child Development*, held at the University of Sussex, July 1984.

[Milner 90] "Action Research: Primary Schoolgirls and New Technology", in the *WiC 1990 Proceedings* and in this volume.

[Morton 86a] Morton P, "Tales From the River Bank", *Your Computer*, October 1986.

[Newton 88] Newton P and Haslam S, "Computing: an Ideal Occupation for Women", *Proceedings of the First National WiC Conference*, University of Lancaster, July 1988.

[Pacitti 90] Pacitti I, "School and Industry Links – An Example of Cooperation", in the *WiC 1990 Proceedings* and in this volume.

[Smail 84] Smail, B *Girl-friendly Science: Avoiding Sex Bias in the Curriculum.*, Longman 1984.

[Straker 85] Straker A, *MEP Primary Project Progress Report No.4*, 1985.

[Virgo 90] Virgo P, "The Women into Information Technology (WIT) Campaign", in the *WiC 1990 Proceedings* and in this volume.

8

Young Women and the Culture of Software Engineering

Flis Henwood[1]

In[2] an attempt to overcome the problems associated with the shortfall in 18 year olds and the related under-recruitment to science and technology courses in further and higher education, employers, trainers and educators have all become interested in the possibility of recruiting women into these areas. The last decade has produced numerous initiatives to encourage women into science, engineering and technology, of which WISE and WIT are two notable examples. Despite these efforts women still represent only a minority of participants in these areas of education and employment. More precisely, they continue to be segregated, within these fields, into typical "women's jobs"[EITB 84, Dain 88]. Researchers have thus turned their attention towards improving our understanding of the barriers women face in taking up engineering and technological work and the last decade has seen a growth in research in this area.

The most influential approach to research on women in engineering to date has focused on the women themselves and their decision to enter (or not to enter) this area of work. Questions are asked such as "Are women who do go into these areas of work different from other women and if so, in what ways?" Comparisons are made between women in traditional and women in non-traditional areas of work using a psychological research framework and focusing on the different "personalities" or characteristics of the two groups. A second body of research, less influential in terms of policy, takes a more sociological or anthropological approach and focuses on the experiences of women in engineering and other male areas of work with the aim of identifying institutional barriers to women's participation in these fields. In this paper, I outline the psychological approach and show how it is reflected in, and reinforced by, the dominant thinking in this area – both at the policy level and in terms of "common sense" or everyday assumptions. I draw attention to the problems with the dominance of this view and argue the need for a re-think on questions of equal opportunities for women in science, engineering and technology.

Early studies of women in engineering tended to see such women as "masculine" and therefore different from other women, and somehow "deviant" [Smithers 81,

[1] Innovation Studies Unit, Polytechnic of East London, Maryland House, Manbey Park Road, Stratford, London E15
[2] Flis Henwood was an invited speaker at the 1990 WiC Conference.

Harding 81]. More recently, however, this "deviance hypothesis" has been rejected in favour of an approach which emphasises similarities between traditional and non-traditional choosers[3]. An influential piece of research by Peggy Newton and colleagues, has made use of these developments in psychology to study women in engineering [Newton 81, Newton 82]. Employing a sex role inventory developed by Sandra Bem (known as the Bem Sex Role Inventory or BSRI), Newton and colleagues characterised their trainee women technician engineers not as more masculine than other women but as "androgynous" – scoring high on measures of both masculinity *and femininity.*

This shift away from the deviance hypothesis and towards androgyny has been welcomed, both by researchers in the field and by policy makers. The perception of women in engineering as masculine is seen as having been a major factor in deterring women from entering this area of work. In an economic climate that has led to calls for more women in these fields, an approach that appears to move away from this construction is bound to be popular. However, there is a danger that in responding to the skills shortage problem by providing "easy answers" to the problems of "getting women in", some important questions will be overlooked; questions that urgently need to be addressed if adequate and effective measures for increasing the numbers of women in engineering and technological work are to be devised.

We need to ask, for example, "Why is being seen as masculine a problem for women?" and "Is this always so or are there positive experiences for women in being associated with masculinity and so-called masculine work?" The androgyny approach, instead of attempting to answer these questions, simply moves away from them altogether in favour of a model of women in engineering that *allows them to be both engineers and feminine.*

It is possible to see this perspective reflected in, and reinforced by, the discourse found in much of the WISE and WIT - type campaigns. Talk here is of overcoming the so-called "misconceptions" about engineering and industry. The emphasis is on dismissing the masculine image of engineering in favour of a more feminine one, often arguing that engineering and technological work require feminine skills, such as good communication. Whilst there are good reasons to examine the need for new and different skills within engineering and technological work, we must remain sensitive to the dangers of simply sweeping aside one image of engineering work and replacing it with a new and different one. First, because this approach makes very simplistic and generalised assumptions about women and their decisions to enter, or not to enter, non-

---

[3]The shift towards an emphasis on similarities, rather that differences, in the literature on women in engineering, has been made possible, in part, by relatively recent developments in psychology, particularly in work on "androgyny". Whereas traditionally, psychologists have seen masculinity and femininity as polar opposites (to be one is to be not the other), more recent developments in psychological theory argue that masculinity and femininity are not opposites but "independent dimensions" [Bem 74]. In this new approach, people are conceived of as having both masculine and feminine characteristics and are described in terms of a relative balance of the two: someone scoring low on both is described as "undifferentiated", high on one and low on another as either "masculine-typed" or "feminine-typed", and high on both as "androgynous".

traditional work, and second, because the problem is *not simply an image problem.*

My own research, on gender and occupation, offers some insights into the question of occupational choice in the context of both traditional and non-traditional choices[4]. My research confirms the view that engineering is understood by many as masculine, as "men's work" and, as such, is rejected by many women. However, it also suggests that the association of engineering with masculinity does not simply deter women in a straightforward manner. Both groups of women in my research, the Personal Assistants (PAs) and the female Software Engineers (SEs) (i.e. the traditional and non-traditional choosers) were attracted to, and deterred by, the thought (and, in the case of the SEs, the experience) of being women in a engineering culture.

So, whilst women are indeed often "put off" engineering by its association with masculinity, they are also, often, simultaneously, attracted by this association. This is because *masculinity signifies status as well as manliness* and it is this status that women accrue when entering "men's work" that encourages some to try for such work. My research shows how those who succeed in entering "men's work" are seen not merely as different, as in "deficient" or "deviant", but also as different, as in "to be admired and respected", and how this, in part, is what attracts them.

The reverse side of the coin to the notion that technology's association with masculinity deters women, is that women are essentially more comfortable with being seen as feminine. From this perspective, a traditional occupational choice is understood as presenting fewer problems than a non-traditional one. Once again, however, my own research suggests otherwise. Neither the choice for traditional, nor the choice for non-traditional work was straightforward for women. For the female SEs, their choice had brought problems regarding their gender identity but had granted them status as women in "men's work", a tension that caused them to feel ambivalent about such a choice. For PAs, too, there was ambivalence; in this case, related to some aspects of PA and secretarial work associated with traditional femininity. In particular, some of the servicing elements (including sexual servicing) were mentioned.

This research leads me to conclude that both traditional and non-traditional choices need to be understood within the context of the relative value and status attached to "men's work" and to "women's work" as well as to question concerning women's (and men's) relationship to both masculinity and femininity. With regard to policy, the research suggests that we cannot increase the numbers of women in engineering and technological work simply by "changing the image" from one of masculinity to one of femininity. First, because women are attracted to, as well as deterred by, technology's association with masculinity and second, because women do not have a straightforward relationship to femininity either.

A second reason why policies that focus on changing the image will not succeed, is that, by constructing the problem as one of "image", they ignore the very real problems

---

[4]The research involved working with two groups of students and their tutors at a college of technology. Using ethnographic research techniques, including participant observation and indepth interviewing, I sought to understand more about the choices and experiences of the two groups, studying as they were on two very different, and gendered, courses: a Diploma for Personal Assistants (all female) and an HND in Software Engineering (90 per cent male).

women experience in these areas of work. In particular, they ignore the ways in which gender is actively reconstructed in the work setting and the problems this makes for women.

Masculinity and femininity are not attributes that are "given" in the individual and then taken into the world of work, as much psychological research in the field suggests. Rather, gender is actively constructed in the work setting and, as Cockburn argues, technology is central to this gendering process:

> "It is not simply that gender difference allots men and women to different kinds of work. Different kinds of work actively create gender difference. The technological incompetence that now characterises women due to their lack of technological training and work is an intrinsic part of what we understand by femininity."
>
> [Cockburn 85a], p59.

For Cockburn, women's exclusion from engineering can be understood in terms of the culture of the technological workplace, particularly its association with masculinity and male power. Several examples from my own research serve to support this view.

In discussions with engineering staff, some interesting perceptions of women in engineering emerged. Most referred to such women in glowing terms: "often the star pupils"; "really strong, determined characters"; "high flyers, the keen ones – they meet the obstacles head on and overcome them"; "hardworking" and "will get there, come what may". This construction of women in engineering is both a partial and a dangerous one. First, it reinforces the belief that most women cannot be engineers (these are "exceptional" women) and second, it serves to invisibilise the average woman engineer. In constructing women who come into engineering as "of the highest calibre", not only will women who do not perceive themselves in this way be put off (as I found with the PAs in my research), but also, extreme and unnecessary pressure will be put on those that do come in, to perform outstandingly, as the following example shows.

The course tutor for the SE course told me the story of "Carol", a woman who was "failing quite badly". Expressing concern that he was wrong to have let her onto the course in the first place, he worried that he had employed some sort of positive discrimination in favour of a woman who had now "let him down". On positive discrimination, he said:

> "I'm not in favour of it because it's not led to equality.. I think, to a limited extent, that's what I got into with Carol.. although I have probably let men on with the same reservations.."

It is interesting here that, although he admits that he has probably let men onto the course with the same reservations as he had about Carol, this man is tortured by the fact that she has not done well and that this might reflect badly on him and on attempts to bring more women into engineering. The discourse from which he speaks about women in engineering has no language or terms in which to see Carol in any context other than a *failed* "woman in engineering". This then leads him back to a position which says "women cannot be engineers" and "engineering is a man's work". In this discourse, women in engineering are understood first as *different from, and "better than" other women*. Then, when, as in this case, a woman fails to make the grade, the assumption behind this understanding (that ordinary women cannot be good engineers) once again comes to the surface, having the effect of jeopardising future attempts to offer opportunities to women in this area.

A further example of the construction of women in engineering and technological work as "different" relates to their perceived difference from male colleagues: being treated as "special", especially by the older men; not being expected to work as hard or to help with unpleasant and dirty jobs; being expected to act "feminine"; always being in a position of having to prove themselves as capable as men; being teased and harassed in a way that draws constant attention to their status as "outsiders" [Newton 82, Griffin 85, Cockburn 87a]. The young women software engineers in my own research mentioned all these difficulties. However, what is perhaps more interesting here, is the ways in which these young women sought to overcome the negative consequences of this emphasis on difference.

The main strategy employed by the female software engineers was simply to reject this constant emphasis on difference and to demand that they be treated "the same as men", a treatment that was considered to represent "equality"[5]. Some of their male colleagues appeared to share this understanding of equality, speaking proudly of the fact that they treated their female colleagues "no differently" from their male ones. Here, they clearly mean to indicate that they do not make their female colleagues the objects of their sexist discourse. However, by equating equality with "sameness" in the way they do, these men can be understood as precluding the possibility of discussion about gender dynamics: indeed, as silencing those who would speak of such things[6].

Several issues arising from my research have led me to conclude that existing policies aimed at increasing the numbers of women in engineering and technological work are unlikely to succeed. In this paper, I have shown why initiatives that concentrate on changing the image of technological work, from a masculine to a more feminine one, are misguided: first because women's relationship to masculinity and femininity is far less straightforward than such an approach suggests; and second, because the problem is not with the image of engineering but with the culture thereof. Serious attempts to encourage women into technological work cannot afford to ignore the ways in which gender is actively constructed in relation to work and in which, to date , masculinity and male power has been preserved by offering a very limited, "same as

---

[5]This confirms the findings of previous research on women in engineering. Newton and Brocklesby, for example, point out from their research that : "most young women basically wanted to be treated as equals" [Newton 82] p35. Being treated as "one of the lads", is welcomed by many young women precisely because it is seen as encouraging "equal treatment with the men".

[6]Indeed, I find it significant that the women SEs were far more likely to speak about their problems *as women in engineering* when talking informally over coffee or in "corridor chats" than they were in the more formal interview sessions, where they were likely to emphasise the need to "merge in" and "not make a fuss". They can be understood, here, as having been "silenced".

men", approach to equal opportunities.

8.1 REFERENCES

[Bem 74] Bem S L, "The Management of Psychological Androgyny", *Journal of Counselling and Clinical Psychology*, 42, pp155-162, 1974.

[Cockburn 85a] Cockburn C, "Technology as a Factor in Occupational Segregation", *EOC Research Bulletin*, 9, Manchester: Equal Opportunities Commission, 1985.

[Cockburn 87a] Cockburn C, *Two Track Training: Sex Inequalities and the YTS*, London: Macmillan Youth Questions, 1987.

[Dain 88] Dain J, "Getting Women into Computing", *University Computing*, 10, pp154-157, 1988.

[EITB 84] Engineering Industry Training Board, *Women in Engineering* occasional Paper No 11., Watford: EITB, 1984.

[Griffin 85] Griffin C, *Typical Girls? Young Women from School to the Labour Market*, London: RKP, 1985.

[Harding 81] Harding J, *Sex Differences in Science Examinations*, in Kelly A (ed), *The Missing Half: Girls and Science Education*, Manchester: Manchester University Press, 1981.

[Newton 81] Newton P, *Who Says Girls Can't be Engineers?* in Kelly A (ed), *The Missing Half: Girls and Science Education*, Manchester: Manchester University Press, 1981.

[Newton 82] Newton P and Brocklesby J, *Getting on in Engineering: Becoming a Women Technician* Final Report to the EOC/SSRC Joint Panel, 1982.

[Smithers 81] Smithers A and Collings J, *Girls Studying Science in the Sixth Form*, in Kelly A (ed), *The Missing Half: Girls and Science Education*, Manchester: Manchester University Press, 1981.

9

Expert Systems - A Women's Perspective

Margaret Bruce[1]
Alison Adam[2]

9.1 Introduction

Although[3] there is a tradition of research on gender and technology and in particular women and computing, the subject of women and expert systems has received scant attention. There may well be a number of issues which are important for women, relating to education, employment and everyday life. How does a novel technology like expert systems reinforce and reproduce gender divisions and what opportunities are there for women to influence the design of this new technology? In this paper we want to begin to explore these issues. The paper also reports expected impacts of expert systems on women's roles, as identified by a group of women during a Technical Assessment (TA) workshop at the 1988 Women into Computing Conference.

9.2 Expert Systems

As a subject, artificial intelligence (AI) has enjoyed, at least in computer terms, a long though rather chequered career. In the 1950's and 1960's researchers were far more optimistic than they are today about the potential to build general purpose reasoning systems. In the 1980's there was a considerable revival of interest in AI and related technologies. Much of this is due, at least in the UK, to collaborative ventures such as the Alvey programme, which is concerned with a number of enabling technologies, some of which are the intellectual descendants of older work in AI.

One of these technologies is intelligent knowledge based systems (IKBS). These have a more practical focus than traditional AI work in that they emphasise the knowledge in a given domain rather than general problem-solving strategies. A subset of IKBS is "expert systems" although often the two terms have been used synonymously. An expert system can be defined as an IKBS where the knowledge of one or more experts in a given area is explicitly modelled, eg a doctor's reasoning for medical

---

[1] Manchester School of Management, UMIST, Manchester
[2] Department of Computation, UMIST, Manchester
[3] This paper was presented at the 1988 Conference.

diagnosis or a judge's reasoning process in arriving at a judicial decision.

There have been many criticisms of artificial intelligence and expert systems, some of which have originated from well-known researchers in the discipline itself [Collins 85a, Collins 85b, Collins 87a, Collins 87b, Dreyfus 72]. Yet this school of research has produced almost nothing on gender issues. Perhaps this should not be too surprising as gender issues have generally been absent from the science studies domain. On the other hand, there are several studies of women and computing, mainly on word-processing and home-working but also on the positive opportunities available for women [Huws 82, Huws 86, Deakin 84]. Yet again, there is nothing on expert systems and women.

There are two important issues involved in such a study. One is the examination of the ideology involved in expert systems; the second concerns the representation of women in jobs in the expert systems field. In this paper we concentrate on the former area. Whatever the technical problems are in building expert systems, it is clear that they carry along with them a materialist view of the world. There is somehow the idea that it is possible, in some sense, to get inside people's heads, extract the knowledge therein and make a true representation of that knowledge. The danger of this materialism lies in the seeming inevitability that it is the knowledge of groups in power which will be formalised in this way. It is hard to see how the experiential knowledge of women in terms of their caring skills can be reconciled with "objective" scientific knowledge [Rose 85]. There is a danger that expert systems could exercise an undesirably normative effect in reifying the knowledge of one or a group of experts.

However, it is quite clear that it is possible to use expert systems for positive ends. There are a number of education projects concerned with the cognitive aspects of the educational uses of logic programming [Ennals 85]. In offering more flexible models of human behaviour this type of work could potentially provide a model for further research which attempts to break down class and gender stereotypes.

9.3 Technology Assessment

Technology Assessment (TA) is about identifying and evaluating the effects of technological change before they occur, such as biotechnology, a new drug, siting of an airport and so on. The underlying assumption of TA is that it is possible to anticipate the range of likely impacts arising from technological change. The attempt is to act as an early warning device to eradicate potentially harmful effects of a new technology before these are unleashed onto society - the classic example being the terrible effects of the thalidomide drug - and to exert some control over which technologies to promote and which not.

Most TA's take for granted that technology is itself apolitical and "gender neutral", that is, the technology will affect men and women in the same way. Even though there is mounting evidence and increasing discussion about the gendered nature of technology, TA's have rarely been conducted to assess explicitly the impacts of a given technological change on women [Zimmerman 85, Bush 82, Bruce 84].

Without being sensitive to gender issues, it is problematic to conduct a TA which fully explores the diverse effects of technological change. One of the major difficulties in devising such a TA is that of developing techniques for critically appraising the impacts of a new technology like expert systems, a technology which is still new and whose potential applications are not yet fully explored.

One intention of this feminist assessment of expert systems is to stimulate awareness of new technology and to think critically about some of the issues which such a technological change can bring, while at the same time introducing participants to techniques of Technical Assessment which they could use in other situations.

9.4 The TA Activity

The session began with a brief introduction to expert systems technology and the areas of its application. Then the purpose of the TA was stated, viz. to identify the breadth and depth of issues associated with a new technology to prevent "silly things happening". The technique used was a structured brainstorm (see [Bruce 84]), a form of creativity exercise to encourage participants to open up their minds to all sorts of possibilities occurring with the introduction of expert systems. The women were then asked the question:

What would happen if women's needs were taken into account in the design of the expert system?

Each woman spent five minutes working on her own to think about the question posed and to write down whatever statements came to mind without evaluating these in any way. These statements were first discussed with women in the immediate vicinity before conveying them to everyone else in the room. The resulting "impact statements" were then discussed by the participants as a whole, particularly in terms of the salient issues influencing gender relations for expert systems.

9.4.1 IMPACT STATEMENTS

The impact statements which women participating in this session produced were wide ranging in the issues they encompassed and detailed in terms of the fundamental social and political questions which they evoked.

9.4.2 NATURE OF WORK

One of the crucial concerns was the role of computers in general of changing the nature of work and working practices. Certainly some jobs may be affected more than others. Car workers may be replaced by robots but expert systems may bring about other changes which have potential impacts on professional and knowledge workers. The participants suggested that expert systems would be used initially to replace or deskill traditional women's jobs in service sectors such as teaching or health, but in the longer term the technology may eventually find applications in areas of traditional male employment like car mechanics, factory work and so on.

9.4.3 DEHUMANISATION

There were concerns about expert systems as a source of dehumanisation. Would they replace human activity in many areas? If so, women may become increasingly isolated, fewer people might work and come together in groups to chat, share experiences and so on. Such trends may exacerbate social disintegration.

9.4.4 OBJECTIFICATION OF KNOWLEDGE

In the construction of the knowledge base of an expert system, value judgements about gender roles could be made and it was felt that these could become objectified as constituting "true" knowledge. This in itself would reinforce gender assumptions and inhibit possibilities for social change. This raised the issue of power in the construction and design of this technology. It is difficult to capture and make explicit social attitudes in creating expert systems. Nevertheless questions about who designs the technology and whose knowledge is used in its construction and application, should be of continual concern. Only by challenging the values inherent in expert systems could the political nature of the technology be made apparent.

9.4.5 SEXISM

There was disagreement by the evaluators. Some of the women thought the technology would enhance prospects for social change, eg in opening up career choices for women by the dissemination of information about career possibilities to a wider group of people. Others thought that if information is still value-laden and gender-ridden then greater access represents no real shift in power. Some of the assessors thought sexism would be exposed. One example was given of eliciting knowledge for an admissions tutor for a medical school. It was impossible to reproduce the exact set of "logical" and "rational" criteria typically applied for the selection of students. In the end the system recruited more female students than usual and it was no longer used! In other words the technology was abandoned rather than the gender prejudices. This suggests that while expert systems appear to make knowledge more widely available, they may act subtly to support the status quo. The democratic view of technology has its roots in the prevalence of technological determinism rather than the alternative view which sees technology as socially shaped so that it is clearly seen as rooted in and reflecting the values of an existing social structure.

9.4.6 FEASIBILITY

How feasible is it to construct useful expert systems? The women focused on two issues here. First of all, the ideology surrounding the technology, including ideas of how it could be used in principle and secondly its *actual* utility were discussed. How expert systems are perceived may be radically different to how they are used. There is a danger that myths about the omniscience of expert systems are created. For instance, dire predictions as to the consequences of using word processors have not come to pass.

9.4.7 DECISION-MAKING

Another issue centred on the quality of decision-making. If expert systems are designed as decision-support systems, helping to make "better" decisions, then what constitutes such a decision and who decides this? The balance between rationality and intuition is all important. But rationality itself is so value-laden that to implement expert systems to act as decision-makers may be dangerous.

The potential exists to expose incompatibilities between expert systems so that differences in people's knowledge and assumptions can be made apparent. This suggests that it would be unlikely that an expert system would be accepted as the ultimate decision-maker. But on the other hand expert systems may be accepted as decision-makers in certain situations and then the assumptions and discourse surrounding the decisions forgotten.

9.4.8 APPLICATIONS

As well as the more philosophical debates about decision-making and the political nature of technology, various applications for expert systems were suggested by the women taking part in the technology assessment. These ranged from their use for safety in the home, eg in fire alarms, to their community use for applications such as careers advice. The latter application could possibly open up new career opportunities. But on the other hand, expert systems could emphasise more traditional careers for women depending on the gender assumptions built into them. The system itself cannot see whether the user is male or female. This could help to reduce sexism, but only if women were involved in the processes of building and using this technology.

On the whole the women in this session were confident about using technology and clearly felt that they were at least in some position to make choices about technology themselves. They did not regard technology as being "out of control" but felt rather that it was necessary to think through the social and political issues surrounding technological change.

All of the examples of expert systems applications cited were about access to education, supporting career choice, medical use and safety. There were no examples of the commercial use of expert systems such as in financial services. Yet this is one area where resources are being allocated by organisations which are creating and marketing expert systems. The women's priorities for the direction of expert systems was related to their own experiences and concerns.

9.5 Discussion

Thinking through the gender assumptions of a new technology is valuable as it adds another dimension to identifying and assessing the impacts of technological change and is another aspect to feed into discussions about the impacts of emerging technol-

10

Removed From Power

Lyn Bryant[1]

10.1 Introduction

Since[2] 1979 the number of women entering university computer science degrees has declined significantly. During this period a variety of initiatives has been made to try to attract more women into science and engineering generally, but the results so far can only be seen as disappointing. While the numbers of women entrants to engineering courses, unlike the case of computing, have actually increased, they remain a tiny proportion of the total.

10.2 Computers, Power and the Occupational Structure

The past decade has also seen an unprecedented growth in the availability of computer systems based on microprocessors and their incorporation into military, industrial and administrative control systems. Computers have become increasingly identified with power and the ability to control information, processes and people.

Within the occupational structure women, in spite of many "pioneers" and the breaking down of legal barriers, are still in a position of substantive inequality. They are still concentrated in a small number of occupations and on the lower rungs of occupational career ladders. A woman is more likely to be a cleaner, a secretary, a nurse or a primary school teacher than a bricklayer, a manager, a hospital administrator or a headteacher. Women at work are less likely to be in positions of power and control, more likely to be looking after or assisting others. Indeed, women's work roles are likely to echo their roles within the family.

The lack of real change in the domestic division of labour and its reflection in the occupational structure has meant that women have tended to come across computers not as the means by which they can exercise increased control, but, at worst, as the means by which their own working conditions are more effectively controlled.

Computers as they have become more important have evolved an increasingly masculine identity, and this identity seems to be conditioning the attitudes of teachers, children and parents. Computers have become part of the male domain.

---

[1]Department of Applied Social Science, Polytechnic South West, Plymouth
[2]This paper was presented at the 1988 Conference.

10.3 Schools, Families and Gender Socialisation

The socialisation processes that go on within families, schools and colleges are crucial in reproducing gender differences in behaviour and expectations and in supporting ideologies which favour such differences.

The ways in which the hidden curricula at school transmit messages about masculinity and femininity and their appropriate behaviours, subject choices and careers have been well documented. However, changing behaviour is not easy, partly because prevailing ideologies have been dented rather than breached and girls tend to be presented with relatively traditional role models at home, in the media and at school. They are subject to controls by teachers, and by boys, which are gender related and tend to reinforce the more passive and domestic "nature" of the girls.

It is interesting that, as McRobbie has pointed out [McRobbie 78], many of the working class girls who challenge the school system do so by deliberately emphasising their physical and sexual maturity, so that even their rebellious behaviour may only serve to reinforce traditional gender stereotypes.

There may, however, be a little hope to be gleaned from the attitudes of some of the women entering degree courses at Polytechnic South West. A substantial number of the students have entered the Polytechnic from Colleges of Further Education. The major reason given for a decision to leave school to pursue "A" levels at colleges of further education, was the rejection of the "social" aspects of school. Many of the women argued that there was less social distance between teachers and students at such colleges, and that judgements made upon them (the women) were less likely to be predicated upon dress and general behaviour. Importantly they also felt that there was less likely to be outright intimidation by boys. Thus at least some of the women are aware of the social processes by which they are surrounded and have taken some positive steps to change their situations.

10.4 Hegemony and Hopes for Change

Why is it that in spite of greater awareness of the problems facing young women in making non-traditional subject and career choices, change seems to be so slow? One important concept that has been used to try to examine the process is that of male hegemony [Arnot 82].

The moral and cultural control that is exercised by men is rooted in meanings that are deeply embedded in the social structure. Accepting views of women and their abilities which "blame the victim" is easy; the views are part of social reality which we have acquired without thinking. It is easy for people to believe that "girls don't take naturally to computers", boys can be defined as naturally more confident, "we would be glad to take more women, they just don't apply".

However, as Gramsci argues [Gramsci 81], it is quite possible to develop counter hegemonies, especially since there are conflicts and variations in practice within a given culture. But it is important not to see the sharing of ideas about good practice and efforts to increase the recruitment of women as sufficient. Much effort needs to be put into staff development programmes in schools, colleges and industries which encourage people to really question the taken-for-granted aspects of gender stereotypes and roles. If we are content merely to operate at the level of numbers of female recruits in the attempt to achieve a "critical mass", all we may be doing is asking future generations of women to continue to "juggle with gender"; trying to balance family and work roles and having to adopt particular strategies if they venture into areas that are seen to be predominantly male in character.

One problem is that many initiatives have been instigated centrally, prompted by the need to use "all the available talent". This utilitarian approach has echoes of the way in which female labour was used in the war; women being drafted in to "fill the gaps". Beliefs about gender differences in suitability to take up particular occupations or positions of power may remain intact, so that while some behaviour modification occurs, the underlying structure remains relatively unchanged.

10.5 REFERENCES

[Arnot 82] Arnot, M, "Male Hegemony, Social Class and Women's Education", *Journal of Education*, vol 164, 1982.

[Gramsci 81] Gramsci, A, "Selections from the Prison Notebooks", 1981.

[McRobbie 78] McRobbie, A, "Working class girls and the culture of femininity", in *Centre for Contemporary Cultural Studies, Women Take Issue*, Hutchinson, 1978.

11

Why Do We Want To See More Women in Computing?

Susan Jones[1]

Before suggesting how to attract more women and girls into the computing[2] profession, we should consider why we think it a desirable goal. A number of possible reasons may occur to us, including the following.

1. The computer industry is short of experienced staff, and the female population represents the largest potential "pool" of intelligent and trainable personnel with which to boost overall numbers.

   This is the point most often stressed when hand-wringing about the lack of women recruits goes on in the national or the computing press. But it warrants further examination. Skill shortages do not last forever; in particular skills associated with using machines of any kind often become obsolete rather quickly, as 200 years of industrial history has illustrated. Because the technology is self-perpetuating, developments in our own industry are exceptionally rapid, and its practitioners strive assiduously to render their own expertise out-of-date. Recent history has also shown that whereas women are busily recruited into the labour force in time of need, they are just as readily discarded when circumstances change.

2. Computing currently offers a range of rewarding careers, and it is only fair that girls as well as boys should benefit.

   This point of view commands respect, but once again it is worth digging deeper. Is it a coincidence that the most lucrative professions are precisely those where women form a minority? In its early days computer programming was not a particularly highly-regarded or well-paid occupation and females were better represented; they were thought to have the necessary "patience" and attention to detail for an essentially low-level clerical task. A cynic might suggest that the most effective way of ensuring a higher proportion of women in computing would be to reduce the average salaries – perhaps to those of infant-school teachers or nurses.

---

[1] Department of Computer Science, City University, London
[2] This paper was presented at the 1988 Conference.

3. In order to become more responsive to society's needs, the computer industry should take in a wider range of abilities, aptitudes and attitudes, some of which are more likely to be possessed by women than men.

This statement raises difficult issues. Generalisations about the typical characteristics of one sex or another can soon degenerate into cliche and stereotype, and exceptions are easily found. Nevertheless it may be useful to pursue this argument and see where it takes us. It is important to look beyond a simple marketing exercise, "selling" the idea of computing to girls, and to consider what might be most in their, and society's, long-term interests. I want to focus on one issue; the current emphasis on the "engineering" model for software development, and its effect on the provision of computing courses in higher education.

Twenty years ago Donald Knuth published the first volume of a book [Knuth 68] then highly regarded by teachers of the new academic subject of Computer Science. It begins:

"The process of preparing programs for digital computers is especially attractive because it not only can be economically and scientifically rewarding, it can also be an aesthetic experience much like composing poetry and music."

A little later in [Knuth 68] another comparison is made:

". . . a computer programmer can learn much by studying a good recipe book . . . "

It is a fair bet that these words would not cut much ice today. The preferred model is that of engineering, and analogies are most often drawn with building bridges or making aeroplanes. These are all metaphors of course; the material of computing is no more like metal and stone than it is like butter and eggs, or words and notes. But the change of metaphor marks an important change in our perception of how best to go about the task of producing computer systems, and the qualities required in those who perform that task. We are repeatedly told that programming as an individual art or craft has no future, that henceforth it must be seen as a "discipline" involving many finely-graded and differentiated skills, to be carried out satisfactorily only within an elaborate infrastructure of "tools" and "methodologies".

My purpose here is not directly to question these ideas, but to point out that they present a prospect very remote from the experience of the average adolescent girl. Her most likely contact with real hardware will have been in the context of word-processing, an application which is interesting only when processing one's own words rather than those of a boss or teacher. The engineering analogy will convey little of a positive nature; while engineering with physical materials at least produces a visible artifact, software engineering may suggest nothing but a nightmare of bureaucracy and jargon with no tangible result.

Those with more experience of the reality may have a different story to tell, but how to make it convincing? Can Knuth's words still be quoted without being totally misleading about the nature of computing? Is it an activity in which creative skill with words or ingredients is a relevant starting point? Can we identify the qualities needed to produce successful computer applications and ensure that they are properly valued, in whatever guise they appear?

At its heart, involvement in computing requires a concern for *structure*, both on a large and a small scale, since large systems must be built out of smaller components which work together harmoniously. Describing how a system is to perform requires the use of an artificial "language" of some kind, with its own syntactic and semantic rules. No matter what the form of this language – whether high or low level, imperative, functional, logic-based, diagrammatic – a high degree of precision in its use is mandatory, as is an ability to foresee the consequences of making any particular "statement".

Other essential characteristics include an interest in the way information is perceived, represented, and communicated, since computers are useful only in so far as they accept and hold information about the outside world, and rearrange it in ways satisfactory to their users. Many well-tried methods of doing this have been developed over the last thirty years, but all but the most stereotyped system design work requires the ability to weigh up alternatives and select a solution – which may not be "ideal" but will best serve its purpose within the current constraints.

No one would deny that many girls have the qualities mentioned above, but they don't always show them in the most obvious way. In particular we can point to the oft-quoted statistics about their tendency to follow arts rather than science courses at school and in higher education. There are no doubt numerous reasons for this, some culturally determined. But in so far as their subject choices represent genuine preferences they show that girls are more skilled with words than with numbers, and more interested in social phenomena and observable natural phenomena than in scientific or mathematical abstractions. (They also appear less interested in competitive games, either physical or mental, or in other rituals which involve the application of rules for rules' sake[3]).

Creativity, rigorous thinking, the ability to examine evidence and consider alternative approaches to a problem, concern for detail and pride in the production of a sound piece of work – all these are fostered by arts disciplines such as languages and history. However, because such subjects involve mental immersion in the thought-habits of people widely separated from the student by time or space, they should also create a sensitivity to different points of view, and a concern for the wider consequences of technical decisions.

Employers in the computing industry are aware of these facts, and often make little or no distinction between science and arts qualifications when recruiting. Neither does there appear to be any strong sex-discrimination where intelligent and well-qualified young people are concerned. The reluctance on the part of arts graduates (particularly women) to take up these opportunities stems from feelings of incapacity, and from a

---

[3] Many women will object to these sweeping generalisations and will certainly consider themselves to be counter-examples. Unfortunately some subjectivity is inescapable in discussions of this kind.

perception that the work to be done is both boring and useless.

I want to return to this point later, after briefly discussing the situation in higher education. For although academic computing qualifications are not necessary for a computing career, many of us are still anxious to see more girls obtaining them. And rightly so – even the most benevolent employer will train only for his own long or short-term needs, and it is important to maintain a supply of entrants with the breadth of knowledge provided by specialised degree courses. But what do such courses currently contain?

A number concern themselves with particular applications such as business data processing – these do not demand advanced mathematical expertise, and attract a reasonable proportion of female applicants. However it would be a pity if opportunities for girls were to be confined to this area; they should have the chance to see the range of possibilities presented within a Computer Science course as well.

Computer Science education is traditionally dominated by those who are "really" mathematicians, physicists and engineers, and who see the bracing mental gymnastics which they undertook themselves as an important rite of passage through which intelligence and competence is established. For a time other approaches were accepted as equally valid; now, under the banner of software engineering, mathematics is back in full force. Syllabuses emphasise formal logic and abstract symbol manipulation at the expense of more practical experience of real applications, machines and programming languages – paradoxically at a time when there are fewer school leavers with mathematical and scientific inclinations, and Computer Science departments are prepared to accept a wider range of entry qualifications.

I do not challenge the necessity for more rigorous approaches to large-scale system building, particularly where reliability is critical. But an emphasis on formal methods of design to the exclusion of all others must, I think, act as a deterrent to candidates who would be able to function satisfactorily even in quite technically demanding areas of the industry. It should be recognised that expressing problems in a formal notation does not of itself produce solutions; it simply enables those with a particular cast of mind to find solutions more easily, while acting as a barrier to everyone else.

There is a danger that this barrier will be particularly effective against girls. Not, of course, against those who are mathematically gifted, but the others who are less likely than their male counterparts to accept the "do it first, understand it later" approach which is their only chance of mastering the subject, (at least to the extent of qualifying them to study what really interests them). "Mathematics is about doing what you're told, isn't it?" was the remark made by a student recently emerging somewhat battered from the A-level sausage machine. I am not enough of a mathematician to judge, but I should hate to think it was true of computing!

We are frequently told by those who influence opinion that new methods of software production are vital because the current ones are slow, unreliable and expensive. Speakers or writers on this theme usually have their own solution to offer, and often present it along with dire warnings about the consequences of failing to take it up. We hear, for instance, of the "software crisis", and read that unless system development is formalised and automated, by the end of the century the entire literate workforce will need to be employed as programmers. An advocate of logic programming comments that "given the dimensions of the problem currently facing software management ... (discussing the merits of structured programming) ... is like arguing over the placing of the deckchairs when the Titanic is sinking" [Hogger 84]. If nothing else, phrases like this certainly reveal that we take ourselves seriously!

Advances in the theory and practice of computing are clearly desirable, but it is salutory to question from time to time whether new techniques can perform all they promise, and if so at what cost. An interesting point of view was expressed recently by Richard Bornat [McCrone 88] that there are limits to the feasibility of large projects, because the hierarchical and mechanical organisation required to complete them conflicts with the essentially creative nature of the work involved. Analogies with hardware engineering are false because the "manufacture" (and even the maintenance) of software is a design task down to the lowest levels. I see a parallel here with the medieval cathedral, where large and complex designs were successfully implemented by thousands of craftsmen, each making a unique contribution to the whole. There are of course striking differences – notably the longer time-scales involved in these "projects", and the fact that the participants probably had a firmer conviction of the ultimate value of the work!

The last point is not irrelevant. Investment in new tools and techniques is expensive, and advanced software engineering methods are most often advocated and adopted in the context of big development projects involving large sums of money and considerable prestige. In practice many of these are concerned with "defence", or with systems designed to provide ever more sophisticated facilities for manipulating exchange rates and commodity prices in the interests of small groups of people. It is hardly surprising that a very abstract approach will be preferred here, if only to allow the participants to conceal from themselves the essential futility of the enterprises in which they are engaged.

While such systems are held up for admiration as the "state of the art", we surely need not wonder why girls and women, unaware of more interesting possibilities, don't wish to be drawn in. Taking a realistic view of the likelihood of rising in an organisational hierarchy, they see themselves as potential cogs in a huge incomprehensible machine, with little control over their work or genuine sense of achievement. And it would be useless to deny the relevance of this picture to some areas of the computer industry.

By contrast there are numerous beneficial uses of computers, and even more exciting possibilities still barely explored. Moreover we have the means to build systems on a sufficiently human scale for their purpose and function to be well understood by their creators and users. Many of us know this from experience, and we need to stress it when encouraging girls towards a computing career. Better still, we should bring to bear what ingenuity and influence we possess to ensure that computer power is used wherever possible to help people to be safer, better-informed, and more satisfied in their working lives.

I want to conclude by looking again at possible reasons for bringing more women into computing.

If we are simply concerned with current skill shortages, I suggest we spare ourselves the worry. I am sceptical anyway about the existence of a "software crisis", in any normal sense of the word "crisis". People can survive quite well without any software at all, and in the long run small variations in the rate of its production are unlikely to matter. It is arguable that too many, rather than too few, resources are devoted to it even now, in comparison with other more pressing needs.

If we want to give more girls the chance of a career in which their intelligence and creative flair will be rewarded, we need to be more imaginative about computer education. The abstract formal approaches currently favoured in deference to the "engineering" model will not be congenial to everyone, and a greater variety of teaching methods is desirable. These need be no less disciplined – courses starting with object-oriented design and "literate programming" techniques [Knuth 84] might have the right flavour, while being academically respectable enough to pass muster with those who are prone to condemn "soft options" and "watering down". Such courses could profitably move off the beaten tracks of systems programming/ business data processing and specialise in different applications areas like education, publishing, lexicography, bibliography, etc. Much core material would remain, but presented in contexts more relevant to those for whom natural language is of primary importance.

The final possible reason for wanting more women in computing, particularly those who are not "natural" programmers and computer scientists, is that they may bring fresh insights to our problems. Within the industry we worry about inefficiency and late completion dates, while those outside complain of systems generating monotony and stress, requiring conformance to arbitrary rules in return for services rendered. We need software built with a concern for quality of communication, going beyond the provision of slick "user friendly" interfaces. But this requires that the industry becomes more mature, less obsessed with the grandiose and the technically sophisticated than with the satisfaction of making something genuinely useful. Our efforts to encourage more women to enter the computing profession will be worthwhile only if they contribute towards that end.

Acknowledgements

This paper expresses my personal views, and not those of the department in which I teach. However, I should like to thank the "real" Computer Scientists at City University, who over the last ten years have cheerfully tolerated the very unscientific colleague in their midst.

11.1 REFERENCES

[Hogger 84] Hogger, C J, *Introduction to Logic programming*, Chapter VIII.2.1, Academic Press, 1984.

[Knuth 68] Knuth, D E, *The Art of Computer Programming, Vol 1*, Addison Wesley, 1968.

[Knuth 84] Knuth, D E, "Literate Programming", *Computer Journal*, Vol 27, pp97-111, 1984.

> "The practitioner of literate programming can be regarded as an essayist, whose main concern is with exposition and excellence of style. Such an author, with thesaurus in hand, chooses the names of variables carefully and explains what each variable means. He or she strives for a program that is comprehensible because its concepts have been introduced in an order which is best for human understanding, using a mixture of formal and informal methods that nicely reinforce each other."

[McCrone 88] McCrone, J, "Project Management", *Computing*, May 12th 1988.

12

Machismo and the Hacker Mentality

Laurie S Keller[1]

In[2] the course of a career in computing which spans 20 years in industry and academia in the United States and Great Britain I have met several people I would call *hackers*. This paper describes some personal observations and speculations. In all the cases I describe here, my judgement has been confirmed by the independent judgements of others who have met and worked with the same people.

Hacker is a term which has begun to appear with increasing frequency in the press over the last half-dozen years. I find that its meaning has shifted somewhat in its transition from the restricted domain of computer professionals to the public domain represented by the press. Certainly a part of that shift in meaning has been due to the explosion of the availability and interconnectedness of data communications networks.

The term *hacker* originally denoted a "hack programmer", the direct counterpart of the "hack writer". This means a writer concerned with the volume of written output and the volume of income, a person with no real aesthetic, ethical or moral orientation who churns out words to order, a writer unconcerned with the quality of the written output, a person unconcerned with the factual content, style, or possible effects of what he or she produces or with its use or abuse once it is paid for. The original hack programmer very quickly turned out copious amounts of program code that worked at least once but was unconcerned with its quality: correctness, clarity, maintainability. He *[sic]* was more concerned with the quickness with which he could deliver the product and the cleverness of the code. Latterly the term *hacker* has come to mean someone interested in penetrating computer systems, usually by means of a data communications network, using fair means or foul, simply to snoop[3] or, more sinisterly, to compromise the integrity of the software or data they find. Their primary purpose seems to be "to have fun".

In giving thought to this shift in the meaning of the term *hacker* and in considering hackers of both types I have met, I find that, substantively, the two types are really the same. The change in the underlying technology from large machines without networks

---

[1] The Open University, Walton Hall, Milton Keynes
[2] This paper was presented at the 1988 Conference.
[3] Some hackers recently have attributed their action to altruism, claiming that they are performing a service for computer installations and network managers by penetrating a system in order to point out its vulnerability [Arnfield 88] [Gold 88]. Steve Gold was one of the men prosecuted for hacking into Prestel.

to smaller machines interconnected by data networks has altered the way in which hackers do their hacking, but the motive and methods remain the same.

In the preceding paragraph I said "his". Normally when I write or speak, I say "his or hers" or "one's" or "theirs", but in this case I use only the masculine purposely. I have never met a female hacker. No one I know with whom I have discussed hacking can recall an instance of meeting or hearing of a female hacker[4]. On this evidence, I must postulate that there are very few, if any, female hackers. Hacking seems to be an entirely male preoccupation.

Certainly most of the men I have met in the course of my career have not been hackers by any stretch of the imagination. However, so far, all the hackers I have come across (including press accounts) have been men. This leads me to speculate about why this apparent gender difference should exist.

A possible explanation for such gender difference is statistical – the number of women in computing is small. Perhaps there are too few women to constitute a sample of sufficient size to throw up an example of a female hacker. I do not know the numbers and so can make no statistically valid assumptions.

A second possible explanation is that, of the small number of programmers who are women, only a very tiny part advance into the realms where the kind of knowledge required for successful hacking is to be learned. Women tend to be concentrated in the areas of systems analysis, customer service, training and applications programming in commercial environments, where the opportunities to learn the details of operating systems and networking needed for hacking are generally unavailable.

However, I find myself drawn to a third explanation, which will, I hope, answer a related pair of questions. Those are: why are all the (observed) hackers male, and why are few men hackers? This third possible explanation which I would like to pose is that hacking is an aberrant behaviour related to *machismo*.

Machismo is an exaggerated form of male posturing designed to demonstrate a high degree of masculinity through the accomplishment of acts of proof, with the object of exciting the admiration of others and (perhaps also) demonstrating contempt for the less masculine. The act of proof is almost always undertaken in a solitary fashion since shared glory is, by definition, not glory at all. Hence being a good team player in football is not, by definition, *macho*, while daring the run of the bulls in the Pamplona festival of St. Fermin [5] is quintessentially *macho*.

Let us compare the behaviour of the hacker with macho behaviour.

The hackers with whom I've spoken at any length tend to describe their behaviour in terms of "overcoming","defeating", "proving [oneself] cleverer than the system's designers", "playing a game" [in which the object is to defeat or overcome a system's safety mechanisms]. These hackers also often express considerable contempt for those whom they deem less clever than themselves – for example those programmers who are concerned with the quality and maintainability of their work and therefore with

---

[4]The *Hacker's Handbook* [Anon 88] mentions one, but at one point puts *she* in quotes, as though to denote irony or uncertainty about that particular hacker's true gender.

[5]Hemingway is a fine example of a macho author and has the advantage, to those who wish to explore *machismo*, of writing in English.

its design and clarity or those programmers willing to work in a team or submit to the direction (especially technical direction) of others. This contempt also takes in network and system designers who fail to exclude hackers from a system. (Indeed, a prevailing attitude I have sensed in the course of these conversations has been a contempt for *everyone*).

In drawing a profile of a "typical" hacker I have always found them to be more or less solitary men. They may work in a group, marry, have families, but they are essentially and fundamentally solitary; they *relate* to no one. They are passively, rather than actively, anti-social. They spend a great deal of time hunched over a computer or computer terminal, face close to the screen, often with the brightness and contrast turned down to "protect" their work from accidental "prying" by others. They often become very possessive of a particular computer terminal. Even in a situation requiring sharing they will often adopt one terminal for their exclusive use and become indignant if some innocent should happen to sit down and log on during one of their absences.

The secretiveness of the hacker extends to protecting his own programs and data with encryption and passwords. Where I have seen these passwords I have found them to be literally inhuman – such as T42Y3A$, one that, in the course of my job, I had to find out from a hacker in order to move his files [6]. As a part of his tendency to secrecy, the hacker does not share his code or his techniques with others and does not normally volunteer help to a colleague with a technical problem[7]. If asked for help, the hacker tends to answer with a rapid flurry of nearly unintelligible jargon (which he refuses to explain) that displays his mastery of the topic and at the same time expresses contempt for the enquirer.

When not actively hacking, the hacker tends to sit engrossed in playing computer games or writing them. Very little of the hacker's work tends to be *purposeful* in the sense that his employer or his colleagues would recognise. He is often given to playing clever pranks that mimic system malfunctions, delighting in pranks that cannot easily be traced to him or, when he finds himself suspected, pranks that cannot be proven against him.

The activity of hacking is more important to the hacker than any objective one would normally associate with the development of software. Perhaps this explains some of the attractions computer games seem to have for hackers. Often these games seem to be a vehicle for nearly ceaseless, frenetic activity aimed at no real purpose in

---

[6]This password resembles nothing so much as something generated by a machine. When I asked about it, the hacker replied that, for him, it had special meaning, and he was very peeved to have to reveal it and change his password to something new once I had finished my task. A similar story appears in Weinberg's *Psychology of Computer Programming* where the sole comment in an entire program which had gone wrong in its author's absence was extremely cryptic. The poor programmer assigned to put the program right decided that this comment must be an important clue since it was appended to a particularly obscure line of code in the immediate vicinity of the error and he devoted several hours to trying to understand it. It turned out to be the date of Mozart's death.

[7]This may, however, be due to the contempt for others I mentioned earlier; contempt was certainly the reason I have been given twice by hackers for not offering aid.

life other than winning a higher score each time the game is played. The game becomes boring only when no further advance on the scores, no higher level of difficulty, exist. It is worth noting that most of these games are not *constructive*, that is, they are not simulations of creative or purposeful activity.

(In the sense that hacking is a solitary and non-constructive activity, it might be termed *masturbatory*. The pleasure or interest is confined to the activity itself, and has no object, such as a lover, and no objective, such as a demonstration of affection).

Recently, a senior police officer discussing his theories of the psychology of repeat killers in a press interview said that he felt that an important factor in the eventual apprehension of such criminals is the curious contradiction that, having committed a perfect crime (that is, having killed but remaining unsuspected), they feel disappointment that their cleverness goes unappreciated. There is a compulsion to try it again to demonstrate one's unsurpassed cleverness. The cleverness is, however, unrewarding in that no one knows that the criminal has carried out this clever crime. Eventually such criminals may subconsciously long to be apprehended so that they can flaunt their cleverness openly, and this longing may cause them to engineer their later crimes so as to result in eventual detection. Only when caught can they achieve the "reward" of being acknowledged by another person as clever. So they offend again and again, each time consciously challenging the police to detect them, and perhaps each time after the first, subconsciously hoping to be rewarded by having their pursuers acknowledge to their faces their extreme cleverness.

My own conversations with hackers engaged in penetrating systems have led me to believe that something similar occurs with them. They challenge a system in secret, penetrate it, and yet their cleverness goes unacknowledged and often unnoticed. So they must try again, to prove their cleverness to themselves. Yet, since this can be deeply unsatisfying, they hope unconsciously at the same time to be discovered by someone with sufficient stature in their eyes who will confirm to them how very clever they are. The problem is thus self-augmenting.

The characteristics which hacking shares with machismo can perhaps explain why hackers are men, and why not all, or even most, men are hackers – for not all men are caught up in the ethos of machismo.

The chief characteristic that hacking and machismo share is the need to prove oneself, not once, but over and over. A young male, daring the bulls at the festival of St. Fermin, for example, is not content with approaching once, standing firm and then withdrawing. The object of the exercise is to approach repeatedly, getting closer each time, daring more, perhaps touching a horn or rolling out of the way at the last possible instant to avoid a trampling or goring. Neither does the hacker rest[8]. Machismo precludes close relationships with others in the proving activity (but not outside it). A group of young men taunting a bull together, drawing its charges off from each other, are not behaving in a fully macho fashion. It is necessary to act alone, to dare the bull as an individual, without the help of others. As I have observed, the hacker is also

---

[8] One hacker expressed to me a deep regret that some day he would have penetrated all parts of the system and that there would be nothing further to challenge. He then casually proceeded to outline a plan to "hold the system to ransom" in such a way that he could remain undetected.

solitary.

In machismo, it is the proving act itself which is significant; its object or objective are not. Hence pointless acts of daring and bravery are perhaps the ultimate demonstration of a man's machismo. Better to die alone in a blaze of glory than to live and work with others for the survival of all. Better to spend one's time penetrating a network or a system or writing a truly clever piece of software than to work in a team and develop worthwhile (but to the hacker's mind pedestrian) software.

While secretiveness is not a characteristic of machismo *per se*, the hacker deems it necessary in order to protect his work so that others cannot copy and use it. Once code is copied by someone else, it loses its association with its author and can be used freely by the copyist as though it were his or her own. This would compromise the hacker's special claims to unique cleverness, since others could then demonstrate the same abilities and, indeed, might learn from them sufficiently that they can surpass the "master".

The truly macho man, of course, has nothing but contempt for the un-macho. The hacker has nothing but contempt for *anyone* less clever than he is.

The demonstration of machismo requires an audience who can affirm and confirm the glory of the macho act. The crowds at the Festival of St. Fermin[9] or at the bull fights act as this appreciative audience. It is no use facing an angry bull alone in a field, unobserved (except, of course, for practice); better to face the bull in full view of a crowd. Here the hacker has a problem. The appreciation of cleverness can only come from others who understand the nature and degree of the cleverness; one's colleagues. In common with the murder mentioned earlier, the hacker's activities often border on or are actually criminal. As such, the hacker's tragedy is that his appreciative audience will materialise only when he is caught or reveals himself.

12.1 The Hacker Mentality, Machismo and Women in Computing

What has the hacker's mentality and its relationship to machismo got to do with women in computing? Based on my own experience and experience shared with me by other women, we find ourselves often the objects of a contempt beyond that misogyny normally accorded women in a man's field. The sheer virtuosity of a hacker may be admired by his male colleagues; to a woman it is intimidating. This is especially true if she asks questions and tries to learn from such a person – where her questions earn her jargon-filled replies and contempt which may engender feelings of inferiority to erode her already fragile self-image – or if she finds herself as adversary in the form of network or systems programmer charged with preventing hacking.

In machismo, the sole role of the woman is as an appreciative audience; no woman,

---

[9]Including especially other young men, potential rivals who can be diminished by one's undertaking a sufficiently daring act, and young women whose admiration is – one hopes – boundless.

no matter how brave or daring, no matter how audacious, can be accepted as macho. By definition, such a woman is stepping so far out of her role as to be comparable to a dog who lectures on the philosophy of Wittgenstein (ie such a thing is not believed possible). The hacking *fraternity*, if it can be so called, while not excepting women as potential recruits, does not actively accept them either, preferring perhaps that women simply stay out of the way, particularly if those women prove unwilling to accept the hacking ethos.

Some university courses encourage hacking by providing a climate in which hacking is subtly or openly encouraged. Such courses place a disproportionate emphasis on speed of coding, the finding and use of inside knowledge and lack of emphasis on design, structuring and especially on team work, while failing to acknowledge broader social and philosophical concerns such as ethics or an examination of the role technology plays and should play in modern society. In many universities, polytechnics and colleges, those who teach computing are male and some have a hacker mentality.

What does this mean for a woman who has already taken a risk to enter such a masculine field? While there are other problems in the relationship of teacher and student such as the unbalanced power relationship between the two, the hacker is by nature not a good teacher for *anyone* and can actively discourage those, like women, who may feel that the risk to their self-image is too great to continue. Those courses which encourage a hacking mentality may so frustrate and intimidate as to drive women away, or to alienate them completely from computing as a profession.

12.2 Conclusion

Undoubtedly, many forms of discourse can be brought to bear on a serious study of the hacker. Given the spread of computers and networks throughout society, the ubiquity of sensitive personal and organisational data about all of us, the potential for the misuse and abuse of that data, and the vulnerability felt by women students entering a "masculine" field, I believe the hacker deserves serious study, and perhaps some therapy as well.

12.3 REFERENCES

[Arnfield 88] Arnfield R, "Facing a hard French line on hacking", *The Guardian*, Thurs, 21 April, p25, 1988.

[Gold 88] Gold S, "Hackers let off the hook", *The Guardian*, Thursday, 28 April, p27, 1988.

[Anon 88] *The Hacker's Handbook*, 3rd Edition, Century Publishing Company, 1988.

13

Child Care Provision in Higher Education :- A Case Study

Gill Russell[1]

13.1 Introduction

Economic forces are now at work, which indicate that the role of women, both in the workplace and in education, can, at last, no longer be ignored. But despite a growing awareness that lack of adequate child care provision hinders women's participation, moves towards providing the necessary facilities are generally characterized by lethargic indifference.

The University of Glasgow established limited child care provision a number of years ago. But since that time, the demand or need for child care provision has had no formal re-examination. This paper will discuss some of the arguments and issues involved in providing child care facilities. It will examine the co-operative effort between staff unions, the Students' Representative Council and others, which is attempting to force a review of the existing provision and report on the progress made to date.

13.2 Existing provision in Higher Education

Child care for both staff and students within higher education, as an AUT survey [Fleury 89] conducted in March 1988 highlighted, has existed in a number of institutions for some years. The survey, covering 81 associations with a response rate of 62%, discovered that 3 out of 4 universities (76%) had some form of child care provision. However:-

- many of the institutions did not offer enough places to satisfy demand (the average number of places was 35);

- the average length of opening was just over $7\frac{1}{2}$ hours but periods ranged from $2\frac{1}{2}$ hours to $9\frac{1}{2}$ hours and 4 institutions were open less than 4 hours;

- only 14% had any type of provision for school-age children;

- less than half (46%) were open during vacation periods.

---

[1]Department of Computing Science, University of Glasgow, Glasgow

Scott [Scott 89] has also examined the relationship between child care and women's access to all post-school education in Scotland (all institutions of FE, centrally funded and universities sector). With a response rate of 74%, the study found that:-

- only 38% of institutions had any child care provision;

- 48% of provision was for 3-5 year olds only;

- 63% of all provision was part-time;

- there was no provision for children over 5.

Thus in many educational institutions, a belief exists that children are born about 3 years old and no longer exist after the age of 5 and that the need for child care starts at 9.00am and ends around midday.

13.3   The Argument For

13.3.1   ATTRACTING STUDENTS

The UK is currently undergoing a fundamental demographic change. Government figures, published in 1988, projected a decrease in the number of 17 year olds overall in the UK until 1994 of about 27%, (a drop of about 30% is expected in Scotland) and a rise of 2.3 million among people aged 25-54.

What does this mean for higher education? The lack of school-leavers should motivate higher education, coupled with the current financial climate, to develop strategies which will increase participation from groups with traditional low levels of participation, in particular women and black students to maintain (and increase) student numbers. This means that institutions will need to re-examine the services and facilities offered to an increasingly diverse group of students. Logically, all institutions will need to re-examine or establish their child care policy as part of this process. Support for these arguments has been found by Scott. When Scottish institutions were asked to assess the effect of child care support on overall takeup rates :-

- 82% agreed that child care could improve access to courses for women;

- 62% of those providing child care said that it had improved uptake;

- only 8% said that providing child care had no effect.

13.3.2   ATTRACTING STAFF

Higher education has a number of significant employment problems to rectify. In academic terms, nearly 20% of full-time teaching staff leave academic careers before they are 30, and more than 70% of academics are due to retire over the next 20 years. Another problem, as the press [THES 90a] recently highlighted, is of low pay for

University clerical and secretarial staff, leading to some institutions experiencing difficulty in recruiting and then retaining such staff. However, this problem is not simply one of pay; the issue of the working environment also needs to be addressed.

In this context, child care provision is an important issue, which, if tackled positively, could help partially to overcome some of the employment problems currently facing higher education. For not only do positive child care policies simply address a problem which faces all working parents, they also indicate a caring and realistic employer – one who not only supports equal opportunities for all employees, but can be seen to do so.

13.4 The Argument Against

While only 4% of the respondents in Scott's survey felt that child care was the sole responsibility of parents, funding was identified as a major problem, along with lack of accommodation and lack of demand. Thus it can be argued that developing a positive child care policy within an institution is largely to do with "resource allocation".

13.5 Child Care at the University of Glasgow

13.5.1 BACKGROUND

The University of Glasgow has had some child care provision on-campus for about 20 years. Set up as a charity, a parent committee now employs 7 staff daily to look after a maximum of 55 children at any one time. A total of 72 3-5 year olds attend every week (children aged 3 do not come every day). The nursery is open school terms only from 9.00am - 12.15pm for both staff and student children, with students having priority. All parents pay the same daily fee, although there is some help available to students via a fund administered by the Students' Representative Council (SRC). The University provides a building with 2 rooms, kitchen and toilet facilities on the ground floor and two rooms with additional toilet facilities in the basement, which also has permanent access to a large enclosed garden. These facilities along with heating, lighting and maintenance of the building are provided by the University. All furniture and other equipment, as well as running costs are paid for through the fees.

13.5.2 THE CURRENT STATE OF AFFAIRS

Some time ago, a closer examination was made into child care provision in the University, in response to the publication of the AUT child care survey, the setting up of a Working Party for Mature Students in the Science Faculty, and the formation of a committee to devise an equal opportunities policy for the University. The main aim was to discover the answer to a basic question, "Does the current provision actually satisfy the current needs of the University's staff and students?". Unfortunately, the picture described in section 13.5.1 has grown somewhat tarnished.

An examination of the children's parentage revealed that only 6 of the 72 children currently attending the nursery (1989/90) actually have students as parents, a further 35 children belong to staff, and the remainder are the children of General Council Members ie former graduates of the University. This situation has arisen because the nursery has experienced difficulty filling all the available places. Advertising the vacant places to ex-University graduate parents now working in local government solved the problem.

Trying to find out how many students had been helped by the SRC bursary, uncovered the fact that no financial help had actually been given to any student for at least two years, because the regulations stipulated that both parents had to be undergraduate students of the University. It was also discovered that the nursery accommodation, which was thought to have been used for other purposes in the afternoon, was actually available all day. Child care provision in the University was not actually determined by the University Court but by the parent-run committee.

13.5.3 SURVEYING THE DEMAND FOR CHILD CARE

In response to these discoveries, three surveys have been conducted, in an attempt to quantify the demand for child care from within the existing staff and student populations.

The Glasgow AUT Questionnaire

A questionnaire was sent to all GAUT members. With a 15% response rate, it found that:-

- 88% of the respondents believed that the University should provide full-time child care;

- 66% had children for whom arrangements had to be made;

- 82% of those who had children felt that they had been hampered in the day-to-day performance of their job;

- 43% had a child minder coming to the house;

- 27% had the children going to a child minder;

- costs fell most frequently in the £40-60 per week bracket.

The questionnaire also identified 42 full-time and 30 part-time children who would use a facility if it existed. Another 36 members of staff answered that they would not use it. However, 22 of these indicated that they answered in this way because they now wanted to continue with their existing child care arrangements. Therefore there were another 22 members of staff, who would have used University child care, had the option existed, when they began to need child care.

The NALGO Questionnaire

The same questionnaire was sent to all NALGO members within the University. With a 14% response rate, it found that:-

- all were in favour of the University providing full-time child care, even though 57% of the respondents did not have children themselves;

- 43% had children for whom arrangements had to be made;

- 100% of those who had children felt that they had been hampered in the day-to-day performance of their job;

- 16% had a child minder coming to the house;

- 44% had the children going to a child minder;

- costs fell most frequently in the £40-60 per week bracket.

The questionnaire also identified 9 full-time children and 8 part-time children who would use a facility if it existed. Another 5 members of staff would have used University child care had the option existed, when they began to need child care, but did not wish to change their arrangements now.

Science Faculty Mature Student Questionnaire

The main aim of this questionnaire was to identify the needs and problems of mature students within the Science Faculty. Child care requirements and the problems student parents face were integral parts of this identification process.

The questionnaire was sent out to 200 mature students, ie all undergraduates in the Science Faculty who started a degree course over the age of 21. A response rate of 35% found that:-

- 4% did go looking for child care on campus;

- none of these students had any success finding child care on campus;

- the pool of subjects which students can choose from is restricted because they have difficulty attending subjects with afternoon labs (this is of significant importance for science subjects);

- students do not have adequate access to library facilities because of child care problems in the evenings and at week-ends;

- finance was the major hurdle students had to overcome in coping with their University course;

- alternative timetabling (evenings/weekends) needs some form of child care provision to succeed.

The questionnaire also identified that the type of provision required is equally split between the under and over 5's and that the ratio between part-time and full-time requirement is 1:3.

13.5.4 QUANTIFYING DEMAND

Table 13.1 identifies the potential number of students requiring some form of child care and a breakdown of the type of provision required. Table 13.2 combines staff and student totals.

Table 13.1 Potential no. of students requiring child care

		Student numbers	Estimated No. of mature students	Estimated No. requiring child care
Postgraduate	Fulltime	1337	1337	54
	Part-time	1173	1173	47
Undergraduate	Fulltime	10210	1021	41
	Part-time	357	36	0
	Total	13077	3567	142

Table 13.2 Under 5's Child care requirements for staff and students

	Part-time	Full-time
Students	18	53
GAUT	30	42
NALGO	8	9
Total	56	104

There are some inadequacies with these statistics, for example the figures do not indicate the numbers of students needing help for more than one child. Neither does the survey reflect the higher proportion of women mature students in the Faculties of Arts and Social Sciences. Currently the exact proportion of mature students within other faculties is being sought. However, these figures do at least present a quantifiable demand, which can be used to support the case for a re-examination and expansion of child care on campus.

13.5.5 THE CAMPAIGN

The campaign for child care in Glasgow University was launched in an article published in the University newsletter. Presently the names of people responding to the article are being collected, so that when all the information has been prepared to put the case before the University Court, their support can be galvanised. The case for better provision is being argued in a number of ways:-

- providing child care facilities will attract staff and students to the University (an unfortunately impossible task would be to survey how many students have not come to the University because of the lack of such facilities);

- inefficient use of accommodation is a wasted resource;

- it is unacceptable that the University Court is not in control of child care policy on campus;

- questioning how much is currently spent on child care (currently the costs are hidden);

- questioning why a fund to benefit the social life of staff is unspent, arguing that children are part of the social life of staff so there already is a fund which could help finance provision;

- the University is currently beginning its career as an equal opportunities employer; there can be no real equality of opportunity without convenient child care;

- the University is proud of the lead it has taken within higher education to develop student services in response to both students academic and personal needs – child care is a personal need for some students.

13.5.6 CAMPAIGN AIMS

What has been clearly established is that a far greater need for child care exists on campus than is catered for by the current provision. However, all child care requirements will never be met. Therefore the campaign has tried to identify different stages of development towards a totally integrated child care policy. These are, in the following order of priority:-

- the development of a positive child care policy;

- an efficient use of the existing nursery building for the 3-5 year olds;

- provision for the under 3's;

- the development of play-schemes during holiday periods;

- the development of after-school care on campus;

- for the University to become involved in initiatives within the local community to provide more child care facilities in recognition that what may be provided on campus is not always suitable, such as on campus after-school care for students who travel to the University.

The over-riding feature which will permeate all these aims is flexibility.

13.5.7 STATUS REPORT

Details currently under investigation are:-

- how best to provide a mix of part-time and full-time care;

- how to be flexible for day-to-day requirements;

- budget details based on the figures presented in section 13.5.4;

- an alternative "financing" arrangement;

- accommodation for "under 3's" provision.

Also, the child-minding association has been contacted to supply an up-to-date membership list for use within the SRC advice service (the local authorities are 4 years out of date). All student enquiries regarding nursery placements, financial help etc are being collected and collated. Two large employers in the area have been contacted to investigate the possibility of a collaborative approach to financing child care. One has responded positively.

13.6 Conclusion

This paper has discussed some of the arguments and issues involved in providing child care facilities within higher education. It is shameful that this society in the 1990's still needs to have the same arguments repeated time and time again. Yet for as long as higher education continues to ignore both the need for women's participation and the needs of those women who do participate, and "advertises itself as an equal opportunity employer without possessing the necessary will or machinery to effect such a policy" (see [THES 90b]) these arguments must be made. The Campaign for Child Care in the University of Glasgow has come some way down the path from asking basic questions about the existing provision. While it still has a way to go, identifying the potential demand is a very necessary first step.

There is now a pool of interested and motivated people within the University, who have identified a strategy to work towards and have initiated steps to prepare themselves thoroughly before presenting their case to the University Court.

13.7 REFERENCES

[Fleury 89] Fleury B, "Universities caring for the very young: an AUT survey of child care facilities 1989", 4, *AUT Bulletin*, April, 1989.

[Scott 89] Scott G, "Child Care and Access: Women in Tertiary Education in Scotland", Scottish Institute of Adult and Continuing Education, *Scottish Adult Education Monographs*, 9, 1989.

[THES 90a] *Times Higher Education Supplement*, 18.5.90

[THES 90b] *Times Higher Education Supplement*, 20.4.90, "Behind the Bastion".

14

Opting Out Of Technology: A Study of Girls' GCSE Choices

Philippa Buckley,
Barbara Smith[1]

14.1 Introduction

In common with similar departments in many other UK universities, the School of Computer Studies at Leeds University has become increasingly concerned over the past few years by the declining proportion of women amongst our students. In 1979, 20% of the students entering Computer Science and related single-subject degree schemes at Leeds were women, but since then the proportion has tended to decrease, reaching just 9% in 1988.

At O and A level the national picture is slightly different from that for degree courses. DES figures for England and Wales show that the proportion of girls amongst A-level Computer Science entrants stayed at about 22% from 1979 to 1983, declining to 17.7% in 1985. At O-level, the proportion of girls amongst Computer Studies entrants remained fairly constant at 30% from 1979 to 1985 (DES, Statistics of Education). More recent figures from the DES show that in 1987-88, amongst school leavers, 9% of girls took GCSE Computer Studies, compared with 16% of boys.

It seems from these statistics that girls in secondary schools are much less likely to choose computing as a field of study than are boys. Underlying the question of why girls have chosen not to apply for University courses in Computer Science is the question of why they also choose to opt out at an earlier stage. This investigation was aimed at looking at this opting out in secondary schools; however, it was decided that the study would not be limited to Computer Studies, but would consider technology subjects in general.

This decision was mainly influenced by the prospect of the National Curriculum, under which Computer Studies is not considered to be a foundation subject: instead, Information Technology will be taught across the curriculum. However, a technology subject is compulsory as part of the set of foundation subjects, and this may mean that the main exposure to, and involvement with, computing as an examinable subject will come from the Craft, Design and Technology subjects. It is reasonable to assume that if girls are at present choosing to opt out of technology subjects in general, this may lead to significant problems in the future.

---

[1] School of Computer Studies, University of Leeds, Leeds LS2 9JT

14.2 The Study

The main objective of the study was to establish whether or not there is a significant difference in the number of male and female pupils taking technology options at GCSE level (the subjects included in the study will be discussed further below). Regional variations were also investigated, and variations between different types of school (girls only, boys only and coeducational). The number of technology options offered in different schools was considered, and the pupils' opting behaviour in technology options was compared with that in more established subjects, such as Physics and History, and in Home Economics, where a difference in uptake between girls and boys is also to be expected.

The study was based on a questionnaire sent to individual schools, asking for information about the school, its pupils and the GCSE options that were being taken by fourth and/or fifth years in the academic year 1989/90.

The questionnaire was sent to 101 schools in five areas of England (not including London). The areas were selected for diversity of location, geography and demography. Usable replies were received from 46 schools, the proportion of schools replying in each area being fairly similar (between 42 and 50%).

However, because of variations in population density, the number of pupils covered by the completed questionnaires varied from 635 in area 2 (a mainly rural area) to 2334 in area 5 (a metropolitan district). Altogether, the total number for which GCSE data was given is 6137, of whom 3161 are male and 2976 female.

14.3 Results

14.3.1 OPTIONS OFFERED

There is a wide variety of GCSE technology options on offer in the schools surveyed. For the purposes of the study, it was decided to include only options offered by at least 5 schools in the sample: this excluded Robotics and Office Studies with Information Technology, offered by one school each.

The computing and related options included in the study were Computer Studies, Information Technology and Business and Information Studies. The Word Processing, Office Studies, Computer Literacy and IT Awareness courses were excluded, partly because in many schools the last two are compulsory or non-GCSE courses, so that there is no evidence as to whether pupils would choose to do them given the option, and partly because the level of typing and keyboard skills in these courses tends to be too high to consider them technology options.

Only 11 schools offer Computer Studies, and as many as 20 schools (46%) offer none of the four computing options. These schools tend to be the smaller ones, covering 31% of the pupils in the survey. Only 4 schools offer more than one of these options.

The most common technology options available in the survey schools are the three Craft, Design and Technology (CDT) options. CDT is a generic term covering a range of studies and is concerned with giving pupils the opportunity to gain experience in identifying, considering and solving problems through the use of a range of materials and technologies. CDT: Design & Realisation is primarily concerned with the process of design, using a variety of tools and materials, which include microcomputers as well as traditional materials such as wood, plastics and metals. The computing content of the course is not fixed, however, and can therefore be significantly higher in some schools than in others. Great emphasis is placed on problem solving, the design lifecycle and the impact of technological change. 31 schools offer this option.

CDT: Design and Communication is offered by 18 schools and is concerned with the analysis of problems and design of solutions. The common core of the subject involves the collation, dissemination and presentation (invariably using microcomputers) of information from a wide variety of sources. One of the main objectives is to foster awareness and appreciation of the value and use of information, with particular reference being placed on the advantages to be gained from the use of computers.

The common core of CDT: Technology concentrates on problem analysis and solving and places particular emphasis on systems design. It covers a wide range of issues such as ergonomics, prototyping and systems modelling and contains a defined computing content which aims to foster interest in the ways in which computers can be used as tools to aid research, analysis and design and as a control device. 20 schools offer this option.

Of the schools surveyed, 10 offer all three CDT options. On the other hand, 12 offer none of them: these are all girls' schools, apart from one, a very small independent co-educational school.

The other technology option offered by the sample schools is Electronics, available at five schools, always in addition to at least one of the CDT options.

14.3.2 LEVEL OF AVAILABILITY OF TECHNOLOGY OPTIONS WITHIN SCHOOLS

Of the seven technology options included in the survey, the number offered at each school is on average 2.3. However, this varies considerably with the type of school: as already mentioned, 11 girls' schools (out of the 13 in the sample) offer none of the CDT options. Eight of these 11 schools offer no computing options either. The average number of technology options available to pupils in girls' schools is therefore very low: only 0.8 options. Boys' schools do rather better: of the 11 schools in the sample, all offer at least one CDT option, though only four offer a computing option as well. The average number of technology options on offer is 2.0. All single-sex schools therefore place much less emphasis on teaching technology subjects than the coeducational schools, where on average 3.3 technology options are available.

Differences between the five areas sampled, in terms of the number of technology options offered, were also considered. However, it was difficult to identify any significant differences, which would in any case have been difficult to disentangle from the differences between types of school, given the small numbers of schools in each area and the varying proportions of single-sex schools. It was, however, noticeable that area 5 (a metropolitan district) has a much higher level of computing in its schools than the other areas. 73% of the schools sampled in that area offer at least one of the three computing options, compared with 50% or less in all other areas. This suggests that significant regional differences may indeed exist, perhaps reflecting different local education authority attitudes to computing, and technology in general, which a larger survey might have been able to identify.

By contrast with the technology options, most of the other options for which information was requested in the questionnaire are much more established in the curriculum of the survey schools. Physics, Chemistry, Biology, Geography and History are offered by all the schools. Home Economics is offered by 30 schools, the exceptions including, not surprisingly, all the boys' schools.

14.3.3 UPTAKE OF GCSE OPTIONS

Table 14.1 shows the proportion of pupils in the survey taking each of the options covered by the questionnaire. Since the first five options are available in all the schools, the percentages given show the proportions of pupils choosing to do these options. The table shows that the reputations of Chemistry, and especially Physics, as boys' subjects, and Biology as a girls' subject, are being maintained.

Table 14.1 Proportion of Pupils in Survey Taking GCSE Options

Option	% Pupils Taking Option		
	Girls	Boys	Total
Geography	46.2	63.3	55.0
History	44.2	46.6	45.4
Physics	22.2	55.4	39.3
Chemistry	35.7	46.1	41.1
Biology	46.1	35.1	40.4
Home Economics	30.1	5.7	17.6
CDT:Design/Realisation	3.6	27.8	16.1
CDT:Technology	1.5	12.4	7.1
CDT:Design/Communication	3.9	16.2	10.2
Computer Studies	4.4	8.4	6.5
Information Technology	8.7	4.7	6.6
Business & Information Studies	10.7	4.4	7.5
Electronics	0.2	3.1	1.7

For the other options in the table, the proportions partly reflect the availability of the various options in the schools, and not solely pupil choice. The table clearly shows, however, the very small numbers of girls taking CDT options. The total percentage of girls taking a CDT subject is at most 9%, assuming that no girl takes more than one of these subjects.

Rather surprisingly, although fewer girls than boys are taking Computer Studies, this is not the case for the other two computing options, Information Technology and

Business and Information Studies. These options will be considered in more detail below.

Table 14.2 attempts to show the extent to which pupils choose to do the various options on offer to them. For the eight subjects which are not offered in all the survey schools, it shows the number of pupils taking an option as a proportion of the number of pupils at a school which offered that option. The last two columns show the number of pupils who are at a school offering the option as a proportion of the total number of pupils.

Table 14.2 Proportion of Pupils in Survey Choosing GCSE Options

Option	% Pupils choosing option		% Pupils who can choose option	
	Girls	Boys	Girls	Boys
Home Economics	31.9	9.5	94.4	60.4
CDT:Design/Realisation	5.7	29.3	62.7	94.9
CDT:Technology	3.5	21.1	43.3	58.7
CDT:Design/Communication	8.0	30.5	48.9	53.1
Computer Studies	16.8	23.3	26.5	36.1
Information Technology	27.2	23.8	31.9	19.6
Business & Information Studies	34.2	19.7	31.4	22.5
Electronics	1.0	14.2	16.4	21.5

It is assumed here that pupils can freely choose to do any subject, and any combination of subjects, which is on offer at their school. In practice, of course, because of timetabling problems, some combinations may not be possible. For instance, if Home Economics is in the same timetable group as one of the CDT subjects, the choice of one would preclude the choice of the other. Information on timetable groupings was not requested in the questionnaire, partly to reduce the burden on the schools and because it would be difficult to collate. It would in any case be difficult to interpret the information, since schools would probably claim that the groupings reflect demand rather than prevent pupils from doing subjects which they would otherwise choose.

Table 14.2 shows that even where the options are available to them, girls choose to do the CDT subjects and Electronics very much less often than do boys. It is interesting to compare Home Economics with CDT: Design and Realisation. These two subjects seem to occupy complementary niches in the curriculum. Home Economics is available to nearly all the girls and about 60% of the boys (because although it is not taught in boys' schools, it is widely available in coeducational schools). Roughly 30% of girls who can choose this option do so, but under 10% of the boys. The position of CDT: Design and Realisation is almost a mirror image of this.

The three computing subjects are in a very different position to the CDT subjects. Although Computer Studies is chosen by fewer girls than boys, the difference is not very great. The other two computing subjects, Information Technology (IT) and Business and Information Studies (BIS), are more popular with girls than with boys. There seems to be a tendency, though not altogether uniform, to view Computer Studies as a boys' subject and IT and BIS as girls' subjects: for instance, no girls' school in the survey offers Computer Studies, whereas five offer IT or BIS (or in one case both). Of the four boys' schools offering a computing option, three offer Computer Studies and one offers BIS. The girls' schools which offer IT or BIS also do very well in attracting girls to take these subjects: 41% choose IT when it is available and 42% choose BIS. On the other hand, in coeducational schools, fewer girls than boys choose to do IT, whereas BIS is again favoured more by girls.

Table 14.3 considers the technology options in coeducational schools only, and shows that in mixed classes, girls are very much in the minority except in the computing options.

Table 14.3 Pupil Mix in Technology Subjects in Coeducational Schools

Option	CDT: Design/ Realisation	CDT: Tech.	CDT: Design/ Comm.	Comp. Studies	IT	BIS	Electronics
Boys	646	274	387	165	148	80	63
Girls	87	23	93	132	110	135	7
% girls	11.9	7.7	19.4	44.4	42.6	62.8	10.0
Number of schools	21	14	14	8	7	5	4

14.4 Summary and Discussion

It has been suggested that girls' schools do better than coeducational schools at attracting girls to subjects such as Physics that are seen as boys' subjects. There is some evidence in the survey that this is the case in the girls' schools offering technology options. As has been stated earlier, the proportion of girls choosing IT or BIS in girls' schools is higher than in co-educational schools. A similar effect seems to occur in the CDT subjects: 13% of the pupils in those girls' schools which offer one of these options choose to do it, which although still very low is better than the overall proportion. The efforts of these schools are, however, outweighed by the fact that most girls' schools in the survey do not offer the technology options: only two schools out of 13 offer a CDT option, and only five offer a computing option.

The study showed that, in the schools surveyed, girls are not lagging behind boys in choosing to do computing options at GCSE, if we include Information Technology and Business & Information Systems as well as Computer Studies itself. However, fewer girls than boys are taking Computer Studies, partly because it is less likely to be available to them and partly because when it is they are less likely to choose it.

It would be interesting to investigate further pupils' attitudes to the three computing subjects, to try to establish why IT and BIS are so much more attractive to girls than Computer Studies. It would also be worth considering to what extent the various GCSE computing options lead to further study in Computer Science. Are A-level Computer Science students drawn equally from Computer Studies and the "girls'" options of IT and BIS, or predominantly from Computer Studies (or conceivably from pupils who have done no computing options at GCSE)? Similar questions could also be asked about entrants to Computer Science courses at Universities and Polytechnics.

An examination of a small sample of 70 UCCA forms of home students who have been offered conditional places on computing degree courses at Leeds University for October 1990, and who took GCSEs in 1988, points to some answers to these questions. Eleven of the 70 applicants had done no examinable courses in computing, or technology in general, so that we are still managing to attract some applicants who perhaps have had no opportunity to take a technology subject at school. Seven of the rest were doing A or AS level Computer Science without having done a technology GCSE. All of the remaining 52 applicants had GCSEs in at least one technology subject: of these, 36 had Computer Studies GCSE, compared with only three who had an Information Technology GCSE, and 32 had a GCSE in one of the CDT options. From this evidence, it appears, therefore, that the GCSE options in Computer Studies, and equally CDT, are the main source of our applicants, and it is evidently Computer Studies, rather than IT or BIS, which leads students to consider degree courses in Computer Science. A more detailed study of the technology background of applicants to computing degree courses would be very worthwhile.

The school study shows that at present the CDT options are much less attractive to girls than to boys. The brief survey of UCCA forms suggests that this may have some bearing on the lack of female applicants for computing degree courses, since the CDT options seem to play a role in encouraging students to consider studying computing further. With the advent of the National Curriculum, this may become a much more important factor, as technology becomes a foundation subject, while Information Technology is integrated with the rest of the curriculum. The present failure of CDT to attract girls shows that schools will face a considerable challenge in selling technology to them. The comparison with the current position of Home Economics suggests that the cultural change required is at least as great as would be involved in persuading all boys to do Home Economics. The success of schools in tackling this challenge may well determine whether or not we see any improvement in future in the number of girls choosing to pursue computing beyond GCSE.

15

Action Research: Primary Schoolgirls and New Technology

Audrey Milner[1]

15.1 Introduction

In order to encourage the participation of girls in New Technology, the European Commission launched a programme of research projects to be conducted simultaneously in each of the member countries.

The UK project, proposed and led by the author and partially funded by the DES, began in January 1987 and finished in September 1988. Eleven primary schools, all in outer London Boroughs, were involved, though particular work was developed in six classrooms, in different schools, across the age range five to eleven years. This paper is based on the final report.

The project concentrated on teaching and learning within the area of Control Technology. Some of the reasons for this decision follow. This is a new venture in schools and so there could be an attempt at the start to make sure that girls are not left behind, that their contribution is valued and that they see the work as sensible and relevant. The area of application (Craft, Design, Technology – CDT) is one in which traditionally boys feel more at home and is thus a challenging area. There is a direct and apparent link with what goes on outside school in broader areas of life and work. Control work in primary schools is likely to be topic based and to depend for its educational success sense on related work such as descriptive writing, technical or scientific writing, planning, the drawing of diagrams and model making. Within the project then, other computer related applications besides CONTROL are likely to be used, thus exploring the wider involvement of girls with new technology.

15.2 The Development of the Project

As the project progressed in each classroom, new approaches were developed. These were not envisaged at the start but evolved gradually from a shared concern to improve the situation. Observations made in the classrooms, while working with the children, and conversations with individuals and groups, form the basis for this report. The examples reported are those which have been found to be typical. They are not reported

[1]North Fursdon Farm, Yealmpton, Plymouth PL8 2EN

in order to provide statistical evidence but to give a glimpse of reality. Teachers will be able to identify with this and so become more aware of what is happening in their own classrooms. It is hoped that this awareness will lead to the development of new approaches, which work well for each teacher, to counteract inappropriate practices.

The following four sections refer to the differences in the behaviour of boys and girls. Assertions are made, followed by anecdotes and justifications.

15.3 Boys' Domination

This section refers to the dominating behaviour of boys. In order to counteract this behaviour, we must be aware of the ways in which it is shown.

- Boys dominate as a result of their demands.

- Boys answer for girls and take over from them.

A girl was working on a number grid and asked me to go back to see how she was getting on. I went back and, as I asked her some questions, the answers came from a boy some distance away.

- Teachers reinforce stereotypes.

- Children are developing a perception of their roles and accept what is set up for them according to gender.

- Boys belittle girls' attempts.

- Boys are chosen by the teacher to be computer monitors which often means that they assume right of access to the computer.

- Boys have greater experience, often outside school, of technological activities.

- Boys domination causes, but could also be said to be caused by, girls' low self image.

In a fourth year junior class, four girls and two boys were working with a town layout that they had designed and made. They were using a control box interfaced to the computer to control vehicles and traffic lights which they had also made and positioned on the layout. The girls were gathered at one end of the table. One boy was at the keyboard, with the other boy beside him. When asked why the group had been chosen for this work, the girls said of the boy at the keyboard that he had got brains, which he smilingly acknowledged. The girls were questioned, "But why have you girls been chosen?". Their first response was, "Don't know". It genuinely puzzled them and as they worked, they continued to speculate. They rejected the suggestion that perhaps it was because they had brains. They were included, "Just because the teacher said 'come' ". Other comments were:

"I don't think it's because we did well with making the cars because we didn't do too well."

"I enjoy building cars and finding out and making things that move."

The teacher, who heard much of this conversation, expressed surprise, bordering on unease, at what he had learned about the group.

15.4 Ways of seeing work and play

An important aspect of girls' apparent reluctance to participate in technological activities, such as model making, arises from the emphasis which is put on "work" in school by teachers and by parents. Girls see model making as "play", whereas writing, reading and number work are seen as legitimate "work" and therefore as more important.

- Work is important. Teachers' direction is needed before play is permissible for girls.

One eight year old girl said that work, for her, was writing, maths, putting a cover on her topic book and sewing. Play is making models with LEGO. Boys build models with LEGO and then play with them. She would only play with LEGO if the teacher told her to do so.

- Play which is seen as a preliminary to writing is seen as legitimate.

Another girl said that she might play with LEGO when she had finished her work, but she would prefer to draw a picture. She didn't see using LEGO as a good use of time, because, "If I did some drawing I would do some writing to go with it". Girls have a compulsion to absorb themselves in what they consider to be legitimate work. Part of that legitimate work is "drawing" in which they almost seem to hide away. It is a soothing way of passing time and the demands can almost be what the children make them to be. It also leads to REAL work, which is writing.

- Work is a legitimate refuge from a situation of potential conflict.

Four girls were busy writing at a table. I asked them why they were not making models. Here is a summary of their replies.

"I don't know how to make them."

"I like drawing pictures. My brother has LEGO but he doesn't let me play with it."

"Most of the time they don't let the girls have a go because they keep the space ships to themselves and they don't let the girls touch a piece. They don't break them up and they keep them for themselves. That's why we are doing our work.".

- Work is directed and hard. Play takes place at choosing time.

Some six year olds girls made comments about work and play. They differentiated between **work** which is something hard: Scottish maths, drawing, writing and reading a book and play which takes place at "choosing" time. So making models and using the computer they regarded as **play**.

- Girls' play is distinguished from boys' play.

15.5 Choice in primary classrooms

"Choice" appears to be a significant factor in connection with encouraging girls to participate in new technology.

- Choice **by the teacher** of particular children to participate in particular activities available in the classroom.

In this approach, unless a teacher is aware of and concerned about the likelihood of gender bias and stereotyping, s/he is likely to match child to task according to existing gender stereotypes.

- Choice of which children are to succeed those already engaged in the activity and ready to leave the activity.

If the choice is left to the children themselves, this can lead to boys' activities being continued by boys, and to girls' activities being continued by girls. A group of six year old girls tried to think how they would set about trying to join in with the model-making and computer work. Their thoughts turned to asking the teacher for help, but only magic, for them, could change the present choice situation, as it had been set up by the teacher, with the boys seemingly responsible for choosing. It was having an effect on the girls and they rightly assumed that the teacher was unaware of this. They themselves were well aware of their role and of patterns of classroom interaction. Some of their comments follow.

"If I had a wishing stone, I would wish that I could play on the computer and the boys wouldn't be allowed to choose."

"We could have a go early in the morning before the register. Then the boys will moan and sulk all day. Then our teacher will tell them off and it wasn't their fault. Then nobody might be able to have a go."

- Choice by **children** from a range of particular activities offered by the teacher.

Though this appears to offer free choice, the actual effect is quite different. Gender stereotyping is likely to affect the choice that children feel able to make. Their earlier experiences with technology will also affect their confidence in choosing an activity. It is too readily assumed, by teachers and parents, that if girls say that they are not interested, they are not interested. Often they would like to be interested, but feel inadequate or feel that they should not trespass in boys' territory.

- Choice by the **teacher** of those activities which are to be an essential part of classroom work contrasted with those which are optional, often referred to as free choice or **play**.

When activities linked with new technology are designated by the teacher as optional, then it is likely that boys will dominate and, for a variety of reasons, already discussed, girls will opt out unless measures are taken to counteract this.

15.6 Anticipation of employment

- For girls, saying that they would not like to have a job connected with computers often means that they think that they will not be able to get such a job.

Responses by girls, when made in gender stereotyped situations, cannot be taken at their face value. A very able eleven year old girl said, "It is on TV that most of the good jobs are to do with computers. They are for boys. I am saying that I don't want a job with computers, because I don't think that I will get a job. In senior school, people teach boys more than girls. My brother told me."

- Even when girls are positive about their achievement in new technology at school, they are not optimistic about their role as women in employment in this field.

In the extract that follows, a nine year old girl is trying to sort out her thoughts. Following a discussion about jobs, one girl said that two girls were the cleverest children in the class, yet when asked about jobs using computers, she said that boys could do everything. When questioned about this, she said that a lady might find flying an aeroplane hard. Men, as boys, were used to playing with cars and aeroplanes. Girls play with dolls which are cute; dolls are mostly like girls. Boys can see male car drivers; she sees few women. Men drive trucks. She then said that driving a plane was a matter of pressing buttons. She then said that ladies get scared when there are accidents. When reminded that she had said that the two cleverest in the class were girls, she said that her teacher doesn't give such hard work and added that she hadn't seen any ladies driving aeroplanes.

- Boys point to the overwhelming preponderance of men in technological employment as precluding the involvement of women.

- Boys are more ambitious than girls about their careers, as are their parents.

- Anticipation of employment links with stereotyped images of a boss, who is referred to as male.

- The change from boy into boss.

Girls have difficulty in reconciling their view of the boys they see in class with the later status in life of these same boys. Work is seen as a world dominated by men, yet, many boys in class "muck about", don't listen and don't know what they should be doing.

- Some girls seem able to assess the situation and, as it were, step outside it, by making their own decisions to be involved in new technology.

A ten year old girl, speaking about ability to use computers said, "I don't see what's different between boys and girls. Girls are more elegant, more ladylike, but I want to be my own self. Girls are not into computers, because that's not ladylike."

15.7   Strategies for change

The illustrations given of what is happening in UK classrooms are not confined to the UK or to primary aged children. Many of the features and situations here described are to be found across a very wide age range, including adult, and apply outside the UK also.

The report has looked closely at what hinders girls from participating in new technology. These detailed statements, though apparently negative, may also be seen as pointers to action.

Close observation in the classroom and open discussion are essential preliminaries to trying to effect change. A second essential is that teachers and children and others involved, should appreciate the need for change. Thirdly, it is essential that they should want it to happen and be prepared to be involved in the change themselves. It cannot be imposed by individual teachers or even as part of a school system. There must be skilled preparation and the motivation to make it work.

Teachers will need to recognise the constraints under which girls are working and then, seek to enlarge their opportunities. Some people are concerned about the effect that this will have on boys. Will it be worse for them? The strategies applied in this project affect both boys and girls and improve the situation for both.

15.8   Suggested strategies for teachers to adopt

15.8.1   OBSERVATION

Teachers must start by knowing what is happening. They can observe in the normal course of events, while children are engaged in activities. What they observe can be changed, step by step, according to their own priorities and inclinations. Particular aspects can be focussed on, in turn, and then changed.

15.8.2 DISCUSSION

In addition to observation, discussion is a way of finding out what is really happening in the classroom. It is generally neglected by teachers, for many understandable reasons. As a result, teachers can be very unaware of the thoughts and concerns of the children they teach.

Particular group or class discussions may be set up, but informal brief questions and comments to individuals are very valuable. Children must feel that their responses are welcomed. The aim, to encourage girls to participate in new technology, must be born in mind as the focus.

Discussion with individuals, followed by discussion in mixed groups, about girls' participation, which often involves boy/girl cooperation is appreciated by the children. They comment that discussions have helped everyone to be open and to discuss together as friends things which they would not normally discuss.

Discussion leads to changes. When children are caused to reflect upon the problem of girls participating in the use of new technology, they become more aware of their perceptions and biases and then begin to counteract them, by cooperating and sharing.

Weeks after a discussion with a group of six year old children had taken place, their teacher said that she had felt very critical, when the discussion was suggested. She had always offered the choice of making a model to everyone and had assumed that that was all that was necessary. However, she appreciated what resulted from the discussion. After it, she said that she was astonished by the apparently different girls who came back into the classroom. From that time onwards, they were not reluctant model makers any more. It seemed as though some submerged part of them had been released by sympathetic consideration of what they had been feeling so strongly. The teacher was particularly interested that these young children were so aware of what was affecting them and had been able to discuss their motives. They revealed thinking that was more mature and analytical than had ever been expected.

15.8.3 COOPERATION AND THE FORMING OF BOY/GIRL PAIRS

As the project developed and ideas were explored, the children came to the conclusion that it would be fairer to work in mixed pairs. With teacher support, instead of the children sitting at tables in their chosen, all boy and all girl friendship groups, they changed to sitting and working in mixed groups. Most of the mixed pairs have worked well, though strategies had to be used to ease the first embarrassing sessions.

Because the children themselves had decided to work in mixed pairs, as a result of exploring their ideas together, they were willing, as pairs, and as a cooperative class, to try to resolve such issues as one of the pair dominating.

Reasons given by girls for working in mixed pairs included the following.

- "Because girls can find out how boys think and two sets of ideas can come together."

- "Because we wouldn't have to work against boys, we would work in the same way, because we wouldn't have our minds set on competition, our minds would be on what we were trying to do and it would be easier to succeed."

On the other hand, they also anticipated some problems. The ten year old children said that hindrances to working together would be shyness and embarrassment and a difficulty in talking with each other, because they were not used to it. They thought though, that it was important to work together and to find out what others think and feel. Even though they had worked in mixed sex classrooms, many ostensibly sharing tables, throughout their school lives, the image of a brick wall, separating the boys from the girls, held a lot of meaning for them all.

Some of the girls thought that working together might be horrible, because

> "boys always want their own ideas and ways. They never let the girls have their ideas and ways, so it is as if the girls' ideas are locked up and forgotten."

At first one boy walked around the table to talk to his friend instead of talking to one of the girls on each side of him. Another older boy expressed misgivings about talking to girls. "I would die first, but I have agreed and would like to do it." A girl said, "It will only be one girl at a time. Try it and see."

15.9 Planning and structuring activities

- New technology as both work and play.

When new technology is seen as an important part of classroom life and not just one of a minor range of choices, girls are able to respond more positively to it. In their developing evaluation of its importance, it becomes to them a combination of both work and play.

- Writing gives validity to model making and to computer control.

Girls are very concerned, as has been said, with doing their legitimate work. As they move in a more committed way into model making and computer control, they are happier with it when they see a link between it and their writing.

- Choosing a project of interest to both girls and boys.

A project which interests both boys and girls could be chosen as a basis for technology work. This then provides an overall pleasant context, which gives particular meaning and purpose to the activities. However, girls often affirm that they are interested in many so called boys' topics. This aspect must not be lost sight of.

- Required work rather than optional.

It is better for girls if participation is assumed rather than being left to their choice. It is important to ensure that the level of entry is suitable to their knowledge and skills. In this sense, it need be no different from the introduction of any subject area. Sympathetic guidance and consideration should be given as they extend their work.

- Equipment and materials.

As the supply of computer related equipment and materials in schools increases, girls' opportunities to participate should increase, provided all related issues are well handled.

- Exhibitions and presentations.

Exhibitions of work and demonstrations given to the rest of the school and to parents can be encouraging for girls. Attention is drawn to girls' achievements alongside boys' achievements. This extends beyond the children actually involved in the exhibition, particularly if, in the introduction, mention is made of the effective participation of both boys and girls.

- Choice and employment.

Reference has been made to choices being made by children and for children. Making choices is of fundamental importance in life. Perhaps children choose without having an understanding of the effect that their choice has. For instance, a choice once made means that alternatives have to be discarded. Choices affect others. Teachers may present choices without realising fully what effect this has on the child. The inevitable gap between resources and demand for them leads to the need for choice.

In the primary school and early secondary school, if choice is handled well, there will be an effect on the way that girls make choices and on their own self image. The ground will have been prepared for enlightened choices to be made at secondary option choice stage and as their careers develop.

16

IT Teaching in Schools - Gender Bias in the Secondary school

Elaine Coleman[1]

16.1 Introduction

I believe that everyone is prejudiced to one degree or another. So how can we, the teachers, the parents and society in general deal with these prejudices to ensure that our children grow up to have respect for each other.

Teachers are expected, by parents, to provide all children (from 5 to 16) with an education that meets the needs of their ages, abilities and aptitudes (Education Act 1944) [Education Act 1944]. What is meant by the term "aptitude"? My thesaurus includes the following alternative terms:-

> inborn aptitude; innate ability; natural bent;
> predisposition; leaning; prejudice ...

Could this be interpreted as encouraging "boys to be boys and girls to be girls" in its traditional sense? For some parents and teachers, it appears to be an excuse for encouraging boys towards and discouraging girls from a variety of technological courses.

> "For a variety of reasons, the interest boys have in technical artefacts
> is frequently reinforced during the late primary years and adolescence,
> whereas that of girls often lacks encouragement."
>
> [DES 89]

Although the HMI's do not say so, I believe that the main stumbling block is the attitude of adults, which children learn, to traditional male and female roles.

My personal opinion is that the classroom should be a place where both boys and girls are able to feel that they have equal access to all aspects of an education programme. It is only possible to create such an environment if we make ourselves aware of our failings and do something positive to rectify the situation.

---

[1]ILECC, John Ruskin St, London, SE5 0PQ

16.2 The Prejudices

Children bring a variety of instinctive and learned prejudices into the classroom, particularly at secondary level when it is crucial for them to play the "correct" male/female role. In a mixed classroom, boys will be more dominant and girls more passive in activities which are traditionally the domain of males.

However it is the teacher who is in a position to direct the behaviour of pupils in the classroom. So just how good am I (a self-confessed prejudiced teacher) at spotting the prejudices? What shape do they take?

Firstly many adolescent boys seek a high profile. They are louder, more demanding and often less well-behaved in their attention-seeking. They have been taught by prejudiced adults to regard the computer as their province and will push girls off a machine. Boys are more likely to have informed opinions of IT from reading computer magazines and consequently more likely to express themselves in class discussions. Boys are less willing to share. Quite often they expect to have sole occupation of a computer while girls are left to share the remaining machines in threes or more and will do so without complaining. They can intimidate the girls by ridiculing the girls' attempts to manage the technology and showing off their own prowess.

So what about the girls. The prejudice is not all one-sided. By adolescence, there are a number of taboos for girls, who wish to be seen as socially acceptable prospective mates to the male species, one being that thou shalt not indulge in boyish behaviour or follow boyish pursuits; to whit – "playing" with the computer.

Girls, generally, have less interest in the nuts and bolts of the computer, as the adult female has in the contents of the bonnet of her car. This does not mean however, that they take the car less seriously but see it more as a utility for getting from A to B. So girls are more likely to utilise a computer as a tool. Until recently suitable software has not been available for that purpose, particularly in the home computer market.

Through adolescence, boys are becoming physically much stronger than girls and a healthy respect of that strength exists on the girls' part, hence their submissive behaviour in the shareout of machines.

When it came to selecting option courses for GCSE many girls in the past would erroneously choose Computer Studies in the hope of learning to type and expecting it to lead them to a key-boarding job. They very soon became disenchanted. Boys on the other hand would expect to learn to program so they could write their own arcade games and earn a fortune. They too were disappointed, I am afraid.

16.3 Possible Solutions

The picture painted above is based on my observations in my classroom over a number of years. I offer no hard evidence. These conditions would still exist if I allowed it but with constant vigilance I am able to encourage my pupils to behave respectfully to each other.

The first thing I did, and still do, was to teach the children that the computer was a working tool, not a plaything, and I banned all games programs from the system. I did not stop the games programmers because there were valuable lessons to be learnt in the programming process.

I also talked to parents about the role of the computer in school and gave advice about purchase and use of home computers. Both pupils and parents were advised on suitability of option courses and we looked for alternative syllabuses that encouraged our pupils to develop the practical skills of the potential computer user of the future.

In the classroom I refused to allow boys to monopolize the computers. In fact I positively encouraged the girls to be equally aggressive, aiding them in displacing boys at terminals. When computer software that interested the girls became available, they had something to fight for. In fact they were more likely to get priority treatment at lunch-time sessions because their intention was more serious, continuing their class-work or homework from other subjects

We have tried to focus discussion so that girls can participate from their experience too. This is where perhaps the teacher has to be most aware. It is so easy to respond to the first hand up or the enthusiastically shouted answer or not to notice the sexist remark and thus let it pass without checking the perpetrator.

We looked at the content of our lower school IT course to see if it could be altered to make it as interesting as possible to both boys and girls. We realised the content was very dry, having been originally based on the content of our CSE syllabus. We decided to look for ways of balancing the theory with the practical work. Over a period of time, through a process of trial and error, we have developed a number of modules that seem to be enjoyed as much by the girls as the boys.

We also looked at the public examination syllabuses and decided that the traditional London Computer Studies course left a lot to be desired. New Information Technology courses were emerging with a practical emphasis. We decided to pilot Southern's course which incorporated a module linked to the RSA CLAIT which concentrates on acquiring basic skills in a variety of software packages and a module concentrating on the use of computers in a number of applications. The move away from studying computer architecture and data structures was much more acceptable to the girls and gave them the confidence to meet the boys' success.

The school has been moving towards a pupil-centred, resource based learning approach. Units of work are ideal for this purpose as it allows both boys and girls to develop an idea in their own style. Celia Hoyle [Hoyles 88] identified the differences between boys' and girls' approaches to tackling problem-solving tasks. Boys prefer an abstract approach while girls prefer a practical concrete style. Boys and girls have a lot to learn from each other and need to learn to collaborate; each bringing their own strengths and skills.

So far, this has been relatively easy for me to achieve. I am a woman who finds computers and the related technology exciting. I think like the girls and I believe in equal opportunities for girls and boys. What about some of my colleagues? I was recently in a local special school reviewing an IT assessment scheme. The teacher was male and seven children were present, one boy and six girls. Each pupil was being assessed and had to have each step of the assessment checked by the teacher before moving on. I wish I had had a stopwatch to calculate the amount of time and attention demanded by the boy and given by the teacher. It must have been about eighty per cent. The girls just sat patiently waiting to be noticed and I had to intervene several times on their behalf. Yet that teacher would be horrified to think he was being sexist.

Somehow it seems to be more difficult for the male teacher to realise his prejudices and to find an effective solution. He has a "natural rapport with the boys" approach to learning and will undervalue the girls even though their methods arrive at an equally worthy solution.

It is very important that we raise awareness in all staff. We need to be much more overt in pointing out sexist behaviour in our colleagues. A useful exercise is to observe a teacher's lesson, noting all the occasions when sexist behaviour on the part of the teacher or a pupil goes unchecked. They should then make a positive effort to notice their own behaviour and work at correcting it.

All schools should have a policy for dealing with gender issues. While most do now have equal opportunities policies, these are paid little more than lip service. The former ILEA produced a lot of material for their schools giving guidance on anti-sexist policy making [ILEA 85].

The policy should demand that teachers consider their own and their pupils' behaviour. They should consider the relevance of the curriculum and its method of delivery for each sex. It is also a good idea to encourage the use of computers for other, less "technical", subjects so that girls do not see them as being solely part of subject areas that they traditionally succeed less well in. They should also make a study of the suitability of the schools resources, not only reading matter but also computer software.

I have made no reference to changing attitudes among toy manufacturers and advertisers. This in itself is a major issue. However, teachers can make themselves heard and should be prepared to make complaints when necessary.

To change attitudes we must rely heavily on those who believe in equality of opportunity. However, the speed of change and the steps to achieve it must be within grasp of those we wish to join us.

16.4 REFERENCES

[DES 89] "Curriculum Matters - Information Technology 5 to 16", DES, 1989.

[Education Act 1944] 1944 Education Act

[Hoyles 88] Hoyles C, "Girls and Computers", *Bedford Way Papers*, Institute of Education, University of London, 1988.

[ILEA 85] *Implementing the ILEA's Anti-Sexist Policy*, ILEA, 1985.

[ILEA 90] *Tools for the Mind*, ILEA, 1990.

17

Girls and Computing - A Case Study

Linda Anderson[1]

Computer Studies is a relatively new subject, having been introduced at university level only some twenty years ago. Its apparently neutral image at that time has gradually become more and more masculine with many of the features associated with mathematics and science.

Against a background of complex reasons for not being attracted to computing, there are girls who nevertheless continue with the subject to higher levels. A case study of a senior girl pupil at Higher Level Computing in Scotland provides an insight into some of the key issues.

17.1 The Background

Girls' experience of education has not always been either a happy or rewarding one. The educational system was created by men for boys and this is reflected in many of the opportunities which girls are offered in the educational system. Although the aim of equality within the science and technological fields is now generally accepted, the methods for achieving it are often based on implicit (and questionable) notions of masculinity and femininity. The philosophical view of the female as being helpless, irrational, submissive and emotional has meant that the "hard" world of machines is not for her. While many would dispute such a picture of the female, these concepts continue to be subconsciously reinforced through the everyday life experiences of the female pupil. This occurs in the media, the school and the home. The school still reflects society's opinions and often it may merely pay lip service to equality. The fact that attention is being paid to attract girls into computing is often regarded by boys as being sexist, an opinion that they are quick to express. This combination of "showing favouritism" and the concept of the "problem of girls" in computing may well serve to discourage girls even more in the future. The underlying opinions of staff, parents and peers have a far greater effect than a few words of encouragement from a committed party. Girls are still often utilised in school for service functions and expectations regarding their behaviour often differ radically from those for boys. Their achievements are seen in terms of hard work and conscientiousness rather than ability.

[1] George Watson's College, Colinton Road, Edinburgh, EH10 5EG

"While boys' performance is often described in terms which stress potential and possession of "brains" and understanding, (even when this performance is poor) it is, by contrast, rare for girls to be described in these terms and their performance, no matter how good, is commonly attributed to 'hard work'."

[Girls and Mathematics Research Unit 87]

This perception inevitably affects girls' opinions of their own ability and the notion that they will get married anyway, and therefore will have to accommodate family commitments, is often reflected in their career choices.

The historical link between computing and mathematics has raised again the spectre of spatial and logical ability. In the 1970's it was widely held that spatial ability was gender linked. More recently doubts have been cast on such a hypothesis.

Given the numerous and long-standing conclusions of sex-related differences in spatial visualization findings of small differences ... are contrary to expectations and consistent with the growing skepticism about this and other sex-related differences.

[Fennema 87]

However as Kelly [Kelly 87] points out:

"Teachers put extra effort into teaching boys to read to make up for any deficiency, whether its origin is biological or social."

Certainly the same could be done to boost girls' spatial ability if it were thought to be of significance.

The curriculum has developed in a sexually differentiated way. This has its roots in the traditional role of the female but has continued in relation to the sexually segregated labour market. Often this has led to seeing "the problem of girls and science/maths and technology" as one of the needs for more skilled labour for this market.

Feelings about the new technology are gender linked. The buildup of the masculine image is strongly linked to that already existing in what we may regard as related fields ie science, maths and engineering. Many girls reject the ethos of competition surrounding computers and the violence associated with many computer games [Skirrow 86]. They may also be alienated by the way in which computers are used for social, economic and military control. The vision of the machine orientated individual (usually a boy), who prefers spending time having a relationship with a machine rather than a person has a negative effect on girls' beliefs about computers.

The role offered by society to its children in their formative years often contradicts the role offered by both education and parents. This may be observed in the six advertisements offered at each commercial break during young children's viewing time (typically Saturday and Sunday mornings). In one such observed period there were three food adverts and three toy commercials. In two of the food commercials the women were portrayed as mothers worrying about their sons . The guilt about not giving them what they wanted or needed to eat was predominant and the boys' behaviour although bad was seen as both typical and acceptable. Two of the toy commercials were directed at boys with all male characters, harsh voices and violent scenes involving military machines and "saviours" of the world. This was portrayed as exciting and active play. The one "advert" for girls was for Princess Barbie and portrayed the vision of girl as princess. There was no activity involved except for smoothing down the party dress. The girl in the advert was dressed in a similar fashion to the doll. The voice overlay was sweet and soft. Very few children will enter primary school without a clear picture of their expected role in society as portrayed by the media in general.

It has been argued that primary school children of both sexes are equally interested in computers and exhibit none of the gender-related differences of their older counterparts. Is such complacency ill-founded?

> "That it (gender gap) is apparent even at the lower end of the primary school was revealed in a study we conducted in an Edinburgh school."

> [Siann 87]

Certainly in the experience of the school involved in this study, the first year course (secondary department) in Information Technology is greeted with enthusiasm by both sexes. Each pupil has a machine of their own to use although co-operation is encouraged. The boys do involve themselves in "showing off" often giving the impression to other boys and girls that they know more than they in fact do. It is also questionable whether the girls see themselves taking the subject by choice in their third year. The impression is often given that they see the subject as becoming difficult when studied seriously.

The difference between what parents say they believe and the way in which they act has an influence on their children's choices. Often the female may be encouraged to study non-traditionally at school while being relied upon to behave traditionally at home. This contradiction may result in girls choosing what they see as an easy option which they believe will avoid complications later on.

Girls usually see their achievements in terms of hard work and seldom in terms of ability. When asked about their ability in a subject they will often underestimate it. In contrast to this, boys will often overestimate their ability even when there is evidence to the contrary. Non achievement is seen as being a result of lack of work rather than low ability in respect of males. It is interesting to read a selection of school reports where the terms reliable, hardworking and conscientious are often applied to females and linked to high scores. The emphasis is on these qualities, not on ability. In contrast the phrase "He has ability but is not achieving" is often used for boys. Where there are boys and girls in a family parents often describe their children in the same terms.

> "By attributing their daughters' achievements to hard work and their sons' to high ability, parents may be teaching their sons and daughters to draw different inferences regarding their achievement abilities from equivalent achievement experiences."

> [Parsons 82]

Girls come to know themselves through their interaction with the world. Such conceptions of personal efficacy affect not only the courses of action they pursue but their thought patterns and their behaviour.

> "Among the different facets of self-knowledge, perhaps none is more central to people's everyday lives than conceptions of their personal efficacy."

[Bandura 77]

Bandura goes on to explain, that people's judgements of their own efficacy, whether accurate or faulty, arise from four principal sources of information. These include performance accomplishments; vicarious experiences of observing the performance of others; verbal persuasion and states of psychological arousal from which they partly judge their capableness and vulnerability. Why is there such such a contrast between what girls can do and what they believe they can do despite evidence to the contrary?

17.2 The Study

The school involved in the study is an independent co-educational school of approximately 1200 pupils in the secondary department. The school has a varied intake in both ability and social background and operates a number of bursaries as well as an assisted places scheme. There is a small boarding house. This is used predominantly by pupils who have come from overseas or whose parents have had to go abroad to work. The school is really a day school in character. It has a reputation for academic achievement but is also noted for its extra curricular work and the emphasis lies on developing the whole child. There is a well established learning support department which has pioneered many developments in this area.

The qualitative data was collected over a period of one year from the only female pupil in a Higher Computing class of twelve pupils. The data was collected by observation and interview. A case study was conducted wherein the subject was asked to provide a life history with help from her mother. This was recorded by her at home. Further questions were supplied in order to develop some of the areas further. The subject preferred to tape record this information herself rather than be interviewed directly. She was very helpful and interested although rather embarrassed by the interest shown in her life. The Computing Department was very co-operative and interested, the Head of the Department being aware of many of the difficulties associated with attracting more girls and very committed to doing so.

The subject came to the school this year to do her fifth and sixth years. This is quite common, and the school has a sixth year of about 200 hundred pupils and an emphasis on preparation for adulthood. Her family live in Portugal and her father is English and her mother is Portuguese. There are two children. She is the elder and she has a brother who is fourteen months younger than her. She chose this school herself after looking through the prospectus and hearing reports from some acquaintances who have children here.

The subject, who we will call Lorna, arrived after the beginning of the session to join a class of students who had either Scottish O grade or Standard grade computing. She had sat an international equivalent of the English GCSE, which differed from that of the other pupils in that she had done no programming. I tried to reassure her about this, pointing out that it might even be an advantage to start from scratch. My first impression was of a shy, embarrassed girl and my Head of Department and I expressed our reservations about her fitting in to a class with no other girls. Lorna contributed little verbally in class at the theoretical discussion time, but often asked questions afterwards when the class was finished. She was obviously embarrassed by the apparent skill with which the rest of the class used the Econet Network, with which she was unfamiliar. The difficulties were further compounded by a new word processor and her need to learn programming. However it became apparent that she was not to be deterred and she worked away quietly and consistently at these problems. Lorna worked co-operatively with another student, a boy who had some difficulty with the work. Despite Lorna's encouragement he gave up the subject a short while after.

That was what was wrong with Willie; I mean, he didn't see computing as a challenge.

17.3 The Subject's Home Background

My father always worked abroad. My mother was permanently with us. My place in the family ... I've always been the one who's responsible for my brother. Also when my father comes home and he's been out of touch with what's going on in school, school is always stressed. He asks me personally how he's (the brother) getting on, whether he's coping being the youngest in his class.

I think I'm more introverted than my brother, very worried about personal relationships. Because I was such a worrier I never liked to be in trouble with the teachers ... I never missed homework. When I had to choose between German and Drama, I immediately chose German, because I hate acting because I'm shy. I'm interested in sport . We always did sports together and competed against each other.

My parents didn't expect us to be the same. My father wanted my brother to be more responsible. I don't like housework. Jobs in the house are repetitive, tedious, nothing to them. I like working outside the house ... weeding, watering, cleaning the pool. I liked helping when we were building the pool.

Lorna's mother sees her daughter as being very determined, especially when she was very young. She was the leader of the two and was quite determined that her brother should play the way she wanted. She maintains that the "responsible" role which her daughter displayed was of her own decision. However she does agree that

Lorna is often given responsibility for her brother. She was a meticulous child with a great desire to organise.

17.3.1 SCHOOL BACKGROUND

I enjoyed school ... never objected to it. I spent five years at my last school ... neatly presented books, high grades, worried by exams but did well. It was difficult leaving my last school. It was small ... 200 pupils in the international side so I knew everyone well. They understood that I really tried. We were the first class to do the GCSE ... I was very worried by it. I became quite ill and had to have X-rays and was very run down. My subjects ... I'm OK all round - I try to be above average . School is very useful to me. I meet a lot of friends, socialise at weekends, sports, clubs, go for new challenges, the competitive side - gives something to life. You can become independent too; your parents aren't there to fend for you. You lose out if you don't work. No good results – no good job. I want to be fairly well off. Sometimes the amount of work gets me down but if you manage to do it all you feel better afterwards.

17.3.2 SELF EFFICACY

I succeed always through hard work, compared to Morgan who did not work hard but always did well. He had this ability. I always have to work hard to be successful. We were all envious of Morgan and his natural ability. Although they (the boys) studied they didn't put in as much effort as the girls do. Take my roommate, she does Biology SYS, Chemistry SYS, Calculus SYS, Statistics SYS and hopes to become a doctor. She attained her grades at prelim and had worked really hard. Compare her to Frank who does some of the same subjects. He can do it on ability. For his Physics SYS he studied only the night before.

17.3.3 CATCHING THEM YOUNG

I think to an extent primary school is more sexist than secondary school. Within primary school for example ... at activity time ... the actual class-rooms are sectioned off and when it's activity time the boys are given building blocks and they build and construct. The girls ... they use the area that's symbolic to the home ... you know with curtains. They are sort of impressed to take the traditional routes, whereas at least in secondary schools they debate the ideas of equality. Another thing about primary school, when you have story telling, the majority of stories are about princesses and things like that and the girls are led into thinking of this like an inferior state ... in the story they're usually captured by some ogre – it's the boy that saves them or something like that.

17.3.4 Teachers' Attitudes

I don't think comments influenced me ... my English teacher used to often bring up the subject (of equality). The boys in the class would say they were better and how women can't cope and I remember a debate about women going out to get jobs and it was really good. I also remember one physics lesson me and my friend took a long time to change these wires in comparison to the boys but the teacher did come round to check and he made a few remarks but they weren't severe enough to influence me.

17.3.5 Subject Choices

My father did advise me to take physics. Physics was set against Portuguese and my dad said since I could speak it it would probably be better to widen my knowledge. In the end I did receive the GCSE merit which is given when you obtain passes in a wide area eg Humanities, Science, Art and Language. I did take core Physics. I didn't think it was my best subject, but I got a "C" which is difficult to get. We had a computer at home, but my brother was on it most of the time, playing games. I don't know what I expected Computing to be like when I chose it - Computing was set against Chemistry. I didn't want to do Chemistry. I was shocked when we started. I expected it to be harder than it was, more on the scientific side like Chemistry or Physics. Why did I choose Computing ... a good friend of my father had been round. He said to me that computers are the subject of the future, when I said I wasn't sure. He's been round the world, seen everything, done everything and because my father had given me the same advice beforehand. Anyway it all helps even if you don't pass your exams at least you'll know something about it. But I did enjoy it . It's very interesting.

17.3.6 Role Models

I do see Computing as a boys' subject, but my views are not the same as they were in the past. One of the reasons was that in our last school all the science, maths and computing teachers were men. Don't take offence, it was even quite a shock to see you teaching computing when I arrived at the school. I remember my mother suggesting that I be a lawyer instead of just watching films about court cases and not stick to my idea of clerical work (I wanted to be a secretary). I always remember my dad telling me to keep an open mind. When we got the newspapers he always told me the reports about equality and talked with me about them. I don't think they would be concerned if I turned round and told them I wanted to be a civil engineer as long as I was happy.

17.3.7 THE FUTURE

I think if computers are used wisely it is extremely beneficial. I would like to go into the business world and computers are used there. My father always achieved high standards. After the war he returned to studying in his own time; he decided to do it. His father had never insisted on work, had never helped him. He has a good job, and has travelled round the world. He has managed to achieve it through ability and hard work. He's always concerned about our work at school maybe because his father never was concerned about him. It is helpful and I really appreciate it. He has many friends around the world so our family is always having friends around. He achieves high standards and is happy ... this influences me to work hard and have fun as well ... a good image for me to follow in the world.

17.4 The Conclusion

The material for this paper has been drawn from an MEd dissertation on the same topic, and is therefore a window on a much larger work. However, it has still been possible to show some connections between Lorna's view of her personal and educational life, and the complex web of reasons why girls often choose not to do computing. Although there are many reasons for Lorna not to have chosen computing, especially perhaps her poor opinion of her own ability in the subject, yet she has persisted. It would be difficult to argue against the fact that her father has played a large part in encouraging her to keep many options open and often to choose the less traditional subjects. It is interesting to note that Lorna saw her organising ability originally as being the stepping stone to secretarial skills rather than management material. Her parents appear to have encouraged more ambitious thoughts. Perhaps the most important outcome of the study has been the change in Lorna herself. Although still beset by self doubts, taking part in such a study has taught her to question many of the assumptions which she previously took for granted.

17.5 REFERENCES

[Bandura 77] Bandura A, *Self-referent thought: a developmental analysis of self efficacy*, National Institute of Mental Health, 1977.

[Fennema 87] Fennema and Sherman, "Sex-Related Differences in Mathematics Achievement, Spatial Visualization and Affective Factors", *American Educational Research Journal*, 14, pp51-71, 1987.

[Girls and Mathematics Research Unit 87] "Girls and Mathematics Research Unit", in *Proceedings of the GSAT Conference 1987* edited by Walkerdine V, University of London, 1987.

[Kelly 87] Kelly A, *Science for Girls*, Open University Press, 1987.

[Parsons 82] Parsons J E et al, *Socialization of Achievement Attitudes and Belief: Parental Influences*, University of Michigan, 1982.

[Siann 87] Siann G, "Gender Differences in Computer Use in Children of Primary School Age", in *Proceedings of the GASAT Conference 1987*, University of London, 1987.

[Skirrow 86] Skirrow G, "Positive Action in Scotland", *Women and Computing in Scotland*, Scottish Institute of Adult and Continuing Education, 1986.

18

Observations of Attitudes to IT in Database Use in Schools

Janet Spavold[1]

18.1 Introduction

By focusing on the teaching of history, this paper discusses the differing approaches to computer based learning used by girls and boys in differing situations. General areas looked at include sex sterotyping and the way this is reflected in IT work; differences in group and individual approaches; perceptions of status; and personality factors which affect children's approaches to computer-based work, as well as their attitudes to computing. More specific areas concern differences in approaches to databases, such as those tied to hardware use; the different approaches which have been observed in query formulation and search strategies, and difference in user effectiveness. Finally the paper offers some tentative comments concerning language and imagery. In particular, it is suggested that the imagery of computer language may affect girls' perceptions of computing.

18.2 Background

The main study on which these observations are based was a year-long project involving two Derbyshire primary schools (A and B). The schools were visited for a morning a week, and during this time they each prepared a database on the 1881 Census for their own area. Using data capture sheets, they analysed and where necessary coded the data ready for entry, then entered it on to a data file on the INFORM database. When sufficient of the data file was ready, they began to formulate queries to interrogate the data file. Later, the two schools exchanged information through the medium of TTNS.

INFORM is a database specially written by Nottinghamshire's software centre for schools' use. It runs on BBC machines, and is capable of extensive record management (for an educational program). The classes used a standard format file. School A compiled a file of 498 records, while School B produced two files, one of 527 records and one of 150. Each record had 17 fields, some of which were coded and others

[1] Department of Information Systems, Leicester Polytechnic, PO Box 143, Leicester LE1 9BH

entered in full.

School A was situated in an attractive commuter village, some six miles north of Derby; School B was an ex-Board school in a more settled urban industrial area. The children were aged 9 to 10 in School A, with 15 boys and 12 girls in the third-year class. The children in School B were aged 9 to 11; there were 13 fourth-years (nine boys and four girls) and 20 third-years (ten of each). Both classes had some previous experience of educational computer use, though School A had used a wider range of software. Neither class had any experience of building and analysing a data file.

Following this study, work was undertaken for the History Adviser for Derbyshire with a view to the integration of IT into the teaching of history. This was a cross-phase project, preparing materials as requested by the staff of a secondary school and its feeder primary schools. On the whole, the school staffs oversaw the compilation of the various data files after the researcher had prepared the material, the format files and the handbooks. The school specifically quoted in this paper as School C is an inner-city multi-cultural primary school, and the class concerned were fourth-years. Two groups were observed, one comprising five girls and the other, five boys. The cross-phase work is currently continuing.

When the first of these studies was undertaken, using Schools A and B, there was a clear set of expectations concerning the outcome of the study as far as the database work was concerned. There was also a clear set of questions to be answered about teaching history by means of computer integration into classroom research, and about the best approaches for the presentation of both the material and the method. But there were no expectations that gender differences would be discernible during the course of the work. These observations were noted more because they struck both the researcher and the class teachers as being significant pointers to differences in the way boys and girls approached computer-based work. Following this first project, the researcher did look for gender differences in subsequent work. This paper collects together these observations, and some suggestions about them arising from discussion with class teachers.

18.3   Attitudes to IT

18.3.1   SCHOOL A

Teachers are already aware of the dangers of stereotypes affecting computer use in the classroom, and there were noticeable differences between the boys' and the girls' approaches in School A. Though so young, the girls were precociously aware of their sex roles in terms of dress and expected behaviour. Only two girls here volunteered questions about how the computer worked, or made any comment relating the project work to outside computer experience. Many of the boys did; their questions covered for example communication via the modem, a range of discussion on networks, and computer use at home. During lulls in the work when using the computer the girls' conversation turned to social topics whereas the boys discussed the computer and their work.

There were also discernible differences over attitudes to the completion of work in School A, which seemed to imply gender differences. It was noted by the class teacher that while the girls preferred to complete a task they were more anxious to finish than to check the accuracy of the work. When running enquiries it was observed that the boys spent considerable time in the early stages checking to ensure that they had covered all aspects of the topic, but that they could be careless about following it through. As a result, work done in mixed groups was organised by the stronger girls, who delegated tasks. In effect, they took a management role, and the boys in these groups took secretarial roles – copying, writing up, etc – quite the opposite of the stereotypes of later life; yet by the time this skill could be of use to them, experience suggests that most girls will no longer see themselves as potential managers. Instead they are likely to do as one girl did, and act as secretary to a male boss: one boy got her to do his data entry for him because he felt idle, and she was happy to comply. In dealing with the keyboard the girls resembled good secretaries: they were methodical and businesslike, with none of the arguments seen among the boys about who would go first.

When new aspects of the work were introduced in School A during the enquiry stage it was noted that boys were more likely to try new enquiries; the girls preferred the security of known approaches. It was a disturbing indicator for the future education of these girls, especially in the sciences, that they were reluctant to guess or offer an hypothesis for testing, showing anxiety lest it should be perceived as being wrong. The boys were more willing both to suggest an hypothesis and to modify it for retesting in the light of their results. Their self-confidence seemed to support them; they did not have the same sense of failure and were therefore more likely to push themselves forward when the girls would retire.

18.3.2 SCHOOL B

There were no discernible differences in the way the boys and girls in School B worked. They were equally likely to persist with difficult queries; they worked in mixed groups which were fluid, not exclusive, and both sexes produced lines of enquiry which were interesting equally to the other. Both sexes here showed considerable interest in the technical side of the work, and questions came from them all. The potential value of the researcher as a role model had greater impact in School B, where one girl commented on it, drawing the agreement of others. There was no similar comment made in School A, nor indeed was there any overt comment made about the appropriateness or otherwise of the work for boys or girls; yet the conditioning seemed well established even at this early age, and the children seemed to come to the classroom already aware of social expectations. If boys and girls are to benefit equally from the IT revolution, attitudes such as those noted in this study will need to be changed as much from outside the classroom as within. The attitudes of the children in School B seem more likely to give rise to equality. These key attitudes seem to reflect the social patterns and expectations of the catchment areas rather than the gender composition of the classes or groups. They are established in the child's social milieu both before school age and during the process of social development which parallels the educational development in school. Maybe one way round the problem would be to run computer literacy courses for parents, together with careers information, from the start of the child's school life.

18.3.3 SCHOOL C

The pattern of better management of work showed in a slightly different way in School C. Here the children worked in separate groups of boys and girls, by choice. All were performing the same task, the entry of data into a database from previously prepared data-capture sheets; but they had to think about the method of entry and check their codings as they did so. The girls worked in a genuinely co-operative group, contributing to discussion, listening to each other's suggestions and modifying their work according to the group decision. There did not seem to be any sense of finding fault for the sake of it, rather that observed mistakes needed to be corrected for the quality of the work. They arranged who did what quickly and efficiently, and took turns at each task. As a result, all the girls in the group benefitted from each other's understanding, and all had a good grasp of both process and theory at the end. By contrast, the group of boys would not share ideas and understanding but preferred to go their own ways, even though it meant that they had areas of misunderstanding. They would not ask their peers for help and advice, and they would not offer help even where they could see it was needed. They would point out errors in their peers' work, not to offer help but to establish the fact that they could see that the other boy had made a mistake. They took data capture sheets in turn, and worked on their own; when it was not their turn, they left the machine to do something else. Their attitude was one of competition rather than co-operation.

18.4 Social Structures in the Classroom

In School B a group of three boys became the most familiar with the system. They assumed a leadership role for the rest of the class, and helped to overcome the others' fears of the system. The less confident children, both boys and girls, increasingly attached themselves to these three, and the social structures in the classroom were sufficiently fluid for this to be acceptable. Once the leadership group was established in School B it was possible for the adults to delegate some of their normal role in helping children. The boys in this group were willing to assist other boys and the girls equally. They may have been helped by the fact that they were among the oldest in the class, so that the younger boys felt it was not a threat to their social positions to ask for help. It was noticeable in this classroom that the leadership group was all male.

One of the early expectations from the study had been that the use of the computer could help the development of personality and confidence, and in the case of one of these boys this was especially clear. He was not one of the brightest children but he rapidly understood the practicalities of the database. He was the only one of all the children to be sure enough of himself and his work to be able to deliver a twenty-minute explanation of what he had been doing to his classmates, the researcher and his teacher with no trace of nervousness and with considerable skill in the use of the charts he had produced. Above all, the confidence gained from the fact that he knew better than most how to manipulate the data on the computer showed in the enthusiasm and clarity of his task. None of the girls could be persuaded to give a similar talk.

School A had more rigid social groupings, especially noticeable in the division of the sexes when the children grouped themselves for play or other activities. No leadership group developed here, and the children did not look to each other for assistance in the same way.

18.5 Keyboard Use

When working on data entry for the first time, the children were organised into groups of three: one read the capture sheet, one operated the keyboard and one checked the screen. The difficulties for adult casual users of keyboards have been studied by Cuff [Cuff 80], and in many ways the children's use of keyboards reflects the problems he described. There was no difference seen in the children in School B or School C as to the speed of their typing or the competence with which they managed the keyboard, but the girls in School A showed greater familiarity and competence. Many of them had a typewriter at home, and were encouraged to use it. Two girls from School B were the only ones of those unfamiliar with the keyboard to show a methodical approach: one scanned the keys in vertical blocks, the other scanned along the lines. The rest looked at random until either they or their partner spotted the key; if the latter saw it first there was a tendency (strongly discouraged) to interfere and press the key. They were all one-finger typists. There were some left-handed children in both School A and School B, and it was with this group that the idea of using the left hand to operate the relevant function keys (at the extreme left of the row) to move between fields, and the right hand on the rest of the keyboard, originated. Eventually twelve children in School A (eight boys and four girls), and four in School B (three girls and one boy) adopted this.

It may be that, if IT is to be widely adopted in education, schools need to introduce keyboard skills at an early age. Typing must no longer be confined to girls about to leave school. A recent report is noted with approval here (see [Times 90] for full details), to the effect that the Secretary of State for Education has accepted plans to add "core skills", including keyboard skills, to the A-level curriculum. Even so, this may be too late in a young person's school life.

18.6 Query Formulation

Gender differences appeared in the children's methods of query formulation. For the boys in School A, success with single-condition searches on the more obvious aspects of the database led by the fourth enquiry session to similar searches utilising coded fields; it was another four weeks before the first girl used codes. In School B on the other hand the older children, boys and girls, were utilising coded fields in the second enquiry session. By the third session the children moved to exploratory enquiry often where several enquiries taking different approaches were made to check that all the relevant data had been covered. Three boys in School A, by the end of the project, had used paths to searches giving a nil result as a final confirmation for their enquiry; none of the girls here came independently to the realisation that a valid search producing a nil result could be as valuable as any other. They tended to show anxiety over a nil result, regarding it as failure.

The School A girls preferred to use repeated short paths, as shown in the many ageband and name frequency enquiries. This repetitive group included the girl with by far the highest reading and reasoning score of all the children (chronological age of 9.2, reading age of 12.11, reasoning quotient of 140, measured by the NFER tests); time after time the girls seemed motivated in their choice of search path by the need to repeat success, and they appeared to measure success by the length of the printout rather than by the usefulness of its content. The boys on the other hand were more interested in the information conveyed by the result, whatever its form.

18.7 Navigation Paths

When the children in Schools A and B began to use the database on their own, they showed differing responses to the fear of getting lost in the system. This fear has been studied in adult users (see [Canter 85, Canter 86]), and shown to be a powerfully inhibiting factor in new or inexperienced users.

The children only used two of the possible paths suggested by Canter, Rivers and Storrs [Canter 85]. These were searching and exploring, as defined by Canter et al, but not scanning, browsing or wandering. The limited approaches were almost certainly due to the task environment of the classroom, where each child had an enquiry formulated before getting access to the computer and for which a specific result was sought. As they considered the results of their searches many children began to ask supplementary questions, and so moved on to exploring, though still with a positive objective. Analysis of the enquiries entered by the children and the routes they used to access data showed a clear preference for many short paths. There were no perceptible gender differences with the early enquiries. But after nine weeks of experience in query formulation, they began to show the use of queries which indicated their growing confidence with the system, a greater degree of familiarity with moving around in the system and a greater willingness to take risks, as they moved from searching to exploring.

Some of the younger children from School A, both boys and girls, proved as willing to move from searching to exploring as the older children from School B were; all of this latter group at some time suggested enquiries indicating exploratory paths. In each case, the willingness to experiment, which had been expected in the older rather than the younger children, was related to confidence and personal security rather than to gender differences. Within each group of the School A children there were the more and the less confident. The least confident children were the slowest to overcome their fear of getting lost and some half-dozen children always sought the reassurance of a confident partner. These children tended to avoid making an enquiry unless firmly encouraged, and they were fairly equally divided between the boys and the girls. Membership of the less-confident group in School A was not limited to the younger children. But most of the children in both schools forgot their fear of getting lost as they became more familiar with the system.

The children from School B showed no discernible gender differences in their pattern of navigation; both boys and girls used single- and multiple-condition enquiries and there were examples of the movement from searching to exploring from both. In School A, however, regardless of age or attainment score, the boys were more adventurous in their navigation paths. The girls, starting with success in obvious single-condition searches (names, ages, occupations), then produced numerous parallel pathways. While this served to reinforce their confidence and initially was allowed with this in mind, it became difficult to persuade them away from variants on these limited searches.

Only three girls from School A showed a more mature approach in their planning of pathways, and showed the ability to move from searching to exploring. In each case, as in School B, the move was prompted because the results of an initial enquiry raised further questions which were immediately pursued.

18.8 User Effectiveness

Most areas of user effectiveness, as defined by Reisner [Reisner 81], showed no gender differences in approach. The one which did concerned the relative efficiency of the queries formulated for the database. It was some time before the children began to recognise that there were degrees of efficiency in the formulation of queries. Some never attempted to take it into account in their queries; the effort of formulating a query which produced the desired result was achievement enough. But some of the children did see the relevance of it and tried to make use of efficiency in their query formulation. These children were all boys, and none of the girls could be persuaded to try similar approaches. Again, the key factor seemed to be confidence and the determination to succeed, which was stronger in the boys than the girls. It may be that while our schools are so inadequately provided with computers, it will tend to be the most determined children who will get time on the machines and the more retiring personalities who will be pushed off; in social terms, the boys will push forward while the girls will retire. While we have primary schools with only one or two machines for the whole school to use, rather than enough for every classroom, we may perpetuate the gender differences because of social expectations and lack of opportunity.

Not all the children saw advantages in the use of the computer for their work, and three of the children in the main study specifically dismissed it in their summaries of the project. It had clearly had no impact on their methods of work, mainly because they did not appreciate the link between data entry and enquiry. There were two boys and one girl who thought the computer had nothing to offer in this way. The majority of the children saw mastery of the computer as enhancing their status among the peer group at school, and the family at home.

18.9 Language and Imagery

Coming to computing from lecturing in both English literature and history, the language and imagery associated with computing has been most striking. Some analysis of computing language is offered here, and some tentative thoughts on its effect particularly on girls and women as users of computers.

Academic and commercial computing are both dominated by male practitioners; one of our concerns here is to break this dominance. It is in many ways a closed world, using jargon in the usual way to impose exclusiveness, which is to be expected. But there is a power and persistence in certain lines of imagery which appear to form a basis for mutual understanding between members of this closed world. It seems that many users of such imagery are unaware that they *are* using imagery, let alone have any conscious understanding of what they are implying by it. We recognise that much of the power of literature derives from its use of imagery, whereby the author can suggest a wider range of meaning through the association of ideas than he could through the simple, primary meaning of words. Words are susceptible of multiple meanings – they can be transformed to metaphors, so that both the literal and the metaphorical meaning can be present at the same time, and the metaphorical meaning can itself be extended and varied according to the individual experience of the reader. Such powerful imagery is present in the jargon of computing, though not generally analysed, and its presence provides a disturbing undercurrent which may be less acceptable to girls and women.

The common denominators are the imagery of sex and violence, used at varying levels of sophistication or crudeness depending on the context. The images of violence often have echoes of sadism in them. Images of sex and violence as used in computing seem to derive from an all-male environment where the absence of real women as colleagues allows a common base for fantasy, perhaps encouraged by the isolated nature of work with a computer. The one-to- one relationship with the computer seems for some men to replace any human relationship quite satisfactorily.

Some examples of imagery drawn from computing and which are based on sexual imagery are the use of the terms "corruption", "violation" or "to violate", "degradation" and "penetrance", generally in connection with programming. The common use of "abort" to indicate the premature termination of a program is another image with a sexual origin, and one which, because of its deeply felt meaning for many women, may be perceived as an offensive trivialisation of a significant emotional event. There are connotations of violence here too. "Chaining" or "chaining to a block" also occurs in programming, and has overtones of both sexual and violent imagery.

Most of the easily identifiable images are based on violence. Some have the same sort of sadistic tendency as the sexual imagery, such as the way the term "thrashing" is used in describing the operating system. Some are dependent on military affinities; the present writer does not much like the combination of, for example, F4, crosshair sights, trigger, target, destroy, containment, ditching, pre-empt or pre-emption, and eliminate. There are various other verbs in use which describe violent death, almost as a casual matter of course. Given the predominant themes of computer games, and the tendency for compulsive games players to graduate to professional involvement with computers, it is perhaps hardly surprising that the adult male computer scientist continues his delight in death and destruction.

A further group of images is medical in origin, using the terms "dissect", "clean cut" and "performing operations on processes". These terms on their own are relatively neutral, but one becomes more uncomfortable with them when they are seen in the context of the common image types of death or mutilation with a sharp instrument. There is something deeply disturbing about the frequency with which these images are applied, implying as they do repressed sadism. "Execute" is common in every area of computing, and the writer has seen an icon of a guillotine for it, which merely emphasises the underlying cruelty of the image. Other similar images are those of "razoring" in artificial intelligence; "disabling" of a system; "timeslicing" in connection with operating systems, and the "binary chop" in information processing. Data is often "chopped up" into segments, as keys or messages may have to be.

One group of images to do with death and injury are so widely used that they have almost lost their point as images. These are the terms "crash", "head crash", "abort", "terminate", "expiring", "kill" and "dying". Some of these have already been discussed. But it is worth remembering that, however much of a cliche each has become, its origin was as an image and its cumulative use adds to the disturbing pattern demonstrated throughout the world of computing. The problem may lie in the fact that most computer users do not recognise their vocabulary as imagery, and are unaware of the implications of the imagery in common use.

The majority of imagery used in connection with computing is essentially inhuman and anti-human, and the inexorable violence of much of it runs counter to the way that girls are brought up. Social conditioning turns girls away from the undercurrent of violence, whereas boys are more likely to be conditioned to accept it. For girls, the emphasis is placed on caring, on the perservation of life rather than its destruction, and it is suggested that such imagery presents girls and women with some uncomfortable mental adjustments. For those in school, the adjustments may have to be made at a time of considerable social and sexual change, in the teenage years, when their impact may be heightened by the emotional awareness of adolescence.

It is possible therefore that the very vocabulary of the subject could be a contributory factor in the rejection of computing by girls.

18.10 Acknowledgements

I am most grateful to Mr S Bacon, Derbyshire Computing Adviser, and Mr H Butterton, Derbyshire History Adviser, for their general help and support. For the Census project, my thanks are due to Mr J Reece, Headmaster of William Gilbert Endowed School, Duffield, and his staff; to Mr D Backhous, Headmaster of Wilmorton Primary School, Derby, and his staff; and to Peter Collins and Michael Sayer, without whose co-operation and classes the project could not have been done. For the cross-phase project, my thanks are due in respect of this paper to Mrs Sue Hearne of Dale Primary School, Derby, and Ms Jackie Overton, of Derby School.

18.11 REFERENCES

[Canter 85] Canter D, Rivers R and Storrs G, "Characterising user navigation through complex database structures", *Journal of Behaviour and Information Technology*, Vol 4 No 2, pp 93-102, 1985.

[Canter 86] Canter D, Powell J, Wishart J and Roderick C, "User navigation in complex database systems", *Journal of Behaviour and Information Technology*, Vol 5 No 3, pp 249-257, 1986.

[Cuff 80] Cuff R N, "On Casual Users", *International Journal of Man-Machine Studies*, Vol 14, pp 163-187, 1980.

[Reisner 81] Reisner P, "Human factors studies of database query languages: a survey and assessment", *Computing Surveys*, 13, pp 13-31, 1981.

[Times 90] The Times, D Broom, *Reformer with a career on the run*, p15, col 6, 28-05-1990.

19

A Study of Computing Experiences of Female A-Level Maths Students

Judy Donnelly[1]

19.1 Introduction

In 1980, 23% of the UK candidates applying through UCCA for admission to computer science degree schemes were women. Following annual decreases, by 1987 women represented only 11% of such applicants. This recent trend is both novel and disturbing because until 1980 there had been comfortable annual increases in the the number of women applicants. Despite increases in the number of places available on computer science courses at both polytechnics and universities, the actual number of female students has decreased; for example in 1980, 423 of the 1754 UK university first-year computer science students were female, but by 1987 only 193 of the 1852 students accepted through the UCCA scheme were women. Many authors have expressed concern over this phenomenon [Evans 87, Lovegrove 87, Soper 88]. In this study I have analysed the replies to a questionnaire which was distributed to A Level maths students in order to assess their past experiences of computing and the impact on future career aspirations. The replies to the questionnaires were analysed to study gender differences.

19.2 Methods of Data Collection and Analysis

The questionnaire was completed by 66 A Level maths students in June 1988. The students were drawn from a total of eight mixed comprehensive schools and further education colleges in the Leeds area. By design, 50% of the respondents were female and all of the students were completing their first year of A Level study. These students were selected for the investigation because the possession of A Level maths is a requirement for entry to many computer science degree schemes.

Students were asked for details of age, sex, A Level studies and types of educational institution they had attended, as well as future career plans and knowledge of computing. They were also asked if they would be interested in attending short courses to gain experience of computing. In order to reduce the chance of bias, the exact purpose of the questionnaire was not revealed until the final question. The introductory

[1]3, Edmonton Place, Chapel Allerton, Leeds, LS7 4LP

information merely stated that the purpose of the questionnaire was to help gather more information about A Level maths students and their knowledge of computing courses available in polytechnics and universities. The final question invited answers that could help to explain why less than 10% of computing undergraduates in universities were women. The information received was analysed using a program written for this purpose.

19.3   Results and Discussion

The 33 female A Level maths students represented the total number of first year female students from the eight participating institutions. Although it should be appreciated that the small number of respondents in the survey precluded a valid statistical analysis, when the answers were analysed for gender differences there were easily apparent differences in the responses and computing experiences between the sexes.

19.3.1   NUMERICAL ANALYSIS OF RESULTS

Approximately half the students were studying the sciences, with the others mainly taking a variety of disciplines. The majority of students were studying at mixed sex comprehensive schools. Almost half the students claimed that no one had influenced their decision to take A Level maths, although it was a favourite subject of only 30% of those of either sex. The majority of students were aiming towards a university degree course. None of the girls was intending to apply for a computing course, but 15% of the boys were considering this option amongst others. Salaries were not the major consideration, but interesting (especially for girls) and worthwhile jobs were of importance.

The majority of girls had never considered computer studies or similar courses, whereas 42% of the boys had considered this option. Most students were unaware of the entry requirements for university computing courses and did not know what Data Processing involved. Most students did not use computing facilities at school/college and although 77% had access to a computer at home, most spent less than 30 minutes per week on computing. A slightly greater number of males said they enjoyed computing, but the difference in confidence between the sexes was significant; only 21% of the girls claimed to be confident in using a computer compared with 58% of the boys. The boys had more practical experience, many more knew some computer languages and had written a computer program. Despite the lack of experience and confidence of the girls, there is hope that they may catch up given the opportunity by higher education establishments; of the people interested in short courses and visits the girls were in the majority. Clearly lack of confidence does not deter the girls from expressing an interest in gaining knowledge such as that which may be obtained by this provision.

Of the maths and science students, 91% intended to enter higher education, yet only 3% were considering computing; medicine and chemistry were more popular choices. 69% of these students has never considered applying for computer related courses. Only 26% of these students use a computer at school/college, although 80% have a computer at home. 80% of the students used the computer for less than half an hour a week, and they were no more knowledgeable or confident than non-science students.

The number of students who considered maths their favourite subject was equal in both sexes, and in this category there were a greater number applying for computer courses than for either medicine or chemistry. More than half of these students had considered a computing related degree course at some stage: they were more aware of the entry requirements, and more likely to use a computer at school or college , although they did not claim more confidence or knowledge.

The students who use computing facilities at school/college were predominantly male, and maths was their favourite subject, but only 7% were intending applying for related degree courses. These students spent more time on computing, and enjoyed it more; they were more confident and knowledgeable.

Of the students who said that they enjoyed computing, 38% had considered related courses, but only 9% were still considering this option. The students who claimed to be confident were largely male. 42% of them had considered related courses at some stage, and 15% were still considering this option.

The students who were interested in short courses were predominately female, and only 3% were intending to apply for a related degree course, although for 28% this had been a previous consideration. These students did not use computing facilities often, although they had access at home. 52% enjoyed computing, though confidence and knowledge were lacking.

Table 19.1 shows that the students who are likely to apply for computing courses are those who are confident, have knowledge of computer languages, and can program a computer. 75% of these students are male. No previous knowledge of computing is required for entrance to university degree schemes. Indeed some university computing lecturers have claimed that students would do better if they had no knowledge of the subject rather than that gained at school. Yet some students who might do well on such courses will not apply because of lack of knowledge and confidence - this particularly applies to girls.

19.3.2 COMMENTS GIVEN BY RESPONDENTS

In the final question students were invited to comment on why there were so few women computer science undergraduates. Lack of knowledge and/or confidence and fear of isolation and/or prejudice were the most frequently cited explanations. Whereas 47% of the female students who commented considered that lack of knowledge or confidence was the reason, none of the male students gave this reason. One female student recorded her own experience: "My explanation is based on what goes on at our school. This being they don't try to interest you to do computer courses. I know we have computers at our school, but not once in six years I've been here has anyone taught me or my fellow pupils anything about computers. It wasn't until we

Table 19.1 Interest in Computer Related Degree Schemes

Positive Answers Given	% Students who have considered computing related degree	% Student intend applying for computing related degree	% Students retained interest
Studying Maths & Science	28	3	11
Maths Is Favourite Subject	50	20	40
Use Computers at School/College	29	7	24
Enjoy Computing	32	9	28
Confident Computer User	42	15	36
Can Write Programs	46	18	39
Interested In Short Courses	28	3	11

chose our options for O-Levels that they offered you a computer studies course. A lot of people weren't interested because they had never worked with computers and didn't know anything about them. Boys knew more about them because they would play and do things with computers they had at home. I know computers are becoming more and more important in our lives and I think people should at least learn something about them at school".

Apart from lack of knowledge and/or confidence, other girls (33%) felt that computer courses and/or the computing industry were oriented towards males. However, only one of the male respondents suggested that the subject was not readily promoted to women students; the majority (80%) of males who commented suggested that either fear of isolation or fear of prejudice was the cause, although none of the girls suggested this was the case.

There is a clear gender difference in the suggestions as to why women students are poorly represented, with girls more likely to believe that this is due to lack of confidence and/or knowledge and boys more likely to believe that girls are scared of encountering isolation or prejudice during their studies or in careers.

19.4 Conclusions

Although previous computing experience is not required for higher education computer studies courses, lack of knowledge and encouragement clearly deters academically eligible female candidates from considering such courses. The provisions of short courses with hands-on experience and a friendly environment could provide the encouragement and confidence required. In the longer term, the situation in which schoolgirls feel that they have less knowledge about computing than boys could be alleviated before the stage at which they are considering post-school career options. This should be done by providing a satisfactory computer education for all pupils in the earlier years of secondary school education.

It could be argued that as most of the respondents were aged 16-18 in June 1988, the numerical results and comments reflect the fact that these students were the victims of the problems associated with introduction of the microcomputer in secondary schools; this occurred from 1980 onwards and the students would have been in the early years of secondary school during this period. At this time many school administrators took the view that the introduction of microcomputers was an urgent consideration to boost publicity and prestige. The micro often arrived at the school before the necessary re-allocation of resources and access for all pupils had been considered.

Two years have now elapsed since the students participating in this survey were questioned. In order to ascertain whether there has been any significant improvement in the computing experience of female A Level maths students attending the eight institutions, this survey will be repeated in June 1990.

19.5 REFERENCES

[Evans 87] Evan A and Hall W, "Programming inequality", *Times Education Supplement*, 3718, p4, 1987.

[Lovegrove 87] Lovegrove G L and Hall W, "Where have all the Girls Gone?", *University Computing*, 9, pp207-210, 1987.

[Soper 88] Soper P, "Where have all the Women Gone?", *Computer Newsletter*, Jan/Feb, pp7-8, 1988.

20

Profile of Glasgow "WiC" Girls

Helen D Watt[1]

20.1 Introduction

In 1989 Glasgow University's Computing Science Department issued questionnaires to the 1,000 schoolgirls who attended one of their one-day "Women into Computing" workshops. 773 girls completed and returned questionnaires (ie 77% response). Some questions focused on background information about the girls' previous experience of computers at school and at home. Others investigated the girls' attitude to computers before the WiC workshop session.

Invitations to the workshops were issued to all schools in the Strathclyde, Central, Dumfries and Galloway regions. The 1,000 available places, on five separate workshops, were allocated on a first-come first-served basis. However the number of places allocated per school was limited.

On arrival at the workshop, each girl was asked to complete a questionnaire.

20.2 General information

All the third-year schoolgirls who completed the questionnaire were in the age-range 13-16 years with the majority being aged 14 years. Table 20.1 shows the exact distribution.

Table 20.1 Age distribution of WiC schoolgirls

Age	Number	Percentage
13	13	1.7
14	547	70.8
15	211	27.3
16	2	0.3
All ages	773	100%

Only 43 (ie 5.5%) of the girls attended all-girls schools. There was no statistical significance between attending an all-girls school and the region in which the girls

[1] Computing Science Department, University of Glasgow

lived. However there was an overwhelming significance (p = 0.0001: a 1 in 10,000 possibility that the results occurred by chance) that if a girl attended a single-sexed school it would be in the private sector and that if a girl attended a state school that it would be mixed-sexed (Table 20.2).

Table 20.2 Type of school – Gender by Sector

	All-girls	Mixed	Totals
Private	38	39	77
State	5	691	696
Totals	43	730	773

20.3 School Computing

Each girl was asked "Have you studied computing at school?". Table 20.3 shows the distribution of their responses to this question.

Table 20.3 Numbers studying computing at school

Course	Count	Percentage
Completed study	107	13.8
Currently studying	365	47.2
Never studied	297	38.4
Don't know	4	.5
Totals	773	100%

Most of the girls were either currently or had previously studied computing at school. However no information was collected on the length of the courses attended. Girls attending single-sexed schools had a higher than expected likelihood of having completed a computing course whereas there was a higher than expected number from mixed schools currently attending a course (Table 20.4).

Table 20.4 Number studying computing by type of school

Observed (Expected)	Single-sexed	Mixed-sex	Totals
Completed course	14 (6.0)	93 (101)	107
Currently studying	6 (20.3)	359 (344.7)	365
Never studied	22 (16.5)	275 (280.5)	297
Don't know	1 (0.2)	3 (3.8)	4
Totals	43	730	773

The girls were then asked if they had taken or were going to take any of a list of computing exams (O-Grade, Standard Grade, SCOTVEC, O Level). Those currently attending a computing course gave a higher than expected positive response whereas both the group who had completed a course and those who had not attended a school course were more negative (Table 20.5).

Table 20.5 Numbers hoping to take a computing exam by previous/current study of computing

Exams Obs (exp)	School computing course				
	Completed	Current	None	Don't know	Totals
Yes	34	330	23	3	390
	(54)	(184.2)	(149.8)	(2.0)	
No	56	14	220	1	291
	(40.3)	(137.4)	(111.8)	(1.5)	
Don't know	17	21	54	0	92
	(12.7)	(43.3)	(35.3)	(0.5)	
Totals	107	365	297	4	773

Analysis of the girls' responses to questions about specific examinations demonstrated the same trend.

20.4   Home Computing

512 (ie 66%) of the 773 girls had a computer in their home. However there was no relationship between studying computing at school and having a computer in their home. Of the 512 girls with access to a home computer only 34 (6.6%) didn't use the machine. Most girls, when asked if they used it for games, programming, writing or other, answered positively to two of the options (Table 20.6).

Table 20.6 Options distribution for WiC girls with home computers

Number of options	Number of girls	Percentage
0	34	6.6
1	198	38.7
2	206	40.2
3	62	12.1
4	12	2.3
Total	512	100%

Since nearly all of these girls used the home computer for games – 467(96.5%) of girls answered yes to this option – there was no correlation between games playing and any of the other activities. Therefore girls using the home computer for programming or writing were not less likely to play games than those who didn't program or write.

However girls were much more likely to use it for both programming and writing if they used it for either of these tasks (Table 20.7).

Table 20.7 Home computer - Programming by Writing

| | Use for programming | | |
Obs (Exp)	Yes	No	Totals
Used for writing	78 (64.3)	70 (83.8)	148
Not used for writing	90 (103.8)	149 (135.3)	239
Totals	168	219	387

Girls using the computer for either programming or writing were much more likely to use the machine for at least 2 or more activities.

In the 512 homes which had a computer, 31.4% of the machines were used by the father whereas only 15.5% were used by the mother. In 52.5% of homes the computer was used by a brother and 36% by a sister. Unfortunately the question to gain this information was badly designed, so that it was not possible to take account of number and sex of any siblings. The question only asked the girls to specify "who in your family uses the computer?". This has been altered in the questionnaire to be administered in June 1990. Despite this inadequacy the figures show that a girl is more likely to use the computer for more activities in a home where either the father, sister or mother uses the machine than if a brother does (Table 20.8).

Table 20.8 Family use of home computer by Number of types of use by WiC girl

	Who in family uses home computer								
	Father		Mother		Brother		Sister		
O	Yes	No	Yes	No	Yes	No	Yes	No	
E									T
0	3	31.	1	33	12	22	7	27	34
	(11)	(23)	(5)	(29)	(18)	(16)	(12)	(29)	
1	40	158	18	180	111	87	62	136	198
	(62)	(136)	(31)	(167)	(104)	(94)	(71)	(127)	
2	78	128	42	163	104	102	81	125	206
	(65)	(141)	(32)	(173)	(108)	(98)	(74)	(132)	
3	32	30	15	47	33	29	31	31	62
	(19)	(43)	(10)	(52)	(33)	(29)	(22)	(40)	
4	8	4	3	9	9	3	3	9	12
	(4)	(8)	(2)	(10)	(6)	(6)	(4)	(8)	
T	161	351	79	432	269	243	184	328	512

O=Observations, E=(Expected figures), T=Totals

20.5 Opinions

The last part of this pre-workshop questionnaire asked the girls their opinions of computing, the answers to which are given below:

Q. Would you like a job in which computing is a major part ?

A.	definitely	think so	don't know	don't think so	definitely not
	66 (8.6%)	260 (33.9%)	357 (46.6%)	73 (9.5%)	10 (1.3%)

Q. Would you like to study computing at university ?

A.	definitely	think so	don't know	don't think so	definitely not
	58 (7.6%)	186 (24.35)	352 (46.0%)	132 (17.2%)	38 (5.0%)

Q. Do you think computing is just for boys ?

A.	definitely	think so	don't know	don't think so	definitely not
	2 (0.3%)	0	4 (0.5%)	21 (2.7%)	739 (96.5%)

None of the above were effected by whether the girls had a computer in their home or not.

Q. Do you think computing is mathematical ?

A.	definitely	think so	don't know	don't think so	definitely not
	75 (9.9%)	301 (39.7%)	175 (23.1%)	176 (23.2%)	32 (4.2%)

Girls who had a computer at home were more likely to think that computing was mathematical than those who did not have a home computer.

Q. Do you think that people working in computing need to be able to communicate well ?

A.	definitely	think so	don't know	don't think so	definitely not
	167 (22%)	327 (43%)	154 (20%)	91 (12%)	21 (2.8%)

No significant difference was observed between those who did and did not have a computer at home in their response to this or the next question.

Q. Do you think that people working in computing spend all their time working at their machine ?

A.	definitely	think so	don't know	don't think so	definitely not
	20 (2.6%)	71 (9.3%)	97 (12.7%)	364 (47.8%)	210 (27.6%)

20.6 Summary

About two-thirds of the girls who completed the questionnaire had access to a computer in their own homes. Of these only a handful did not use this facility. The majority of these girls used the home-computer for playing games. Some girls, especially in families where either parent used the machine, also used the computer for programming and writing.

There was no observed difference to the uptake of computing courses at school or to the girls' opinions about computers between the girls who had and those who did not have access to a home computer. Girls who were currently attending a computing course seemed more likely to take computing exams at school than those who had completed a course. Those who had no school experience were very unlikely to take examinations in computing in the future. More than sixty percent of the girls attending the WiC workshop had some experience of computing at school.

If a girl attended a single-sexed school then it was more than likely that this school would be in the private sector. Girls from state schools were more likely to be attending a computing course in their third-year than girls from the private sector.

The opinion of all the girls showed that this group certainly did not think that computing was just for boys. They were also aware of the facts that people working in computing need communication skills and do not spend all day sitting in front of their machines.

The "Women into Computing" workshops which these girls attended aimed to alter the opinions of those who were not aware of these facts and to provide all the girls with a more positive feeling towards working in or studying computing in the future. Information on the effect of these workshops on girls' attitudes is described in [Watt 90a].

20.7 Acknowledgements

I would like to express my appreciation and thanks to: Mary Bryson, Computing Science Dept, University of Glasgow, who painstakingly entered all the questionnaire responses into the computer; Keith Oakley, Dept of Psychology, University of Glasgow, for his advice on coding and interpreting the information from the questionnaires and to my children, Susanne and Jeffrey, who helped to collate and code the original questionnaires.

20.8 REFERENCES

[Watt 90a] "Education and Industry Partnerships can change Attitudes", in proceedings of *Women into Computing Conference*, 1990.

21

The Gender Gap in Secondary School Computer Use

Peter Glissov[1]

21.1 Introduction

This paper reports on research into pupil attitudes to computers, with particular reference to the mixed/single-sex issue. The survey which forms its empirical basis was carried out as part of a research thesis concerned mainly with an investigation of the gender gap in school computer use. From the literature it is clear that various factors have been identified as applicable from a social psychological point of view (eg [Tittle 86, Culley 88a, Foon 88]). However, two structural social factors in particular stand out, namely social class variables (See [Lepper 85, Harvey 85, Dutton 85, Siann 86, Levin 89]) and whether or not a school is co-educational. This paper focuses on the area of the pupil sex composition, i.e. single-sex versus mixed-sex schooling, often referred to as the co-ed issue (cf [Ormerod 75, Smithers 82, Deem 84, Vasil 87, Foon 88]).

It has been argued that the mixed-sex school environment produces certain group dynamics that are detrimental to girls' interests in computers. [Culley 88a], in a study of option choices in (English) secondary schools, concludes that "... research suggests that in girls-only schools there is no shortage of enthusiasm for computing: computer studies is a popular option and computer clubs thrive [2]." This situation can equally be viewed as an argument about girls being disadvantaged in the competition for resources ([Stanworth 81, Durndell 90c]). There is, furthermore, ample evidence to support the idea that if the learning situation is made relevant and non-threatening, then females will actively enjoy learning about computers ([Stockdale 87, Cooper, Watt 90b]).

There is evidence to suggest that these factors may interact, a point that earlier research has not taken fully into account [Foon 88]. Elsewhere it has been argued that young children show great enthusiasm for working with computers, but invariably it seems easier for boys to benefit more from the exposure to computers, so that they acquire, if not a more positive attitude toward, then a higher degree of interest in using computers. The result of this process is that college first year students present themselves as highly differentiated along sex/gender lines [Siann 90, Durndell 87].

---

[1] Department of Psychology, Glasgow College, Cowcaddens Road, Glasgow, Scotland.
[2] See [Stockdale 87, Sanders 87] for examples of positive action in this respect.

The results presented in this paper substantiate this research and suggest, in addition, that important changes take place, particularly in the secondary school years.

21.2 Method

21.2.1 QUESTIONNAIRE

A questionnaire was developed, based on one used previously in a study of primary school children [Macleod 88], to gauge the pupils' attitudes towards, and use of, computers. It consisted of three main parts:

1. respondents were asked factual questions about their use of computers (a) within the school setting, and similar questions about their use of computers (b) outside the school, eg at home or at friends';

2. the main body of the questionnaire consisted of about 50 items concerned with attitudes to computers. These items were presented in the form of a 5 point Likert-scale with response choices ranging from "strongly agree" (score of 5) to "strongly disagree" (score of 1);

3. the final section was a sentence completion exercise where the respondents had to choose words from a list of gender oriented choices which would meaningfully complete each sentence. A typical example, with the choice of answers in brackets () would be as follows:

   "Interest in technology is usually shown by ..... " (Women=1; Men=2; Men and women alike=3; Not Sure=4).

21.2.2 DESIGN

Three Edinburgh secondary schools were chosen for their particular policy on single/mixed-sex education, as well as their particular socio-cultural background characteristics. [3]

The schools thus fell into two main groups based on the sex-composition of the pupil populations. Common to all schools was the variable of Age, based on three stages of the school career, namely first year (s1), third year (s3), and sixth year (s6) of secondary school. The respondents were not volunteers, and the sample of 286 pupils comprised 141 females and 145 males.

---

[3]This was done by selecting schools that are operated by the same merchant company, and thus charge identical fees, and comparable in terms of socio cultural background of the pupils.

21.3 Results

21.3.1 FACTUAL QUESTIONS

The first part of the questionnaire contained a range of factual type questions regarding the respondents' use of computers, firstly in, and secondly out of, school, and the results will be reported accordingly. [4]

21.3.2 SCHOOL COMPUTER USE

On all the questions that asked if the respondents had used various types of equipment and software, boys reported significantly more experience, with the exception of playing games, be that for "fun" or "learning".

In addition to the overall sex differences there were rather more subtle differences when comparing the two types of sex-composition. Boys showed no differences in computer use due to sex-composition. However, a significantly greater number of mixed-sex girls reported having used a word-processor, printer, and database, as opposed to their single-sex peers. The difference between the girls in their experience of word-processing is summarised in Table 21.1. (These figures are reported in somewhat more detail by way of illustration, but also because word-processing is an area traditionally considered a female domain.)

Table 21.1 Percentage of girls ticking number of texts produced using a word processor

Number of Texts:	Nil	1-5	6-10	>10	
In mixed-sex environment	34.8	53.5	15.2	6.5	N=90
In single-sex environment	63.3	33.3	00.0	3.3	N=46
Total	53.7	36.8	5.1	4.4	

The pupils' experience of writing computer programs was also investigated. Overall, the results show a significantly higher number of boys saying they have written a program (57%) than for girls (33.5%). Unlike their use of database and word processing software (mentioned earlier), single-sex girls now reported significantly more experience than did mixed-sex girls. This difference between the two types of school was also reflected in the results for the boys. These results are summarised in Table 21.2.

---

[4]The data presented in this section was analysed for statistical significance using X2 tests. Individual levels of probability etc. are not presented for the sake of brevity, but an alpha level of .05 was used throughout.

Table 21.2 Percentage of respondents answering "Yes" to:
"Ever written a computer program?"

	Mixed Sex	Single Sex	Total
Girls	25.5	43.6	37.6
Boys	48.8	71.0	64.8
Total	36.7	58.2	

It is, however, not only the formal education at school that reveals a gap with respect to girls' and boys' computer use, as shown in Table 21.3. When asked if they had used a computer outside formal classes there was no difference between either of the mixed- and single-sex groups, whereas there was a significant overall gender gap with 61.4% of girls answering "yes" compared with 72.4% of boys.

Table 21.3 Percentage of respondents answering "Yes" to:
"Ever used a computer outside lessons"

	Mixed Sex	Single Sex	Total	
Girls	57.4	63.4	61.4	(N=140)
Boys	72.1	72.5	72.4	(N=145)
Total	64.4	68.2		

21.3.3 COMPUTER USE OUTSIDE SCHOOL

Turning now to the use the children make of computers outside school hours, either at home or at friends', it was – in view of the within school results – not surprising to find that the boys reported a much higher rate of usage at home than the girls did, as summarised in Table 21.4.

Table 21.4 % of respondents answering "Yes" for each level of usage outside school

	Never	Once a month	Once a week	A few times weekly	Daily	
Girls	35.5	40.4	10.6	09.2	04.3	N=141
Boys	16.0	21.5	11.8	27.1	23.6	N=144
Total	25.6	30.9	11.2	18.2	14.0	

The results revealed that there was no significant difference between the mixed-sex and single-sex settings on any of the home use measures.

Furthermore, the results showed a significant difference between girls and boys in computer ownership, with 41.3% of girls and 66.2% of boys saying that they own a computer. However, there was, as with the home usage results mentioned above, no difference between the sex-composition groups for either sex.

When asked if there is an adult, other than those in the immediate family, with whom the teenagers could talk computers/-ing, Table 21.5 shows that there are fewer girls who have adults with whom they can talk about computers.

Table 21.5 Percentage of respondents answering "Yes" to:
"Is there another adult(s) to speak about computers to?"

	Mixed Sex	Single Sex	
Girls	15.2	20.4	N=139
Boys	32.6	29.7	N=144

In addition, Table 21.6 shows that the boys were much more sex biased, in so far as they generally responded in terms of same sex adults with respect to whom they can talk about computers.

Table 21.6 Percentage responding affirmatively to:
"If so, tick appropriate sex of other adult(s)"

	Female	Male	Both	
Girls	8.1	7.3	6.5	N=124
Boys	7.7	22.5	1.4	N=142

NB: Percentages for respondents answering "Not Applicable" are not shown.

21.3.4 ATTITUDINAL ITEMS AND COMPUTED VARIABLES

In order to extract major trends in the attitudinal items which formed the second part of the questionnaire, a "classic" factor analysis was carried out (principal axis with oblique rotation). It revealed no clear factors pertaining to gender differences and in general this approach was not considered particularly helpful in terms of the results reported here. Consequently the factor analysis was not utilised further. Instead 5 variables were computed from the raw-scores of conceptually linked items. These were:

1. School Use, computed from items of computer use, such as "How many pieces of text (for example notes, letters) have you produced using a word processor";

2. Home Use, calculated in identical fashion, eg "How often do you use a computer outside school". For both these usage variables the maximum possible score = 10, possible minimum = 0;

3. Positive Attitude, computed from affective type items like "computers are exciting" and other items measuring an attraction, or positive attitude, for want of a better expression, to computers;

4. Negative Attitude, calculated identically to Positive Attitude. Max. possible score for both Positive Attitude and Negative Attitude= 14, min.= 0;

5. Computer Attitude measured a general attitude to computers and was computed simply by subtracting the Negative Attitude score from the Positive Attitude score, forming a convenient summary of the previous affective measures. Possible max.=14, min.=-14;

6. Androgynous Outlook was an accumulation of scores on items which expressed a general non-stereotyped, or androgynous, gender perception. This score was a count of the number of times a respondent circled the "both men and women" choice option in the sentence completion section, mentioned in the Methods section above. The max. score= 7, min.= 0.

These variables were then subjected to analyses of variance, the results of which are summarised in Tables 21.7 to 21.12. These tables show mean scores on the computed variables by Sex-composition (mixed/single sex school) and Year at school (first, third, and sixth year respectively: s1, s3, s6) for each Sex. In all tables the total number of subjects are 286; including 141 females and 145 males:

Table 21.7 Computer Use At School

Year	Mixed-Sex			Single-Sex			Total
	s1	s3	s6	s1	s3	s6	
Girls	2.20	2.40	1.13	1.44	1.71	2.64	1.93
Boys	2.27	3.62	3.50	2.92	3.26	3.21	3.11
Total		2.49			2.55		

Table 21.7 shows significantly higher computer use with the school year, or the respondents' ages (p=<.025). There is also a significant difference between the sexes (p=<.001), with boys using computers to a greater extent than girls. A 2-way interaction occurred between Sex-composition and Year showing a gradual increase in school computer use with age for the single-sex pupils whereas the mixed-sex pupils showed a peak in their third year computer use to return to the level of the first year (p=<.033). Special note must be made of a highly significant 3-way interaction here (p=<.003), the result of which is that in the mixed-sex situation the girls' and boys' scores on the School Usage variable steadily grow apart with age, whereas the opposite effect is found in the single-sex environment.

Table 21.8 Computer Use At Home

Year	Mixed-Sex s1	s3	s6	Single-Sex s1	s3	s6	Total
Girls	0.90	1.50	0.07	1.56	1.47	0.39	1.07
Boys	2.80	1.92	1.79	3.00	2.44	1.82	2.39
Total		1.52			1.85		

Home Use showed no significant main effects. It can be seen in Table 21.8 to be lowest at the 6th year point for all groups, with a significant 2-way interaction between Sex and Year ($p = <.001$), resulting in Home Use of computers to be particularly low for the older girls. No further significant differences were found.

Table 21.9 Positive Attitude to Computers

Year	Mixed-Sex s1	s3	s6	Single-Sex s1	s3	s6	Total
Girls	5.17	3.50	2.87	4.45	4.77	4.03	4.20
Boys	5.75	5.77	3.64	5.97	5.44	4.54	5.30
Total		4.37			4.93		

The patterns of Positive Attitude toward computers show significant main effects for Sex and age. Thus boys were found to respond significantly more positively than girls ($p = <.001$), and a general tail-off with age was also found ($p = <.001$). These results are summarised in Table 21.9. This growing disaffection with computers appears to be particularly accentuated for the mixed-sex girls, but the difference was not statistically significant for this sample.

Table 21.10 Negative Attitude to computers

Year	Mixed-Sex s1	s3	s6	Single-Sex s1	s3	s6	Total
Girls	2.33	2.35	3.73	1.48	1.77	2.10	2.12
Boys	1.56	2.92	1.71	1.89	2.92	1.79	2.17
Total		2.42			2.02		

In Table 21.10 the mean scores on the Negative Attitude variable are summarised. The results show that there is a main effect with age showing that the s1 group holds the least negative view of computers, ($p = <.059$). Highly significant 2-way interactions occur with Sex and Year ($p = <.007$), and Sex and Sex-composition ($p = <.025$), giving a rather complex picture. Nevertheless, it can be seen in Table 21.10, that as far as sex differences are concerned, the boys from the two types of schools show a similar pattern of a peak in their third year, but in the main their negative Attitudes stay level. Girls, on the other hand, show a rise in Negative Attitudes with age, and the mixed-sex girls more so than their single-sex sisters.

Table 21.11 General Computer Attitude

Year	Mixed-Sex			Single-Sex			
	s1	s3	s6	s1	s3	s6	Total
Girls	2.83	1.15	-.87	2.97	3.00	1.93	2.08
Boys	4.19	2.85	1.93	4.08	2.53	2.75	3.13
Total		1.94			2.92		

The general Computer Attitude, with mean scores presented in Table 21.11 summarises the results of the previous two variables, as presented in Table 21.9 and 21.10. The overall picture presented here is that of a general decline in positive regard for computers with age ($p=<.004$). A main effect was also found with respect to sex differences, with the girls generally less positive than the boys ($p=<.034$). A similar pattern occurred between the two types of schools with a more negative view held by the pupils in the mixed-sex situation ($p=<.056$).

Table 21.12 Androgynous or Non-Stereotyped Attitude

Year	Mixed-Sex			Single-Sex			
	s1	s3	s6	s1	s3	s6	Total
Girls	4.20	3.75	4.20	3.48	4.56	4.11	4.06
Boys	3.40	2.69	3.07	3.76	2.59	3.18	3.16
Total		3.55			3.62		

Table 21.12 illustrates a highly significant, and large, sex difference on the Androgyny type score, which measures a tendency to non-stereotyped gender perception ($p=<.001$), with boys more stereotyped than girls. Further, a significant 2-way interaction of Sex with Year was found ($p=<.001$), resulting in the boys being more sex-stereotyped in their responses with age, in contrast with an increase in scores with age for girls.

21.4 Discussion

21.4.1 MAIN FINDINGS

A significant sex related difference was found both in pupils' attitude towards and use of computers, with boys scoring higher on both counts. The very positive views that pupils hold about computers generally diminish during the school years, particularly for girls in the mixed-sex school environment. In the main, a polarisation of girls' and boys' attitudes characterised the mixed- sex environment. Speaking of differences between the girls in the two groups, it appears that mixed-sex girls are indeed "turned off" computers in comparison with their single-sex peers.

21.4.2 COMPUTER USAGE

As far as school usage is concerned, the results showed a general peak in the 3rd year at secondary school, but a decline is evident amongst the girls, especially in the mixed-sex setting. This is in line with previous research ([Wilder 85, Foon 88, Durndell 90c]).

Mixed-sex girls were found to have significantly more experience of database and word-processing software and associated hardware, whereas single-sex girls had more experience of programming. The two groups of girls reported no difference in their use of computers outside formal lessons (which was still significantly less than the boys'). This difference could be due to a different emphasis in the teaching styles of computer related subjects. Certainly there was an apparent difference, during our visits, in the appearance of the computer labs between the girls-only school and the other two schools. The equipment in the girls-only school looked somewhat outdated in comparison – and little used – and I understand that girls from this school went to another school to use the computers there for their sixth year maths projects.

Wordprocessing highlights not only the sex-composition aspect, but is also an important example of computer use where one would expect – according to traditional sex related divisions of labour – that girls would, at least, equal boys; but they didn't. This serves to underline the depth of the wider gap in experience which was significant on all measures of school use and knowledge of computer languages. This finding is in line with previous research ([Breakwell 86, Dambrot 85, Vasil 87]).

The students in the mixed-sex school environment tended to polarise along more gender stereotyped lines than their single-sex counterparts on measures of computer use and measures of affective type attitudes toward computers. The sex difference in the mixed-sex group grew bigger with age, whilst the sex differences remained at about the same level between the single-sex pupils throughout the school career. These trends can only be interpreted in terms of a polarisation effect.

No significant differences in home computer ownership and use between the two groups of girls were found, but a large difference between the sexes existed on these measures. This trend was also reflected in the number and sex of the adults with whom the respondents speak about computers. In summary, the results with respect to home use show a consistent fall with age in computer use for all groups, which is particularly evident in the mixed-sex girls.

21.4.3 ATTITUDES

In this study sex differences were found to be a salient aspect of attitudes toward computers. In the literature, however, the evidence is rather less clear. There are cases where sex differences, in the main, were not found, eg [Harvey 85], and where the usual sex difference was reversed with girls registering more positive attitudes to computers than boys [Loyd 87]. On the other hand, ample evidence showing sex differences can also be found [Miura 87, Loyd 87, Levin 89, Shotton 89]. On balance, with the results from this study, the evidence for sex differences in attitudes must now be considered to be well documented. These seemingly contradictory findings can perhaps be explained through the various methodologies employed. In this study I have focused on the evidence relating to the school sex-composition in a social psychological framework. Taking structural social factors into account does, on the whole, seem to produce results showing sex differences, suggesting the possibility that sex often interacts with other factors. Another explanation may be that research has focused on different age groups, where younger computer users will probably not show traditional sex related patterns of use or attitudes.

A more technical point of interest could be raised here. The separate measure of positive and negative attitudes to computers is perhaps slightly idiosyncratic. The point of this is to stress the fact that these attitudes are constructs, and highlight the possibility of subjects simultaneously harbouring both feelings.(The advantage of this conception lies in the separate analysis of these factors which it affords.) In Tables 21.9 to 21.11 it can thus be seen that the variation in positive attitudes can be described wholly in terms of main effects for sex and age (Table 21.9). The variation in negative attitudes, however, lies not in main effects on their own, but in interactions between sex on the one hand, and age and sex-composition on the other (Table 21.10). I would therefore tentatively suggest that an understanding of the gender gap should be sought at two levels.

- First, the reason for the polarisation of attitudes with age in the mixed-sex situation should be found in the rise in negative attitudes due to an interaction between sex and age, and sex and the mixed-sex environment. That seems to suggest that the nature of the polarisation phenomenon should be described in terms of an active "turn off" of the girls by the mixed-sex environment, rather than a passive lack of positive attitudes on the part of the girls themselves (Table 21.10).

- Second, the pattern of the attitudinal results, with their sex and age effects, accords with the pattern found in the analysis of the Androgynous type measure, see Table 21.12. The highly significant sex difference and interaction between sex and age here is suggestive of an underlying mechanism of gender, but more of that below.

The documented general decline in positive views with age is also in line with previous research [Wilder 85]. The younger and presumably less experienced pupils show a high level of enthusiasm for and use of computers which peaks somewhere around the third year. In line with [Wilder 85] these findings can possibly be explained by a developmental shift in the respondents' understanding of what is meant by "computer". However, considering the findings from a previous intervention study of primary school children [Siann 88b], it seems more plausible that the change is due to what I would call a "sobering" effect which comes with experience and the realisation that computers cannot match earlier (unrealistically optimistic) expectations, which is a qualitatively different conception from the developmental model.

21.4.4 IMPLICATIONS

The results show that there is a significant gender gap in computer use, as reported widely in the literature, perhaps with the exception of very young users. When considered with structural social factors, some interesting interaction effects can be discerned which were not evident before, and which have important policy consequences. For example, with respect to positive attitudes to the use of computers it was found that the sex-composition of the schools interacted with sex, so that although all categories of respondents showed a decrease with age, this was significantly more pronounced in the case of the girls in the mixed-sex school environment. These results from the attitude scores are congruent with the home usage scores, but largely do not reflect school usage. It arguably follows that school computer use does not have quite the smoothing out effect – in terms of attitudes – that has been suggested in the literature [Miura 87]. It rather seems to suggest (as one would expect) that there are dynamics within the mixed-sex girls' environment which are stronger than that of mere exposure to school computer use. The related drops in positive attitudes toward computers and home usage point to strong out-of-school influences on girls getting bored with computers, at least in the mixed-sex situation.

In spite of the clear trend for the mixed-sex girls to show less interest in computers, it ought to be stressed that certain difficulties in generalising from this study exist. First, in order to systematically investigate the effects of sex-composition, the socio cultural background of the respondents was held constant. Hence, there are problems in applying the results to populations from different socio cultural backgrounds. Second, one must be cautious in applying results obtained from an all-girls school, to girls-only groups within a mixed-sex setting, as there are additional complications in the latter with regard to a number of questions. Tacit messages, for example, may be broadcast when "removing" girls from mainstream teaching. The break-up of mixed-sex teaching may also result in dysfunctional dynamics in boys-only groups. Furthermore, situations which could provide rich opportunities for teaching equal opportunities may be sacrificed.

21.4.5 GENDER DIFFERENCES – BEYOND SEX DIFFERENCES

Finally, an inherent "weakness" in the current approach to so-called gender differences will be discussed. Most of the questionnaire based research falls into the (sub)category of sex and gender research that [Deaux 84] called "sex-of-subjects" research. She argued that to treat sex as a variable is too crude a measure, which is useful mainly in establishing whether sex differences exist and their extent. It might be psychologically more helpful to explore the underlying processes that cause the gender differences. This point was taken up in a theoretical paper by [Archer 87], in which he argued that it is the "social processes in which gender plays a part" that should be studied.

Here I would like to return to the findings regarding the Androgyny type measure mentioned earlier. The measure used here was a *post hoc* measure and clearly it is a very crude measure of gender stereotyping. Nevertheless, it can be argued that the large sex differences on a measure of a socially determined attitude indicate that gender (as opposed to sex) may be a crucial factor. One researcher who has researched the gender argument extensively is Sandra Bem. She argues [Bem 81, Bem 87] that although we are born with a given biological sex, the consequences are socially reinforced and perpetuated from that moment on. Whether a person develops into a masculine or feminine person (not the same as male and female), depends therefore not only on their biological sex; that is to say, that social and psychological factors intervene. [5]

Hence, I would argue, along with Archer, that the sex differences are relatively unimportant – from a psychological perspective. The first step in a new direction is possibly to look in more depth at what we mean by gender. Is it really a dichotomy in the same sense as sex? We often talk about gender as being either feminine or masculine, but does it make sense to talk of gender, the social construct, as if we were talking of biological dimorphism? We ought perhaps to ask ourselves why we, as a science, have adopted this "standard" dichotomised approach to sex differences. Two questions in particular spring to mind: Is it not because it is, in a cognitive or perceptual sense, such an easy thing to do? And is it not an approach prescribed by values reflecting a deeply sex divided society?

If we accept that gender is socially negotiated, then it is also possible to accept that gender is not necessarily a dichotomous entity. When we can conceive of gender differences as being more than just comparing females and males on various measures, then, I would suggest, we might be more successful than the largely quantitative approaches of the general body of social psychological research in this increasingly important area.

21.5 Acknowledgements

The author would like to express his gratitude to the pupils who filled in the questionnaires at the schools in Edinburgh, namely (alphabetically): Broughton High School, Daniel Stewart's and Melville College, George Watson's College, The Mary Erskine School, and Wester Hailes Education Centre. Thanks also to the following staff members at the schools (respectively): J. Scott, P. Caton, A. Brobbel, E. McCamley, A. Goodall. Finally the following individuals deserve a special mention: Anne Knox, Gerda Siann, Alan Durndell, Hamish Macleod, and Jackie Glissov.

---

[5]It is impossible to do justice to Deaux's and Bem's works here, so interested readers are referred to the original literature. (A good review of the androgyny issue can be found in [Cook 85]) This argument is "constructionist" in character, and is akin to the approach taken by authors like [Keller 85] and [Kelly 85] in their analysis of the gender gap in science.

21.6 REFERENCES

[Archer 87] Archer J, "Beyond Sex Differences: Comments on Borrill and Reid", *Bulletin of the British Psychological Society*, 40, pp88-90, 1987.

[Bem 81] Bem S L, "Gender Schema Theory: A cognitive account of sex typing", *Psychological Review*, 88, 4, pp354-364, 1981.

[Bem 87] Bem S L, "Masculinity and Femininity Exist Only in the Mind of the Perceiver", In *Masculinity/Femininity: Basic perspectives*, Reinish, Rosenblum and Sanders (eds), N.Y. & Oxford: Oxford University Press, 1 in "The Kinsey Institute Series", 1987.

[Breakwell 86] Breakwell G M, Fife-Schaw C R, Spencer J and Lee T R, "Attitudes to New Technology in Relation to Social Beliefs and Group Memberships", *Current Psychological Research Review*, 5, 1, pp34-47, 1986.

[Cook 85] Cook E P, "Psychological Androgyny", New York: Pergamon Press, *Pergamon General Psychology Series*, 1985.

[Cooper] Cooper J, Hall J and Huff C, *Anxiety as a Consequence of Sex Stereotyped Software*, Princeton: Princeton University, Unpublished manuscript.

[Culley 88a] Culley L A, "Option Choice and Careers Guidance: Gender and computing in secondary schools", *British Journal of Guidance and Counselling*, 16, 1, pp73-81, 1988.

[Dambrot 85] Dambrot F, Watkins-Malek M, Silling M, Marshall R and Garver J, "Correlates of Sex Differences in Attitudes toward and Involvement with Computers", *Journal of Vocational Behaviour*, 27, pp71-86, 1985.

[Deem 84] Deem R (Ed), *Co-education Reconsidered*, Milton Keynes: Open University Press, 1984.

[Deaux 84] Deaux K, "From Individual to Social Categories: Analysis of a decade's research on gender", *American Psychologist*, 39, pp105-16, 1984.

[Durndell 90c] Durndell A J, "Choice and Image: Gender and Computer Studies in Higher Education", in this volume.

[Durndell 87] Durndell A J, Macleod H A and Siann G, "A Survey of Attitudes to, Knowledge About and Experience of Computers", *Computers and Education*, 11, pp167-75, 1987.

[Dutton 85] Dutton W H, Kovaric P and Steinfield C, "Computing in the Home: A research paradigm", *Computers and the Social Sciences*, 1, 1, pp5-18, 1985.

[Foon 88] Foon A, "The Relationship Between School Type and Adolescent Self Esteem, Attribution Styles, and Affiliation Needs: Implications for Educational Outcome", *British Journal of Educational Psychology*, 58, pp44-54, 1988.

[Harvey 85] Harvey T J and Wilson B, "Gender Differences in Attitudes Towards Microcomputers Shown by Primary and Secondary School Pupils", *British Journal of Educational Technology*, 16, 3, pp183-187, 1985.

[Keller 85] Keller E F, *Reflections on Gender and Science*, New Haven and London: Yale University Press, 1985.

[Kelly 85] Kelly A, "The Construction of Masculine Science", British Journal of Sociology of Education, 6, 2, pp133-154, 1985.

[Lepper 85] Lepper M R, "Microcomputers in Education: Motivational and Social issues", *American Psychologist*, 40, pp1-18, 1985.

[Levin 89] Levin T and Gordan C, "Effect of Gender and Computer Experience on Attitudes Toward Computers", *Journal of Educational Computing Research*, 5, 1, pp69-88, 1989.

[Loyd 87] Loyd, "Gender and Computer Experience as Factors in the Computer Attitudes of Middle School Students", *Journal of Early Adolescence*, 7, 1, pp13-19, 1987.

[Macleod 88] Macleod H A, Siann G and Glissov P, *Cognitive and Motivational Factors in Primary School Computer Use*, Edinburgh: Scottish Education Department, Microelectronics in Education Committee, Project Ref MEC/IRD/19m, 1988.

[Miura 87] Miura I T, "Gender and Socioeconomic Status Differences in Middle-School Computer Interest and Use", *Journal of Early Adolescence*, 7, 2, pp243-254, 1987.

[Ormerod 75] Ormerod M B, "Subject Preference and Choice in Co-education and Single-sex Secondary Schools", *British Journal of Educational Psychology*, 45, 3, pp257-267, 1975.

[Sanders 87] Sanders J S, "Closing the Computer Gender Gap in School", *Proceedings of the Fourth GASAT Conference*, University of Michigan, Ann Arbor, Michigan, USA, 1987.

[Shotton 89] Shotton M A, *Computer Addiction? A study of computer dependency*, London: Taylor & Francis, 1989.

[Siann 86] Siann G and Macleod H, "Computers and Children of Primary School Age: Issues and Questions", *British Journal of Educational Technology*, 2, 17, pp133-144, 1986.

[Siann 88b] Siann G, Glissov P and Macleod H A, "Cognitive and Motivational Factors in Primary School Computer Use", in proceedings of *Women Into Computing: First National Conference*, University of Lancaster, 20-22 July 1988.

[Siann 90] Siann G, Glissov P, Macleod H A and Durndell A J, "The Effect of Computer Use on Gender Differences in Attitudes to Computers", *Computers and Education*, 14, 2, pp183-191, 1990.

[Smithers 82] Smithers A and Collings J, "Co-education and Science Choice, *British Journal of Educational Studies*, 30, 3, pp313-328, 1982.

[Stanworth 81] Stanworth M, "Gender and Schooling: A study of sexual divisions in the classroom", *Explorations in Feminism Series No. 7*, London: Women's Research and Resources Centre, 1981.

[Stockdale 87] Stockdale, *Proceedings of the Fourth GASAT Conference*, 1987.

[Tittle 86] Tittle C K, "Gender Research and Education", *American Psychologist*, 41, 10, pp1161-1168, 1986.

[Vasil 87] Vasil L, Hesketh B and Podd J, "Sex Differences in Computing Behaviour among Secondary School Pupils", *New Zealand Journal of Educational Studies*, 22, 2, pp201-214, 1987.

[Watt 90b] Watt H, "Profile of Glasgow 'WIC' Girls", in this volume.

[Wilder 85] WilderG, Mackie D and Cooper J, "Gender and Computers: Two surveys of computer-related Attitudes", *Sex Roles*, 13, 3/4, pp215-228, 1985.

22

School and Industry Links - An Example of Co-operation

Irene M. Pacitti[1]

22.1 The School

St Gerard's Secondary School is situated in the mainly working class area of Govan on the south side of Glasgow. Since the 1960s it has been a six-year denominational comprehensive school. A large number of the pupils come from districts designated for priority treatment by Strathclyde Region under the terms of its policy on urban deprivation; almost 50% are entitled to free school meals.

Over the past few years the roll has fallen by about 25% to its current figure of about 450 pupils. This downward trend has been accelerated in recent years by the Parents' Charter, which allows them the right to place their children in schools other than their designated local school.

Many adults also attend the school to take leisure and certificate classes. There is a properly established crèche, under the supervision of a trained nursery school teacher – a facility which has enabled women students to attend many of the classes.

Extensive links have been established with the local community. The school's facilities have been used in the evenings by clubs and sports groups. Representatives from local industry have addressed pupils and it is hoped that this will increase. Prior to the 1988 Govan bye-election, the various candidates participated in a forum organised by the school. Further contacts have been established by providing service to the people in the neighbourhood and beyond.

22.2 Work Experience

A number of pupils have participated in work experience and work shadowing organised by the school, notably in hospitals but also in a local primary school and in industrial and commercial establishments. Many have also experienced more traditional pupil employment such as paper and milk rounds, and work as weekend shop assistants. There is an arrangement whereby upper school pupils in their non-classtime may help with the crèche – a valuable opportunity for anyone wishing to proceed to pre-school education supervision.

---

[1] St Gerard's Secondary School, 80 Vicarfield St, Govan, Glasgow G51 2DF

The school has various schemes to help pupils secure employment when they leave. These will be looked at firstly through the co-operation between individual departments and then through the different avenues of approach that have existed in the school. In particular, mention will be made of the Guidance Department, which has much expertise in securing work experience. More recently the school has become involved in COMPACTS (see later in this paper) and soon there will be the introduction of the TVEI extension. All of these have had a certain influence on the school.

22.3   Some Cooperative Initiatives

22.3.1   BACKGROUND: THE GOVAN INITIATIVE

Govan Initiative Ltd is an amalgam of private and public sector interests led by Strathclyde Regional Council and involving the City of Glasgow District Council, the Scottish Development Agency, Glasgow Opportunities and major business, industrial and commercial concerns in Govan. It is at the helm of one of the most important and economic initiatives in the West of Scotland and is scheduled to continue its work through 1991.

Goven Initiative Ltd offers advice on business developments, grants and loans, training, physical and environmental improvements and the promotion of Govan as an area of the city which is ready for further development. An experienced staff team from both the public and private sectors take a personal and particular initerest in all areas of strategic concern.

22.3.2   THE YOUNG ENTERPRISE SCHEME

Until recently, the school participated in the Young Enterprise Scheme with the support of the Business Studies Department and in conjunction with the Govan Initiative. This scheme was for upper school pupils and took place mainly in their own time.

The most recent project, undertaken in 1988, was the design, production and marketing of Christmas cards. These were of a very high standard, much sought after and appreciated by those who purchased them.

Under the aegis of the Home Economics Department, the pupils produced a very successful Christmas Dinner for OAPs in the area, which involved the pupils preparing and cooking the menu, setting up tables and serving the meal. Earlier in the first term, following a visit to a local craft shop, some pupils had become very keen to produce some goods to sell. With the cooperation of the owner, this became a reality and they were thus able to raise money to subsidise the meal.

Departmental co-operation exists in the school and in particular in the SCE (Scottish Certificate of Education) Standard Grade Course in Social and Vocational Skills, which involves the Departments of Business Studies, Home Economics and Technical Studies.

The aim of this course is to develop the pupils' self-confidence, initiative and cooperative ability. Communications skills are also developed. These play a large part in the pupils' own organisation of the course as THEY must choose a plan and then effect it themselves by letter writing, form-filling and use of the telephone.

Basically the plan of the course is as follows:

Term 1 - Enterprise theme

This has taken the form of the pupils producing some very attractive classroom theme plaques in their metalwork class. They also produced various nameplates in plastic and wood which they sold in the school.

Term 2 - Leisure activity

Term 3 - Residential stay at one of the residential centres used for this purpose.

Term 4 - Work experience which will be arranged by other means already existing within the school.

Term 5 - Community event chosen and organised by the pupils themselves.

22.4 School Careers Structure

22.4.1 THE GUIDANCE DEPARTMENT

The longest established expertise is in the Guidance Department, among whose remits has been the placement of S4 pupils in work experience. This is particularly important for those who will be returning to study for their Highers in S5 and S6, but placements are sometimes secured even for those who intend to leave at the end of the year. In addition, work experience is often secured for S5 and S6 pupils who wish to pursue different avenues in their careers.

This work experience has so far taken place during the last week in May and first week in June, prior to pupils' return following the April/May study leave for the SCE exams. This option will remain open, but new school initiatives currently being developed may afford the pupils additional work experience.

Placements are organised following a set plan of action involving school, employer, parent/guardian and pupil. Some of the steps are detailed below.

Participating employers are sent a "letter of understanding", detailing responsibilities and the insurance position. The employer must provide written confirmation of having read the letter and agreed to these conditions. At the end of the work experience, a report is sent to the school on the conduct of the pupil during the week. The parent or guardian receives a letter giving details of the scheme and both he/she and the pupil are required to confirm in writing that they accept certain of its conditions. The pupil receives a note reminding them of expected behaviour. Pupils must also sign a form guaranteeing among other things that they will not disclose confidential company information.

In the recent past, it had become more difficult to place pupils as job vacancies had become scarcer. Nevertheless the Guidance Department had managed to place most of those who wished to participate in the scheme. Recently there has been a marked upturn in the interest of employers. Guidance staff have been engaged in placing the present S4 from February onwards. By March there were five avenues active, with enquiries from more prospective employers coming in every day. Pupils have been sent to venues which include local nursery, primary schools, hospital, police and the Royal Mail. Two S5 boys have been placed on work shadowing in engineering firms.

22.4.2 THE CAREERS OFFICER

The two careers officers attached to the school also have considerable experience in cooperating with local industry. They visit the school once a week during the first two terms of the session, with the remit of interviewing each pupil during S4 prior to considering tertiary or further education, YTS or job placement. They have up-to-date information on the qualifications and/or skills required in the marketplace and are able to offer advice to the pupils according to their talents, skills, interests and aptitudes.

One of the careers officers is responsible mainly for S4. If S5 or S6 seek counselling, they will see the senior careers officer to discuss their prospects. In addition the careers officers are in attendance at all parents' evenings.

22.5 New Initiatives

22.5.1 COMPACTS

In September 1989, an empty classroom was revamped as an office environment and COMPACTS arrived in the school. Having originated in the USA, COMPACTS is an initiative between school and industry, now taking place in many cities in the UK, including several locations in Glasgow. COMPACTS takes the form of a contract signed towards the end of S2 for commencement in S3 between pupil (who has to complete a Personal Action Plan), school (through the Guidance teacher in charge of the year group) and industry (through the COMPACTS officer in the school who is the link between education and employer). For successful candidates, the scheme guarantees a job placement at the end of the contract expiry date.

The Personal Action Plan is an undertaking by the pupil to fulfil certain conditions during S3 and S4. These targets are for 90% punctuality, 80% attendance and certain educational goals to be reached. Observance of these targets involve the whole staff with normal attendance patterns being the criteria in the first two. The educational goals are determined by normal classwork, viz attempts made at work according to ability as well as actual grades attained. In addition there is an assessment of pupils' social skills which involves observation of their behaviour both with their peers and with those in authority over them.

Various means are employed to help those who have signed up. During S3 a series of lessons helps them bridge the gap between school and the workplace. These include sessions devoted to self-understanding and confidence building, as well as discussion of issues such as equal opportunities.

Among other strategies used to encourage the pupils to meet their targets are prizes for good attendance, good performance in pursuit of other goals and for those who have improved on a previous bad report. The "magic" figure of attainment for each of these categories has to be reached by the end of S4. Already some pupils have dropped out as they cannot visualise themselves achieving their goal. COMPACTS will also drop a pupil who fails to achieve the attendance criteria even with perfect attendance in S4 and this will indubitably have an effect on their academic performance.

The pupils have to demonstrate a link with industry three times during their contract. This can take the form of a talk by an industrialist, a mock interview session and one week's work experience (at the end of which the employer will return a report on them to the school). These all take place in the S4 year.

New contacts will be set up to provide pupils with further work experience. This will take place early in the session, and it is expected that the first COMPACTS people on work experience will be out of school in late August/early September 1990. This work experience does not preclude them from going out again later in the S4 year under the usual arrangements made by the Guidance department.

The school's part of this bargain is to produce young persons who have been reliable in attendance and punctuality *and* have reached their own educational goal.

22.5.2 TVEI

The extension programme of TVEI comes into operation in autumn 1990. The advent of TVEI has meant a large technical input to the school, and we have benefited further in equipment in the Business Studies, Computing, Technical, Home Economics and Art Departments. It also means a slant towards technological input throughout the curriculum.

95% of pupils select technological subjects voluntarily. In an attempt to attract the remaining 5%, an extra slot has been created in the timetable, giving 80 hours technical activity through short courses.

For technology activity in S3 during 1990-91, the school is offering courses in Craft and Design, OIS (Office and Information Skills), Computing Studies and Home Economics: in addition there are short courses in Electronics (from SEB ie Scottish Education Board), Photography and Computer Applications - probably DTP (both these latter from modules from SCOTVEC, Scottish Vocation and Education Committee). To encourage technical application awareness, there will be enhancement of other courses in various departments: Art (development of dark room), Craft and Design (CAD) Music (electronic instruments), Computing (second computer room).

Careers education will be supplemented with Computer Assisted Careers Education Software (Micro Doors and Open Doors) situated in the library and overseen by the librarian, who will also supervise the development of a careers library. In addition there will be liaison between the librarian and the Guidance Department.

A careers officer will be attached to the TVEI unit to advise the guidance staff in all aspects of career education. He/she will support and assist in the preparation of a short careers education programme, and will assist the librarian in future development of the careers library.

During 1990-1991, this short careers education programme will be achieved by pupil extraction in groups. To help develop the programme, several supplementary new appointments will be made – an Assistant Head Teacher, Principal Teachers in Guidance and Information Technology – as well as a TVEI co-ordinator in the school. In addition, guidance and counselling will be refined and extended by increasing one-to-one interviews. This will be effected by the involvement of the COMPACTS officer and team in the school and by the assistance of the guidance and supplementary staff.

Pupil personal and social development will be through student centred learning methods and will be in electronics and probably PLD (Pupils with Learning Difficulties). Residential experience will be at outdoor centres eg Blairvadoch or Faskally and Religious retreats eg Langbank.

In order to meet the schools/industry liaison requirement, there is already the involvement of S3 pupils in COMPACTS. The target is 100%, but this will be reviewed. The problem will be to find out how to accommodate non-COMPACTS pupils.

An Equal Opportunities Committee has also been established. It has already reviewed the school handbook and subject choice materials. It will further look to the attendance of staff at in-service training, organised by Division/TVEI Unit, and will oversee dissemination/training within the school.

By Easter 1992, the pupils will be required, in conjunction with the Guidance department, to produce a record of achievement similar to a CV. This activity will be supported by the Departments of English, Computing and Business Studies.

The management and monitoring of this will be by the co-ordinator of TVEI, along with the TVEI Committee which will consist of the Co-ordinator, the COMPACTS Liaison Officer, the supplementary staff and the principal teachers in subject areas as and when required. The Line management structure will be: SMT (Senior Management Team) ↔ TVEI Committee ↔ PTs ↔ teachers. An annual report will be issued to all staff and the school board. Times will be made available to allow arrangement of the school's TVEI programme to be undertaken. Hence the committee will be given time to meet SMT and PTs within PAT (Planned Activities Time). PTs will report to teachers within DM (Departmental Meeting) time.

22.6 Conclusion

This, then, has been a description of how the school in which I am currently employed attempts to bridge the gap between school life and the workplace. It is not necessarily to be taken as any sort of role model of what should happen in any other school.

22.7   Acknowledgements

I wish to express my thanks to the following St Gerard's staff members who helped in my research for this paper: Mr Andrew Tarbert, Head teacher; Mr Jim Braidwood, TVEI co-ordinator; Mrs Ella Sherry PT Guidance; Mrs Pauline Elliot, Guidance liaising with COMPACTS; Mr Eddie Welsh, PT Business Studies; Miss Martina Boyce, PT Home Economics; Mrs Margaret Finnie, Home Economics; Mr Alex McFarlane, Senior Teacher in charge of Computing; Ms Gerry Maclean, School Librarian; Mrs Isabel McMurchie, COMPACTS Officer in the school.

23

Choice and Image: Gender and Computer Studies in Higher Education

Alan Durndell[1]

23.1 Introduction

This paper reviews a sequence of studies carried out on newly enrolled higher education students covering four successive intakes from 1986-1989. The latter two studies,
(covering 1988 and 1989), where factors involved in the choice *not* to study computing were investigated, will be given greater weight.

Interest in the relatively low level of female participation in the physical sciences,
engineering, computing – and sometimes mathematics – is now widespread. In the
UK, the UCCA figures, eg [UCCA 89], document a rising trend of female participation in university education in most subjects, including engineering. Computing
however, is special in that the level of female participation over the last decade has
fallen from 25% to 11%. The recent GASAT (Gender and Science and Technology)
conference [Granstam 86] revealed that this appeared to be an international trend, at
least within northern Europe (ie Germany, Holland, Denmark). Sweden provides an
interesting example, as institutional support for gender equality has possibly gone further than in any other country in the world. Yet whilst 60% of all first year university
and college students are now female, 47% of chemical engineering students are female, and 23% of civil engineering students are female, only 8% of computer science
and engineering students are females [Swedish Institute 89]. A mirror image is provided in the UK by Morris el al's study [Morris 90] on psychology applicants, which
shows that the discipline of psychology is experiencing huge increases in demand for
places, and that there is some concern that applicants can be 75-80% female. Why do
males and females choose in this fashion?

23.2 Study 1

The first study was based on 928 students enrolling on a wide variety of courses in
1986 [Durndell 87, Siann 88a]. The findings form part of what is now a reasonably

[1]Dept of Psychology, Glasgow College, Cowcaddens Roads, Glasgow G4 OBA

consistent literature, spanning the USA as well as the UK [Linden 87] about gender, attitudes and experiences of computing. Girls tend to have less experience and use of computers than boys and are less likely to have their own computers. Conversely, there tend not to be gender differences in certain attitudes to computers, in that in general computers are seen as necessary, useful and linked to the future. Similarly, as reported in [Siann 88a] neither male nor female computer scientists are negatively stereotyped.

23.3 Study 2

The second study was based on 387 students, again enrolling on a wide variety of courses [Durndell 90b]. Both open ended and fixed answer material was collected on why they chose their particular courses. They were also asked to account for the relatively low female participation in technological subjects. Computing students of both genders were found to be somewhat more instrumental in their approach to course choice, ie money and jobs were relatively important to them, rather than an intrinsic interest in computing. This relative lack of gender differences *within* a particular discipline grouping is becoming a common finding – cf [Kolmos 90] on engineering students.

There was support for the idea that computing had a rather boring image, and open ended material indicated that girls sometimes feared harassment if they found themselves in nearly all male groups. School teachers were widely criticised for encouraging pupils to go into sex stereotyped directions, and there was some support for the idea that girls were more interested in computers as a means to an end rather than as objects of interest in themselves. The "we can I can't" formula also received support – females thought that females in general had the ability to do computing, but that they individually did not [Sanders 87].

23.4 Study 3

The third and fourth studies, on enrolments in 1988 and 1989, will be presented in somewhat more detail. Building on the findings above, it was decided to target courses that contained large numbers of females, who, whilst under the Scottish system were qualified to study computing, chose instead to study either in business or natural science areas. They were asked specifically why they had chosen *not* to study computing ([Kelly 88, Culley 88a]) and their answers were of interest as they represented students who could potentially be attracted most easily into computing.

The third study [Durndell 90a] had as its 210 subjects 55 male and 68 female business students, and 30 male and 57 female natural science students. They were given a questionnaire during their first year enrolment session. Apart from background information, the questionnaire asked them in an open ended format to consider why they had chosen *not* to study computing. Subsequently they were presented with a 5 point scale going from 1 – of no importance to me, through to 5 – very important to me, with which they were asked to evaluate a series of factors that might be involved in their decision not to study computing.

Apart from the common response that the student was not interested in computing, the open-ended answers could be seen to reflect three main themes which to a large extent were produced by both genders.

1. In the words of a male business student, "computing needs a new image". 17% of the students volunteered comments about their desire to work with humans rather than machines, and appeared to be put off by the image of sitting all day in front of a screen. For example, business females commented "The thought of just punching a keyboard all day just would bore me", and "Computing doesn't allow enough contact with people". Business males commented "didn't want to spend my life watching little green figures, nor a TV monitor" and "Computing restricts you to working with machines rather than people". Natural science females commented "no satisfaction working with a man-made brain, the human one is more interesting" and "didn't want to be stuck behind a computer terminal and monitor for the rest of my life" and a male commented "no ambition to be a tool or machine operator".

2. Many respondents, including 42% of business students, volunteered comments to the effect that computing was too specialised a subject with too narrow employment opportunities. They were happy to study computing as one small part their studies, recognising its uses, but that was all.

3. The third theme was two pronged. On the one hand a surprisingly large number of respondents (8% of males as opposed to 36% of females) volunteered comments that they had had little or no contact with computers before coming to higher education and therefore were unlikely to choose to study computing. 46% of females specialising in maths for business gave this response, indicating that maths and computing were clearly separate for them. On the other hand, 19% of respondents made negative comments about their contact with computing at school, mainly concerning how boring it was, and commented that this contact had helped convince them not to study computing.

The statistical results are shown in Table 23.1, where the suggested items are arranged in order from the highest (most important) to lowest (least important).

Table 23.1 Average score of importance for suggested items in choice not to study computing

Item	Average Score for the whole sample	't' test Male vs female	Average female score	Average male score
The subject matter would not be interesting	3.51	N.S.		
I am more interested in people than objects.	3.43	p = .001	3.69	3. 02
I don't mind using computers, but they are not an end in themselves to me.	3 17	N.S.		
Studying computing removes you from contact with people.	2.83	p = .005	3.05	2.50
I do not have the required abilities.	2.63	N.S.		
I would have difficulty getting a job with a computer qualification.	2.61	N.S.		
I am not qualified to study computing.	2.56	p = .003	2.80	2.19
The prospect of being in nearly all-male groups is off-putting.	1.82	p = .001	1.60	2.16
Video and computer games turned me off computing.	1.69	N.S.		
Males can be hostile to females with abilities in computing.	1.52	p = .005	1.66	1.30
Computing has a rather unfeminine image.	1.34	p = .02	1.42	1.20
I was advised not to study computing.	1.32	N.S.		

(N.S. = not significant)

23.5 Study 4

Study number 4, based on 1989 enrolments, targetted the same groups of students as study number 3, 127 female and 78 male. In general the open ended and fixed answer responses were broadly similar to study 3, except that one additional item "I do not want to be sitting in front of a terminal all day" displaced "The subject matter would not be interesting" from the top of the list. Additionally, subjects were asked about their use of computers and given an Information Technology (IT) quiz that was also used in the 1986 study. 16-18 year olds in the 4 target courses in 1986 and 1989 were compared in this way. Tables 23.2 and 23.3 show the results.

Table 23.2 % reporting experience of computing in previous 2 years, 16-18 year old polytechnic entrants, by gender and year of intake.

	1986			1989		
	Male	Female	Overall	Male	Female	Overall
Used computer at school	42	52	48	67	61	63
Used own computer	24	9*	14	49	18*	29
Used family computer	24	29	27	26	38	34
Used friend's computer	65	46*	53	50	31*	38

(* = gender difference p < .05)

Table 23.3 IT quiz score, 16-18 year old polytechnic entrants, by gender and year of intake for 4 target courses.

	Female Mean	Male Mean	Male-Female difference
1986	2.54	4.60*	2.06
1989	4.10	6.02*	1.92
Improvement 1986-1989	1.56	1.42	

(* = gender difference p < .01)

23.6 Discussion

It would appear that computing has a severe image problem in general, and that this is accentuated for females. Both open-ended and statistical results confirmed that students of both sexes perceived the lack of human orientation or contact that they associated with computing to be a very strong factor in their choices to avoid studying computing. They wanted contact with people, not machines, and in accordance with gender stereotyping, females found this on average even more important than males (who still found it important however). The contradiction between the many negative remarks about computing made in this study and the generally positive attitudes to computers found in other studies, eg [Gardner 86], could be interpreted as the difference between thinking computing is useful and advantageous for society as a whole, but not something that the particular individual wishes to be very involved in (another version of "we can I can't"?). Indeed "we can I do not want to" appears to be a more serious problem. It was also notable that it was not primarily an unfeminine image that was the problem, cf [Siann 88a], but the perception of a lack of human contact, which of course does have gender stereotype overtones to it, in as much as females might be expected to value human contact more than males.

The results in relation to perceptions of harassment of females in nearly all male computing groups failed to support the hints from the earlier study [Durndell 90b].

The relevant factors were all given very low importance, and the gender difference was in the opposite direction (ie with males rating it more important) in one case.

The females with a very strong mathematical background were of particular interest, as the school link between maths and computing has been criticised, eg [Lockhead 85, Collis 87], as being off putting for girls. The samples investigated here tended not to extrapolate from their interest and ability in maths to computing, and a surprisingly large number of them appear to have successfully avoided computing at school. Whether they would become more interested in computing following computer contact on their courses is an interesting question.

It can also be seen that the reported use of school computers and the use of students' own computers and family computers, have increased in 1986-1989, but use of a friend's computer has decreased. Gender differences have generally been maintained, with boys more likely to report use of their own computers and friends' computers. Girls were more likely to report using a family computer. The IT quiz scores indicated a general improvement in knowledge, but the gender gap in favour of males remained.

Although these studies provide some evidence that the situation in schools is improving, there still seems to be cause for concern, cf [Kelly 85, Askew 88] and [Newton 88]. The problem appears to be two edged. That such a large number of recent school leavers, particularly girls, can report little or no contact with computers implies either a lack of sufficient computer equipment in schools and/or a lack of organisation in letting pupils use it. At the same time, the fact that so many recent school leavers who have had school computer contact found the experience negative and boring, is cause for deep concern. Furthermore, this seems to be a problem which relates to boys as well as girls. A core curriculum, including computing, which delays choice until the mid teens, and possibly some single sex tuition, cf [Siann 90], may be good ideas, but if the content of computing is not chosen with great care, taking on issues of gender and human orientation, then the subject will remain relatively unpopular. (Many examples to combat this have of course been given at WiC and GASAT conferences.)

The same applies to higher education, where attempts to widen the courses and combine computing with other disciplines should be supported, as this would combat the "narrowness" and lack of human contact that is perceived to be part of computing. The experience of City Polytechnic [Ward 90] and others support this. There is still a problem however, image and reality must be approximately the same. Attracting females into traditional computing courses which have not changed may result in a large dropout or be unethical. Many computer specialists and employers would also no doubt argue that the stereotype of computing as not involving human contact is inaccurate, and that real computing jobs involve considerable communication and discussion with people. Alternatively there is now a well developed feminist critique of the whole basis of science and technology, eg [Bleier 88, Bentley 87, Elliott 87]. As [Everts 90] points out, attracting more females into computing would not necessarily automatically humanise or alter computing, without an associated thorough re-organisation of the content of the discipline and the way it is taught.

There is also considerable debate at the moment as to what extent employers will

want computer scientists and computer engineers, or business-oriented specialists
with some systems skills in the future (eg the comments of [Virgo 89b]). If the demand
is going to be the latter, then the mixed courses (with large proportions of females)
will be what is in demand, whilst all graduates would be expected to have some basic
computer literacy. (These issues have also led to confusion in the literature between
Computer Science, Computer Studies – the UCCA term – and Information Technology.)

Finally, it can be concluded at present that the gender gap in computing has hardly
begun to close, and that the image of computing as not having a human face is helping
large numbers of females (and males) to choose not to study computing. Strategies to
combat this are available though.

23.7 REFERENCES

[Askew 88] Askew S and Ross C, *Boy don't cry: Boys and Sexism in Education*,
Milton Keynes: OUP, 1988.

[Bentley 87] Bentley D and Watts M, "Courting the positive virtues", in Kelly A (ed),
Science for Girls, Milton Keynes: OUP, 1987.

[Bleier 88] Bleier R (ed), *Feminist Approaches to Science*, New York: Pergamon,
1988.

[Carlsson 90] Carlsson K, *The Percentage of Women on Study Programmes in Technology at Lulea and in the Rest of Sweden, 1980-1989*, Lulea, Sweden: University of Lulea, 1990.

[Collis 87] Collis B A, "Sex difference in the association between secondary school
students' attitudes toward mathematics and toward computers", *Journal for Research in Mathematics Education*, 18, pp394-402, 1987.

[Culley 88a] Culley L A, "Option choice and careers guidance: Gender and computing in secondary schools", *British Journal of Guidance and Counselling*, 16,
pp73-81, 1988.

[Durndell 87] Durndell A, Macleod H and Siann G, "A survey of attitudes to, knowledge about and experience of computers", *Computers and Education*, 11, pp167-
175, 1987.

[Durndell 90a] Durndell A, "Why do female students avoid computer studies?", *Research in Science and Technology Education* (in press), 1990.

[Durndell 90b] Durndell A, Siann G and Glissov P, "Gender differences and computing in course choice at entry into Higher Education", *British Educational
Research Journal*, 16, pp147-162, 1990.

[Elliott 87] Elliott J and Powell C, "Young woman in science: Do we need more science?", *British Journal of Sociology of Education*, 8, pp277-286, 1987.

[Everts 90] Everts S, "Social responsibility in technology and feminist visions", in Granstam I (ed), *Contributions GASAT 1990*, Jönköping, Jönköping University, Sweden 1990.

[Gardner 86] Gardner J R, McEwan A and Curry C A, "A sample survey of attitudes to computer studies, *Computers and Education*, 10, pp293-298, 1986.

[Granstam 86] Granstam I (ed), *Contributions GASAT 1990*, Jönköping, Jönköping University, Sweden 1990.

[Kelly 85] Kelly A, "The construction of masculine science", *British Journal of Sociology of Education*, 6, pp133-154, 1985.

[Kelly 88] Kelly A, "Option choice for girls and boys", *Research in Science and Technological Education*, 6, pp5-24, 1988.

[Kolmos 90] Kolmos A, "Women and men in engineering education – different approaches?", in Granstam I, (ed) *Contributions GASAT 1990*, Jönköping, Jönköping University, Sweden 1990.

[Linden 87] Linden K, Lebold W and Armstrong P, "Gender differences in computer knowledge, literacy and competency", in Daniels J Z and Kahle J B (eds), *Contributions to the 4th GASAT Conference*, University of Michigan: National Science Foundation, 1987.

[Lockhead 85] Lockhead M E, "Women, girls and computers", *Sex Roles*, 13, pp115-122, 1985.

[Morris 90] Morris P, Cheng D and Smith H, *Preliminary Report to the B.P.S.: How and why applicants choose to study Psychology at University*, Psychology Department, Lancaster University, 1990.

[Newton 88] Newton P and Haslam S, "Computing – an ideal occupation for women?", in proceedings of *Women into Computing Conference*, Lancaster University, 1988.

[Sanders 87] Sanders J, "Closing the computer Gender gap in school", in Daniels J Z and Kahle J B (eds), *Contributions to the 4th GASAT Conference*, University of Michigan: National Science Foundation, 1987.

[Siann 88a] Siann G, Durndell A, Macleod H and Glissov P, "Stereotyping in relation to the gender gap in participation in computing", *Educational Research*, 30, pp98-103, 1988.

[Siann 90] Siann G, Macleod H, Glissov P and Durndell A, "The effect of computer use on gender differences in attitudes to computers", *Computers and Education*, 14, pp183-191, 1990.

[Swedish Institute 89] Swedish Institute, *Fact sheets on Sweden; Equality between men and women in Sweden*, Stockholm, Sweden: Swedish Institute, 1989.

[UCCA 89] UCCA, *26th Annual Report 1987/1988*, Cheltenham: UCCA, 1989.

[Virgo 89b] Virgo P, "Gender and computing in the 1990's", Paper presented to *SIACE Conference on Bridging the Skills Gap; Women and Education in Scotland*, Strathclyde University, 1989.

[Ward 90] Ward J, "City Poly solves conundrum of how to get women to do computing courses", *Women into IT Newsletter*, March, p12, 1990.

24

Computer Attitudes, Interface Preference And Simple Task Performance

**Konrad Morgan[1], Shirley Gibbs[2],
Hamish Macleod[3], Robert Morris[3]**

24.1   Introduction

This paper was prompted out of concern at the gender imbalance that is often found in computing today, the consequences of which are feared likely to become more significant as the shortfall in skilled computing staff increases. This absence of females from computing subjects can be traced from the earliest sectors of our national education system through further and higher education into industry. If this trend is left to continue the authors fear it may pose a threat to the economic success of information technology in the United Kingdom; and be a sad reflection of the continuing gender inequality in our country. To try and increase awareness of the problems in such gender research, this paper aims to review past research which attempted to investigate the possible psychological, social and environmental differences for such gender imbalances in technical subjects, and to report on the gender differences found in the results of a study conducted by the authors at Napier Polytechnic in the years 1987 to 1989.

24.1.1   GENDER AND COMPUTER ATTITUDES

Some studies have shown that there are no differences in the rates of computer anxiety between the sexes [Gressard 84]. Instead they found that computer experience was a much better indicator of the level of computer anxiety, most anxiety was shown by those of both sexes who had less experience of computer systems. Some confirmation for this finding comes from two other studies which used computer attitude scales. First is a controlled study in which students who had to use a computer in an assignment were found to develop more positive attitudes towards computers than

[1] School of Information Science, Portsmouth Polytechnic, Portsmouth
[2] Computer Studies Department, Napier Polytechnic, Edinburgh EH14 1DJ
[3] Department of Psychology, University of Edinburgh

those who did not[4]. In this study males and females did not differ in their rates of computer anxiety either before, during or after the course [Eastman 87]. Second is a study which measured attitudes to computers [Loyd 87], and which also reported that girls exhibited a more positive attitude towards computers than boys. This may reflect a change in attitudes (the study is more recent), or may be a biased sample. Surveys have shown that the careers advice given to school leavers was highly sex stereotyped where computing was concerned [Culley 88]. It should be noted that that many of these studies could have had their findings affected by expectancy effects.

24.1.2 GENDER DIFFERENCES IN DEGREE OF ATTRIBUTED COMPUTER SYSTEM ANIMISM

Some research has also shown that males and females vary in their attribution of characteristics towards computers [Wise 87]. Males tend to use more animate descriptions (less mechanical) as they become more experienced, while females tend to show the opposite trend. It is possible that this difference in the degree of preferred attributed computer system animism, particularly where it occurs in the fundamental design of a computer system (as for example in Unix "Demons"), may result in a significant gender difference in rates of acceptance using such "animised" systems. Some researchers have highlighted other potential dangers which are inherent when humans start attributing animism to what are [Gaines 84, Shneiderman 87].

24.1.3 SELF RATED GENDER ROLE MODELS

In a survey of 1,600 students' gender attitudes towards computers and video games [Wilder 85], both boys and girls rated computers and video games as being more appropriate for boys, and this trend showed as early as kindergarten. The boys in the survey rated their liking for the computer more strongly than did the girls. Both sexes showed a dramatic decline in their reported liking of computers after middle childhood. The second part of the same study compared the computer attitudes of 334 (141 Female, 193 Male) college freshmen. The sex typing found in the school population was found to be attenuated in this group. However one interesting factor did emerge, that being that males rated their computer expertise as being higher than that of comparable experienced females. This female underestimation of computing expertise has also been reported by others. Researchers who have looked at the subject preferences of the sexes have reported that females were under represented in the sciences overall, particularly in the so called "hard" sciences, such as physics [Deboer 86]. Both sexes were equally represented in biology and chemistry, and although females out performed males, the females rated their performance as lower than the males. There is evidence that in the UK computer based gender role expectancy is found as early as primary school [Hughes 85a, Hughes 85b, Hughes 87, Siann 86].

---

[4]However there have been reports that levels of computer anxiety were not changed by attendance of a computer literacy course (Electric Learning, 1981)

Figure 24.1 Number of Initial Applications to Napier Polytechnic's BSc Computing Degree

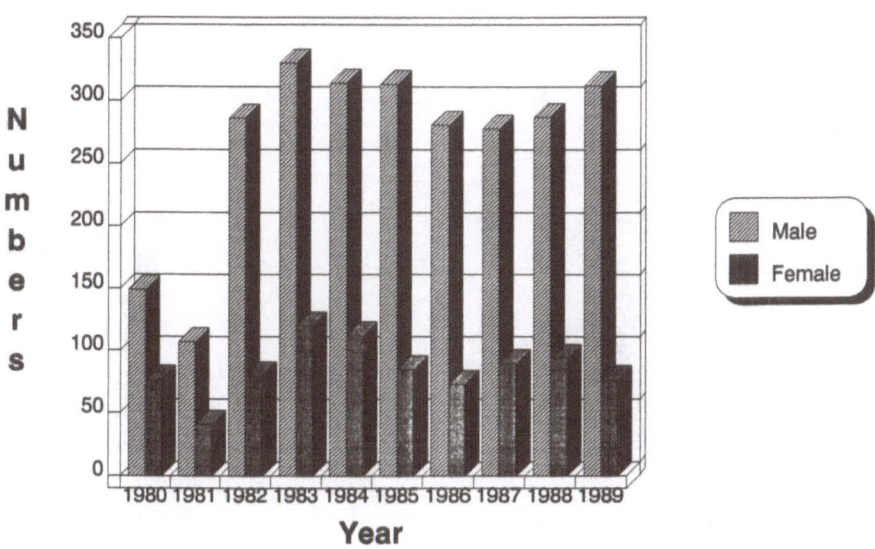

Figure 24.2 Number of Entrants to Napier Polytechnic's BSc Computing Degree

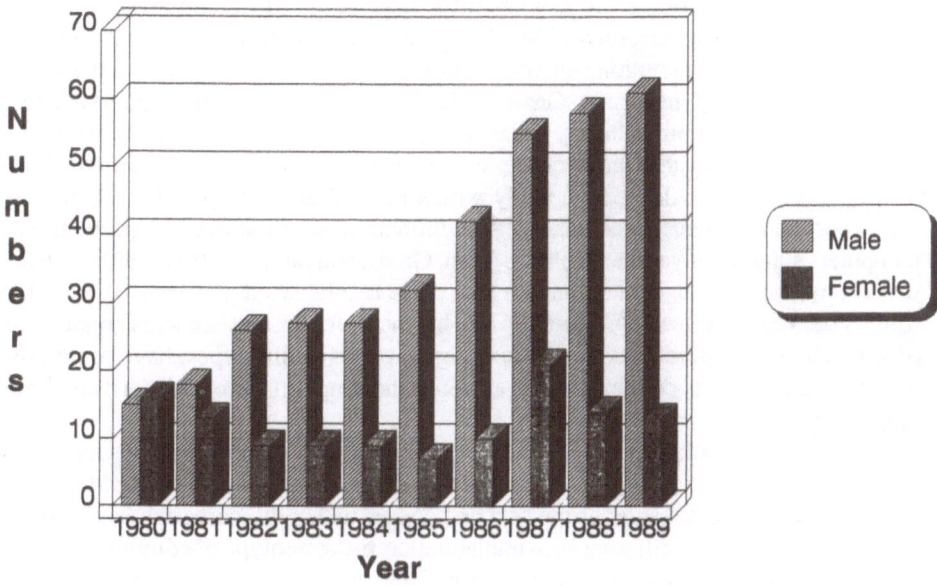

Figure 24.3 Number of Students Awarded Napier Polytechnic's BSc Computing Degree

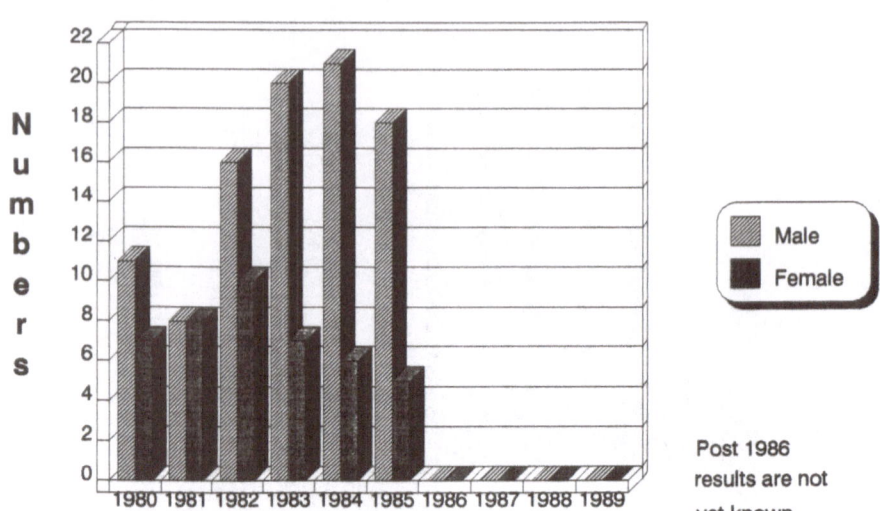

24.1.4 DIFFERENTIAL OPPORTUNITIES GIVEN TO THE SEXES IN EDUCATION

Many researchers attribute the gender differences to the differential opportunities given to the sexes in education [Chen 86]. Research has shown that males receive more of the teacher's attention and more computing time than girls in computer based teaching situations [Omerod 81, Gerver 85]. This may not be totally due to a selective gender role bias in teaching, since there is evidence that when girls are given equal access to computers they tend to use them less than males. These latter findings have been contradicted in a study which used a large sample size (3,085). In this experiment females given positive discrimination were found to adopt the use of computers significantly more than boys (Fish, Gross, and Sanders, 1986), although the positive discrimination element means that these results are not strictly comparable [Sheingold 83, Lockheed 84, Miura 86]. It has been found that students (regardless of sex) who show more realistic and investigative personality types, have more positive attitudes towards computers than students showing artistic or enterprising types [Abler 87].

A study which looked at the sex ratio of 5,533 entries to computer courses at US summer camps found a significant sex difference favoring males [Hess 85]. This 3 to 1 difference became larger as the cost and course difficulty increased. The authors postulated that sex role differences in mathematics, the stereotype of computers, male-oriented software, and the symbolic and viso-spatial features of programming were responsible. The last two reasons are particularly unconvincing since some of the most able programmers have often been women. Some research has shown that while females are less likely to enroll in programming classes, those who do are successful, and make up the majority in groups who are exceptionally talented [Linn 85a]. Other research by the same author [Linn 85b] found that females have different strategies for risk taking, help seeking, and more importantly attributions about success or failure. Other research has shown that when the computer based learning strategies of both sexes are compared males tended to adopt the more successful learning strategies spontaneously. This was termed the shifting method of cognitive engagement. Females tended to stick to one form of cognitive engagement throughout the task, regardless of its success [Mandinach 85]. Similar gender ratio patterns in maths and science education have been reported in the UK [Whyte 85]. Many researchers believe these differences can be explained by the gender roles which are often enforced upon girls by their teachers and career advisors in secondary education [Spear 85, Newton 81, Whyte 85].

24.1.5 SUMMARY OF THE REVIEW ON GENDER DIFFERENCES

As yet there are no universally accepted explanations for the sex differences found in computing. A large (non-computing specific) meta analysis of 127 different studies with a sample sizes from 7 to 25,000, and ages from 2 months to 30 years found that males were more active than females[5] [Eaton 86].

The authors concluded that social influences served merely to increase this natural difference. Certainly there is evidence that social and cultural effects play a very large role. Several researchers have surveyed the sex roles portrayed in the mass media [Braun 86, Siann]. These researchers have found that males are portrayed as being the predominant users, and being in a dominant role in any mixed sex portrayals. One other factor in the lack of females in computing may be the male harassment of females who work in traditional male occupations. Research has found that the rate of such harassment is 75%, compared to 50% in the general population [Lafontaine 86]. Perpetrators of such harassment included supervisors, peers, subordinates, and clients. This reflects the existing sexist attitudes that too many men seem to hold, viewing females as "sex-objects" rather than human beings, or fellow workers. The task of addressing such unfair practices will take considerable time, but it can only be hoped that a time will come when such unfair pressures are removed.

24.2 Experimental Methodology

This study involved students completing a series of questionaires and using a database program specially designed and developed to have two interfaces; one a command line, and the other a direct manipulation system. The two interfaces were matched for functionality and as far as possible error opportunity.

---

[5]Although age and situational variables seemed to be equally important.

24.2.1 INTERFACE PERFORMANCE MEASURES

Two performance measures were recorded by the interface systems.

Errors. The system recorded the precise part of the users input that caused the rejection, with details of the actual and mean length of time between each error, and the type of the error (the type and sequence of commands to be issued are preset, and are identical for all users).

Commands. The system recorded the details of all the commands issued during each session along with the actual and mean amount of time between each command.

24.2.2 QUESTIONNAIRES

As well as the behavioral data gathered from the interface system the study took a measure of the subject's psychological, social and environmental differences, and how these differences influenced the subject's attitude and behaviour with regard to new technology, and preferred interface type. A series of questionnaires were created for the study, each with a specific purpose. One was a Technology Attitudes Questionnaire (TAQ), which measures various aspects of the subject's experience and background with new technology. The other questionnaires were post session evaluation attitude measures, called the User Evaluation of Interactive Computer Systems questionnaire (UEICS). Versions of this questionaire were developed for both interface systems.

Technology Attitudes Questionnaire

The technology attitude questionnaire was designed to take a measure of the user's previous exposure and attitudes towards new technology, and in particular to computers.

The TAQ contained 55 questions which investigated the following areas:
a) Personal details. b) Adaptability and history of adoption of new technology. c) Self Esteem. d) Working style (in new situations). e) Liking of machines f) Understanding of computers g) New technology based stress and fear. h) Impersonal (non-humanness of computers). i) Frequency of damaging mechanical and electrical devices j) Early attitudes and Family history with regard to interactions with machines.

Post Session Questionnaires

The post session questionnaires were designed to take a measure of the users' attitudes towards the interface they had just used. The direct manipulation interface and command line versions consisted of 27 and 25 questions respectively. Both versions had a similar format, which included:
a) Personal details. b) Physical aspects of the system. c) Aspects specific to interface. d) Syntactic evaluation. e) Semantic evaluation. f) Feedback (including errors and on-line help). g) System performance evaluation.

24.2.3 PROCEDURE

Subjects were spilt into groups of 12 and issued with unique subject numbers. The subjects experienced both interfaces using a standard counterbalanced order within subjects design. Prior to participation, subjects completed the technology attitudes Following completion of a session on a particular interface, subjects completed an Evaluation of Interactive Computer Systems questionnaire (UEICS2 - also developed by the authors). At the end of the whole experiment subjects were asked to comment on their impressions and feelings with regard to the interface.

Subjects

Group One

These were 72 second year B.A. commerce students at Napier Polytechnic. The sessions were part of their coursework, and attendance was compulsory. This group was computer naive and keyboard literate.

Of the 55 who took part, 33 used both interfaces, 42 used the command interface and 46 the direct manipulation interface. 10 of the subjects were male, 45 were female. 3 of the subjects were non-uk nationals (european exchange students). The youngest in the subject group was 18, the oldest 24, 4 subjects were left handed.

Group Two

These were 26 first year postgraduates in a systems analysis and design course. Again attendance was compulsory. The subjects had both typing and previous computer experience. Of the 26 who took part, 21 used both interfaces, 25 used the command line system, and 21 used the manipulation interface system. 14 of the group were male and 12 were female. 24 of the group were right handed, 1 was left handed, and 1 claimed to be ambidextrous. The youngest member of the group was 19 and the oldest was 36.

This was an "intermediate" group of subjects, a third of whom had done some touch typing and 4/5ths of whom had some previous experience of using computers at various levels of competence.

Group Three

The subjects were split between 26 first year HND office studies students, and 75 first year business studies degree students. 25 subjects (split between both groups), completed the experiment. 8 subjects from the HND completed both interfaces, and the remaining 3 were taken from the second group. Of the 25 subjects 21 were female, and 4 were male. They were aged between 17 and 40 approximately [6], the average age being about 18. All but one of the subjects were right handed.

---

[6] Some of the female subjects declined to provide their personal details

24.3 Results

24.3.1 ANALYSIS ON SEX DIFFERENCES

The TAQ and Overall Session Data Correlations With Sex Differences
To look at the sex differences within the subject populations we combined the TAQ data with the overall session recordings, allocated a sex code of zero for females, and one for males respectively, and then performed a Kruskal Wallis anova by ranks with the following results:

In Session Recordings
Females were found have made fewer errors ($p < 0.05$), had a slower inter-error time ($p < 0.05$), issued their commands faster ($p < 0.085$), and have been younger (than the male subjects) ($p < 0.01$).

Working Styles
Females were found to be less likely to enjoy hobbies which involved doing things in a specific order ($p < 0.064$), less likely to enjoy repairing machines ($p < 0.06$), and were more afraid of looking silly if they were seen by other not to know how to use the computer ($p < 0.05$). Females used digital watches less ($p < 0.01$), played fewer video games ($p < 0.05$), and read less about computers ($p < 0.05$).

Early Childhood
In their early childhood females were less likely to have been allowed to use dangerous equipment ($p < 0.01$), were less likely to have been encouraged to explore how machines worked ($p < 0.05$), and more likel y to report having been frightened by some kinds of equipment ($p < 0.05$).

Post Command Line Interface Session Questionnaire And Command Session Data Correlations With Gender
The post Command line system questionnaires were combined with the command line in-session recordings. The resulting data file was then analysed on gender using a Kruskal Wallis anova by ranks, with the following results:

In Session Recordings
Females were found to have issued more commands ($p < 0.01$), attempted more trials ($p < 0.01$), issued their commands faster ($p < 0.01$) and tended to be younger than the males ($p < 0.01$).

Comments About The System
Females felt there were too few operations required to complete a task ($p < 0.05$), and that the system was too fast ($p < 0.05$).

Post Direct Manipulation Interface Session Questionnaire Data And Session Data Correlations With Sex The post direct manipulation interface system questionnaires were combined with the direct manipulation interface in-session recordings. The resulting data file was then analysed on gender using a Kruskal Wallis anova by ranks, with the following results:

In Session Details
Females tended to have longer sessions ($p < 0.05$), made fewer errors ($p < 0.05$), issued more commands ($p < 0.064$), made errors more slowly ($p < 0.05$), and tended to be younger ($p < 0.05$).

Using The Direct Manipulation Interface System
Females found the mouse harder to control (p < 0.05).

24.4   Conclusions on these findings

Reference to the computing degree figures from Napier reveal that female students perform well in the assessments leading to the award of the degree in computing. This includes a low withdrawal rate for female students. Anecdotal material from Napier lecturers appears to confirm that female students achieve a high standard for examinations and coursework. An example of this is that in the first year of Napier's degree (1980), a male and female student were jointly awarded the class prize. It is believed that by encouraging more girls to enrol on Napier's computing course the standard of attainment will be maintained, and that areas of expertise currently absent from the industry will be provided by these additional female graduates.

In the results from the experimental analysis the females were found to have made fewer mistakes, perhaps by being more accurate and careful, but also less exploratory. The traditional sex stereotypes discussed in the literature review were also found. Females were less favorable in their attitudes towards computers, and more concerned about looking silly if they were seen to make a mistake. These sex stereotypes were most strongly shown by the fact that females were significantly less likely to have received encouragement to use dangerous equipment, and explore how machines worked. On the negative side, and probably connected to their lack of exposure to machines females were significantly more likely to have been frightened by a machine in their childhood. There was also some (weak) evidence that females found the command line system easier to use. It is possible that this could have been due to problems derived from the differences in visospatial ability of females that has often been reported in the literature.

Our exploratory findings appear to show some evidence of gender differences in our subjects' early experiences with machines. These differences appear to have existed both at home and at school, and to have continued throughout the formative years of our subject population. It does not seem unwarranted to postulate that these influences had an effect on the subjects' attitudes as users and potential users of computer systems. If these findings can be generalized it may be that we can start to put forward reasons for the lack of coherent findings presented in the gender differences review in our introduction. It could be that a large part of these apparent gender differences are due to environmental role models enforced upon children by their teachers, parents and peers. Since these role models would vary due to geographic and socioeconomic factors it might not be surprising to find the inconsistent results described in the literature review. If this is indeed the case it is only by removing these restrictive role models from our society that we can truly begin to resolve the problems outlined in the introduction of this paper.

24.5 REFERENCES

[Abler 87] Abler R M and Sedlacek W E, "Computer Orientation By Holland Type And Sex", *Career Development Quarterly*, , Vol 36(2), 163 169, Dec 1987.

[Braun 86] Braun C M, Goupil G, Giroux J and Chagnon Y, "Adolescents And Microcomputers: Sex Differences, Proxemics, Task And Stimulus Variables", *Journal Of Psychology*, Vol 120(6), 529 542, Nov 1986.

[Chen 86] Chen M, "Gender Differences In Adolescents' Uses Of And Attitudes Towards Computers", *International Dissertation Abstracts*, Number : 210aac8612723, 1986.

[Culley 88] Culley L, "Option Choice And Careers Guidance: Gender And Computing In Secondary Schools", *British Journal Of Guidance And Counselling*, Vol 16(1), 73 82, Jan 1988.

[Deboer 86] Deboer G E,"Perceived Science Ability As A Factor In The Course Selections Of Men And Women In College", *Journal Of Research In Science Teaching*, Vol 23(4), 343 352, April 1986.

[Eastman 87] Eastman S T and Krendl K, "Computers And Gender: Differential Effects Of Electronic Search On Students' Achievement And Attitudes", *Journal Of Research And Development In Education*, Vol 20(3), 41 48, Sept 1987.

[Eaton 86] Eaton W O and Enns L R, "Sex Differences In Human Motor Activity Level", *Psychological Bulletin*, Vol 100(1), 19 28, Jul 1986.

[Gaines 84] Gaines B and Shaw M, *The Art of Computer Conversation*, Prentice/Hall International, 1984.

[Gerver 85] Gerver E, "Women, Computers And Adult Education", 1 Vol, University Of Strathclyde, Pilley C, *Women And Computing In Scotland*, Report Of Conference Held By The Joint Working Group On Women And Computers, 14th June 1985.

[Gressard 84] Gressard C and Loyd B H, "An Investigation Of The Effects Of Math Anxiety And Sex On Computer Attitudes", paper presented at *The American Educational Research Association*, New Orleans, 1984.

[Hess 85] Hess R D, Miura I T, "Gender Differences In Enrollment In Computer Camps And Classes", Special Issue: "Women, Girls, And Computers", *Sex Roles*, Vol 13(3 4), 193 203, Aug 1985.

[Hughes 85a] Hughes M, Macleod H and Potts C, "Using LOGO with infant school children", *Educational Psychology*, 5, 287 301, 1985.

[Hughes 85b] Hughes M, Macleod H, Potts C and Rodgers J, "Are Computers only for boys?", *New Society*, 11 Oct 1985 .

[Hughes 87] Hughes M, Brackenridge A and Macleod H, in Rutkowska J and Crook C, *Computers, Cognition & Development*, John Wiley & Sons Ltd. 1987.

[Lafontaine 86] Lafontaine E and Tredeau L, "The Frequency, Sources, And Correlates Of Sexual Harassment Among Women In Traditional Male Occupations", *Sex Roles*, Vol 15(7 8), 433 442, Oct 1986.

[Linn 85a] Linn M C, "Fostering Equitable Consequences From Computer Learning Environments", *Sex Roles*, Vol 13, Nos 3/4, 229 240, 1985.

[Linn 85b] Linn M C, "Gender Equity In Computer Learning Environments", *Computers And The Social Sciences*, Vol 1(1), 19 27, Jan-Mar 1985.

[Lockheed 84] Lockheed M E and Frakt S B, "Sex Equity: Increasing Girls' Use Of Computers", *Computing Teacher*, 11, 16 18, 1984.

[Loyd 87] Loyd B H, Loyd D E and Gressard C P, "Gender And Computer Experience As Factors In The Computer Attitudes Of Middle School Students", Special Issue: "Sex Differences In Early Adolescents" of *Journal Of Early Adolescence*, Vol 7(1), 13 19, Sept 1987.

[Mandinach 85] Mandinach E B and Corno L, "Cognitive Engagement Variations Among Students Of Different Ability Level And Sex In A Computer Problem Solving Game", Special Issue: Women, Girls, And Computers, *Sex Roles*, Vol 13(3 4), 241 251, Aug 1985.

[Miura 86] Miura I T, "Understanding Gender Differences In Middle School Computer Interest And Use", Paper Presented At Symposium : *Gender Differences In Computing: Policy Implications*, American Educational Research Assc, 1986.

[Newton 81] Newton P, "Who Say's Girls Can't Be Engineers?", in Kelly A, *The Missing Half*, Vol. 1, Manchester University Press, 1981.

[Omerod 81] Omerod M B, "Factors Differentially Affecting The Science Subject Preferences, Chances And Attitudes Of Girls And Boys", in Kelly A, *The Missing Half*, Vol. 1, Manchester University Press, 1981.

[Sheingold 83] Sheingold K, Kane J H and Endreweit M E, "Microcomputer Use In Schools: Developing A Research Agenda", *Harvard Educational Review*, 53, 412 432, 1983.

[Shneiderman 87] Shneiderman B, *Designing The Computer Interface*, Addison-Wesley, pp448, 1987.

[Siann 86] Siann G and Macleod H, "Computers & children of primary school age: Issues and questions", *British Journal of Educational Technology*, 17, 133-144, 1986.

[Siann] Siann G, Durndell A, Macleod H and Glissov P, "Stereotyping In Relation To The Gender Gap In Participation In Computing", Unpublished Paper.

172

[Spear 85] Spear M, Whyte J, Deem R, Kant L, and Cruickshank M, *"Girl Friendly Schooling*, Methuen, 1985.

[Wilder 85] Wilder G, Mackie D and Cooper J, "Gender And Computers: Two Surveys Of Computer Related Attitudes", Special Issue: Women, Girls, And Computers, *Sex Roles*, Vol 13(3 4), 215 228, Aug 1985.

[Wise 87] Wise G, Robinson-Staveley K and Nelson L, "Report From The Cognitive Motivation Laboratory", *Newsletter Of The Human Information Processing Group At Princeton University*, USA: Princeton University, 3, 1987.

[Whyte 85] Whyte J, Deem R, Kant L and Cruickshank M, *"Girl Friendly Schooling*, Methuen, 1985.

25

An Analysis of Attempts to Remember that Some Students are Female

Karen Shipp,
Dianne Sutton[1]

25.1 Introduction

The[2] Open University has been teaching students using multi-media distance education methods for over twenty years. Undergraduate students with no formal academic qualifications can study for a degree. Associate students follow individual courses, some of which are non-assessed.

Each course in the undergraduate programme is classed as being worth either a half or a full credit. A full credit involves on average fifteen hours of work per week over the academic year, which runs from February to October.

Six credits are required for a BA and eight for an honours degree. Courses are at different levels – foundation, second, third and fourth level. Honours degrees require a certain number of higher level credits to have been obtained.

Students can choose courses from the six areas of study offered – arts, social science, education, maths, science and technology, although a number of courses are inter- or multi-disciplinary. Much has been done in recent years to promote maths, science and technology courses and to encourage women to take these courses.

Open University students do not receive grants, they fund their studies themselves, although there are various schemes to allow disadvantaged students to participate. Many employers fund part or all the cost of courses for their employees. Undergraduate courses in 1988 cost about £166 for a full credit; additionally there are set books to buy, perhaps a summer school to pay for, and the cost of travelling to tutorials.

The Open University has always used a multi-media approach to teaching including the use of television, radio, audio cassettes, video, face-to-face tutorials in study centres, summer schools and the use of computer terminals.

Until recently practical computing was performed using either terminals in study centres linked by telephone to centralised mainframes, or at summer schools where microcomputers have been introduced in recent years.

---

[1] Academic Computing Service, Open University, Milton Keynes
[2] This paper was presented at the 1988 Conference.

Computing is used by all faculties and in 1988 over twenty courses were involved. It mostly involves students running applications packages or using computer assisted learning packages, although some courses teach programming.

In recent years it has become obvious that to maintain credibility, computer science courses in particular could not continue to expect students to do practical work in one hour chunks at study centre terminals, so the home computing policy was devised. This stipulates that for certain courses students must provide their own access to an IBM-PC compatible micro in the same way that they provide their own access to a television or cassette player. The University provides all the course software. For 1988, which was the first year of the home computing policy, about 5,000 students were involved, growing to 13,000 in 1989. For 1988 the University arranged a discount purchase scheme whereby a suitable microcomputer could be acquired for around £500, and also a hire scheme which cost the student £150. Some students already possessed, or had access, perhaps at work, to suitable hardware. The financial aspect alone may be off-putting to a large number of women. For 1988 there were three courses involved with two more in 1989 and others in later years.

25.2 The 1988 Home Computing Courses

The three 1988 courses, all of which are still running in 1990, were as follows.

M205 Fundamentals of Computing

- This course requires the student to spend two to three hours each week on practical work, using UCSD Pascal.

M371 Computational Mathematics

- This course requires the student to spend about 24 hours over the year running both teaching and applications packages under GEM.

DT200 An Introduction to Information Technology: Social and Technical Issues

- This course consists of six blocks, each of which is studied over a period of approximately five weeks, and each of which has 15 to 20 hours of practical work associated with it. The practical work involves using a word processing package, a database package, a spreadsheet package, interrogating an on-line database, up- and downloading questionnaire data, analyzing the data and writing a report using any or all of the packages.

- The student is also required to use a supplied modem to access a computer mediated communications system called COSY. Most tutoring is done using this medium.

The numbers of students involved are shown in Table 25.1.

Table 25.1 Open University Home Computing Policy: 1988 Course Populations

Course	Total U/G	Total Ass.	Male U/G	Male Ass.	Female U/G	Female Ass.	Percentage Female
DT200	1383	0	1018	0	365	0	27
M205	2435	599	2055	457	380	142	17
M371	248	19	198	18	50	1	19

Note: DT200 was not offered in the Associate Programme in 1988.

25.3 A Summary of Home Computing Courses

1988 Courses

- M205 Fundamentals of Computing – full credit

- M371 Computational Mathematics – half credit

- DT200 An Introduction to Information Technology: Social and Technical Issues – full credit

1989 Courses

- T102 Living with Technology: a Foundation Course – full credit

- M353 Programming and Programming Languages – half credit

1990 Courses

- M357 Data Models and Databases – half credit

- T202 Analogue and Digital Electronics – full credit

... AND more courses in future years.

25.4 DT200 – Two Ways of Considering Women

This is a multi-disciplinary course. It does not set out to teach students to be program-mers or experts with Lotus 1-2-3 but looks, as the title suggests, at issues. The issues include gender-related ones. It is also innovative in that a large proportion of tutoring is done using the COSY CMC system rather than face-to-face.

You can see from the numbers that it has the largest proportion of females of any of the home computing policy courses. Whether this is because it is the only one that isn't a Maths course has yet to be proven.

Open University courses are produced by Course Teams. The Course Team for DT200 is drawn from the Technology and Social Science faculties and includes members from the Institute of Educational Technology and the School of Education. It consists of about two thirds males and one third females. The Team has joint chairs, a male technologist and a female social scientist.

I asked a number of members of the course team what effort, if any, they put into making the course material attractive to women students. The response was almost universal:

"What an interesting question!   WE DIDN'T CONSIDER IT"

Closer questioning shows that they were all very conscious of the need to cover gender-related issues in the course material, and this they appear to have done successfully, but the issue of trying to attract women students to the course in the first place wasn't really addressed.

One explanation for this is that the course was a new one and it was felt that there was a large enough pool of potential students waiting for such a course that the question of attracting students at all never arose.

This was not the case with M205, the course with the largest number of students, which is discussed below.

25.5   Creating M205 – Questions, Issues and Ideas

25.5.1 INTRODUCTION

M205 is a foundation course in computing, based largely on UCSD Pascal. The course was an interesting one to study, from the point of view of the course team's attempts to make the material accessible to women. This was because a number of members were very aware of the issue, team members held a wide range of views on the subject, and some of the course material was particularly amenable to analysis, as is shown below.

25.5.2 METHODS OF ANALYSIS

I used three methods in my analysis of this course. These were:

1. a study of the first week's reading material;

2. an analysis of the topics chosen for the example programs which were provided. This included a survey to discover whether these topics were felt to be male or female oriented;

3. interviews with the course team.

25.5.3 COMPOSITION AND ATTITUDE OF THE COURSE TEAM

The course team consisted of 23 members including designers, producers, editors, authors and external consultants. Four of these were women, though of the eighteen academics involved only two were women.

I interviewed twelve members of this team, and three members of related course teams who had a special interest in attracting women to computing courses. I asked them about their attitudes, experiences and opinions on making material accessible to women. I shall be quoting liberally from these interviews in the following sections.

Amongst the academics there was a high level of enthusiasm and interest in making the material attractive to women. It was clear that the issue had been in most people's minds, and had been discussed at course team meetings.

- "Any who recognised sexism changed it – *if* a better and less sexist suggestion was made."

The views of the individuals in the group varied enormously. Here are some examples of the range of opinion.

- "The team wanted to write the course as if there was no gender. But there is a need to challenge people's ideas about what the norms are."

- "The worst problem I had in trying to carry out this sort of programme was trying to convince my male colleagues that there is a problem and that it is worth addressing."

- "You are not trying to change people's ideas, you are trying to teach them computing. If you feel that way, go and join the social scientists!"

Several people's views had developed over the time that the course was being created.

- "When working unconsciously I always think of men's names, so I had to make a decision to choose women's names consciously."

Some problems were only noticed when it was too late to change them. The women in the group played an important part in keeping the issue on the agenda.

- "It is important to have someone on the course team to think about these issues."

- "The presence of women makes men less likely to scoff. They do still joke about it and seem flippant, but their underlying view may be changed."

- "If there is a woman on the course team it can suppress the bad undercurrents."

The academic editors – one female, two male – were very alert to the issue, and some of the other academics depended on them to remove any sexual bias from their written material.

- "I agreed with x that wherever possible we would use the female pronoun to emphasise that the course is for women, not just for men."

- "There was a case where there was a male analyst and a female programmer. So we swapped them round."

- "In some units I put 'she', in others I randomly selected 'he' or 'she', and in others I did the opposite of what was expected. The objectors didn't get their way, but there was no absolute policy."

- "One author produced an example about a tennis club which had members and 'lady members'. Everyone sat on him. . . . This backfired because there was a tennis club secretary. While he was male it was clear that he was a retired bank manager type of honorary secretary. When we changed it to a woman, everyone assumed it was a typist sort of secretary."

Three male academics held the view that it was unnecessary to consider female students whilst writing course material. They felt that the subject matter was asexual and their sole aim was to write good teaching material. They did not think of students as being male or female, and considered that students of both sexes would best be served by concentration on the subject of study rather than on the sex of the reader. These men experienced a degree of irritation with members of the team who were consciously trying to encourage women.

- "I never gave it a second thought. I don't have any hangups about it – should I?"

- "You should not make a political point in a technical place."

There was a reasonable tolerance to issues of sexism being brought up.

- "When the issue was raised, most retreated to the position of not using gender at all. If the issue was not raised, they were happy to continue using 'he'."

- "When men wanted to use 'she' I thought 'has his wife been getting at him?' "

- "The attitude of the meeting was that they *would* change it, but didn't think it *that* important. And if you complained multiple times, they would think 'oh no – x on his hobby horse again'."

There was also a healthy degree of self criticism.

- "I have come to take the lack of positive discrimination for granted. Given a subject where women's numbers are so disastrously low, this is a major omission."

- "I didn't have the energy and push to redo all their examples."

- And of a different course – "we gave the material to a cross section of students to criticise. We were going to change the material as a result of their comments. No effort was made to balance the men and women in this group."

The course team members who were involved in the design and creation of the course but who were not academics came up with some unexpected and interesting points. They included a software designer, a BBC producer, and two graphic designers. In many ways they were very well placed to influence the 'feel' of the course. They could have responded to requests from the course team to produce the material in a style which would not be alienating to women. But as no request was made, they did not have this aim in mind. The attempts made by the authors fell into two groups. These were:

- **Language** – references to men and women in the text;
- **Examples** – the choice of topics for use in programming examples.

Other issues raised were:

- **Television** – who do you point the camera at?
- **Visual appearance of printed material** – what impression do you try to create?

25.5.4 LANGUAGE ISSUES

One course unit was written using "he" throughout as a generic term to cover both sexes. As the successive drafts passed through other hands, the academic editor changed all the "he's" to "she's", the publishing editor changed all the "she's" to "he/she's", and the academic editor changed them all back to "she" again.

There were five positions on language:

1. **Always to use the masculine**

   - "I'll be using the term 'he' because it is accepted practice that it means both."
   - "Just because you throw 'she' in everywhere it won't change anything, it will only put people's backs up. It trivialises the issue. It is going over the top."
   - "I would find the use of 'she' offensive. I would feel someone was getting at me. There are certain constructs in the English language which you expect to find."
   - "Using 'she' breaks the flow of the text, and draws attention to the text in a way that it shouldn't be drawn."

2. **To avoid indications of gender**

   - "Doesn't anti-sexism mean not mentioning sex?"
   - "The technical content is sexless"
   - "The editors made attempts to neutralise the thing"

3. Occasionally to use the feminine

- "I sometimes use 'she' instead of 'he' to shock people. This makes them question their assumptions."

- "It's good to make people go 'uh?' now and then. We shouldn't be surprised it's a female, but we are."

4. To use feminine and masculine equally

- "As for using 'he' or 'she' alternately in examples, I have tried this with some success, and have actually convinced a man who felt it unnatural that if he used it often enough it would become 'natural'. He later came back to me and agreed that it was a matter of getting over the habit of always using 'he' and that now he had consciously worked at fitting 'she' in half the time, he found the 50/50 solution perfectly 'natural'."

5. Always to use the feminine

- "When talking about professionals I always use 'she'."

It seems that a compromise position was reached, with many references to gender being removed, and "she" being used in key places to emphasise that a senior professional was a woman.

The first unit of the course was both written and edited by people who were determined to avoid a male bias. There was therefore surprise when a male student wrote complaining that it had a male sexist bias. I combed the text of that week's reading in the hope of comparing the number of "he's" and "she's". There was not one reference to gender. All the managers, analysts, programmers etc mentioned were sexless. I concluded that the student had automatically assumed that they were male, without registering that their sex wasn't mentioned. This is why it is important to use 'she' sometimes. The only other bias was in the cartoons used to lighten the text. No one had noticed that all the characters in the cartoons, mostly computing personnel, were men.

When lists of names were used, there was a tendency to use the names of famous men. An example using the "Mr Men" characters was rejected partly on the grounds of its being frivolous. Although the characters are all male, I felt that this example from the world of children would have presented a familiar face to women with children, amongst a lot of new and unfamiliar material.

I feel that the removal of references to gender, the removal of jokes, and of personal style can lead to a text which seems formal and impersonal. This style of writing increases the impression of being a technical document *about things* rather than a teaching document *for people*. Several academics put forward the view that women in general are less interested in the technology for its own sake, and more interested in the application of the technology to real life situations. These two factors combined suggest that a formal style of writing may increase women's feeling of alienation from the subject.

25.5.5 TOPICS IN PROGRAMMING EXAMPLES

From the 217 files which were provided as part of the course to students on disk, I extracted 50 topics. Many examples had a number of files – incomplete programs for the student to work on, answer files containing a complete correct program, data files, alternative approaches to the same problem, or developments of the original problem.

I then asked 40 people to give their immediate gut feeling as to whether each topic was a female topic, or a male topic, on a scale of one to five – one was clearly a male topic, three was a neutral topic, and five was a clearly female topic.

I was interested in the immediate gut feeling, because I believe the problem of women not taking up computing is more to do with their unconscious assumptions than with their conscious views. Once a woman begins to think about whether she wants to go into computing, and to weigh up the pros and cons, there is at least some hope that she can make an informed decision. But I believe that most women do not get that far – computing is not even within the realm of things they think of considering – they just feel it is not for them. They may consciously *think* that women can do anything that men can do and that no fields of work should be closed to women, but the unconscious *feeling* may still be that it is not for them. It is very hard for a person to get to the root of feelings like these, and to understand the source of the feelings deeply enough for them to loose their power.

The group of 40 was composed of four groups of ten:

1. men who work in computing;

2. women who work in computing;

3. men who don't work in computing;

4. women who don't work in computing.

I divided the groups this way because I wanted to know how different men's view of what was a male and what was a female topic was from women's view. It is wonderful if the men who produce the course material are trying to find topics which are not particularly male-orientated. But how well can they judge this from the point of view of the women they are trying to attract?

I also wanted to know whether we women who are already in computing are any better equipped to advise on suitable topics, or whether we have absorbed different ideas about sexual stereotyping as a result of our work in this male dominated profession. We may have thought more about these issues, and as a result have different perspectives from women who have not yet entered the field. We may have been atypical women in the first place, to enter a field which puts most women off.

The results were not as I had expected (see Table 25.2). Averaging all the scores for all topics to give a rough measure of how "masculine" overall the programming examples had been, I found that all four groups gave the same result. On a scale where 1 represented a masculine topic, 3 a neutral topic, and 5 a feminine topic, the average score was 2.8. This indicated that the material was considered just slightly masculine. This was not a surprising result for such a predominantly male course team.

The women gave 38% of the topics a score between 3 and 5 indicating that the topic had some degree of female orientation, and 60% a score between 1 and 3, indicating some degree of male orientation. The men placed 39% of topics in the former group and 56% in the latter.

Did the different groups agree though about *which* topics were male and which female? Performing a students t test, I found that there were only 4 topics where the men's view was significantly different from the women's. These were a credit broker example, which the women felt to be more masculine than the men did – and three examples which the women felt to be more feminine than the men did – to do with simple clerical tasks.

When I compared the results for women who work in computing with women who don't, there were *six* topics on which there was a significant difference of opinion. Women working in computing considered card games and betting to be less masculine that other women did. They thought that squaring numbers and summing squares were neutral topics, while women not working in computing found these topics masculine. Computing women disagreed with non computing women on "population census data" and on "spotting a given character", considering the former a female topic and the latter a male topic, while non-computing women placed them the other way round.

It seemed that the most important two groups to compare were the men who work in computing, therefore representing the authors of the course material, and the women who work outside computing, therefore representing students we have so far failed to attract. Here I found *no* significant differences of opinion!

Table 25.2 Significant Differences of Opinion on Sex of Topics

Group A	Group B	Number of differences between groups A and B
women	men	4
women in computing	women outside computing	6
men in computing	women outside computing	0

This was a very small sample on which to base firm conclusions. However, it does suggest that we should not assume that being women we automatically understand the feelings of women who are not attracted to computing. We need objective studies to find these things out.

When I sorted the topics into perceived order of "femaleness" a number of groups emerged (see Table 25.3). These were, in decreasing order of femaleness:

1. **simple clerical tasks/games**, eg spotting a given character, guessing a letter;

2. **topics to do with relationships/feelings**, eg a dating agency, greeting someone, feeling bored;

3. **word processing type activities**, eg splitting a sentence, replacing a word;

4. **sexually neutral real life activities**, eg tennis club membership, student exam results, population census data, booklists;

5. **mathematical topics**, eg squaring numbers, sequences of numbers;

6. **financial topics**, eg credit brokers, exchange rates, banking;

7. **male work activities**, eg warehouse work, crime;

8. **Male leisure activities**, eg cricket, football, betting, cards.

Table 25.3 Average scores given to programming topics, by group

	Non computing women	Computing women	Computing men	Non computing men
Simple clerical tasks/games	3.6	3.0	3.2	3.1
Feelings/ relationships	3.4	3.2	3.5	3.0
Letters/ word-processing	3.2	3.2	3.1	3.0
Sexually neutral real life	3.0	3.1	3.1	3.0
Mathematical topics	2.7	3.0	2.7	2.6
Financial topics	2.4	2.5	2.6	2.5
Male work activities	2.3	2.4	2.5	2.4
Male leisure activities	1.5	1.8	1.8	2.0

(1=male-oriented 2=faintly male 3=neutral 4=faintly female 5 =female oriented)

There was a depressing tendency for simple things to be considered more feminine, and complex things more masculine. It seemed that both men and women could not picture an important *man* doing a simple task like sorting odd from even numbers, while both felt that a more complicated numerical task like dealing with a mathematical sequence would involve a man.

I also noticed a tendency for topics to be more "female" as they became more people orientated – "*student* exam results" was more feminine than "*analyzing* exam results".

All this puts us in a dilemma. Do we pander to sometimes unhealthy sexual stereotypes, so that more women feel the course material to be written with them in mind? Or do we ignore these stereotypes in the belief that financial and mathematical topics are just as relevant to women as to men?

I believe that we ignore these unconscious feelings at our peril. I think we can look for the healthier aspects of this sexual stereotyping, like the interest in people and the preference for real life examples over abstract mathematical examples. And if we have to use a financial example, for instance, then we should try to make it seem less alienating by referring to women professionals and customers in the example. I don't think we should fall into the trap of feeling that supposedly female topics which are treated as being not really serious – like things to do with children, and with relationships and feelings – are embarrassing aspects of sexual stereotyping which we must get away from. It is the absence of a sense of the importance of these things which can make computing such a barren field to work in. It is the failure to assert the importance of these things which results in the vast resources and potential of computing remaining in the hands of moneymakers and warmongers.

25.5.6 TELEVISION – WHO DO YOU POINT THE CAMERA AT?

"When we go to places we see things as they are, and can't distort them.
You point the camera, and film what you see."

This was the view of a television producer, who had been pleased to find an example of a female analyst advising a male programmer when filming on location. This was the only occasion, in 16 programmes, where a woman was shown in a senior position. No other senior women were interviewed or filmed, and all the commentaries and introductions were given by male academics.

It is worth thinking for a moment about the influence of Open University television programmes.

Who sees them? They have a much wider audience than just those people who are taking a particular course. They are perhaps the most public face of the Open University. They can influence people who have not yet decided whether to go into computing.

Who is filmed? Mainly men, it seems. Course team members spoke of the difficulty of finding good examples of women working in the fields they wish to make films on. One course team had considered and rejected the idea of using female actors to increase the proportion of women in a computing environment. Another team decided that they would have to go to the United States to find a workplace where there were women in senior positions.

Who is presenting? Men again, it seems. Television is a potent but unobtrusive way to have influence. Nobody thinks it unnatural or contrived to see a woman presenter or lecturer. It is not that women look at a film on computing, see a female computer expert and think "ah – I could do that too". But it chips away at their unconscious assumption that computing is only for men. This makes them less likely to reject the possibility of a career in computing. To see only men in a programme about computing simply reinforces the idea that computing is not for women.

25.5.7 VISUAL APPEARANCE OF PRINTED MATERIAL

The two graphic designers on the team were professionally trained to be able to create a desired visual impression. Not having been asked to think about attracting women with their material, each responded differently to their task.

The designer of the covers for the course texts considered computing to be a "hard" subject. Because this was a foundation course in computing he wished to "soften" this "hard" effect. He therefore chose cover illustrations which were linked symbolically rather than literally to the content of the text – a stone wall for modularity, footprints in the sand for first steps, tiny cars on a complex road network for data in a computer. He used soft rather than brash colours, and he used a flowing script typeface for the titles.

The designer of the illustrations on the other hand approached the course as she approaches all science and technology courses. This meant that illustrations would be precise, clean and angular, as opposed to the more flowing illustrations she might provide for an arts course.

I asked this second designer to describe the differences you might expect to find in consumer items which are designed for a particular sex, for instance the difference in style between an electric drill and an electric food mixer, or an electric shaver designed for men and one designed for women. She felt that things for men would be more angular, solid and bold than those for women. There seemed to be a parallel here. I felt that designers could inadvertently be giving computing materials a "male" appearance. This could be because of their own underlying assumption that it was a "male" subject, and also because the design culture which has built up around computing has developed to attract the men who represent the majority of buyers.

It was pointed out that there is very little choice of typeface for mathematical and scientific texts, because only certain typefaces have the full range of technical symbols. This can lead to these texts all having a rather similar appearance.

One designer mentioned that financial constraints mean that inessential illustrations are excluded, and that this course was visually very boring to work on. Another pointed out the liking that technical authors have for lists. This can break up the visual flow of the text.

There were many choices to be made in the visual design of a text, and the main constraints seemed to be the need for ease of legibility, the form of the text supplied by the authors, and financial constraints. Given these limitations there was still scope for influencing the "feel" of the text. For instance the text in an arts course might have decorative rules as a visual stop to break up the text, whereas you would not expect to find these in a text on, say, heavy industrial machinery.

> "You could do a psychologically misleading design. There are visual cues as to what sort of material you have picked up – you never get a two column novel. If briefed 'this is for women' then you'd think of stereotypical ways of making it for women – less technical manual style. Instead of round black bullets in a list, use little roses, pastel shades."

Clearly we don't want to go to absurd extremes, or to introduce bad design. However, there seems to be scope for discussion and for greater use of the designers' skills here.

25.5.8 SOME CONCLUSIONS AND QUESTIONS

This section summarises some of the conclusions I came to as a result of this study.

Despite widely varying viewpoints, the team as a whole did make a conscientious effort to design and revise material so that it would not be alienating to women. These differing views were held and discussed without too much hostility, and several people developed their views on the subject as a result of this. This tolerant attitude is not always easily maintained, and I think it is a tribute to the fairness of the chairman, and the tact of individual team members that so much was achieved.

Whatever its roots, the primary prejudice we have to counteract is that in *women*. It is women who do not apply for computing courses. I think there are two factors at play – one a quite reasonable and rational distaste for certain aspects of the computer industry – and the other an unjustified but compelling assumption that it is "not for them". We need to counteract this assumption.

Because we are contending with such deeply rooted prejudices, I believe that we have to move the issue out of the unconscious, into the conscious mind. Then it will be accessible to rational thought. This can only be done by shocking people occasionally with something unexpected or "unnatural" which brings them up against their unconscious assumptions. It is therefore important sometimes to present women in roles we might expect to be filled by men, and vice versa. I believe that neutralising gender is not enough to stop people assuming that professionals such as managers, credit brokers and analysts are male. It would be valuable to do research to find out the extent of this assumption.

Given that all the programming examples in this course were written by men, the slight bias towards "maleness" was not surprising. However, I believe that a positive female bias needs to be achieved to counteract the a-priori feeling that computing is for men. In programming examples I would suggest that this can be achieved by:

1. more emphasis on real life examples, in place of abstract mathematical examples;

2. avoidance of predominantly male work and leisure topics;

3. less emphasis on the world of finance;

4. an approach which links the technology with its applications. In this respect I feel it may have been a mistake to cover hardware topics in the first unit of the course, rather than starting with practical software examples and later describing the hardware which supports the software.

It is important to have several women on each course team, not because men are *unable* to produce good female-oriented material, but because the presence of women can alter the attitude and behaviour of some men. There are some men who would otherwise neglect the issue – there are after all so many other issues to consider. There are some men who would ridicule other men who brought the topic up. It is hard to be a woman holding the fort but I think it can be equally hard for the men who are trying to attract women students. We need each other's support.

We should not forget to enlist the help of graphic designers and others who are involved in the presentation of material. It is not just a matter of whether the illustrations are of men or of women. There is a whole wealth of expertise that we could tap, about how visual appearance can differentially attract or repel the sexes.

I believe that to some extent women have the psychological advantage. Our minority position can put our friendship and approval at a premium. We have been brought up to be sensitive to other people's feelings, giving us a greater intuitive awareness of the sort of games that people play. We are more aware of their motives and their ego trips. We are more aware of how far we can go with certain individuals, and we are trained in tact. If we use this tact and intuition *consciously*, rather than just blindly avoiding offending people, we can have greater power than our numbers might suggest.

26

Home-based Computing for Women Students

**Gill Kirkup, Ruth Carter, Laurie Keller,
Jenny Lewis, Chris Saxton, Dianne Sutton[1]**

26.1 Introduction

The Open University (OU) has always recruited a significant proportion of women into its courses: by 1988 32,992 women were registered as undergraduates (46% of total) and 46,555 women had graduated with BA degrees (49% of total graduates). As with all institutions of higher education, women have been much less well represented on courses in maths, science and technology – including computing courses. However, unlike many institutions the OU has managed to encourage women onto courses where computer use is a significant element, see Table 26.1.

This table represents not only women who are interested in using a computer but women who are able to make *their own arrangements for access to equipment*.

26.1.1 HOME COMPUTING POLICY IN THE OU

The OU has always used practical computing for its students. Facilities were formerly provided through a national network of terminals in local study centres connected to a central service. Additional facilities were provided at summer schools. These facilities were adequate only for small amounts of use and in the 1980s the University saw the potential of personal computers for students, both to expand the potential for teaching Computer Science, and also as a learning tool for other courses.

A University specification was set up based on an IBM PC compatible microcomputer running an MS-DOS system. Students were advised that in order to study certain courses they would have to ensure good access to specified equipment. The University arranged a special purchase scheme through certain suppliers, and a limited pool of machines available for rent. During the first three years of the policy, 1988-90, students studying "home computing courses" qualified for a small fee discount. However, studying home computing courses involves students in a significant extra expense. There were three courses in the policy in 1988, seven in 1990 (see Table 26.1), by 1992 there will be thirteen and this will continue to increase.

[1] The Open University, Walton Hall, Milton Keynes MK7 6AA

Table 26.1 Women students registered on OU *home* computing courses in 1990

Course Title	No. of women	% course students
An introduction to I.T	603	34.0
Fundamentals of Computing	846	22.0
Computational Mathematics	60	23.0
Programming and programming languages	213	15.0
Data models and data bases	214	22.0
Living with Technology	1670	28.0
Analogue and Digital Electronics	35	2.5
TOTAL NO. WOMEN IN 1990	3641	

26.1.2 LOOKING OUT FOR THE INTERESTS OF WOMEN

Those of us at the University who are concerned about women's education were very worried about the effect of this policy on the recruitment of women to these courses. We know that women find the costs of studying with the OU more onerous than men. We also knew from our own research and that of others that women have less access to computers in the home than other family members [Culley 88b, Gerver 86]. In the first year of the policy, fewer women did register for home computing courses [Kirkup 89], but it was not clear which factors were most discouraging, and whether women were disadvantaged once they had registered. The University has been concerned to monitor the success of this expensive innovation, and those of us concerned in particular with women students have been keen to monitor gender effects.

This paper describes some of the issues that members of the OU Women into Science and Engineering (WISE) Group have explored. The WISE Group has been active since 1984 [Carter 90a, Carter 90b], and a Women into Computing (WiC) group has been active since 1988. We do not have an integrated programme of research intervention, but we explore aspects relevant to the different areas of the University in which we work.

26.2 Student drop-out and special support initiatives

26.2.1 DROP-OUT AMONGST WOMEN ON HOME COMPUTING COURSES

In the first year of the policy, extensive surveys were carried out, one of which was of students who had "dropped out" of one of the three home computing courses (this includes those who began studying but gave up in the first three months, as well as those who signed up for a course but withdrew before fees were paid or materials received). Questionnaires were sent to 380 students (99 women and 281 men) who were in this position. The aim was to establish whether there were significant differences in the personal circumstances of the women and the men who dropped out and whether there were differences of influence causing the women and the men to take the decision to drop out. The proportion of women studying on home computing courses was 19%. The proportion of women among the students who dropped-out was 26%. So women were over-represented in the drop-out group.

Of the students in the drop-out group who indicated a desire to overcome a fear of computers as being a significant factor in their decision to register for a home computing course, 61% were women. Of the students who were influenced into registering for a home computing course by a spouse or another person (not an employer), 65% were women.

Of the students giving cost of loan or purchase as the most significant factor influencing their decision to pull out, 40% were women. Many students (56 of the women and 44 of the men) stated "change in personal circumstances" as the most significant factor. The following quote from a woman student indicates the interplay between the pressures of family circumstances and of cost.

> "Change in circumstances involved moving due to husband's career, necessity of finding full-time job after years of part-time, finances went through a sticky patch, child care was not sorted out. Looking back, it would have worked out ok by now, but at the time I panicked. Also we had not and still haven't a phone."

120 students began studying, but withdrew within the first three months. Of these 120, 33% were women. When asked which of 10 factors was the most significant factor influencing the decision to withdraw: 20% of the women and only 6% of the men said "difficulties with course material"; 30% of the women and only 12% of the men said "study time in excess of what was expected"; 15% of the women and only 4% of the men said "lack of tutorial support". Overall, of the students giving a course-related difficulty as the most significant factor, 58% were women.

This survey indicates the multiplicity of inter-related factors which make home computing difficult for women.

26.2.2 REGIONAL INITIATIVES

Since cost is so obviously a barrier for women, initiatives to provide free or cheap access are a primary focus of work. Places are offered to new undergraduate applicants on a "first-come first-served" basis *within* each region of the country, as is the option of renting one of the limited supply of rental machines. For example in the Yorkshire Region in 1991 there will be roughly 300 places for the first year course: Living with Technology, but less than 100 rental computers available (cost £55 per annum). Students from disadvantaged groups tend to apply later in the application period; they also tend to be offered places after the quota of computers has been allocated. They then become further disadvantaged by the University's expectation that they will buy their own machines (minimum cost about £550 in 1990). Women, unemployed, with lower incomes on average than men, or without access to the "household" income, are particularly hard hit.

Strategies explored to counter this in the Yorkshire Region fall into two groups: first, those that give students access to computers outside their homes. The Region has been able to negotiate with some further education colleges and polytechnics for OU students to use their computer facilities. In one rural study centre, the local branch of the OU Students Association has raised enough money to buy a machine and has arranged for it to be installed in the public library. The disadvantage of these schemes is that access is restricted by opening hours, and difficulties associated with travel and childcare may hamper every visit.

The second group of strategies helps to increase the availability of *home-based* computers, in line with the official university model that unrestricted access to a computer at home is what is required. Approaches to the two Government Task Forces in the Region have each yielded six extra machines, made available to unemployed students at the subsidised rental. Similarly, a special fund within the University has agreed to supply six machines, on an experimental basis, for unemployed women who will be following a specially designed course at an adult education college. Approaches are also being made to potential commercial sponsors. In 1990 British Gas North Eastern Division made five £100 grants available to disadvantaged students towards the purchase of a home computer. Hopefully, other companies will follow their lead.

For the future, the Region is looking at ways of setting up a home computer exchange, whereby students who wish to sell their home computers can be put in touch with applicants who might want to buy one second hand at a reduced price. However, all these initiatives have demanded extra work from the University's regional staff, and there is as yet no *national* set of special access schemes for women.

26.3 The computer keyboard: is it sexist?

There are also the more subtle aspects of disadvantage suffered by women students. One of these – the keyboard – was investigated by one of us at an OU summer school. Many courses have week-long summer schools as an essential part of a student's study. At least two of these have a significant element of computing. The summer school week for the Mathematics foundation course has long included a major computer exercise, and very simple computing is taught as a part of the course. A significant proportion of students has considerable difficulties in undertaking the computing work at summer school. This involves: logging on to a terminal (VT200); running two prewritten programs and providing simple commands (such as RUN) and numeric input for these; coding a simple program of about 10 lines in BASIC and then modifying this program to call a pre-written subroutine and to carry out a different type of calculation. Some of the problems students had were simple ergonomic ones: the on-off switch on the terminal was very difficult to locate (even with stickers on the terminals pointing to it and signs above each terminal showing where it was located), the attached printer had to be switched on or the computer simply waited for the student to realise the problem, and so on.

A significant number of students, however, had genuine difficulty with the keying of commands and numbers. (The best student finished the entire exercise in 35 minutes, the worst took over five hours, and the average seemed to be between two and two-and-half hours). Many students were obviously very unfamiliar with the QWERTY layout, having to search the entire keyboard for each keypress.

A questionnaire was given to students asking about their experience of keyboards, including typewriter, calculator and other keyboards. This included a question on age and one on gender. Given women's greater exposure to keyboards in office work, it was hypothesised that women as a group would find keyboard use easier.

A surprising result was that women were *more* disadvantaged by the keyboard interface than men. Less surprisingly, the younger a person was, the more likely he or she was to have encountered and used a keyboard to the point of acquiring some facility in using it. Among male students, 43% used a keyboard often, 21% used a keyboard regularly, 17% used a keyboard occasionally. Among female students, 28% used a keyboard often, 12% used a keyboard regularly, and 40% used a keyboard occasionally. Significantly, 25% of the women used keyboards rarely, once or twice or never, whereas the percentage for men was lower at 20%.

A greater percentage of men than women indicated that they found keyboards easy or very easy to use and a greater proportion of men than women said they used non-typewriter- type-keyboards (other than calculators) occasionally or regularly. It would seem from this that the humble QWERTY keyboard was not simply a barrier to computing for non-typists; it was more of a barrier to these women studying mathematics than to men.

26.4 New uses of computing and their potential effect on women

26.4.1 CAN COMPUTER-MEDIATED COMMUNICATION HELP?

The University is experimenting with the use of computer mediated communication (CMC) as a communication and a teaching medium. We are exploring how this can be used to benefit women. Where women are a minority in a local tutorial group they are often afraid to ask for help, because they feel that their fellow male students don't need it and they will be wasting group time. Sometimes "non-technical" men on computing courses have the same reservations. How do we get over this problem and show women students that they can ask for help with the technology or make comments without feeling pigeonholed into a stereotypical role? Women-only computer self-help groups and a women-staffed telephone help line, although demonstrably successful in some institutions, have not been possible before now at the OU.

One home computing course, Introduction to IT, uses CMC as part of its multimedia teaching strategy. All students are encouraged to participate, to gain marks for assignments. They all have the hardware necessary to do so although telephone costs which are carried by the student affect participation rates and can be shown to favour waged male students rather than unwaged female students.

An interesting aspect of computer conferencing is that individual students are identified by default just by initials and surname, although one can ask for further information about an individual. The additional information shows forenames. This genderless identifier can be used to advantage by women, and others who may feel an audience's reaction to what they say is coloured by visual cues such as sex, colour and disability.

It is possible for a female student to make a comment in a conference without fear of it being immediately dismissed because "she's only a woman". Interestingly, although this anonymity has been used to advantage by some women, and some disabled students of both sexes, a surprising number of students choose to announce their sex by signing their contribution Sue, Mary, John or whatever. Yet despite its potential, so far, women have spent less time logged on to CMC than men. The social/gender relations of CMC are only beginning to be investigated and we need more work on the participation (and lack of it) by women.

26.4.2 INTRODUCING HOME COMPUTING INTO MANAGEMENT COURSES

The University is now introducing obligatory home computing into other areas of the curriculum, where women have also been under-represented eg management education. Up to 1988, 32% of all registrations for OU management courses were from women, and in 1989, 17% of MBA students were women. Unlike the undergraduate programme, the School of Management must be self-financing, therefore course fees are high: between £475 and £750 for a short course, £1575 for the first year of the MBA. The majority of students are sponsored by their employers, although some bursaries are awarded in special cases. A new policy requires that computers will be used to support the course objectives, and for some courses home computing will be essential.

Two surveys of student opinion on the inclusion of "hands on" computing were carried out by the School. The first survey was of Diploma level students (who need no formal entry qualifications) and the second survey covered the first year of the MBA (honours graduates or equivalent).

Diploma students

These students are usually significantly more advantaged with respect to access and experience than undergraduates. Similar percentages of women and men described themselves as frequent users of computers at work. The percentage of women who were users of word processing packages was higher (at 64%) than the percentage of men (53%), while for spreadsheets the opposite result held. This probably reflects the occupations of Diploma in Management students.

More men had access to a suitable machine than women. A third of women said the cost would put them off buying a PC, while fewer men felt this (but of course fewer of them needed to buy). When asked about their enthusiasm for computing ("If you were told that it would be essential to have access to a computer for a future course, how would you react?"), 12% of women (18% men) said they would be even more enthusiastic, while 20% said they would take it reluctantly (like 13% of the men).

MBA students

Although these are graduate professionals, far more MBA women than men (48% to 21%) said they would need training to get a new PC from its arrival in a box to being a working computer. However, since 37% of the men admitted that they did want training in getting the disk operating system to carry out basic housekeeping, they appear to be demonstrating more confidence in their ability to unpack and plug in the components. In fact, half of the men and 65% of women said they needed basic training on a range of standard packages.

In terms of their current experience of computing, similar percentages of MBA men and women had some experience of using operating systems on IBM compatible PCs. Three quarters of both women and men had word processing experience. For databases, the picture was more complex; the proportions with no experience were similar at about one third, but while more women were used to maintaining databases, fewer felt confident about setting them up.

As usual, more men than women had access to IBM compatible PCs at work (62% to 44%), but for home access the gap narrowed (31% men, 26% women). More women had no access or were not sure that any could be gained. However, when asked about purchasing arrangements and told the machine would cost at least £500, similar proportions of women and men said they would have to pay themselves and that this cost *was* acceptable. 39% thought that they needed to purchase and that cost would be a problem, whereas fewer men held this view.

In many ways women on these courses are "elite", and respond more like their male fellow students than like women undergraduates. And yet they too are more disadvantaged with respect to computer access than men. Money is less likely to be a problem, but the data implies that their experience of the more quantitative uses of computing is considerably less than their male equivalents.

26.5 Conclusion

It is likely in the future that more institutions of further and higher education will expect students on courses such as management studies and technology to use a PC as a tool. It is important that we work with colleagues in these disciplines to promote the interests of their women students with respect to computing. What comes out of our various pieces of research is that the ways in which women students are disadvantaged with respect to access and experience of *home* computing are varied and still not properly known. As a group we hope to integrate our interests and consolidate them into a more coherent research programme. At the same time we need to support and extend positive action initiatives. Our problem as educators is how to develop institutional policies which are supportive of a range of women students, and don't further alienate women from subject areas in which they are already a minority.

26.6 REFERENCES

[Carter 90a] Carter R and Kirkup G, "Women into Science and Engineering WISE: Activism and Institutional Change", Contributions *GASAT Conference*, Jönköping, Sweden, 1990.

[Carter 90b] Carter R and Kirkup G, *Women into Science and Engineering (WISE) Report 1990*, Unpublished Report obtainable from authors at Open University, Walton Hall, Milton Keynes.

[Culley 88b] Culley L, "Girls, boys and computers", *Educational studies*, 14, 1, 1988.

[Gerver 86] Gerver E, *Humanising Technology: Computers in Community Use and Adult Education*, Plenum Press, 1986.

[Kirkup 89] Kirkup G, "Equal Opportunities and Computing at the Open University", *Open Learning*, 4, 1, 1989.

27

Making a Place for Women in Computing

J. K. Bansal[1]

27.1 Introduction

The Computing Department at Birmingham Polytechnic has been in existence for only five to six years. Prior to this it was a section belonging to the Computer Centre. The second group of students has just graduated this year. Interestingly, of the three first class honours students, two were female, one of whom was from an ethnic minority background.

27.2 Birmingham Polytechnic asks "Is there *really* a problem?"

Headlines hitting the mass media state that there is a crisis in computing skills shortages. However, inspection of the student statistics at Birmingham Polytechnic reveals that the percentages of female students on computing courses lie in the range 25-30%. These exceed the national average percentage which stands at only 12%. The next logical step then is to investigate why some academic establishments have a higher success rate than others in attracting females onto their computing courses.

27.3 On the road to success

This section of the paper proposes to look at the reasons which in the author's opinion have led to this success.

27.3.1 GETTING THE BALANCE RIGHT

Unlike the traditional computer science degree, the computing degree at Birmingham Polytechnic (BSc Computing Information Systems) attempts to achieve a good even

---

[1]Faculty of Computing and Information Studies, City of Birmingham Polytechnic, Perry Barr, Birmingham B42 2SU

mix of soft and hard computing topics with particular strong emphasis on systems analysis, organisational concepts and communication skills. The major strength behind this course is that the systems analysis and design units have been developed using expertise from the Structured Systems Analysis and Design Methodology Research Centre (SSADM) which is located within the Computing department. Table 27.1 shows the percentage of females on each year of the degree course.

Table 27.1 Percentage of females currently on BSc Computing Information Systems

YEAR	FEMALE PERCENTAGE
One	32% (19 out of 59)
Two	29% (15 out of 51)
Three	29% (15 out of 50)
Four	24% (9 out of 37)

The skills of a systems analyst are allied to the skills that women are reputedly good at (eg communication, good listeners, extracting information, creative and social skills) [Adam 90]. Hence the attraction to courses such as the BSc CIS degree. As can be seen from Table 27.1, the female representation on the BSc Computing Information Systems degree course is increasing at a steady rate.

27.3.2 TIME MANAGEMENT

The figures on the HND Computing course also reveal a good proportion of females (see Table 27.2).

Table 27.2 Percentage of females currently on HND Computing

YEAR	FEMALE PERCENTAGE
One	26% (13 out of 53)
Two	22% (8 out of 37)

The timetable of the HND Computing course has been modified to fit in with school hours (10.00 am to 2.30 pm) thereby enabling mothers studying on the course to drop the children off at school and pick them up at the end of the day.

In addition to this, funds are actively being sought from various sources, particularly local industry, to provide female mature students with personal computers so that assessed practical work can be completed from home. This would be an innovative feature of this course which is certain to be favoured by busy mature women students who need to manage their time well. Homeworking is a key area which is definitely worthy of detailed consideration [Gabriel 90].

27.3.3 OPEN DAYS - BOTH SIDES OF THE COIN

When prospective students arrive at the polytechnic on an open day, introductory welcome talks are given by senior members of staff and a departmental video is shown. To put the students in the complete picture, current students from each year of the course get a 30-40 minute slot to share their opinions and experiences (the honesty of the current students shows quite well here!). In this way, the prospective students do not get a biased view of the department and its courses.

27.3.4 INDUSTRIAL LINKS

The polytechnic has been successful in increasing its links with local computing companies who are willing to employ females on a part-time basis or on part-time placements. This facility is useful for women who have a desire to build their computing skills and yet continue their family roles simultaneously. Two women currently on the degree course have been able to combine their studies and maternal roles with success. Both have completed their second year on the degree and have found suitable placements for their sandwich year.

27.3.5 PART-TIME STUDY WITH A DIFFERENCE

The part-time Polytechnic Diploma in Computing course shows mixed levels of success. Students on this course attend either on day release or one evening per week for a two year period. Table 27.3 shows the percentage of females on the Polytechnic Diploma in Computing.

Table 27.3 Percentage of females on Polytechnic Diploma in Computing

YEAR	FEMALE PERCENTAGE
One	16% (11 out of 69)
Two	28% (10 out of 36)

The newest course in the Faculty is the MSc Information Management which got off the ground last year. This course provides a more flexible structure within its part-time mode of study. Students can choose to attend either *short courses* in concentrated blocks or attend one evening per week over a 6 to 10 week period. The course allows for individually selected programmes of study (core modules and optional modules) which can be modified at scheduled points during the length of the course.

The MSc Information Management is based on a credit points scheme. If half of the total number of credits have been attained then students can choose to take leave and are awarded a Postgraduate Diploma in Information Management. The MSc qualification is open to these students providing they return to complete the project at some defined point in the future. Students can qualify for this MSc by choosing the route which suits their needs best.

The MSc Information Management course has attracted a significant proportion of females. Thirteen female applications were received out of a total of seventeen. Table 27.4 shows the background in terms of qualifications and age of the nine females that were accepted onto this course.

Table 27.3 Background of females on MSc Information Management

QUALIFICATIONS	AGE
BSc Hons Mathematics	32
BTec HNC Public Administrator	36
MSc Technical Communications	34
BSc Mathematics for Business	42
BA Government	45
BSc Mathematics, ACA, PGCE	34
Secretarial Teaching Certificate	41
BSc Management Science; Diploma in advanced Marketing Techniques	25
A-Level Commerce (Private Tutor)	36

Two points are worth highlighting. Firstly, the majority of female applicants came from a mature age category (mid 30s to early 40s). Secondly none of these applicants had a strong computing background. The computing stream of modules form one quarter of the MSc course but this did not deter these mature women from applying.

27.4 Other Initiatives to show the way forward

Establishments must seek to create a good working environment. One way of achieving this would be to offer various incentives to the female workforce. Organisational policies must allow women returners to rejoin work at the same level at which they left (not lower). Better child care facilities is another area which is of major concern. If half of a working mother's earnings are allocated to child care then one must surely ask "Is it really worth the effort?". According to Teresa Gorman MP, child care facilities should be treated as a business expense. She asks "Why should cars, sports facilities, Christmas parties, uniforms, telephones and concessionary coal attract tax relief on gross pay but not child care facilities?" [Nicholle 90].

Certain academic establishments provide a crèche facility for students only but not for female staff. If this policy was changed so that female academics could also have the crèche facility made available, they would be more inclined to think that they are working in a good environment which cares about their needs.

Role models exist but these need to be more widely dispersed. Not surprisingly, women tend to join organisations where other female employees already exist. This has led to a *clustering* effect. Certain Polytechnics have a good male/female staff ratio, others do not. There is no doubt that the "safety in numbers" syndrome (working in women groups) gives the females a sense of security and also boosts their level of confidence. The solution to this problem would be for organisations to have recruitment policies which make firm commitments to encouraging women returners [Guardian 90]. Prospective female job applicants or prospective female students can obtain reassurance from conversing with a female interviewer or admissions tutor who is seen inadvertently as the role model.

27.5 Concluding Remarks

Birmingham Polytechnic has achieved certain levels of success in attracting a higher than national average number of females onto its computing courses. Complacency must not be allowed to set in. On the contrary, there is so much which remains to be accomplished.

By updating their skills (via higher education/returning to work) women will not only be bringing satisfaction to themselves but more importantly they will be doing the *nation* a big favour. Therefore the onus lies on the Government, employers and educationalists to take steps and put forward incentives which make the option of returning to work or education an appealing one.

It only takes one person/organisation to take initiative; the trend is set with others following. The author aims to encourage the Polytechnic to adopt some of the above approaches in order to increase not only the female student representation on computing courses but also increase the proportion of female academic members of staff. The latter will lead to strength in numbers, thus increasing the likelihood of achieving this sizeable task which lies ahead.

This paper has outlined measures being taken by Birmingham Polytechnic in planning to be one of the first in encouraging very capable women to be involved in computing either by returning to higher education or by returning to employment in the computing field. Such plans are not trivial. They require a continuous supply of determined effort, time and money. For those who acknowledge that women will be an important resource in eliminating the skills shortage that is looming in the not too distant future, the benefits will be numerable.

27.6 REFERENCES

[Adam 90] Adam A and Bruce M, "Do Women Make Better Knowledge Engineers?", *Computing*, 8th February 1990.

[Gabriel 90] Gabriel C, "Housework", *Computing*, 12th April 1990.

[Guardian 90] Lancashire Polytechnic Advertisement, *The Education Guardian*, 5th June 1990.

[Nicholle 90] Nicholle L, "Women Wait for Major Tax Break", *Computer Weekly*, 15th March 1990.

28

Initiatives for Recruitment of Female Undergraduates

Janet Johnson[1]
Dave Arnold[2]

28.1 Introduction

This paper[3] presents a summary of activities on student recruitment in the Electronics and Computing Sectors in 1987 and 1988 in the School of Information Systems at the University of East Anglia. Some of the background is given first, followed by an outline of initiatives to stimulate interest from women (both school leavers and, at a more local level, mature entrants). Thirdly, a brief look is taken at initiatives with teachers. Some of the initiatives to make the university more accessible are described – BTEC tie-ups and access courses. There is also a description of some new courses at UEA – Electronics Design and Technology and Open Entry Science.

28.2 Background

The School of Information Systems was founded in 1985 and comprises three sectors: Accountancy, Computing and Electronics. In 1987 application rates of females to the school were buoyant for accountancy courses but low in computing and very low in electronics. In earlier days, when computing was first developed at UEA and before the foundation of the School of Information Systems, female application rates had been somewhat greater. From the few statistics available, computing was attracting 15-20% of applications from women in the period 1973-1982 (see Table 28.1). The degree programmes then were Computer Studies and joint degrees between Computing Studies and a number of other subjects. There was a small number of mature women applying for places. The figures for the 1988 admissions round show a 13.8% female application rate.

The development of scientific computing over the past ten years or so has occurred at the same time as a diminution in computing's attractiveness to women. It is not possible to say if this is the causal link, as changes in admissions policy as well as

---

[1] **21 Chalfont Walk, Norwich NR4 7NH**
[2] **School of Information Systems, University of East Anglia, Norwich NR7 4TJ**
[3] This paper was written for the 1988 Conference.

changes in the degree courses' perceived attractiveness to women students may both be factors – but the circumstantial evidence appears strong! The School has been concerned for some time over its relative lack of success in attracting women to study these subjects.

Table 28.1 Application Rates

Year	Male	Female	Total	Female as % of total
1973	121	15	136	11.0
1974	122	15	139	12.2
1975	109	18	127	14.2
1976	115	22	137	16.1
1977	158	33	191	17.2
1978	205	46	251	18.3
1979	348	74	422	17.5
1980	402	80	482	16.5
1981	524	127	651	19.5
1982	453	82	535	15.3
****				
1988	313	50	363	13.8

With the first appointment in March 1987 of a woman member of staff in the Electronics Sector in a non-administrative position, the sector has become much more aware of issues of gender, and "women's issues" has assumed a more prominent role.

Coming from a background in technical authoring, applied social research and academic publishing, the new member of staff was entitled Research Assistant, Marketing and Funding, with responsibilities to devise strategies for increasing applications to the undergraduate courses. Success would be measured in terms of an increase in numbers of bodies arriving to study electronics or computing at UEA. It was expected that the post would be funded on temporary contracts, renewed year by year, for three years.

The first step was to look at the existing intake – which was almost entirely young men, mainly with a hobbyist interest in computing and electronics. In addition, some Norfolk students were quite partisan in their choice of university and wanted to study in the area so as to avoid moving too far away from home – a desire which had been expressed by many other students at student recruitment fairs in the region. From discussions with admissions officers from other universities at these student recruitment events, it appears that this may be a phenomenon which particularly affects universities with rural hinterlands.

It was also immediately evident that any increase in female application rates would be of benefit, both to the the social mix of the department and in terms of numbers and quality of students.

In the Spring of 1987, UEA took a hands-on demonstration of some electronics projects to the Women's Training Roadshow. The contacts made there were committed to advancing women's share in the economic and cultural life of the city, and stressed that recruitment from one gender alone halved the potential pool of talent that the courses could draw on. It has also been important to remind members of faculty involved with admissions that the demographic trends, with the fall in the numbers of 16–18 year olds, were not on their side and that they would be in a stronger position in the future if they could think about widening access and strengthening local links, especially if student support is eroded still further.

28.3 Measures Taken to Stimulate Interest from Women

28.3.1 SCHOOL LEAVERS

A recruitment package is being developed in conjunction with the Audio-Visual Centre at the University. In 1988, the UEA Audio-Visual Centre put on a day for Norfolk TVEI Extension which was based around a series of Department of Trade and Industry videos. From contacts made on the day, the idea of working on a joint project which would help the work of recruitment and which would be of interest to the longer-term interests of the Audio-Visual Centre, took shape.

A member of the school's Computing Sector with an interest in making computing available to people with Arts backgrounds already works with the School of Development Studies on a project on problems of computerisation in developing countries, and with members of UEA's Sainsbury Centre for Visual Arts, on a project to catalogue and classify a forthcoming exhibition of Chinese Bronzes. This interest in the broader based applications of computing has led to an interest in cooperating on the creating of a database around three main areas:

1. courses in Electronic Engineering;

2. potential employers;

3. specialisations within Electronics.

The system will also be used to maintain a contact list of organisations which promote the study of electronics and the employment of women and to help to record systematically all the information and contacts which are being built up.

The database will be a supporting package containing supplementary information which will be sent out with a video which outlines opportunities in electronic engineering for women. The video project is still in the process of development; it is currently at the planning stage – finding engineers and students to take part – in readiness for shooting in the autumn term.

A series of interviews will be shot by video. Some have already been done, at a Conference on Artificial Intelligence, Culture and Society, which was held in Sweden in May 1988, with a view to making some useful cross-cultural comparisons. Further interviews will take place with young practising female engineers and with girls at local schools. A rough cut of the video will then be made and will be shown to the engineering professors who have expressed an interest in the work. This dialogue and a series of questions raised by the video will be examined in the teachers' material. The interviews will concentrate on why the respondents took up engineering, their problems and difficulties, and will include, it is hoped, some good footage of the excitement of electronic engineering and why the women enjoy it.

Once the video is completed, it will be sent with the database and a supporting pack of teacher documentation to all interested schools who have the Key Database software.

The video material will also be available for study to determine why women decide to take up electronic engineering, or to avoid it. The qualifications which are needed for the study of engineering and computing are also needed for the take-up of many other careers which do not have the same imbalance of male and female – for example, banking, pharmacy and medicine.

Some pointers have been given by Dr. Kay Sanderson who worked on a Rowntree Project with Dr. Rosemary Crompton of UEA's Department of Social and Economic Studies. Dr. Sanderson reports that recent research suggests that choice of career depends on how women see themselves or project themselves into the future. Medicine, for example, is a profession with unsocial hours and long training and often hazardous and unpleasant conditions of work; so this combination of circumstances is not necessarily a negative factor in career choice. In banking and accountancy, many women gravitate to positions where personal social interaction skills are needed, such as customer liaison and support. The inter-personal nature of the perceived final job may be a pointer in career choice and one which should be investigated.

28.3.2 PUBLICITY

The research will be of practical value if it helps in drafting publicity which will be attractive to a wider audience. A new Electronics brochure has been drafted mentioning that engineering can be a social profession, rather than dwelling on the hi-tech equipment that the student will be using. This hunch needs further examination.

Work in the Electronics Sector is currently centred around organising the publicity for a new degree, including drafting of course brochures in gender-free English, with as many positive and welcoming messages as possible. The title of the new degree, Electronics Design and Technology, is intended to be attractive to a different market. Detailed statistics on admissions need to be collected from the first intake onwards, and compared with those for the students from the other two degrees.

28.3.3 MATURE ENTRANTS

Community links began to develop locally when the Electronics Sector and some members of the Computing Sector took a display to the Women's Training Roadshow in Norwich – an event sponsored by the National Council for Women and attended by a good number of local schoolgirls.

One spin-off from the roadshow was the setting up of an equal opportunities network within local schools. The School was then approached to put on a taster session in electronics for women returners as part of the Cooperative Development Agency's New Opportunities for Women fortnight. This has run for the past three years and has been successful in opening up new directions for many local women, both in terms of study and employment.

The coming fortnight of New Opportunities for Women will see three workshops being put on as the School of Information Studies' contribution:

- Computing Sector will be putting on basic computing;

- Accountancy Sector will provide a session on spreadsheets and databases;

- Electronics Sector will provide a further taster session on circuit design.

28.3.4 WOMEN'S ENTERPRISE AND EMPLOYMENT TRAINING UNIT

Another area of community involvement is with the Women's Enterprise and Employment Training Unit (WEETU), a pressure group set up to fight for recognition of women's employment potential, which is funded with the aid of a grant from Norwich City Council and has recently received sponsorship from the NatWest Bank. We are lucky in Norwich in having a council which is concerned about the employment prospects of its native workers. Norwich is experiencing a boom at the moment and there is a fairly buoyant employment market; however, concern has been expressed that many of the new jobs are not available to local unemployed workers because they lack modern employment skills.

WEETU will be putting on a series of counselling sessions for women returners in the Advice Arcade – a community facility based in the centre of the city next to a large supermarket. A training session will be provided for the volunteer counsellors on providers of training or education for non-traditional careers. A women's cooperative named Boudicca Training, which aims to provide high quality training in the city and its environs, is currently being formed with encouragement and support from the City Council and the Cooperative Development Agency. It is hoped that WEETU's funding from the City Council will make it a desirable partner for cooperative training ventures which could apply for European Social Funding; Boudicca could then be sub-contracted to provide part of the training.

28.4 Initiatives to Make the University and its Courses more Open and Accessible

28.4.1 TEACHER INITIATIVES

An Electronics Teachers' Forum is in the process of development to provide information and support for electronics teachers in schools in East Anglia; however, there are many problems with this initiative, as the teachers concerned are not experienced in this kind of liaison work and the current pressure of GCSE work has left many teachers too busy to develop extra-curricular links. The forum started as a result of a further contact made at the Electronics Now day. Responding to requests from local teachers for help and opening our doors to them and their students in a supportive and helpful manner will become increasingly important in the future, if universities become more regionally based.

In Norfolk the first teacher network to develop was an equal opportunities network and UEA keeps in touch with their work, attending their conferences and monitoring their progress. This is helpful when it comes to advising the electronics teachers, because there is a successful model which has already applied for and received GRIST funding. This network also grew from a very small core of enthusiasts.

The Electronics Sector also helped our local science teachers by providing the final game for the Science Olympiad – Musical Notes. The event was designed and staged by the post-graduate students of the Sector. The event was recorded by video this year and the tape will be taken to the yearly Science Teachers' Conference in Birmingham, hopefully providing Electronics with some publicity amongst science teachers.

28.4.2 BTEC LINKS

A growing proportion of students in electronics arrive via non-traditional routes – in particular with BTEC qualifications. When the Sector was founded it was envisaged that this proportion should be kept to roughly a third of the intake. This target may have to be revised. To maintain a high profile in the locality, the School has entered into negotiations with local colleges of further education, partly in an attempt to solve some of the wider issues (eg grant problems) faced by some BTEC entrants.

The local City College has recently had an access course in Technology approved, to run alongside their Science Access and Social Studies Access courses which are already successful in attracting students. The Technology Access Course will feed both the University's courses and the City College's HND courses. The City College has also formed a committee to try to develop and strengthen the routes to higher education for BTEC students.

Links have been made with Lowestoft College, with several of their students being offered places at UEA this year, subject to good grades in their BTEC exams. Lowestoft College is keen to develop this link which they believe helps their recruitment. They have therefore been helpful in raising the maths content on their courses to be more in line with University requirements and to ease students' transfer to degree programmes. The College is quite forward looking with fairly aggressive publicity. It also has a marketing director whose brief is specifically to market the College – a growing trend among colleges of further education.

28.5   The Development of New Degree Courses at UEA

28.5.1   ELECTRONICS DESIGN AND TECHNOLOGY

The Electronics Sector decided to widen the spectrum of possible entrants by developing a new degree in electronics with fewer pre-requisites in maths or science subjects for entry. There has been criticism of the over-emphasis on the mathematics content of the Electronics Systems Engineering degree; looking at other universities' offerings, it was apparent that reducing the emphasis on mathematics was one option which could be taken. So many engineering degree courses are merely "wall to wall mathematics with a bolt-on project at the end" – memorable quote from Colin Ledsome of the Design Council, himself an engineer. This avenue is a solution which has been adopted by many engineering departments, although it is one which is viewed with concern by many academics and the trend should be properly considered and balanced with the overall objectives of the degree level engineering courses.

28.5.2   OPEN ENTRY SCIENCE

A further development within the University, which has been attracting considerable interest from career teachers, is Open Entry Science.

The University has developed a new general degree in science, designed especially for those who have not studied science since "O" level. This may seem something of a paradox, but research has shown that there are significant numbers of school-leavers who would be interested in a teaching career. The first year of the programme will contain the essential basics of mathematics and physical science, similar to the Science Foundation Course offered by the Open University. Optional courses are available in further maths, physical science, biological and environmental sciences (again similar to the Science Foundation Course offered by the Open University), chemistry and computing. Opportunities exist within the existing arrangement of science teaching at UEA for students to develop and follow their own interests in the second and third years. Students who do well in their first year can transfer direct to the first year of an honours programme, and students who are "late developers" and who complete their general degree to a sufficiently high standard, can do a further year and receive an honours degree. An investigation of the possibility of EEC sponsorship for women applying for this course is being considered.

28.6   Conclusions

The work outlined so far is still in its early days; monitoring and evaluation is needed. Areas which should be developed are those which open the University and the School up to the locality. Measures which will stimulate women's interest and confidence to ask for technological education will be of value both to the University and to the region in the future.

29

Industrial Placements: Women's Experience

Carolyn Whitesmith[1]

29.1 Introduction

Coventry Polytechnic has been placing students on industrial training for many years now and has noticed significant gender differences in proportions of students returning to the company of their placement after their final year. There also appear to be differences in what employers expect/will accept from industrial trainees depending on sex, and on whether they had previously employed the opposite sex. This paper uses both statistics and individual case studies to examine differences between male and female students' experiences during industrial training placements. It investigates whether these differences are a result of students' or employers' attitudes. There are also cases where either students or employers appear to have differing attitudes as to suitability for industrial training and suitability for permanent employment. The paper looks at this phenomenon and considers what, if anything, can be done about it.

29.2 Girls on Sandwich Courses: Background

The industrial training programme on the B Sc in Computer Science at Coventry Polytechnic seeks to provide students with experience of both live information systems and various functional areas within organisations, while allowing them to make a full and useful contribution to the activities of the placement organisation.

The programme lasts for a minimum of 48 weeks and is undertaken outside the Department of Computer Science. The participating companies vary extensively in terms of size, location and type of work provided. The work undertaken is supervised by the Polytechnic to ensure that it is suitable and the student is required to keep a diary and write a report on the work undertaken to meet the requirements for the British Computer Society Professional Development Scheme.

The taught M Sc in Information Technology includes a ten week project based at an external company (unpaid). The aim of this project is to provide the student with the opportunity of developing skills learnt on the course through the production of an individual complete piece of work. These employers are also diverse, but the aim

[1] Dept of Computing, Coventry Polytechnic, Coventry CV1 5FB

of an identifiable project related to information technology means that as a complete project is undertaken, a fuller range of skills can be employed and hence assessed.

29.3   Differences in Rates of Return

The Association for Sandwich Education and Training (ASET) has reported that the percentage of female students who returned to work for their industrial training employer was very much less than for males - 30% as opposed to 70%.

>   Are employers not happy with female students?
>   Are female students not happy with employers?

Polytechnic figures and individual cases imply that employers are as keen to have female students back as male students - about 70% for both. But when female students were asked why they had not returned, there appeared to have been a conflict of expectations between student and employer. Many students who had not returned had experienced a feeling of being a woman in a man's world, or that despite being valued and respected by the people they worked with, personnel management did not regard them in the same light as their male colleagues. One student, who was so highly regarded by the department she worked for, that she was acting as project leader and had two other staff responding to her, was recommended by her manager for sponsorship through her final year. However, the personnel department, who had the final say, showed no interested in her work with the company or on her degree course, and persisted in judging her on her O and A level results. The same company asked another female candidate for sponsorship why she hadn't taken up secretarial work.

Another question to be addressed is whether employers have lower expectations of female industrial trainees. Sometimes a company which has happily accepted a fairly weak female student may complain about a male student of the same calibre. The opposite (weak male followed by weak female) has not given rise to complaints so far, but this may be because of lower expectations of females. On the other hand it may be that even a weak female is better than a weak male.

Women students have no problem in finding placements, usually securing them before the men. One possible (and worrying) explanation for this could be that employers are willing to take females on for what they envisage as one year. but when choosing a male they have a longer term possibility in mind, leading them to be more selective. Employers appear to believe that male students are a better long term prospect whereas in reality young men are much more likely than their female counterparts to get as much experience as possible, then leave for more money elsewhere. The recent British Computer Society survey [BCS 90] has shown that women are much more likely to stay with a company for long periods of time (9 years).

29.4   The MSc Experience

The MSc in Information Technology for Management is a conversion course designed to give people with a degree in anything but computing and a certain amount of life experience the skills to handle IT from a management position. There are three taught terms, with exams, the successful completion of which entitles the student to progress to a project. The successful completion of the project results in the student being awarded an MSc.

The students choose their own projects, and in many ways have a lot more control of the area in which they work. They are also more mature and possibly have more idea of what they want to end up doing. Their project is also an identifiable whole. It may therefore come as no surprise that a much higher proportion of female MSc students return to the employer who commissioned their project. The fact that they are looking for employment immediately after the project finishes may also influence these students - rates of return being approximately equal for males and females.

29.5   Conclusions

If employers are really concerned with retaining female industrial training students then they need to clarify their own ideas. Do they want mobile high fliers or do they want loyal staff, who may also be high-fliers given half a chance, but who happen to be female?

We also need to look fairly closely at how female students choose their industrial training placements. Do we need to supply them with more information about employers (including the number of women in IT with that employer and also the number in positions of high status)? Do they need more counselling - not to try to succeed in obtaining an industrial training placement as soon as possible, but to aim at obtaining the most appropriate training placement for their own abilities and career aspirations?

29.6   REFERENCES

[BCS 90] *Women and WIT: A survey of the female professional members of the British Computer Society*, a British Computer Society report.

30

Does a Masculine Management Style Deter Women Applicants?

Nicky Gunson
Peter Fielder[1]

30.1 Introduction

For the last three years I have been involved in research into the managerial factors which contributed to the success or failure of IT projects. Since completing the research, I have become a lecturer in organisational behaviour in a Department of Management Studies which provides a variety of undergraduate and post-graduate management courses, including several MBA courses.

This paper looks at the content and marketing of the MBA courses at Glasgow University in the light of some of my research findings and asks whether the philosophy of management reflected in the course content is in itself a deterrent to potential women applicants.

30.2 Management Style

As part of my research, I interviewed a large number of IT managers about their jobs; virtually all of them were men. It was only as a result of positive effort to locate them that I was able to include two women in a sample of twenty five. Nationally the percentage of women IT managers is 1.6%. Most of the IT project teams that I studied consisted entirely of men.

What, if anything, is the effect of this overwhelming male dominance on management style. Is there a distinctive female style of management, and how does it differ? Some female managers felt that there was a definite difference in the way men and women managed. They suggested that women used more interactive, participatory, people-centred methods whereas male managers used more quantitative, computer-based decision aids, tended to be more autocratic and to rely on their status as a way of enforcing decisions. Certainly there is some evidence from management literature that writers have made a distinction between what they describe as "masculine" and "feminine" styles of management.

---

[1] Dept of Management Studies, University of Glasgow, 57 Southpark Avenue, Glasgow G12 8LF

Hofstede included the masculine-feminine as one of his four dimensions for analysing national management style [Hofstede 80]. He shows that the countries with a low masculinity/high femininity style coincide with countries with a higher status for women: Scandinavia, Denmark, Finland, Netherlands. These countries also score low power-distance, low-medium uncertainty avoidance, medium individualism. Examples of countries with a high masculinity dimension to its management style are Japan, Australia, United Kingdom, Canada, Ireland, New Zealand, the USA, Austria, Israel, Germany, Switzerland, South Africa and Italy. Hofstede established the dominant management style of the countries by asking a large number of managers a set of questions. How important is it to you to:

1. have an opportunity for high earnings?
   utmost importance/very/moderately/little/very little/no importance.

2. work with people who cooperate well with each other?
   very little/no importance/little importance/ moderate/very/utmost

He concludes that in countries with masculine cultures performance is what counts, money and material standards are most important and ambition is a driving force. **Big** and **fast** are beautiful and **machismo** is sexy! In countries with feminine cultures like Scandinavia the "quality of life" is more important. People and the environment matter, *service* is the main motivation and small is beautiful. Hofstede feels that the major differences between cultures relate to the way they view the relationship between men and women. In masculine cultures the sex roles are clearly differentiated; men are assertive and dominating, women are caring and nurturing. A dominant woman is unfeminine, but is allowed to manipulate in the background. In feminine cultures the sex roles can be more flexible and there is a belief in equality. It is not viewed as unmasculine to have a caring role. To sum up, in masculine cultures high earnings are all important and cooperative group working is not regarded as important. In feminine cultures the main aim is to live in a pleasant area and little value is placed on the need to get *recognition* for a good job done.

But is "masculine" management effective in the long term? Or will management failures force the introduction of more "feminine" methods because they are actually more successful? I decided to look at IT, an area with which I am very familiar. Many computer systems turn out to be at least relative failures, and most failures are not technical failures, but are failures of management. Can this be related to management style?

Introducing organisational change is essentially a political process. Political, negotiating and manoeuvring skills are more important then technical skills. Many workers dislike disruption or redirection and feel that their control, skills, status and interests are threatened. Their competence is invested in the old system and they dislike risk. The management techniques used to prepare people for change have not always worked in the past and this failure has led to underperforming and failed computer systems.

One of the chief reasons for inadequate computer systems is the failure of communication between the user and the technical staff on the project team. Users find it difficult to specify what they need in technical terms and IT personnel often have insufficient knowledge of the business side of the organisation. Few IT personnel have training in interpersonal or communications skills and many are not interested in the human dimension of the systems they are designing. This mismatch is particularly significant at the requirements analysis stage of the systems development cycle, and considerable errors, misunderstandings and inconsistencies can be built into the system at this stage.

There has also been a failure to develop innovative design methodologies in response to system failure. In the past many computer systems were designed to replicate existing information flows, but the design of systems is becoming increasingly linked to the organisation's business strategy and needs to be strongly related to decision making patterns. The older methodologies (SSADM, Jackson, Yourdon etc) do not allow for the increasing importance of understanding organisational issues and politics. They assume that the organisation has a unitary goal whereas in fact each sub-unit may have its own goals, which may conflict with each other as well as with the overall goal of the organisation. Ralph Cornes (*Computer Guardian*) compares structured methodologies with communism "economically inefficient, sociologically outdated and intellectually unsound ... rooted in the 1960's and irrelevant to modern applications ... inflexible, bureaucratic, incomplete and based on the misconception that systems work is purely technical when it is socio-technical".

The third main failure in the management of IT projects is the failure to involve the users in the process of system development and implementation in order that they feel "ownership" of the system once it has been introduced. User-participation in many IT projects is limited to the initial requirements analysis with little or no involvement in the design and development stages. Participation can be "token", with one user designated to liaise with the technical department or on the steering committee but very little attention being paid to them. Users have little control over the acceptance of completed systems, sometimes being obliged to accept them even when they fail to meet business requirements.

These failures in the management of IT projects can be seen as a sub-set of management failures in a wider sense. There is growing recognition that "something" is wrong with UK management, but so far no-one has isolated the problem factors. Amongst these is the "masculine" management style operated by most managers, both men and women, and perpetuated in most management courses due to their failure to present alternatives.

All managers, including IT managers, need to develop more "feminine" management styles, including more consultation, more participation, more feedback before decisions and so on. Although in the short term this may seem to take more time and thus appear inefficient, in the longer term it is worthwhile because it *works*, as managers will have the support of their workers for decisions and changes. The success of IT projects in the future may depend on both the presence of women in the project teams and the team adopting a "female" style of project management. Thus it is important to encourage more women both to do IT courses and to become managers.

30.3 MBA Courses

Although there is a higher proportion of women on the MBA courses than there are women IT managers, they are still in a small minority. Are women choosing not to take MBA's because of the content of the course, or because they do not see the relevance of an MBA to practical management problems?

There are two MBA courses at Glasgow University. The International MBA is a full time course which ran for the first time this year. It has attracted 20 students (19 of them men), equally from European and non-European countries. The students are honours graduates or equivalent and normally have some commercial/industrial experience.

The Executive MBA is a part-time course aimed at working managers. It attracts students from throughout central Scotland. Typically they are in their early to mid 30's and are sponsored by their employers. Total enrolment is about 40 and the syllabus contains substantial work on the application of quantitative analysis to business decisions, as well as managerial finance and investment management. In addition a variety of elective courses are offered, including business policy, competitive manufacturing management, financial management, international management, the introduction of enterprise, manufacturing policy, marketing management and project management. Each student also produces a supervised dissertation.

Over the last ten years the number of women studying for the EMBA has increased gradually, though it is still very low as can be seen from the following table:

Table 30.1 Executive MBA Part-Time 3 Years

Year	Female	Male	Total
1979	2	16	18
1980	1	29	30
1981	0	31	31
1982	0	25	25
1983	2	26	28
1984	1	26	27
1985	1	32	33
1986	0	34	34
1987	3	45	48
1988	3	43	46
1989	5	44	49

The particulars sent to potential candidates emphasise the importance of the "quantitative analysis of business decisions" within the course, which women without a mathematical or scientific background might find off-putting. Many potential women managers may even feel that managerial problems are exacerbated rather than eased by the application of quantitative rather than qualitative analysis. Glasgow University is not alone in having a low proportion of women on MBA courses. Though the numbers are gradually rising throughout the country they are still far below those for men, as can be seen from the following table.

Table 30.2 Ratios Male/Female Students on MBAs

Ashridge	12:1
Glasgow	9:1
Dundee	7:1
Cranfield	7:1
Imperial Coll	6:1
Aston	6:1
Edinburgh	4:1
Napier	4:1
South Univ	4:1
LBS	4:1
Heriot-Watt	2:1

The glossiness of Glasgow's MBA brochure accurately reflects the expensiveness of the courses. Students are often sponsored by employers, many of whom may still be reluctant to sponsor a woman, mistakenly believing that their return on investment is likely to be less in terms of time with the company. It is also much less likely that a woman could afford the fees herself. The second deterrent is that many courses insist on a period of managerial employment. It is less likely that a women will have reached a managerial position by her mid-thirties, because she is more likely to have had a career break.

Does the course content of MBAs reflect the dominant culture of the country concerned? In the UK which, according to Hofstede, has a high masculinity dimension, the MBA courses on the whole emphasise the financial, quantitative, sides of management and little emphasis is placed on teaching methods or on developing participatory or cooperative ways of working. Very few MBA courses concentrate on communication skills, interpersonal relations and techniques of organising participation.

In reality it may be relatively easy to effect a gradual change in management style, because it will be demonstrated that it works and in any case reflects gradual changes in society. What may be more difficult is to change the content of MBA programmes and IT courses! The logic of this is that new qualifications more relevant to the present situation will be developed and the current MBA and IT courses will gradually become obsolete both in content and in form. The content of these new qualifications will include far more emphasis on the people mangement skills, and will be more flexible. The flexibility will allow a relaxation of the requirement for a certain laid down period of management experience, and will allow managers to opt in and out of the course as their pattern of life allows by introducing a modular approach. Cardiff Business School has a modular course which has a 2:1 male/female ratio. Hopefully this flexibility will also make the courses more affordable for a wider range of potential managers and not just those who have already "made it" see as potential management material. In addition, many women will not be attracted to IT careers because of the one dimensional technical perspective that currently dominates the profession.

30.4 REFERENCES

[Hofstede 80] Hofstede G, *Culture's consequences: International differences in Work Related Values*, Sage Publications, 1980.

31

IT: Issues including Role Models and Routes to Promotion

Anne Leeming[1]

This paper[2] discusses some issues which affect women in the IT community. They turn out to be primarily social issues rather than issues which are directly related to or caused by the nature of IT itself. I offer them primarily as a basis for discussion and in the hope that they might help to focus our attention on the lack of women entrants to IT and hence lead us on to explore some possible solutions.

First of all, let me say that I am speaking from the perspective of being very closely involved, for seven years now, with running an honours degree in "Business Computing Systems". The syllabi for this degree come from three sources; the first one is computer science, a good third of the courses taken by the students, especially in their first year, being in this area; another large portion is from the systems analysis and database area and the remaining courses are from the business school perspective. The proportion of women has ranged from 30% to 8%. This degree is run jointly by the Department of Computer Science and the Centre which, until 1988, has been in the Business School.

Again, the comments on group and individual behaviour which follow are not the results of detailed recorded observations but impressions gained as I have worked closely with the students over the last 7 years. They must therefore be interpreted in the way in which they are offered, ie as hopefully useful generalisations and not hard facts.

31.1 Women on computing degrees

Women or girls do not come onto computing degrees because within the schools this type of course is *simply not seen*. We found until four years ago that it was difficult to attract *all* of the students into this area. We attributed this problem to a lack of understanding by school staff of the prevalence and importance of business applications of computing. However, recently we have seen a growth of interest and knowledge among school leavers and mature students. Our total numbers grew to quota level quite fast, though not the numbers of women entrants. The university is largely seen

[1] City University Business School, London EC2Y 8HB
[2] This paper was written for the 1988 Conference.

as an engineering institution which probably contributes to its invisibility to women entrants. It should be noted that our numbers, due to space and other, eg UGC quota restrictions, are quite low when compared with other institutions.

When the women do come, they are very good at the business and organisational disciplines they are being exposed to, and very rarely have any trouble with the technical subjects. They do tend to opt for the more business-oriented options, thinking that they will not be able to tackle the technical subjects.

At job hunting time they have different expectations, usually for jobs of a lower status than the men. On the whole they plan for a shorter timespan than the men do and they rarely set about finding their jobs with quite the same determination and sense of priorities. They seem to me to be demonstrating the attributes of the stereotypical woman quite well. In my experience only one woman graduate did not get a permanent job in the computing field and that was due to other factors.

During the course, both gender groups follow the expected patterns of behaviour, both individually and when in groups for case study work. There are of course honourable exceptions to this. What I am saying is that the women follow pretty closely the expected female behaviour patterns of caring for the group and being sensitive to everyone's needs – super when it comes to users! I might also point out that one third of the staff in the Centre are women who have had good but not outstanding careers in the computing industry and who are very aware of their position as role models.

31.2 Role Models

There is a major point to make about role models. The students do see women teaching and directing courses and, very occasionally, managing staff. However the managerial model they see in the Centre is a man director who frequently makes decisions according to two very simple and commonly used principles: these are to promote to those tasks which carry external status and managerial control according to a) length of service and b) friendship with him. It is quite noticeable among university staff that there are few close friendships across gender lines. There are not that many women lecturers! This may well produce the most appropriate results but it does not produce the right model for either the women or the men students. In addition the women get the usual paternalistic and sexist attitudes from some, but definitely not all, the staff.

31.3 Equal Opportunities and Promotion

The subject of equal opportunities is an open one in the Centre with what is often genuine interest and sympathy for the situation. However none of the men would accept responsibility for changing, let alone acknowledging that they need to change, their attitudes. Whatever one thinks of the situation is largely immaterial; it has to be accepted and included as a major part of the whole task.

Women do get promoted, to the jobs with a large "people" content which stop them doing the things that get them status in the eyes of the University. There is nothing new in all this, neither do these activities show any sign of changing. I do not think we can expect them to change very much without commitment from the people at the top.

We have few ways of climbing the ladder to positions which will enable us to really improve the way our institutions work. Here are two ideas:

1. analyse and copy the masculine way to power and ignore the demands of the students. This would mean that women lost the attributes which actually are highly valuable;

2. alternatively, try to swamp the institutions with women, as is happening in the accountancy profession. This means we must concentrate hard on how to get young women into computing.

We have got to find some sort of middle way which preserves the best of what is available from both women and men in the profession.

31.4   Some possible ways of working

Let us try to use those attributes of the work and the organisation of the job that might be considered to appeal to women. Some of these are:

1. information systems of quality need designers who are sensitive; analysts who are intuitive as well as logical; in fact they need the qualities that are commonly thought of as being feminine. I do not believe that all women necessarily possess these characteristics, nor that men do not. That is patently untrue, but this is beside the point if this observation gives us a possible lead into a way of encouraging more women into the profession. The point here is that the job *needs* those qualities that women often are very proud to possess; this could be part of an information campaign;

2. working conditions: the industry has two quite strongly growing trends which could be seen as favourable to women in the present economic climate – the trend towards contracting, which might be helpful in a male and female job sharing environment, and the trend towards consultancy, which again is exploitable in a small business or home-working environment;

3. routes to other jobs: two reports in the last year highlighted shortcomings of management training in British industry. These included the lack of IT experience among managers and the lack, in management generally, of the so-called feminine skills I mentioned above. Here are two ways in which a discerning young woman might prepare herself for a future career.

31.5 Summing Up

Perhaps it is not so difficult to pinpoint what is wrong with the situation. What is harder is to find ways of dealing with these dangers and problems. It seems to me that we have to find ways of describing the job content that information system/technology graduates are likely to pursue which stress the "people side" of the job and also show that the industry, whether it knows it or not, badly needs these qualities.

32

Information Technology – Art or Science?

Kathy Buckner[1]

32.1 Introduction and definitions

The purpose of this paper[2] is to show that the traditional view of information technology as a science rather than an art is due to historical factors rather than any real requirement. This traditional view has prevented many potential students from considering training in information technology.

What is information technology? Many definitions have been put forward. The British Computer Society has defined information technology as:

> "the application of appropriate technologies to information processing, current interest centres on computing, telecommunications and digital electronics."

or, to put it another way, information technology involves

> "the electrical acquisition, storage and dissemination of vocal, pictorial, (textual) and numerical information."
>
> [CACA]

From these statements we can see that a major component of information technology or information studies (as it is probably more correctly known) involves not only a knowledge of the hardware and software in use but also a knowledge of the methods and means of using the available technology to acquire, store and disseminate information.

So what is this "information" with which we are concerned? [Spencer 85] states that:

> "Information is the organised useful knowledge derived from processed data" and that "data refers to raw material or unorganised facts".

Information can be either verbal, pictorial, textual or numeric and this is critical to the argument – only a small proportion of information is numeric. Increasingly textual

---

[1] Queen Margaret College, Clerwood Terrace, Edinburgh EH12 8TS
[2] This paper was written for the 1988 Conference.

and pictorial (or graphical) information is forming a larger proportion of "information" as a whole. It is also likely that as technological advances occur information transmitted by voice will become increasingly important.

More and more companies are developing a wider perception of information and now see it as a major resource which requires effective and considered management - the gathering and use of information can no longer be left to chance. A result of this is that an increasing number of companies are recruiting information analysts and information officers. Students from information technology courses are well qualified to meet this need.

What does the study of information technology involve? There are many aspects to the study of information technology and some of the major areas of interest are outlined below:

- **Hardware:** Micros, mainframes, input/output devices, storage facilities, peripherals etc;

- **Software:** Applications packages, programming languages, evaluation of software;

- **Information Management:** Classification systems, retrieval methods, indexing methods, sources of information, presentation of information;

- **Information Analysis:** User information requirements analysis, systems evaluation, systems selection, installation, training, types of information system eg management information systems;

- **Communications:** Hardware, software, electronic mail, teleconferencing.

Whilst an interest in computing and information is desirable for students entering this field of study, actual experience via a computer studies "O" level, "A" level or higher is not essential. No previous experience of computers is currently assumed on the HND Information Studies taught at Queen Margaret College. Neither is it necessary for students to have a science or mathematical background[3]. The reasons for this will become apparent later.

32.2 Development of Information Technology as a taught syllabus

The perception of many teachers and careers officers of information technology as a science subject requiring a high level of mathematical attainment at school, stems from the development of the subject from computer science.

---

[3]During 1985-1987, only 15% of male and 15% of female students had a Maths Higher or equivalent.

The early development of computers (and computer science as an academic subject) was in response to a need to rapidly manipulate and analyse an increasing volume of what was primarily numerical data. Early uses of computers for banking and payroll applications, for example, utilised the number crunching capability of the computer extremely well. The technology of the time required that this numerical manipulation was carried out by programming the computer using machine code or high level languages; applications packages were simply not available and neither was ready access to user friendly machines. Users of the information generated by the computer often had no direct access to the machine themselves and used an intermediary to program their requests into the computer. The computer professionals of that time were programmers and systems analysts who were classified as scientists capable of understanding and programming the "number crunchers".

During the late 60s and early 70s query languages were developed to extract information from large mainframe databases and this led to a gradual improvement in the interface between user and computer. Information technology specialists were employed to interpret non computer users' information requirements into terms which the systems analysts and programmers could understand. At that time there were no further education training courses available for such people and they came into information management roles from diverse backgrounds such as geography, physics, librarianship etc. Information had by this time begun to be perceived as not necessarily "numeric" and its use in Management Information Systems was being recognised.

The development of microcomputers at about this time meant that users began to have control of their own information which no longer needed to be held centrally. Gradually during the 70s and continuing into the 80s there was an upsurge in applications packages for increasingly powerful microcomputers. Today's microcomputers are capable of many of the tasks which previously required mainframes. Employers have begun to appreciate the benefits of a good information policy within their organisation and to look for people who can assess their information requirements, identify appropriate hardware and software and implement effective information systems and training programmes. A degree in computer science or mathematics is no longer a prerequisite to using a computer or to a career in information technology.

Some possible careers for qualified information technologists are indicated below.

Information Analysts
Information Support Officers
Information Officers
Computing Support Officers
Information System Analysts
Systems Analyst
Information System Manager
Management Information Analyst
Business Analyst
Computer Training Officer

Many of the positions indicated require (according to a selection of job descriptions in job advertisements) staff to have good verbal and written skills (as well as technical expertise). These are skills which "arts" students already recognise they can excel at and in fact may be better at than their "science" based contemporaries.

32.3 What's Wrong with a "Science" Perception of Information Technology

Two main problem areas which might reduce the potential pool of students putting themselves forward for enrolment on information technology courses have been identified.

Firstly, if information technology continues to be perceived as a science based subject by careers officers and teachers, then it is likely that only students with a science and/or maths background will be encouraged to enrol. This will reduce the potential pool of students considerably by cutting out the arts based students.

Secondly, as it is widely accepted that pupils at school taking science and maths are still predominantly male, this may lead to a smaller proportion of female students enrolling on information technology courses than is desirable.

As information technology courses are not numerically based, students can appropriately be taken from the "arts" side of the curriculum. Tables 32.1 and 32.2 show the figures for students at Queen Margaret College.

Table 32.1

Students on the HND in Information Studies at Queen Margaret College: Art/science highers (or equivalent) expressed as a percentage of all highers

	Female		Male	
	Art	Science	Art	Science
1985	86	14	71	29
1986	86	14	61	39
1987	84	16	91	9
85-87	85	15	72	28

Table 32.2 Students on the HND in Information Studies at Queen Margaret College: Mean number of art/science highers attained per student

	Art	Science
Female	3	0
Male	2	1
85-87	3	1

This is backed by the Pamela Morton of Thames Polytechnic in her Report to the Women's National Commission [Morton 84] who stated that:

"the country will need systems analysts, design and data processing skills
for which science subjects are not such a good background as arts".

With the diversification into the field of "information", the computer has become
the tool or the means to do the job rather than the object of study itself.

There is a growing need for information technologists, information managers and
analysts within society and it is now recognised that the people entering these roles
do not have to enter the profession as skilled programmers. Whilst it may be an advantage for an information technologist to be able to program, or have a knowledge
of programming techniques, it is by no means essential.

32.4 Marketing Courses

Studies in information technology can be as easily defined as an art as a science. There
need, therefore, be no bar to female arts students wishing to embark on this course
of study. The emphasis should be shifted in order to present courses in information
technology as an art to the schools, to inform the staff and pupils of the potential
jobs market and to make the courses attractive to female as well as male students.
This type of publicity should increase the overall number of students applying for
and completing information technology courses as well as increasing the number of
females in the computing profession.

There are several ways in which those involved in higher education can assist in
the marketing process:

a) contact careers officers and discuss courses with them, emphasising the vocational aspects and entry requirements;

b) discuss courses with school guidance teachers; encourage them to visit the college and provide an opportunity for potential students to visit the college and
   see the activities undertaken;

c) be prepared to visit schools and discuss the course with potential students and
   staff.

Marketing of information technology courses is still a matter of education. Many
careers officers, teachers and pupils do not know what is meant by the term and so are
unaware of the possibilities for the future, both in terms of applicability to both males
and females and in terms of employment possibilities. With appropriate marketing in
schools there seems to be no reason why more women should not be persuaded to
embark upon a career in the "information" or "technology" side of computing.

32.5 Experience at Queen Margaret College

That it is possible to attract young women to information technology courses is
demonstrated by the situation at Queen Margaret College (see Table 32.3).

Table 32.3 Students on the HND in Information Studies at Queen Margaret College: Percentage of female/male students in each year

	Female	Male
1985	39	61
1986	64	36
1987	81	19
1988	75	25
1989	52	48
1985-89	62	38

We are in the extraordinary position of having more female than male students on our information technology course. However, this predominance of women students spans all subject areas and stems from the history of the College, which was founded in 1875 as the Edinburgh School of Cookery (later renamed the Edinburgh College of Domestic Science). For most of its life it has provided courses in such topics as Domestic Science, Institutional Management and Dietetics. In 1972 the College was merged with the Edinburgh Schools of Speech Therapy, Occupational Therapy and Chiropody and the new whole was named Queen Margaret College. The courses taught remain predominantly arts or health care based, with a large proportion of female students.

Many students obtain information about the College from an initial interest in one of the better known courses such as Drama, Communications Studies or Physiotherapy and hence discover the HND in Information Studies as an alternative option.

From October 1990, the HND in Information Studies is to be replaced by a new BA degree course in Information Management.

32.6 Conclusion

I have shown that the traditional view of information technology as a science is not necessary, and could be a hindrance. Modifying this viewpoint allows the target population for information technology training to be increased dramatically.

Students, whether male or female, who enter information technology courses without having a mathematics or science background, should not be made to feel disadvantaged; neither should female students be allowed to feel intimidated by or inferior to their male counterparts.

32.7 REFERENCES

[CACA] "Information Technology and the Accountant", *Chartered Association of Certified Accountants.*

[Spencer 85] Spencer D D, *Principles of Information Processing*, Charles E. Merrill Publishing Company, 1985

[Morton 84] *HMSO*, 1984

33

Women: The Hidden Users of Computers

Valerie Looney[1]

33.1 Introduction

Look carefully at the issues surrounding women in computing and there seem to be many contradictions. At one extreme you have an industry crying out for skilled people (an estimated shortage of over 30,000), but which is neglecting to consider seriously women for that employment and which is primarily seeking young male computing graduates, who are absolutely at a premium. At the other extreme, you have the decline in the birth rate, adolescent girls socialised away from science and technology, and the decline in applications for computing courses of all kinds from women of all ages. It's a depressing picture and one which this paper seeks to address.

33.2 The Computer Industry

The computer industry in this country has its origins in the early 1960s. It has grown and expanded over the last twenty years, changing all our lives as a consequence, both in the work arena and the domestic scene. The application of the new computer-based technologies has altered the very nature of work, often making tasks lighter and sometimes changing the existing social relationships. As Cynthia Cockburn writes, "The relationship between jobs shifts too, so that the whole unit – firm, factory, office, institution – acquires a somewhat modified internal power structure. Skill, responsibility, rewards and costs have to be redistributed" (p14 in [Cockburn 87b]). The range of employment in computing is wide and varied but it is an industry run by men, often on the backs of women. Despite being a new industry, companies in the computer field fall into the same categories as others with regard to the employment of women; some of them are very resistant to top level female employees. "Women represent a respectable percentage of positions in programming, systems analysis and sales (of small systems at least) but the numbers of women actually making it to the board room are rare" (p4 in [Morris 89]). Although the shortage of skilled personnel in the industry might be interpreted as good news for women it should be remembered that initiatives being taken to overcome industrial problems by employing more women

---

[1] School of Social and Historical Studies, Portsmouth Polytechnic, Portsmouth PO1 3AS

do not address women's problems in the computing industry. The computer industry is no different from any other in the way it treats its female employees. This is likely to continue whilst a "competitive enterprise culture" endures. Sadly, for a brand new industry, computing has fallen rapidly into a traditional, conventional form with regard to female employment.

New generation computers and increasingly sophisticated computer languages which enable more complex tasks to be achieved with fewer instructions are reducing the need for high numbers of low level programmers. Future demand will be for a smaller number of more highly skilled theoreticians and electronic engineers to develop computer languages and to design and build the new hardware. But if the development of the technology itself is shrinking, the need for advice on its applications is creating a growth in demand for intelligent, creative people who can find out what users really want and translate it into a system designed to meet those expressed needs; people who have real understanding of the user domain and can see the usefulness of the computer as a tool – the "bridging" graduate. The computer industry is also suffering from a critical shortage of articulate and computer-literate consumers. These are the starting points for the course at Portsmouth which is still in its infancy. Emphasis is placed on the students' main discipline area and they are encouraged to think of themselves as historians or social scientists first, and users of computers second – that way we hope to subordinate the technology to the user and only investigate the possibility of computer use when the subject has been assessed as suitable, which usually means in conjunction with other methods of analysis. Computers are not treated as exclusive tools but as possible members of a whole repertoire of analytical techniques available.

33.3 The Portsmouth Experience

In 1987, an internal directive was issued from the management at Portsmouth Polytechnic that information technology was to be incorporated into all degree courses. There was no mention of additional resourcing, and at the time we were already engaged in "rationalization" and severe cost cutting exercises across all faculties. In the School of Social and Historical Studies, the task of implementing the directive fell to two members of staff, who together were responsible for initiating and running an existing first year course in Statistics, Data Analysis and Computing for the three single honours degrees in Sociology, Politics and Social Policy and Administration. In previous years, Statistics had been the main element of these three separate first year courses, but one member of staff had at least one year's experience of teaching statistics via the computing package "Minitab" to the Social Policy students. Despite numerous hardware difficulties, this had gone reasonably well. In the early summer of 1987 it was decided to extend the Minitab course to the Politics, Sociology and History degrees.

The History degree was the real problem, because it had never had either a statistics nor a computing element before. Members of the History staff were in the main extremely antagonistic to the insertion of this alien component into their degree, not least because the timetable was already extremely full and they anticipated that some of their own history courses might not run. This generated a high level of anxiety amongst the lecturers. However despite these reactions permission was sought from the CNAA to incorporate a Statistics, Data Analysis and Computing course into the first year to start Autumn 1987.

CNAA permission to proceed was granted in late summer, too late to amend the prospectus for incoming students, many of whom were dismayed at the inclusion of the new course, and some of whom made it quite clear that if they had known, they would definitely not have accepted the offer of a place on the Portsmouth History course. (Two intending students failed to register at this point, giving as their reason the Statistics, data analysis and computing course (SDAC) – they were both men. It is not known whether they managed to obtain places on History degrees without a computing element). The rest grumbled but still decided to register.

It had been decided, that because of scarce computing resources, uncertain start dates and there only being limited staff input, all four degrees would have to share the same basic lecturing structure, ie a lecture plus a one hour workshop period, at a computer terminal for every student per week. The lectures included basic statistics and a ten week course in information technology, which allowed for "hands-on" word-processing, an introduction to spreadsheets and databases, and some lectures and seminars on the impact of IT in society. The workshop periods were essentially designed to explore elementary descriptive statistics by way of the Minitab package. There was no exam in the subject, but all students had to complete four assessments over the year.

In Social Policy and Administration, the SDAC course, which had already run the previous year, was relatively unproblematic, except for the hardware proving unreliable at crucial assessment submission times. Sociology and Politics too, although experiencing initial teething problems, survived the year intact and without major alterations to the course. The same cannot be said for History. In November, 1987, six weeks into the Autumn term there was a student revolt, which was only just contained. As a result, the SDAC course was rewritten, and renamed Data Analysis and Computing for Historians, and there was a reduction in student hours allocated to the course. The IT and society lectures were refocused on The Early Modern Period and given to a historian to write and deliver and the same historian volunteered to be a Historical liaison officer/representative to the computing course development team. This has been a most fruitful partnership, providing the essential context in which to develop the course.

33.4 Feedback, Evaluation and Discussion

The group of students who had this experience during their first year, have just completed their finals. As a result of that first year experience the feedback and evaluation procedures were extended and provide the basic data for this paper – together with assessments of the two subsequent years. It is realised that the initial experience of the history cohort of 1987 at Portsmouth was probably very damaging to any prospect of eventual recruitment into the computing industry and we think it highlights the importance of that initial educational impact. It gave us substantial food for thought as regards the appropriate and meaningful content such a course should have, and what is feasible and what not. We think we have managed to improve the course and make it more relevant and appropriate for people who do not regard computing as their primary interest but who can see the opportunities that computers bring to their main discipline, providing that they have the skills to exploit them. Ultimately, we may be able to provide the computing industry with individuals well able to become managers, with good communications skills and basic computer awareness, ripe for specific company training. In this category there are more women than men. More importantly there are more "mature" women. Unless the computing industry can see the value in hiring older female staff, many educational establishments are wasting their time. British computing is still a man's world and isn't very keen on becoming co-ed. At the moment the main focus of women's relationship to technology is as its (largely) passive recipients, ie consuming technology, whereas men's relationship can be described as more active, including as it does, generation, construction, assembling and consuming technology[Griffiths 85]. What we need to do in education, it seems, is to meet women at the point at which they are in their relationship with technology, ie as consumers and to build on that. Women easily see the benefits to be had from word-processing documents for example, in building a database of information which can be used to support an academic argument and in using spreadsheets to analyse historical financial data, and with the changes in the computing industry outlined earlier in this paper, there is some hope that we can provide a more suitably equipped and enthusiastic work force in the future. Industry needs to be more flexible in seeing the benefits of older female workers, and women need to have the vision and confidence to apply for jobs in a rapidly changing industry where their skills are desperately needed. "Computing should attract women: it is clean, light work where the best results are obtained by *intelligence* applied in co-operative work groups" [Scholfield 90].

In analysing the data provided by the questionnaire feedback and the interviews carried out with the finalists at Portsmouth, we are able to make some comments particularly on this last point of "co-operative work groups". The assessment for both the SDAC and the Data Analysis and Computing for Historians courses was by four assignments, where group effort was actively encouraged, although all final reports had to be individually written up and presented. Women enjoyed this type of work much more than the men. For some it represented the redeeming feature of the course, maybe the only redeeming feature; it meant working as a team of equals, sharing out the tasks and keeping each other going in order to meet set deadlines. There were more groups of women-only members than mixed groups and there were no women who decided to work entirely on their own, whereas there were several men. As Anne Lloyd and Liz Newell write "One way in which women can more easily learn about technology is with other women, in a non-competitive and stress free environment" [Lloyd 85]. The most difficult problem for these working groups to solve was to get the balance of input about equal between the participants. Where there was a significant imbalance it caused considerable ill feeling, and our crude assessment methods did not do justice to some of the students, whose input was not reflected in their written work. We must develop more sophisticated and fairer methods of assessment if the "feminisation" of higher education is to develop without losing all of the undoubted benefits accruing from the traditionally held attributes of technology such as competitiveness, assertiveness, aggression and dominance. Technology has traditionally been seen to be about control and women have rejected its goals and values. Even when we try to utilise the very considerable talents that women can bring to collective project work, we are strait-jacketed by the means by which we assess such efforts. We are still assessing by individual written documents when they may no longer be the most appropriate method. Comparisons could be made between the use of the dominant culture in Japan, where large numbers of people are employed in software factories, divided into small working groups all working on separate modules for the production of large systems. This labour intensive and non-mechanistic parallel/concurrent development of modules is proving to be very successful in terms of known application problem areas. It is argued that it works because the Japanese culture of work supports it (the ideas of conformity and co-operation predominating)[Cusumano 91].

The brief survey[2] carried out at Portsmouth as part of the on-going evaluation of the SDAC course involved students who completed the course in the summer of 1988. They experienced the first run of the course being incorporated into the History degree with all its attendant problems. Students' ignorance of the existence of the course and unreliable hardware facilities throughout the duration of the course aggravated the problems. Staff felt unwelcome, unsure and under pressure. Despite all these negative points, two years on, many of the students felt that the course had been beneficial in terms of making them more computer aware; they had been alerted to other analytical tools available to them in their study of History, and they could see that there might be a "pay-off" in terms of their employability. They had not been offered the opportunity of an option in a computing subject during their second year, but it is interesting to note that some would have considered taking such an option if it had been available. From the interviews, one of the most interesting comments was

> "Now the dust has settled after that awful first year, I realise that there was
> a genuine attempt to add to my skills as a historian operating in the late
> twentieth century, whereas at the time I had the feeling that the course was
> trying to make me into a statistician and a computer person combined,
> which I strongly resisted".

It has been very important for the staff involved in teaching this course to get the feedback from this small survey. The course has changed quite dramatically since those early days. There is now much closer liaison between History staff and the SDAC staff members, the latter being more obviously tolerated if not exactly welcomed. This has resulted in more relevant and appropriate areas of study being closely integrated within the total History syllabus, particularly this year with the introduction of Probate analysis. Students are certainly less anxious generally about the course, and no doubt because a precedent now exists, they are less resistant to the integration

---

[2]For further details of the results please contact the author

of computing into their main discipline area. They see "computing in its place – as a tool to aid analysis" and the women students in particular have become quite enthusiastic about the possibilities and potential which a more skilled exploitation of computing would give them. Second year students are now suggesting possible areas for computer development for staff consideration at course team meetings. The collective approach to assignments is non-threatening and some excellent work has resulted – although the staff do have difficulty in judging these on the individual level deemed necessary for grading students in their degree.

33.5 Conclusion

In conclusion, the Data Analysis and Computing for Historians course at Portsmouth Polytechnic leads us to suggest that most mature women returners to education demonstrate high levels of aptitude for training in computing which many of them did not anticipate. Industry could benefit from this if it were sufficiently flexible to consider an older female work force. The increasing importance of computers in all walks of life is clear; effective decision making and management already demand familiarity with computing. Women are now trying to redress some of their historic disadvantages, by breaking out of subordination, and becoming more visible. Are men and industry ready to change? In the face of the current skills shortage, our industrial survival probably depends upon it.

33.6 REFERENCES

[Cockburn 87b] Cockburn C, "Technological Change: Short Change for Women", *Social Studies Review*, May 1987.

[Cusumano 91] Cusumano M, *Japan's Software Factories*, Oxford University Press, (forthcoming in 1991).

[Griffiths 85] Griffiths D, "The exclusion of women from Technology", in *Smothered by Invention*, Faulkner W and Arnold E (eds), Pluto Press, 1985.

[Lloyd 85] Lloyd A and Newell L, "Women and Computers", in *Smothered by Invention*, Faulkner W and Arnold E (eds), Pluto Press, 1985.

[Morris 89] Morris J, "Women in Computing", *Computer Weekly*, 1989

[Scholfield 90] Schofield J, "She's gotta have IT", *The Guardian*, 8/3/90.

34

Encouraging Women Returners into Computing Courses in Higher Education

E C P Sears[1]

34.1 Introduction

The statistics on women entrants to computer courses in higher education have shown a worrying trend over the last few years. In spite of the numbers of women on other engineering courses increasing, albeit slowly, there has been a marked decline in the numbers of women applying to and being accepted for computing courses [Lovegrove 87, Dain 88].

This decline is likely to be exacerbated by demographic changes. In the years to the mid-1990s the number of 18 and 19 year olds will fall – between 1964 and 1977 live births fell by 35% [NIACE 89]. The competition for these school leavers will grow as higher education institutions try to comply with government proposals that they should increase student numbers [DES 87].

Employers, aware of the difficulty of attracting young people have turned their attention to more mature recruits, particularly mature women, and have been designing employment packages that will be attractive to them. Higher education could do the same. For those institutions which are less attractive to younger students, for example, city centre colleges of higher education as opposed to universities, attracting women returners makes sense. Such students, currently under-represented, are hard-working and well motivated.

However, any developments in this area need to pay careful attention to the needs of a different group of people from those they are used to recruiting. In attracting mature women, institutions need to consider not only the reasons for the lack of women applicants in general, but also the needs of mature women in particular.

[1] Management Division, Southampton Institute of Higher Education, East Park Terrace, Southampton SO9 4WW

34.2   Reasons for the lack of women applicants

Many reasons have been found for the lack of applications from women. The computer is seen as a male preserve, with computers more likely to be bought for boys than girls [Chivers 87]. Computer games are designed with boys in mind [Turkle 88] and girls are often excluded from the use of computers in schools [Whyte 85]. The general lack of positive role models in non-traditional areas is detrimental to the encouragement of women into technology fields [O'Leary 74] and the socialisation of women at home in stereotypical roles and attitudes is reinforced by teachers at school [Pratt 85]. These factors do not help increase girls' confidence.

The influence of peer group pressure experienced by children strengthens that of adults in discouraging girls from following computing courses [Chivers 87]. Those girls who are not discouraged, find themselves in a minority in the classes and have to contend with ridicule from boys [FEU 85]. While these problems are not exclusive to computing, the linking of computing in schools with mathematics has compounded the problems, in that mathematics is traditionally seen as a "boys' subject" where teachers are more likely to be men [Croydon 86].

34.3   Problems in encouraging women returners

Mature women face the same problems as younger students, although sometimes these problems are exacerbated by the break in their contact with the education system, and they face additional problems. Lack of confidence is accentuated in those who have, for some time, undertaken the demanding but undervalued role of bringing up a family. Women sometimes find that this can lead to a questioning of their own worth and their ability to deal with higher education, which tends to be less "friendly" to women returners than, say, further education, where courses are specifically designed for women in their position [Cowperthwaite 89]. This lack of confidence can be heightened by a feeling among women returners that they lack the study skills for degree level work. This can be due to the type of information sent out by institutions which, with the best of intentions, gives a brief resumé of course content, which is not necessarily easy to understand.

Mature women are also concerned about balancing their commitments. They are concerned about the time management of running a home and undertaking a demanding course where there is always more studying that could usefully be done.

On arrival at the college of their choice many mature students (both male and female) find that the student culture is based around 18 and 19 year olds. They do not feel happy in the student bars or canteens [Bourner 87] and there are few other places for them to go. Yet these are essentially the places where social contact is established and reinforced, and the supportive networks built up which could overcome the lack of confidence and fears about ability to cope.

In addition, the organising institution's culture is rarely geared to mature women [Ball 89]. The bureaucracy of enrolment and grant applications tend to make one feel insignificant and insecure. Teaching is unlikely to be geared to school terms and hours and mature women may well feel out of place [Cowperthwaite 89].

Various studies [Cowperthwaite 89, UDACE 88, Chodorow 78] have found that women respond better to a more informal and student-centred teaching approach, which is now widely used in further education, but less prevalent in higher education where lecturers use formal lectures more frequently.

To help the integration of mature students, thought needs to be given to the most suitable forms of teaching to encourage learning. Whilst this does involve a commitment in staff and possibly finance, there is evidence that those entering higher education with non-standard qualifications do no worse than those with "A" levels [Bourner 87].

34.4   Possible action

There are four areas where action can be taken. Firstly, curricula can be made more "women friendly". Women are skilled in the inter-personal area which is very relevant for systems analysis [Lovegrove 87] and the introduction of courses where the emphasis is on, for example, business applications of information technology rather than the hardware side, would help to achieve this.

This would affect two other areas. Entry qualifications could be reviewed and made more flexible, with less emphasis on "A" levels; and a more diverse range of teaching methodologies could be used – systems analysis teaching can have a high inter-personal skill content which can be taught through a student-centred approach. If work is designed so that students are successful early in the course, with emphasis on hands-on experience, then confidence can be built up [Cowperthwaite 89].

The last area is that of the organisational culture change. This is difficult to deal with and needs to be tackled over time. However, demographic changes work in a positive way – higher education staff are beginning to see the point in trying to attract mature women as their usual recruits become scarcer. As more mature women come into higher education, they provide a focus for newer mature students and can help to change the environment [Ball 89].

34.5   Southampton Institute of Higher Education

Before 1989, Southampton Institute had little experience of recruiting mature women to full-time courses. When a degree in Information Systems was first proposed, the approach of the course team was not fixed. In fact, we did not consider targeting recruitment at mature women when the curriculum was first discussed. However, during the development of the degree we concentrated on:

- developing a course where information technology and business would be linked;

- widening access to the course;

- trying to integrate elements of the course through the use of student-centred workshops.

Research among local employers suggested that a course combining information technology with business studies would be the most appropriate. It was also agreed by the team that the degree should start at a foundation level, so that it would attract those who were interested, but lacked appropriate qualifications. With the two elements – business and information technology – given equal weighting in the first two years, there is less time for more technical elements. This is not seen as a disadvantage, as the team wants the graduate to be aware of both fields and to be able to act as a link between programmers and the end user, but with an understanding of the needs of both.

The four-year thick sandwich course was validated by CNAA in July 1989 for a start in September of the same year. This did not help with recruitment, but it did encourage the team to be more flexible in terms of entry requirements. While applications are welcomed from those with "A" levels, no particular academic standards are set and, because the course is to concentrate on business applications rather than engineering, a high standard of mathematics is not required. In the publicity, emphasis is placed on motivation and an interest in information technology.

As non-standard entrants are to be encouraged, fairly detailed interviews have to be carried out and this is done on a group and individual basis. In order to encourage the mature women who do apply, women lecturers attend both sets of interviews. Group interviews are held to enable the women to see that other similar women are applying and to help them establish initial contact with each other. The group interviews are kept fairly informal and concentrate on providing information about the course. We feel that it is important that there should be at least five mature women on the course to provide support for one another (the "critical mass" idea).

Initial publicity had consisted of an article on the women's page of the local newspaper as well as more standard advertisements. The course leaflet stresses that applications are welcome from women and mentions the course being structured around school terms and hours (although this means a departure from Southampton Institute's usual terms). This change had been agreed on the advice of Southampton City Council's Equal Opportunities Unit.

The course structure is weighted towards workshop and tutorial time, with each lecture being balanced by a tutorial of equal length. It had been agreed that, depending on the students accepted, additional time might be needed for mathematical or particular skills development workshops.

The first series of the weekly workshops are designed to develop the skills needed on the course, both those deemed necessary by the course team and those the students feel that they need. This is done in an atmosphere that stresses co-operative working rather than competition. The group from the first year of the course consisted mainly of mature women and younger students from ethnic minorities and we encouraged them to think in terms of what each could offer to the others.

Initially the workshops are led by a systems analysis lecturer and a behaviouralist, and concentrate on developing a skills inventory which will then be worked into a skills development programme agreed with the students. The skills developed in the early stages of the workshops, such as presentation skills, are reinforced through tutorial work where students learn to practise their skills.

The course team meets regularly, and lecturers also meet on an informal basis. There is a lot of cross-fertilization of ideas which come from the different backgrounds of the lecturers and are shared in joint workshops and tutorials. We feel that it helps the students to see lecturers working together and that it ensures the integration of the course as a whole.

34.6   Where do we go from here?

The women have found adapting to the Institute's environment difficult. They are often seen by younger students as part-time and do not find the social life offered to students as a whole, attractive to them. At present they are a minority group at Southampton Institute, but as more mature students are recruited, more varied interests can be catered for.

Earlier this year an Access Co-ordinator was appointed who has been looking at ways of encouraging more mature students. Meetings have been held with the women returners from this course and those involved in student support (for example, the Student Counsellors and the Careers Officer) to establish the problems and to investigate what could be done. One problem mentioned by the students is the library opening hours, which they would like extended, so negotiations are underway with the library staff about this. The Students' Union has been asked to consider a representative for mature students on the same basis as for ethnic minority students. The consultation system will continue, so that the women returners can feed back their problems as they progress through the course.

We have found that where students experience problems, the informal support that they receive from others is invaluable. This has been particularly useful as the students currently ending their first year have not followed an "Access to Higher Education" course prior to starting the degree. The students feel that the tutor system is essential in helping with difficulties on the course and with personal problems.

Until now there have not been any access courses locally which lead to degrees in information systems. However, Southampton Institute has been approached by two local further education colleges hoping to set up courses which will provide a foundation to the degree. They are concerned that the course team be involved in the design of the access course and that the team has some input during the course. This is a development that we welcome and will be happy to support. We feel that staff in further education have well-developed skills in dealing with non-standard entrants and can provide a high degree of support. An access course gives students time to learn to cope with education, to face and deal with personal problems and to develop confidence without the heavy pressure of degree level work.

We need to develop more links with local employers who can help with third-year placements and we need to look in detail at staff development needs in the light of Southampton Institute's commitment to taking more mature women students.

34.7 Conclusion

Generally, there is still work to be done to ensure that the policy of widening access is supported in practice. However, at the end of the first year the course team feels that we have created a model for other courses within Southampton Institute; the mature women on the course are looking forward to helping next year's first year settle in, and the lecturers have commented on how rewarding they have found teaching mature students – hard work and challenging, but definitely rewarding. We feel that encouraging women returners has enhanced the quality of the course and enriched our environment immeasurably.

34.8 REFERENCES

[Ball 89] Ball C, *Aim Higher. Widening Access to Higher Education*, I Royal Society for the Encouragement of Arts, Manufacture and Commerce (RSA), London, 1989.

[Bourner 87] Bourner T, "Entry Qualifications and Degree Performance: a Report of a Research Project on the Relationship between Entry Qualifications and Degree Performance on CNAA First-degree Courses", *Development Services Publication*, Council for National Academic Awards, London, 10 March 1987.

[Chivers 87] Chivers G, Davidson M and Cooper C (eds), *Women and Information Technology*, John Wiley and Sons, Chichester, 1987.

[Chodorow 78] Chodorow N, *The Reproduction of Mothering*, University of California Berkeley Press, California, 1978.

[Cowperthwaite 89] Cowperthwaite P, Johnston R, Ryves M (eds), *Access in Action. Breaking down the Barriers*, NIACE/Replan Central Unit, London, October 1989.

[Croydon 86] *Girls and Information Technology*, Equal Opportunities Commission, Manchester, 1986.

[Dain 88] Dain J, "Getting women into computing", *University Computing*, 10, pp154-157, Blackwell Scientific Publications, 1988.

[DES 87] *"Higher Education – Meeting the Challenge*, Department of Education and Science, Cmnd 114, HMSO, W London, March 1987.

[FEU 85] *Changing the Focus: Women and Further Education*, Further Education Unit, London, 1985.

[FEU 88] *Information Technology and the Wasted Resource*, Further Education Unit, London, 1988.

[Lovegrove 87] Lovegrove G L and Hall W, "Where have all the girls gone?", *University Computing*, 9, pp207-210, Blackwell Scientific Publications, 1987.

[NIACE 89] *Adults in Higher Education: A Discussion Paper*, National Institute for Adult Continuing Education (NIACE), Leicester, 1989.

[O'Leary 74] O'Leary V E, "Some attitudinal barriers to occupational aspirations in women", *Psychological Bulletin*, 81, pp809-826, 1974.

[Pratt 85] Pratt J, Whyte J, Deem R, Kant, Cruikshank M, *Girl Friendly Schooling*, Methuen, London, 1985.

[Turkle 88] Turkle S and Kramerae C, *Technology and Women's Voices*, Routledge and Kegan Paul, London 1988.

[UDACE 88] *Developing Access, The Discussion Paper*, Unit for the Development of Adult Continuing Education (UDACE), Leicester, April 1988.

[Whyte 85] Whyte J, Deem R, Kant L, Cruikshank M, *Girl Friendly Schooling*, Methuen, London, 1988.

35

Women Returners and Higher Education - Initiatives at Sunderland Polytechnic

Marilyn Ramshaw[1]

35.1 Introduction

This paper mainly discusses the issue of encouraging women returners into computing, based upon experiences at the School of Computer Studies and Mathematics at Sunderland Polytechnic. The courses run are computer studies with a business bias, rather than computer science.

Successful strategies for encouraging women onto our computing courses have included offering the option of a modern language with a degree in business computing and links with a local women's skill centre. The former initiative increased the number of young women on the course from four in 1986 to sixteen in 1989 and the latter led to an average of seven women returners a year for three years on the HND in computer studies (with a business bias). Both these courses were mixed.

Though the closure of the local skill centre in 1988 forced us to seek new ways of attracting women onto our courses, the awareness we had gained of the ability, enthusiasm, and dedication of mature women remained.

The School's three women lecturers were asked to look into new methods of attracting women students. Based on our own experience, and discussions with women already on the School's courses, (especially those from the skill centre) it emerged that there were several reasons why women were not inclined to take up computing courses in higher education. The reasons can be summarised as :-

1. inability to attend lectures because of family commitments (for mature women);

2. lack of information about the courses;

3. lack of confidence.

In an attempt to address these problems the following proposals were drawn up and approved:

---

[1] Sunderland Polytechnic, School of Computer Studies and Mathematics, Sunderland SR1 3SD

1. re-design of the HND Computer Studies timetable to suit mothers, and to include time for extra counselling;

2. organisation of an open day for women interested in computing;

3. setting up of a Women in IT Roadshow;

4. establishment of "access courses".

35.2 The Problems

35.2.1 FAMILY COMMITMENTS

In 1989 the Polytechnic did not have a nursery, and for financial reasons it proved impossible to remedy this. However efforts were made to at least cater for women with school-age children. The HND course was rescheduled so that all lectures, and tutorials for at least one tutorial group, would fall between the hours of 10 am and 2.30 pm. The timetable was also changed to allow work to be done at home during half term holidays. This proved difficult to organise as the Polytechnic's catchment area for mature students spans six different local authorities.

35.2.2 LACK OF INFORMATION

It was also apparent that relevant information about our courses was not reaching prospective students. A major publicity drive was undertaken, based on the new timetables and the access courses which were being developed. The spearhead of this campaign was to be a well publicised open day to be held during the primary school term. The aim of the open day was to attract up to 30 attendees from whom we hoped to gain 8 applicants. In fact over 70 women attended, from backgrounds which varied in a number of respects – social, age, experience and qualifications. Each woman was given advice on the suitability of her qualifications or past business experience to the courses on offer. A few were directed to access courses, the majority being suitable for HND, BA or MSc courses. The confidence gained from this advice session prompted many women to apply for courses. Most candidates opted for the HND because of its shorter hours.

The programme included a hands-on session using software and worksheets prepared by the staff and supervised by current female students. A free crèche was provided. [2] By the end of the day, attendees who had initially felt that they couldn't cope with a full-time course were fired with enthusiasm. Another means of dispersing information is a "road show", where we go out to women's organisations and to girls' schools in the state and private sector.

---

[2]An internal report giving details of our experiences in organising and running the open day can be obtained from the School. It includes details of the methods used for publicity, the response, the format and content of the day and the events which took place.

35.2.3 LACK OF CONFIDENCE

It may have been a long time since women were last in education, and they may not have enjoyed the experience or succeeded. Women are often encouraged to leave school early to start work, and seldom consider a career. Often this lack of self fulfilment in their teens coupled with the working class environment of the North East has reduced their self esteem and stifled motivation and aspirations. Taking the first step – deciding to return to education – is hard enough, but what about competing with younger students straight from school, and what about failure? How does a mature returner with no confidence cope with such anxieties?

One solution is the provision of part-time access courses with an IT component, run during school hours at local FE colleges. Following negotiations, some existing access courses have been modified to include an IT module. Other new access courses have been and are being developed, primarily designed for mature returners. Topics include study skills, confidence building and development of personal skills.

Many women who enrolled on our course were anxious about computers. They were also worried about competing with youngsters straight from school. To ease the step into the course we ran a two day "taster" course for the women, prior to its commencement. These two days were spent on micros, allowing the women to become familiar with machines, keyboards, printers etc and helping to overcome their initial fears of the computer. The group size was twenty, small enough for them to start to get to know one another.

We have found that counselling is required throughout the course, in order to maintain confidence. This is a crucial role which must be played by the lecturers. The importance of this led us to timetable a half hour a week slot for group counselling. These group sessions proved very helpful in removing the feelings of isolation experienced by some women.

All lecturers operate an "open door" policy, allowing students to come to discuss personal problems in private. Much time and effort must be spent on these sessions, and we have found that the students are only prepared to talk to lecturers who teach them, not to the polytechnic counsellors. In the main these sessions consist of assisting the student in overcoming some confidence crisis, and involve listening, understanding, reassurance, and motivation.

35.3 The Women's First Year

As of the end of May seventeen of the twenty four mature women are still on the course. Of the seven who left, two did not have the aptitude and ability to handle the course and after much counselling they were advised to leave. Arrangements were made for them to be interviewed for more appropriate courses. One woman, who left for personal/health reasons, is returning this year to restart the course; another decided that she did not like computing and opted to transfer to a teaching degree. Two women, both of whom had part-time jobs in addition to being wives and mothers, could not cope with the work load. The seventh women left the area due to a change in her husband's job, but arrangements have been made for her to continue with a course at another polytechnic.

All those who remain have passed the assessed coursework modules of the course, and are about to start their end of year examinations in June. We are confident that at least three will do well enough to be transferred to the second year of our degree in business computing. Nine of the women have already secured industrial placements, and will start their year's training after their summer vacation.

We asked the 17 women and 19 mature men on the course to complete a questionnaire on the problems they had experienced during the year. The problems and subjects selected as causing most difficulty or second most difficulty are listed below:

Table 35.1 Problems found during first year

WOMEN	MEN	PROBLEM
8	2	learning again
5	2	family needs
2	0	guilt(no time for family)
2	1	technical aspects of course
1	0	lack of family support
0	3	work load
0	1	meeting deadlines

Table 35.2 Subjects which were found difficult

WOMEN	MEN	SUBJECT
5	11	systems analysis and design
5	2	computer systems
0	3	business studies
2	1	programming

35.4 Conclusion

Women CAN be encouraged into computing but they often have special needs which must be taken into account. These needs are not necessarily difficult or expensive to accommodate, perhaps only requiring a change of course hours and the extra help and support of teaching staff. Women are interested in computing as a career, but they need information about courses and how to find them. Ideally a knowledgeable interviewer should discuss women's experience and qualifications and advise them of the most appropriate courses. Entrance requirements should be made more flexible. Once on courses much counselling is required both on a group basis and individually. This can only be successful if the lecturers are involved in teaching the women, and are sympathetic to their needs.

36

Women Returners: New Initiatives and Experiences

Jacquie Powney,
Janet Toland[1]

36.1 Introduction

The numbers of women students in the Department of Computing at Newcastle upon Tyne Polytechnic are little different from those of other comparable departments (14% this year, 11% last year). The Department offers a range of courses including part-time and sandwich HND's in Computer Studies, a BSc in Computing for Industry, a part-time BSc in Applied Computing and a conversion MSc in Software Engineering. There is also a conversion post-graduate diploma in Software Development which is for women only.

Part-time courses attract more women than full-time courses; HND level courses have more women students than degree level courses. The BSc Computing for Industry, which recruits mainly school-leavers, attracts very few women.

36.2 Tackling the problem

In November 1988, the Department decided to tackle the problem by initiating two campaigns, one aimed at school girls and the other at women returners. The latter was to be tackled first, with the following three approaches:

1. widen access for mature students;

2. develop material and organise events aimed at women;

3. develop women-only courses.

---

[1] Department of Computing, Newcastle upon Tyne Polytechnic, Ellison Place, Newcastle upon Tyne NE1 8ST

36.3   Approach 1 – access

Course entrance criteria were examined and, where possible (ie without devaluing the course), amended to take into account past work experience as well as paper qualifications. As a result, candidates with non-standard entry qualifications are interviewed and counselled as to the suitability of the course for them. This is a very time consuming activity.

Many mature students prefer to start their studies on a lower level course than we can offer. In these cases we direct them to the many local colleges with which we have close working relationships. Specific feeder courses are another method of introducing prospective students to the subject of computing. The provision of such feeder courses for mature students is discussed later.

Most places on our full-time HND and degree courses are filled by people applying through the PCAS system. This process, which starts in September/October for the following years's intake, is problematic for mature students, most of whom tend to apply much later.

36.4   Approach 2 – publicity

We thought that a possible reason for women not applying to us was that they didn't know about the variety of careers and courses available in computing. Two courses of action were planned:

- production of a leaflet aimed at women;
- provision of day courses/open days for women.

36.4.1   LEAFLET

The leaflet, available for distribution in September 1990, will become part of the portfolio of leaflets which the Department of Computing has developed for publicity purposes.

36.4.2   DAY-COURSES/OPEN DAYS

The day courses have been judged a success in terms of enjoyment, information gained by those attending, women applying for places on our courses and the large numbers of women who wished to attend the events. Three such courses have been held so far. The time was split between information giving and practical sessions. We used three computer laboratories, each with facilities for 15 students, which determined numbers for each event.

Publicity for the event consisted mainly of large bright posters displayed in libraries, sports centres, adult education centres, play groups, career offices and employment offices. Advertisements were placed in the local paper and press releases appeared in the "freebies". The articles and advertisements in the papers produced the greatest response, though posters may have a longer term effect, as most are left on display long after the events have taken place.

In response to each enquiry, details on the event and an application form were sent out. Due to the limitation on numbers, women had to apply for a place rather than just turn up on the day. This approach worked in that very few women who had been given a place failed to turn up, in contrast to another departmental event where places did not have to be reserved in writing and many people failed to appear.

The Polytechnic prospectus, departmental and courses information were sent out in advance so that the women were not coming in "cold".

The talk on careers was given by a female manager in a local company which takes some of our students for their industrial placement. She based the talk on her own experience in the industry and this approach was welcomed by those attending.

Each delegate had "hands-on" experience on three different machines. Worksheets were available and assistance provided by staff (male and female) and current students (female). We avoided the "electronic office" approach to the practicals, concentrating on system design using a toolkit, system development using a 4GL and system management using a standard package. After participants had been told of the courses on offer, there was time for an informal chat (and a cup of tea) with members of the department. A free crèche provided for the third day-course cared for 5 children. A lot of work goes into the organisation of these events and on the day, some lecturers are involved all day. Their success has been questioned by some members of the department on the grounds that each event produces comparatively few applicants for our courses. However, those of us involved in the organisation view these days as part of a long term educational process. Benefits will not be reaped overnight, but seeds have been sown.

36.5 Approach 3 – Women-Only Courses

Two types of course were envisaged; a post-graduate conversion course to be run by the Department of Computing at Newcastle Polytechnic, and feeder courses to be run by local colleges but with a Polytechnic kitemark.

36.5.1 FEEDER COURSES

We are currently developing a women-only feeder course in conjunction with South Tyneside College. The course should start in September/October 1990. Students on the course will be given a provisional place on a Polytechnic Computing or BIT course. Polytechnic staff will be involved in the interviewing process and will act as course moderators. The Training Agency has provided money for the development of the course and the local authority and college management have approved the necessary resources.

36.5.2 POSTGRADUATE COURSE FOR WOMEN

The Postgraduate Diploma course in Software Development was run at Newcastle Polytechnic for the first time in the academic year 1989/90. The course is a one year conversion course aimed at women with qualifications (HND, degree, or professional) in subjects other than computing. The course is targeted specifically at women returners, but is open to all applicants including women who have just finished a degree course. This course is funded by the Training Agency.

COURSE CONTENT

The subject content of the course is based on a previous course run by the Polytechnic, tailored to women returners by the introduction of a four week foundation unit, which provides an intensive introduction to programming skills. The Communications Unit also has a substantial input to the foundation unit, helping students who may not have worked for some time to build confidence, and to focus on future career plans.

The course is timetabled between 10 and 4 to give students time to deliver and collect their children from school. Students are only entitled to four weeks holiday from the course, which does not cover half-term or school summer holidays, but the Polytechnic runs a playscheme for school age children during half-term holidays. There is also a term-time playgroup for 3-5 year olds, but this has only 8 places. The lack of childcare during the summer holidays does cause difficulties for women with school age children. The Polytechnic Directorate have announced plans to improve childcare facilities in 1990/91, but no details are available.

The four month industrial placement is an integral part of the course and gives students experience of working in a computing environment. This is very beneficial as it provides a re-introduction to work for women who have had a career break. It also gives students a substantial period of work experience as well as a qualification. During the industrial placement, students are usually involved in the day to day work of the organisation as part of a programming team. This year's placements are with organisations such as British Gas, Scottish and Newcastle Breweries, and the Regional Health Authority.

ENTRY PROCEDURES

The students who apply for the course are interviewed, and given an aptitude test which consists of pattern matching and logic skills. No completely reliable statistics are available, but the testing procedure does seem to give a general indication as to whether a potential student is likely to be a successful programmer. There is a correlation between the score in the logic part of the aptitude test, and the overall marks achieved in the Pascal programming unit.

Aptitude tests are useful in giving some guidance as to whether a student from a completely unrelated background is likely to succeed on a computing course. However, a test taken under examination type conditions can be very stressful for women who have been away from education for a number of years. If an applicant has performed badly in the aptitude test, this is talked through at the interview, and the applicant is given the opportunity of trying again. Some scores improve dramatically on a second attempt, whereas others stay much the same. A poor score on an aptitude test does not necessarily disqualify the student as other factors are taken into account as well.

STUDENT PROFILES

There are 12 students currently on the Post Graduate Diploma, from a wide range of backgrounds. Two were programmers in the sixties but have not programmed for 15 years and need their skills updating to reobtain employment in computing. Many students have had successful careers in other disciplines, eg social work and administration, but wish to change direction. Others have been unemployed since completing arts degrees.

On a conversion course of this nature, the varying background of students can cause problems. Students with a science background are definitely at an advantage compared with students from arts and social science backgrounds. On the other hand, the advantage of a mixed input is that group working can be used to encourage students to share different skills and learn from each other.

Group working techniques are used throughout the course, both because they are thought to be a valuable and economic teaching method and because team working skills are in demand in the computing industry. Group working skills are developed during the foundation unit and drawn on throughout the course by the use of group assignments. 40% of the final assessment for the course is from two workshop exercises which students complete in small groups. This tactic has been very successful; the students have "gelled" well, and are very supportive towards each other. This is helped by the fact that numbers of students are small, and that the students are all women.

ISSUES

The course began with a four week foundation unit, which included an intensive introduction to programming. As well as spending twenty timetabled hours at the Polytechnic, students were expected to spend a considerable amount of time working on their own. Six students dropped out during the foundation unit. Four students left because they were offered jobs, one due to family illness, and the sixth because she found the course too demanding. The fact that the course is very intensive does cause problems, particularly for women with family commitments. One solution would be to offer the course part-time over two years, but Training Agency funding is not available for part-time courses unless it can be proved that relevant part-time employment is available upon completion of the course.

The Polytechnic computing facilities are available until 9.00 pm on weekdays and on Saturday mornings. Twenty four hour opening, seven days a week, would allow students greater flexibility.

Relatively few students on the course have children. The fact that the course is intensive and that it covers school holidays make it very difficult for women with patchy childcare arrangements to cope. The Training Agency does offer up to £50 a week towards childcare costs, but this is only available to lone parents. Of the two students with small children, one is a lone parent, the other has a husband whose work is home-based so that he can pick the children up from school. Various options for childcare facilities have been suggested to the Polytechnic Directorate; we await a decision.

We will not be able to judge the success or otherwise of the course until the first year is complete; by that time we hope to be on our second run through.

36.6 Future Plans

In 1990 the Department of Computing is to be involved in the 1990 WISE event for the first time. This is the first step to addressing the problem of lack of women on the BSc Computing for Industry. Our work in encouraging women to follow a career in computing will continue over the next few years, but we will need new ideas to keep the campaign alive.

37

SWIM: Scottish Women Returners study Information Technology Management

Helen D Watt[1]

37.1 Introduction

This paper describes an Information Technology Management Course, designed with women in mind, at the University of Glasgow. The course (SWIM), which lasts for 30 weeks, is held during school hours for mature women students whose first qualification is in a subject other than computing science. It was designed to assist women in developing their confidence and updating their skills so as to take up careers after a break, while at the same time combating the shortages of skilled IT staff. Funding for the course was obtained from the Training Agency.

The Department had previously (in 1987/88 and 1988/89) run intensive 20 week courses for arts and social science graduates, also funded by the Training Agency. Experience gained from teaching these non-science graduates plus the feed back received from trainees attending the courses were invaluable in deciding the content of the new course.

The need for such a course was apparent as industry was actively seeking more people with IT skills. The report of the "Women into IT" Campaign Feasibility Study stated that

> "Shortages of skilled staff are far and away the most significant obstacle to the more widespread and effective use of IT and have been for the past five years."

and

> "Most of the predicted IT jobs of the future will demand business aptitudes, people orientated skills and 'Multi-tasking' management potential more than technical ability."

There especially seemed to be a need for people who would be able to fulfil the vital task of bridging the gap between computer professionals and business professionals by being able to communicate with both. It was therefore decided that the Glasgow

---
[1] Computing Science Department, University of Glasgow

approach would be to take people with all the organisational and multi-tasking skills, which being a homemaker demands, and transform them into the computer literate managers of the future.

The Training Agency approved and funded 24 places on the course, which was to run from September 1989 to June 1990. All classes would be held between 09.30 and 15.00 and there would be no teaching during school holidays. Participants would also be offered an optional period of a 12 week work placement to take place after completion of the course.

The new course was advertised in early August. Applicants were asked to complete a standard application form and return it together with a current Curriculum Vitae and a letter stating why they wished to take the course. Suitable applicants, from which the final 24 were selected, were interviewed in the Department.

Most of the trainees had degrees in arts and social science subjects, typically English, French, and History. A minority had been in part-time paid employment but most were full-time carers and homemakers. In fact some had never embarked on a career as their family commitments had started immediately upon obtaining their first qualification. Only one or two had previous computing experience and few had keyboarding skills. The majority had not encountered any formal mathematics since their schooldays.

All these factors have been taken into account in the way course material is presented. Modules are taught completely from scratch in a constructive and practical way.

37.2   Aims of the Course

The main aim of the course is to allow women to update their skills and to learn modern information management techniques in a supportive atmosphere. The emphasis placed on the acquisition of practical skills is reflected in the proportion of time which is allocated to "hands-on" activities.

SWIM is designed to provide experience in the organisation, manipulation and distribution of information. These activities are central to almost every use of a computer. It also provides familiarity with terms encountered in the use of computers in a variety of situations.

The course sets out to teach a broad range of topics within the field of computing/IT and related disciplines. Topics covered include:-

keyboarding skills; drawing packages; word-processing; spreadsheets and business graphics; database management systems; integrated software packages; desk-top publishing; accounting applications; electronic mail; principles of programming; computer project management; operating systems including Macintosh, MS-DOS and Unix; human-computer interaction; filing systems; networks and communications.

Other course features include:-

> presentation skills; assertiveness training; time management; field trips; counselling; experience of working individually and in groups; continuous assessment/feedback and optional work placement.

Students should gain an appreciation of the problems of producing, purchasing and installing computer systems in a business. They should also be conversant with the principles of the Data Protection Act and the need for security.

By completion of the course, students should be well equipped to make rational decisions about when and how to use computers. They should feel at home with automated support of their professional work in any chosen career and be able to interact successfully with technology suppliers and computer professionals.

Comparing a computer to a car, the overall objective of the course is to teach course participants to drive the car, not to delve under its bonnet.

37.3 Structure and Content of the SWIM course

The course is structured into 3 terms of 10 weeks. Due to the Autumn school break, there is a one week holiday between the end of week 2 and the start of week 3. There is also a two-day registration and introduction programme before the start of the term.

During this pre-term period the successful applicants are officially welcomed to the department and shown round. They are given more details about the course and meet the staff. Administrative tasks such as registration for computer use and library facilities, and filling in Training Agency forms, are also undertaken.

More importantly, this pre-term session is an opportunity for the women to get to know course staff and each other in a relaxed atmosphere. For many of them, coming on the course was a big step to have taken, and they were nervous. A buffet lunch was provided on the second day to help trainees to mix and thus overcome any fears and generally break the ice.

During the 30 week course, trainees have daily access to two laboratories equipped with a sufficient number of Apple Macintosh computers to allow individual access to equipment and software. Both laboratories are sited within the Computing Science Department, giving trainees the opportunity of becoming involved in the activities of staff and other students in the department. During the third term the group also has access to a laboratory containing IBM-PCs. Thus trainees can gain hands-on experience of using packages and operating environments on different types of computers.

During the first 20 weeks of the course, new material was introduced by following each two hour formal teaching session (in the morning) with a 2 hour practical session (in the afternoon) based on the material presented. Formal teaching was accompanied by a practical demonstration achieved by using an overhead projector linked to an Apple Macintosh.

At the end of each module, this pattern of morning lectures was broken to allow trainees to spend a few days concentrating on more substantial practical projects. Each project pulled together all the material presented in that module and built on the experience gained during previous exercises and modules. Whereas re-inforcement exercises were done individually, projects varied between individual and team activities. These projects were assessed and feedback was provided to the trainees.

One hour per week was allocated to a review session with the Course Director. This provided the trainees with the opportunity to raise issues which are pertinent to the whole class and to have any material presented during that week revised or re-inforced.

During the last 10 weeks only a few lectures are presented. Two and a half hours each morning are spent in the IBM-PC lab. In weeks 21-25 the afternoons are used for projects using the Macintoshes, whereas weeks 26-30 are devoted to a substantial individual project using any of the material and software previously introduced in the course or investigating new software. Trainees can use either the Macs or the IBM PC's for this.

During this final project, trainees can obtain assistance any afternoon by contacting either a tutor or any member of the course lecturing staff. Throughout the remainder of the course, tutors are on duty in the laboratories to provide practical guidance and support.

37.4 The Trainees

Considering the shortage of time between placing the advert and the start of the course there was a good response. The 24 candidates chosen came from a variety of backgrounds.

The common factors were that they all lived within travelling distance of the University, that they had experienced a career gap, and that they hoped that this course would provide them with sufficient knowledge to return to employment.

For a variety of reasons, many of the women found the first few weeks of the course very difficult. Most found that they needed time to adjust to this new way of life. Coping with the course and the amount of travelling involved, added to their normal family responsibilities, was very tiring during this initial period. For some there was a conflict of interest between their wish to attend the course and other commitments, for example one woman was moving house. Others were having an internal struggle with themselves because at some stage in the past they had made a conscious decision not to learn to type. This caused severe problems when learning how to use a keyboard and seemed to give them a mental block when it came to learning word-processing. A few were frightened that they would break the equipment and couldn't believe that the worst that was likely to happen was that they would delete a file or not save the work which they had done.

All the women set themselves too high a standard, expected too much of themselves and became frustrated at the length of time it took them to do even the simplest things compared to the experienced course tutors. They also made things more difficult for themselves by not taking the exercises at face value and reading into them more than what was required, or by quietly getting themselves more and more confused before asking for help. Once they realised that the tutors were there to help and not to judge or criticise, this problem mainly disappeared. As the trainees got to know one another and to become aware that they were not the only ones experiencing problems, they began to help each other and a warm and friendly developed in the laboratories. Although they could use either laboratory, the majority went to the same one each day and in some cases always used the same machine.

Even during the initial difficult period it was obvious that the trainees were keen to succeed. During the first few days of the course the women learned how to use a drawing package. They were eager to obtain printouts of their work to take home to show the children: "What mummy did today", as a few told me. They thought of this as playing, not realising that they were learning important skills like using the mouse and the pull-down menus, opening and closing an application, sending things to the printer, cut and paste instructions etc.

During the first week a large amount of basic terminology was introduced. Questions such as "What is IT?" were addressed and followed by examples from real-life. This prompted considerable discussion and nicely led into the first assessed exercise which was to write an essay on "How IT has affected an area which interests you". This project was given out in week two of the course and had to be handed in as a laserprinted document at the end of week three. The trainees were also told at this time that they would have to give a 10 minute presentation to the class during week five, which could be based either on the material in their essay or on a separate topic. The one week break between weeks two and three of the course allowed the women time to digest the material presented in the class and to think about their essays. This was particularly useful for those women who were experiencing difficulties with the use of a keyboard.

For many, writing the essay was difficult because of the length of time since they had last done anything similar. They also had to make decisions about the layout of their final document, such as choosing font, style, where to place rulers and how to use tabs. A few of the women had teaching backgrounds, which assisted them in the preparation and presentation of their material to the class. However, for the majority, this was their first experience of presenting material in this way. In general the trainees required a lot of counselling and support during this time. However they experienced a great sense of achievement when they realised that they could present material both as a written document and orally.

Unfortunately one of the trainees had to leave the course in the middle of the first term due to family commitments.

Throughout the remainder of this term each of the women continued to experience her own highs and lows. Difficulties with the material varied considerably depending upon each individual's previous experience. The review sessions were exceedingly useful during this period as they provided a weekly opportunity for problems to be aired and ironed out. Individual counselling was also available as and when necessary. In these cases it usually turned out to be an external problem which was affecting an individual's work and thus causing frustration. Having someone who was prepared to listen was often sufficient in clarifying the situation and changing the mountain back into a mole hill.

All of the women welcomed the 3 week vacation at Christmas and came back at the start of the 2nd term with renewed energy. On the whole very few major problems occurred during this term. Some trainees began actively to study the job adverts which appeared in the press and a few began to apply for the positions advertised. Two left to take up interesting jobs. The fact that they were attending this course had assisted them in obtaining these positions.

The trainees' growing confidence became apparent in the second term, not only in their appearance but also in their new liveliness in lectures and group discussions. The standard of project work continuously improved.

In the third term there was a smooth transfer to the use of different equipment, with most trainees appreciating the challenge of learning to use different packages in a different operating environment. The realisation that the skills which they had learned were transferable was very important to the class as a whole.

Another two women left to take up employment, on the one hand disappointed at not being able to complete the course but on the other excited at the thought of taking up their new positions.

At the time of writing, the course is in its 26th week and the 19 remaining women returners are beginning to get their teeth into their individual projects. Most are beginning to think about the type of jobs they will seek. A lot of doors are now open to them which were previously closed. Some already have jobs lined up or are going on to do further courses. The fact that they are attending this thirty-week course has made employers look at them in a different light and has definitely helped when it came to interview selection.

Some of the class wish to take up the option of doing a 12 week work placement.

37.5 Future Intentions

The department had hoped to re-run the course in 1990-91. There seems to be a demand for a dedicated course of this kind which can cater to the needs of people wishing to re-enter the workforce.

If the second year of the course had gone ahead, I would have made a few minor alterations. I would have started in the first week by placing the women into small groups in order that they could gain more confidence and support from each other. Although each woman would still have individual access to equipment and submit her own work, a group approach would have reduced the initial feelings of frustration and assisted the trainees to discuss their own problems more openly.

Unfortunately however, the Training Agency has refused funding for the course for next year on the grounds that it is too expensive.

I am both disappointed and surprised at this response This course has been beneficial to all the trainees, has had an exceedingly low drop-out rate (1 in 24) and even prior to its end has produced successful outcomes (4 in 24). It would be easy to reduce the costs by providing less equipment and/or less assistance. However I feel that this would seriously impair the quality of the training provided and thus be less beneficial to the women who would take it. To run a course of this type properly each woman needs to have access to modern equipment and up-to-date software. I also feel that practical hands-on sessions require supervision by an adequate number of professional staff. The ratio of tutors to trainees on the current course during practical sessions has been 1:6. When this is added to lecturers' time, preparation of handouts, administration, provision of manuals, books, disks, etc, the cost of running a high quality course tailored to returners' needs is expensive.

37.6 Conclusions

This course has proved that there is a need for a course on Information Technology Management which caters to the needs of women wishing to return to employment after a career break.

SWIM has allowed the women to update their skills, build up confidence and learn modern information management techniques in a supportive atmosphere without them having to pay fees or travel which for many would have been prohibitive.

With the shortage of skilled staff becoming more serious, I hope that others will consider running a course of this type and that this paper will assist them in this venture. I have found assisting the current trainees to learn new skills and prepare them to restart careers a rewarding and worthwhile experience.

38

WISE UP: A New Course for Women Returners Run at Reading

Jennifer Stapleton, Shirley Williams,
Jane Goodwin[1]

38.1 Introduction

The course under discussion here is aimed at helping women return to the software industry. This is achieved by helping them to regain confidence in their existing skills in the computing industry and to update and consolidate their knowledge of software engineering; hence its name – Women In Software Engineering UPdate. The course covers the entire software life cycle from feasibility study to maintenance, looking at methodologies and tools for each phase[2]. For instance, formal methods of specification are introduced; very few women who have been out of the industry for any length of time will have experienced these more rigorous approaches to software specification. The course teaches aspects of project management, costing, general information gathering, data analysis, programming in C and systems analysis using Yourdon and JSD. In addition confidence building topics are covered, including such subjects as interview skills and CV preparation.

38.2 Motivation

It is a well recognised fact that more people are going to be needed in computing as this decade progresses. Many of these are going to be women who have taken a career break, but very few opportunities exist for them to return to the job in which they were once professionally competent. There is a need to jump the significant hurdle of technologies which have advanced leaving the potential analyst or programmer behind. This is more a problem of recruitment than anything else. The type of mind that could cope with the thought processes involved in computing ten to fifteen years ago has kept the logical approach that it once had and has gained in maturity of outlook. However, since there is a perceived need amongst employers for up-to-date knowledge targeted to a specific programming language or design methodology, women

---

[1] Department of Computer Science, University of Reading, Whiteknights, Reading RG6 2AX

[2] A syllabus may be obtained from the authors.

must look for the right form of retraining.

In 1988, Hilary was one of the women facing this problem. She had been a programmer for eight years but had not worked in computing since 1982. She attended a general women returners short course at Reading University and then proceeded to look for a course in computing that was more than the usual "BASIC for Beginners" offered by Adult Education. When this failed she investigated Employment Training opportunities locally and again found that they were too low level for her requirements. She mentioned this to the tutor of the women returners course and the idea for WISE UP was born.

It was felt that situated as we are in Silicon Valley there must be many women locally who had been in computing in the past. This idea was reinforced by the fact that many people meet their spouses at work: the large number of computer professionals working in the area made it very likely that the concentration of women facing the same problems as Hilary would be quite high. This has indeed proved to be the case.

38.3 Getting Going

The major problem that we faced was how to fund the course so that it would be accessible to women who had no personal source of income until they had completed the course: Catch 22! Fortunately the Training Agency has a special fund for women, ethnic minorities and disabled people in its HTNT special programmes budget. So the course would be free to all course members. However the Training Agency insist on a work placement being an integral part of any course that they fund. So we had to find suitable industrial placements for the course.

We were very fortunate in being in contact with Usha Seegobin of DEC College in Reading (Digital had sponsored the general women returners course). Usha is very committed to solving the problems faced by women in employment and in particular in helping competent women return to the job scene. With Usha's enthusiasm as a base we were also able to persuade IBM, ICL and Hewlett-Packard to provide work placements for the course. We encountered several problems during this process as we needed to find someone within these organisations who also felt strongly that women were an important resource that remained largely untapped. We were often discouraged as we were passed from one department to another. However, Usha's dedication and enthusiasm at all the meetings we held with our industrial partners proved a mainstay.

We felt it was important that the industrial partners took a significant part in the planning process so that they would feel that they were not just supplying a service to Reading University. Hence our draft syllabus was circulated to all our partners, who commented on its content. Most of the comments were incorporated into an upgraded syllabus which contrived to meet all criticisms. We felt able to withstand the criticism that academics do not understand the problems of industry since all of us have worked outside the academic environment (one is indeed a very recent entry into academia).

It was originally planned that the industrial partners should also supply women speakers to talk on their specialist subject. This proved to be too difficult to coordinate and was ultimately dropped. However, they were able to provide a panel of women returners who spent a day with the course members discussing the problems and delights that they had encountered when restarting their careers. We were also hoping to receive hardware from each of our industrial partners which would be dedicated to the use of the women on the WISE UP course. However this also proved to be a thorny problem so we decided to use University equipment.

While all this preparation was proceeding we were still unsure that the course would be able to proceed as we had no firm contract with the Training Agency. We originally submitted a proposal which included a large amount of money for the considerable preparation time required. This was turned down as being too expensive. With persistence we found what sort of figure they would countenance and submitted another proposal on that basis. This was accepted after a close examination of our aims, syllabus and in particular of the potential market for the course. They wanted to be absolutely sure that there were women of the right calibre in the Reading area who would benefit from the course. The Training Agency agreed to fund two pilot runs in 1990 and insisted on giving us extra money so that each student could be given copies of the course textbooks.

We saw our market as women with school children so we decided that the course would run within one school term(ie for twelve weeks), five days a week between the hours of 9.30 am and 2.30 pm. Because we would be accepting applications from several counties we did not plan for a half term break. In addition to solving the possible logistic difficulties, we felt this would ensure that women considered their child care difficulties more closely.

38.4 Recruitment

Having finally received the go-ahead from the Training Agency to run the first pilot course from January to March 1990, the next problem was to find the women we knew were out there. Fortunately one of our number is very experienced in marketing short courses and knew the procedures for circulating leaflets and posters to local libraries. So we ran off two thousand brochures and two hundred posters. From these we managed to obtain one response! However, we also circulated a couple of press releases to all the local papers. From these we received a far greater number of replies, most of which were from the type of women that we were targeting. However, some were from women with unsuitable backgrounds for our course who wanted to break into computing: this is an area which needs attention, but it would require a different approach. We also received applications from men who faced the same job re-entry barriers; one male systems analyst had spent three years looking after his aged mother and now could not find work because he was out of date. Because of the source of funding we were unable to help these men but there is obviously a need here that is not being addressed.

Also as part of the recruitment campaign we held a very successful open evening during which we outlined the course contents. Each of the industrial partners sent a representative who gave a short talk on some aspect of women returning to computing generally or to their company. They also talked about what their company expected to get out of the placement. This is very much a two-sided affair. The course members experience real work in a modern environment which is to their benefit and the companies get some work done for free while having a look at the capabilities of potential employees. After the more formal part of the evening, the potential applicants discussed their concerns informally over coffee with ourselves and with the industrial partners. This proved to be a very useful exercise as we were able to allay many fears of lack of competence.

Following the open evening we held informal interviews to discuss employment histories and work expectations. To make the interviews as unintimidating as possible, we saw the applicants in pairs so that they could see that someone else felt just as scared as they did. One industrial partner asked to sit in on the interviews and this was agreed to, on the understanding that the final decision as to whom we should select would be ours alone. However pressure of work prohibited her from attending, so we cannot comment on how that would have worked.

We were given funding by the Training Agency for fifteen places but recruited sixteen students in case anybody should drop out. (In the end, sixteen was a preferable number because it made working in pairs possible without always having a wallflower to be grafted onto two others).

We successfully recruited a group of women who would work well together. All but one were graduates. Some were programmers and some analysts. Some had scientific and engineering backgrounds but the majority had worked in commercial environments. The majority were aged 35-45, but the actual age band stretched from 27 to 50. The length of career breaks varied enormously from two years to seventeen years. So we knew we were going to be addressing a wide variety of experience levels. Most of the women lived locally and had young families, but one whose children were grown up travelled into Reading daily from the Swindon area, a distance of about 50 miles.

38.5 The First Days

On the first morning we were in very early, as were most of the course members. They were obviously nervous (and so were we). We used the well known icebreaker of pairing the students and getting them to chat for five minutes before introducing their partner to the group. This quelled nerves and by coffee time everyone was talking, mostly saying how they hadn't slept the night before. The rest of the first day was spent on administrative tasks (distributing user IDs for the equipment they would be using, obtaining library cards and filling out the seemingly endless Training Agency forms) and on a course overview.

The next day was entitled "In at the deep end" as the students were introduced to modern hardware and operating systems including the use of mice and windows. Working in pairs lessened the strain and the exercises were designed so that the students succeeded. Part of the next day was spent on confidence building before diving into C. By the end of the first week we were relieved that all the course members were still with us: they all stayed for the full length of the course.

Most days, we followed the pattern of introducing a new topic, using this in a small group exercise, a bit of playing with computers and a recap. Throughout their time at Reading, the women worked hard and fast and it soon became obvious that it was quite acceptable to work at a rate in excess of that acceptable for full-time courses because the working day was only five hours (less time for coffee and lunch). This indicates that employing part-timers may be a way of getting better value for the salary paid than with full time staff who must necessarily take time to relax. This appears to be contrary to the received wisdom of many employers.

38.6 Industrial Placements

An extremely important part of the course was the industrial placements that all course members undertook. The placements, like the normal course days, ran from 9.30 to 2.30. The first two weeks of the course were purely classroom-based. In the second week the course members were given details of the placements on offer and asked to rank them in order of preference. For many of them the location of the company was as important as the tasks, since although all the companies had supplied work in the Reading area, the drive from home could be as much as an hour for some after depositing children at school.

The placements began with an introductory day in the third week of the course, during which the women were given fuller details of the work that the companies required of them. They were very nervous of the introductory day beforehand and required a great deal of support from each other and from the course tutors but all subsequently expressed themselves happy with what they had found.

The companies took varying numbers of course participants. ICL had a serious staff shortage in analysis at the site where they were offering placements so offered work to eight students. Digital and Hewlett-Packard offered three places each and IBM offered two (this was mainly because most of their sites are inaccessible to those living to the East of Reading where most of our women came from). The majority of the placements were in pairs but two students were asked to work alone which they handled very well considering that they were going into an unknown environment and tackling work in areas with which they were unfamiliar. It had originally been proposed that the placement groups worked as teams to provide mutual support but the companies could not provide appropriate tasks for this way of working. The tasks that the students were given were all jobs that needed to be done rather than manufactured for WISE UP. The students all appreciated this very much. They felt that during their eighteen days on placement (two days a week for nine weeks) they really got back into the swing of working without the pressure of feeling that mistakes would not be tolerated since all the companies knew that they were still learning. A problem that did arise was that they felt a lack of continuity when working three days a week in the classroom and two days a week on site. However as time progressed, they came to value the break from the placement because it gave them time to reflect on problems that they had encountered. In this way the time on placement could be used more fully.

38.7 The End

The prime aim of the course was to get women back into computing who had become out of date through taking a career break. So its success can only be judged on how easily they found jobs afterwards. To this end we spent one day introducing them to companies who were geared up to providing flexible working for women in computing. This was a very interesting day for the women as it gave them a chance to focus on the problems that they faced in finding the sort of working schemes that would be near their ideal. Almost all of them wanted to be able to work in a computing environment during school time, to work at home some of the time and if possible to have long school holidays as free as possible to spend time with their children.

One company who came to talk to the course was a tiny startup company run by two women who arrange job-sharing for professionals. Not much was expected from them. However they sent three of our students to one local company who were so impressed that they offered all three jobs. (Two of the three had other job prospects which they eventually took up). The other two companies were ICL CPS and FI plc. Unfortunately FI did not come over very well and none of the women opted to apply to them, which seems strange since they are one of the prime employers of women requiring flexible work in computing. One student was accepted by ICL CPS. Two students have found work for themselves in the Civil Service at sites near to their homes. The women on placement at ICL were almost all verbally offered work on a part-time basis (one was rejected because she was not British born). However due to a recruitment freeze, these offers were withdrawn, dashing the confidence of some. All of them had turned down other job offers on the strength of the possibility of working in an environment they knew. IBM offered a six-month contract to one of the two women that they had on placement. Unfortunately Hewlett-Packard and Digital were unable to employ any of their placement women due to head-count freezes. Two months after the course had finished, over half of the students had found flexible work that was both interesting and challenging. Most of the others were awaiting verdicts on interviews. Two decided to defer job-hunting for family reasons.

We were very fortunate in getting the BBC to film our course for the "Women Mean Business" series. Following the program several companies contacted us to say that they would be interested in offering the women on our course the sort of working conditions that they wanted. A similar response came after a feature in *Computer Weekly*. So the "demographic time-bomb" is already ticking away but employers just do not know how to find the women who would solve their staffing problems. This is a problem that needs to be addressed with some urgency.

38.8 Conclusions

We had timetabled one day a fortnight for confidence-building topics. These were run by a trainer who was a personnel manager. Practically all the women on the course felt that this was time that could have been usefully spent expanding the technical content and that their confidence grew naturally as the course progressed. They did find useful the days spent on CV preparation and interviewing techniques.

The group worked very well as a mutual support network . They very soon became aware of each other's strengths and weaknesses: the ace programmers helped the analysts who were weak at programming and vice-versa. The class soon formed itself into recognisable groups based on their backgrounds. For instance, the scientific programmers worked well together because they approached problem-solving in a similar way. However, the class was in no way "clique-y": there was none of the competitiveness which is sometimes obvious in undergraduate classes. This was probably because they were working towards a common goal and were mature enough to realise that helping others in no way would imperil their own chances of success. This supportiveness of each other is demonstrated by the fact that they have decided to meet on a fairly regular basis until all have found employment. They circulate possible jobs to likely candidates in the group even if it means putting themselves in competition for a particular job: they are aware that the best one will win.

A side effect of the course is that we have become a mini employment agency, keeping our ears to the ground for likely openings for the course members and forming a central point for them to discuss job opportunities before going to interview.

A weakness of the course that the women highlighted was the shortage of machine time available to them. The first week of the course was spent teaching them the rudiments of the C programming language and since this was out of University term-time, the machines were freely available to them. During term time, they were allotted the hour 1-2pm for continuing their learning of C. We arranged weekend and evening access to the University equipment and some of the students took advantage of this facility. They felt that this was too restrictive and difficult, but the pressure on machine usage within the University made this insurmountable. If we had had the hardware that was originally proposed this would not have been a such a problem although we could not have offered much more time to use it.

Otherwise they felt that the time on the course had been well spent. The general view was summed up by one of them. when she said, "Enjoyable, mind-bending, and I feel so much better for it!". WISE UP will be run again in September and this time Hilary, who set the whole thing going will be attending. We can only hope that it is what she has been looking for.

39

Women Returners: Finding the Gaps

Cynthia McLain[1]

39.1 Introduction

A Commercial Computing Course for women returners was introduced in 1989 by the Sheffield Women's Technology Training Workshop. The course represented a deliberate move towards commercial computing from the more technical courses previously offered. It has proved very successful and substantial extensions in this direction are being planned. This paper describes the Workshop and the course, and summarises our experiences and the lessons learned.

39.2 The Women's Technology Training Workshop at Sheffield

39.2.1 HISTORY AND ORGANISATION

The Women's Technology Training Workshop (WTTW) was set up by Sheffield City Council. It provides training in computing and electronics to women over 25 who are unemployed, threatened with unemployment, or wishing to return to work. Funding for the project was from Sheffield City Council and the EEC Social Fund. The first trainees were enrolled in March 1984.

The Workshop shares a building with the Sheffield ITEC and an open access community drop-in workshop called SPRITE. A single administrative unit called Tritec has been established to cover all three projects but WTTW remains a women-only teaching area. WTTW has a staff consisting of three computing tutors, two electronics tutors, a maths tutor (who also organises placements) and a job-share post which currently comprises general studies teaching and child care development work.

39.2.2 COURSES

The Women's Technology Training Workshop offers up to 48 part-time places a year, with all courses beginning in September. Until the year 1988/89 all trainees followed the same course, a combined electronics and computing course, for which there were

---

[1]TRITEC, Thomas Street, Sheffield S1 4LE

no entry requirements, and which ended with a six-week work placement. The course content included both City and Guilds Electronics and RSA Computer Literacy and Information Technology assignments.

In 1988/89 a modular series of short computing courses, each module accredited by the South Yorkshire Open College Federation, was begun. These courses, better known locally as "Computers for the Terrified", encouraged many women to attend the workshop and develop their interest in the use of computers.

39.2.3 EXPERIENCES

The majority of women on the full year course hoped to apply their newly acquired skills in computing or electronics by going straight into work. However, a few decided to continue their studies. Although the course was not particularly designed to be an access course, most applications to Sheffield Polytechnic were successful.

39.3 Commercial Computing Course

39.3.1 NEED FOR THE COURSE

The perceived need for a commercial computing course was influenced by two factors. The Women's Technology Training Workshop was providing an environment where women could build confidence in their own skills, and was successful in recruiting and training women with no formal qualifications. Experience showed however that some women who enrolled on the course would have enjoyed and benefited from a more intensive and structured computing course.

The short course provision also showed the need for a more advanced commercial computing course. A survey of the women attending the courses identified the following groups:

  (i) women in work, full or part-time, needing upskilling;

 (ii) women returners, with previous office skills, now finding these skills out of date;

(iii) women returners wishing to learn new skills to enable them to re-enter the job market.

Questions were being asked by the women on existing courses about further training which would enable them to apply for jobs advertised locally, jobs for which they were not sufficiently trained.

39.3.2 STRUCTURE OF THE COURSE

The guidelines for the new course were surprisingly easy to establish. The target group was to be women returners who had at least three years of previous office based experience, or who had worked at first levels of management or organisation. The work experience could be paid or voluntary, and applications should be encouraged from doubly disadvantaged groups, ie black women, women with disabilities, and single parents. The course was to be part-time, three days a week, with a work placement at the end of the formal training period.

Staff resources, timetabling and the necessity for quick response to both student and employer needs led to the use of the City and Guilds 7261 Information Technology modular course as a base structure. Modules chosen included spreadsheet, word processing, databases, videotext and data communications, thus involving both computing and electronics tutors in the work on the course.

The course was marketed with the slogan:

Commercial Computing for Women: Secure your Place in the Future!

It was resolved to enrol a pilot group on the course for the year 1989/90, and initially eleven women were accepted.

39.3.3 EXPERIENCES

Of the eleven trainees initially enrolled on the course, eight are still attending and will complete the course with a work placement ending in July. Students have enjoyed the course, though a return to learning and formal study is always hard, and staff recognised a considerable development of study skills as the course progressed. Several trainees have already been appointed to posts or are awaiting a reply, whilst three are considering offers of further study.

Enrolment for a similar course in 1990/91 is presently taking place, with the experiences of the past year providing a valuable guide in the evaluation of next year's prospective trainees.

39.4 Conclusions

39.4.1 WHAT LESSONS CAN BE DRAWN?

The increasing demand from employers for women returners following the demographic changes in the workforce continues to reinforce the need for retraining. The success of the small pilot scheme means that similar courses will be provided by the Women's Technology Training Workshop.

Short course provision must continue, since these have proven themselves as a means of introducing women to the training facilities provided at the workshop. Crèche provision, which was introduced for the short courses in 1989/90, was helpful to many of the women.

The use of City and Guilds Information Technology modules will continue, but with greater emphasis upon electronic communications, ie data communication, teletex, and electronic mail. The course structure appears appropriate. However, the following questions need further examination:

(i) is part time over a year the most effective method of delivery?

(ii) would an intensive modular method be more appropriate?

(iii) should provision be made for advanced modules?

It appears from the eight students still on the pilot course that personal motivation is the principal component in success. All the members of the group had previous school qualifications, some possessing higher education qualifications. Despite this, women who had a recent introduction to learning on one of our courses or elsewhere found their return to study much easier. Age did not appear to influence performance, though previous work experience was of benefit.

The single sex teaching of the workshop provided a necessarily supportive and welcoming environment for the women of the group, with help in child care provision being available where needed. However, with their newly-found confidence in their own skill and ability, none of the group has expressed a continuing need to remain within a single sex environment.

39.4.2 COMMENT AND DISCUSSION

Should it be concluded that if more advanced training were provided, it should be carried out in an "open" environment, with both women and men trainees? Some observers consider that a *continuing* women only provision can be positively detrimental to further study and job search.

Secondly, should it not be possible for women wishing or needing to take "time out" from their job, to be enabled to continue to up-date their skills, or start the re-training process within the home environment? Data communications, on-line computer based training, electronic mail all could be used in an innovative programme ensuring that women are able to return to paid employment when they wish, and not at a low paid low level.

In this paper we have identified two complementary "gaps". The first refers to the needs of business and industry for staff trained in the newer technologies and in particular computer based technology. The second refers to the training required by women returners to meet the needs of these employers.

We have found that training in information technology has proved particularly attractive both to women returners with previous managerial experience in business or the community and to women with academic qualifications in disciplines other than science and engineering. We have also been very pleased to find that employers fully realise that these women are more stable and dedicated employees than the typical male computer staff whose average stay in a company is between two and three years. During two world wars, women "plugged the gaps" but afterwards returned to their hausfrau status without question; by contrast in 1990, it is women who are now stable employees.

40

'Managing With Computers' at the Women and Work Programme

Lisa Payne[1]

40.1 Introduction

Managing with Computers is a course for women returners run by the Women and Work Programme at Coventry Polytechnic. The course has some interesting components which will be outlined in this paper. The paper will also discuss the aims and philosophy of the course and why I feel it works.

40.2 The Women and Work Programme

The Women and Work Programme is a national training and research organisation which, since April 1988, has been located within Coventry Polytechnic. It aims to enable women to maximise their achievement and more fully to fulfil their potential.

The Programme employs a small all-female staff and uses a wide network of additional female staff, many of them self-employed, to deliver training as required. Much of the training is delivered within various end-user organisations, with the remainder being provided at the Programme's base in Coventry. Training is usually delivered to all-women groups, although this is not always the case.

Courses cover a range of topics within the areas of management, business and personal development. Some are fairly general whilst others concentrate on specific skills; some are for "general" participants whilst others are targeted at very specific groups.

40.3 Managing with Computers Course

40.3.1 RATIONALE

For the past two years Managing with Computers has been a 10-week, 3 days per week, course for 14-16 unemployed women funded by Coventry City Council as part

[1] Women and Work Programme, Coventry Polytechnic, Priory Street, Coventry CV1 5FP

of their initiative on unemployment. It is designed to assist women who are not in work to gain employment in areas previously denied to them.

40.3.2 SELECTION

We feel that it is essential that all applicants are interviewed, as women returners frequently lack confidence and self-knowledge and hence find it impossible to do themselves justice on an application form. There are no course requirements for educational achievement or age; indeed efforts are made to ensure a fairly balanced group. Criteria are adopted which give priority to women from Coventry's inner city Priority Area and to black women. Women under 25 are discouraged from applying as they seldom have the personal maturity to fully benefit from the course. It is important that no educational requirements are sought as many women severely underachieve at school and leave with very few, if any, formal qualifications. The selection process endeavours to identify women who would benefit from exposure to computers, by ascertaining the applicant's level of comfort when dealing with numbers or patterns. The educational profile of those accepted ranges from women with no formal qualifications to some few graduates.

40.3.3 COURSE STRUCTURE

The course comprises 192 hours: computing (84 hours), management (18 hours) and personal development (36). A placement and its review require 42 hours. The remaining time (12 hours) is spent on various visits and visiting speakers.

40.3.4 COMPUTING

The computing area covers standard business software; wordprocessing, spreadsheets, database, project management and accounting software. An introduction to programming is provided in the form of a few hours of Basic. A very small amount of theory is also included. The aim is to provide a useable level of skill in these areas but to provide a broader base, and a degree of confidence, on which other computing topics could be built as and when the need arises.

40.3.5 MANAGEMENT

The management aspects are very important. Typically the course participants arrive not knowing what management is about but feeling very strongly that it is not relevant to them and never could be; that it is something "other". During the interviews, and thereafter during the course, time is spent in trying to make management relevant to the participants; to get them to see that the skills they have developed whilst running a home and family are "managerial", that these skills could be transferred into a work context; that THEY could, at some stage in their lives, be a manager. Management is treated in a practical, non-theoretical way, covering topics such as time management, people and resource management, managing new technology and decision making.

40.3.6 PERSONAL DEVELOPMENT

The management training helps to increase participants' horizons. This is supported by a programme of personal development. The usual "returner" topics such as career planning, constructing a CV, preparing job applications and interview techniques are also covered, as are presentation skills, both written and verbal, and assertiveness training. The discussion of barriers to gaining employment, at the start of the course and again towards the end, brings pressing issues out into the open. It allows participants to help each other in resolving what appears to be irresolvable. This helps individuals to see that during the course their view may have changed; what appeared a very long list of problems initially has become reduced to one or two challenges and a series of minor wrinkles.

In addition the Programme provides a counselling service allowing for individual discussions with participants. We ensure that participants realise that they are in charge of their own lives; that they have personal responsibility for their own development and progress. This is central to the course philosophy. The counselling sessions are provided to ensure that participants realise that they are supported and that they can discuss issues and problems with the tutors. However care is taken to ensure that they do not come to depend upon the tutors.

40.3.7 VISITS AND SPEAKERS

Visits and visiting speakers are important in broadening participants' horizons. They provide the opportunity of talking with a range of women about how they have made progress with their careers and how they organise their lives both in work and domestic contexts. The visits also help participants to understand the breadth of computer applications in a modern work situation.

40.3.8 PLACEMENTS

Variation in experience is mostly gained through a work placement. Each participant has a week long shadowing placement in which she observes, and talks with, a woman manager at work. These managers all work in a computerised environment, although their personal level of computer usage varies widely. The participant is required to observe the manager in her dealings with other staff, thinking about her management style and methods of interaction. Questions need to be asked about the use of computing facilities. In most placements participants are allowed to use the computers themselves. This can vary from simply using a wordprocessing package to produce their placement report to using a management information system to answer some real queries.

No matter what the culture of the workplace and level of involvement with computers, the participant sees and comes to appreciate a real working environment. For women who may have been out of work for several years this is critical in building their confidence to return to work. They can see that people who work are not really any different from them, that the women managers are just people who have a job to do. Often they find that the manager got there by a combination of hard work and helping themselves "up the ladder".

Reporting from the placement is both verbal and written. The course includes frequent feedback from small group work which provides practice in talking in front of a group. However the placement presentation is still nerve-wracking. Participants benefit hugely from the self-confidence generated by getting successfully through it. The written report is also important. Many participants find report writing very difficult but the high quality of the work presented is often a reflection of the great efforts made.

40.3.9 BRIDGING DAYS

After completing the course, participants are not forgotten. They are invited back to the Programme after about 6 weeks and then again after 6 months for "Bridging Days". These are days of review, reflection and discussion. The aim is that participants who may not yet have gained employment will be re-energised. Participants who have secured work can use this as an opportunity to review their progress and their plans for the future.

40.3.10 OUTCOMES

The course has been very successful in its aim of helping women to decide what their personal aims are and in helping them achieve these aims by gaining relevant employment or by entering directed training. Of the 14 participants completing the course in the Spring of 1989, 2 had entered further training and 10 had gained employment one year later.

40.4 The Underlying Philosophy

The underlying philosophy of training at the Women and Work Programme is that learning is most effective when it is suited to the individual's needs and is participative. To this end very little of the teaching is in the form of lectures. Efforts are made to make even the small amount of computer theory that is covered as interactive as possible. For these participants formal learning may have been completed many years previously; a formal lecture is rather intimidating and the concentration span very limited.

The teaching is made student-centred by relating the concepts covered to the women's previous knowledge and experiences. This is typically achieved by encouraging small group discussion or practical activities which facilitate the appreciation of points and ideas. It encourages women to bring out relevant experiences from their own lives. In addition to making the subjects relevant this technique allows women to start to appreciate, often for the first time, that they do have skills and that these are worthy. The participants often have very little by way of formal qualifications. Their life experiences have encouraged them to demean the skills they have acquired and thus to demean themselves as people.

Self-reliance is important to the long-term success of the participants. If we guided participants too heavily during the course, they could be at a loss for this support when the course ended. From the very first day we ensure that the trainees appreciate that it is they who are responsible for their own learning. The Managing with Computers course provides them with opportunities and challenges. Whilst dependency is discouraged, support is provided. There are opportunities for discussion with tutors but these are on the basis of equality. Guidance and information may sometimes be offered but decisions must always be made by the participants. Typically, it is appropriate to give the guidance needed for them to acquire relevant information. Tutors are not the only form of support for participants. They support each other, sometimes very heavily. The course encourages this. From the very beginning much work is done to form the participants into a coherent group. Many group exercises are undertaken, some of these designed primarily to encourage mutual support and cooperation.

The course is primarily a computing course. While it is the other aspects of it that make it special, it is its focus on computing that attracts the participants and the computing skills they are able to gain are very important. However, being fluent in one database package will not assist in a situation which requires use of a different package if there is still a fear of computers or a lack of self-confidence. The course heavily encourages participants to believe, realistically, in their existing skills and in their ability to learn and progress further. All aspects of the course are designed to facilitate this.

The women on the course typically enter with very low horizons and expectations of themselves. They may see themselves as working with computers and find themselves attracted to jobs as VDU operators and wordprocessing posts. This is because such posts are most common; are often advertised as being appropriate for people with little or no experience and are what they hear their friends talking about. Often they have no appreciation as to a typical day in such a job. The course aims to avoid producing "VDU fodder" but to encourage women to raise their expectations. Observations during the placement often resolve this. Anecdotes about working conditions and culture typically punctuate the placement presentations. Most women, once they realise what work such as VDU operation involves, decide to look for something else.

40.5 Conclusion

The Managing with Computers course is viewed as being a computer course with additional topics. In practice, it is these other aspects which make the course a success. Courses are readily provided which deliver training in specific computer applications. The problem with this type of training is that the participants benefit only by the acquisition of specific skills. This helps them little in learning other skills in the future. More importantly, their personal goals and self-image have not advanced; their newly-acquired skills can even become a straitjacket limiting their horizons.

Managing with Computers views participants as "whole people" and aims to advance them in many ways simultaneously so that not only do they acquire new skills but they have the self-reliance and assurance to fully exploit them.

41

Why do Women Normally Re-enter the Work Force?

Sue Syson[1]

41.1 Introduction

According to statistics quoted at a recent conference, 51% of women return to a different job after a career break and 63% of women in the 25-45 year age group work. Figure 1 shows the percentage labour force participation of females in EEC countries in 1986 [EEC 89].

In order to encourage women both to join and to remain with an organisation, employers will need to provide attractive conditions of employment and on-going training opportunities.

41.2 The Experience of Women's Skills

In 1984, long before the terms "demographic" and "women returners" were linked, Women's Skills was established as a Company Limited by Guarantee, to train women in an environment sympathetic to their needs. The following observations and subsequent discussion are based on the experience of the Centre and its staff.

The training, which is for women only, is provided by a local further education establishment at the request of the Company.

Our experience has shown that women generally re-enter the workforce either due to economic necessity ("we need the money") or for personal satisfaction ("now it's time for us"). But whatever the reasons, the difficulties encountered are similar: problems with organising childcare; lack of confidence; inadequate educational qualifications; lack of opportunities for part-time work; financial problems.

Women's Skills aims to help overcome these barriers by providing confidence building, training, child-care support and information about part-time work options.

---

[1] Women's Skills, 4th Floor, Sun Alliance House, 16 Albert Road, Middlesbrough

41.3 Confidence

Increasing numbers of women are now bringing up children without support from a partner. The demands of children, housework, parents and work itself all assist in creating feelings of guilt and inadequacy. Women feel unable to say "no" to demands from others, whilst at the same time trying to achieve their personal goals.

Women recruited by Women's Skills need the additional support and help which the organisation provides, in particular in relation to overcoming difficulties of self-image. Yet having completed the 46 week course, which covers computing and business studies, a number of ex-trainees are now working in highly paid jobs where computers are an everyday management tool. They include women who, prior to the course, were unable to secure any form of job or training which would lead to a career.

41.4 Educational Requirements

Women often don't know or understand the heights to which they can aspire. In the North-East of England where unemployment is still high, women see the computer course run by Women's Skills as a way back to work. During the course their aspirations and hopes often change. The work-placement allows them the opportunity to experience areas of work which they had never imagined. Women with few or no educational qualifications prior to commencing our course, are taking degree and HNC courses at the local polytechnic. The staff at the Centre are at present negotiating exemption from some course modules on higher education courses.

The RSA and City and Guilds are now looking at accreditation for "unpaid" work, including work in the community or for a voluntary organisation. Through the work of The Learning From Experience Trust the RSA are looking at qualifications such as the Advanced Diploma in Organisation of Community Groups, which they believe may have immediate relevance for people involved in unpaid work. This type of accreditation will help society to value the work many women undertake in an unpaid capacity.

41.5 Child Care

The fact that from April 1990, employers' contributions to child-care are not taxed indicates the government's concern about the care of our children. But despite minor concessions, Britain lags far behind other European countries in the provision of child-care, for example only 1.7% of industrial employers provided work place nurseries for the under 5's compared with 63% in West Germany [Ashton Tate 90].

Available child-care options currently include:

1. child-minders (most local authorities keep registers);

2. local authority nurseries (not many available);

3. private nurseries (may be expensive for those on a low income);

4. playgroups (only for short time periods);

5. nannies or au-pairs (share-a-nanny);

6. workplace nurseries.

The lack of affordable pre-school child-care in the UK, with only 9% of employers offering any child-care facilities and the average cost of running a nursery at £100 per head per week compared with average female full-time pay of approximately £180 per week is forcing management to look at part-time work as an option [Personnel 89]. The problem of care for older dependants is one that will be of increasing importance as the population generally gets older.

41.6 Part-time Work Availability

In 1986 women formed 88% of the part-time work force in EEC countries [EEC 89]. The issue of part-time availability of work is being addressed by an increasing number of employers, particularly large industrial companies and enlightened local authorities. Flexible working, career breaks, term-time working and job sharing are just some of the options being considered. However, there is still a long way to go in changing the attitudes of employers, who will need to be more flexible, and to change their management procedures.

On the side of potential employees, two areas requiring more work are confidence building and the acquisition of educational qualifications. These areas are linked in that increased confidence will enable women both to ask for the kinds of courses they need and to cope more easily with conventional methods of teaching.

41.7 Conclusion

Women want to train, they want to work and they will be needed - it is up to those with power to insist that management take into account the needs of the women rather than women continually accepting the needs of others.

41.8 REFERENCES

[Ashton Tate 90] The Ashton Tate Partnership, *Target*, Vol 3, no 2, March 1990.

[EEC 89] Commission of the European Communities, *Women in Graphics*, no 30, December 1989.

[Personnel 89] *Personnel Management*, Institute of Personnel Management, August 1989.

42

The Women into Information Technology (WIT) Campaign

**Philip Virgo[1],Carol Beech[2],
Pat Pearce[3]**

42.1 Introduction

The objective of the Campaign is to broaden the main human resources priorities and policies of IT employers as well as educators and trainers. The means is an employer driven campaign on the scale of IT year sustained over the time necessary to achieve the objective. The legal vehicle is the WIT Foundation.

42.2 Background

In 1986, as part of her work on the Women into Science and Engineering Campaign, Pam Morton of Thames Polytechnic identified that the number of women entering Computer Science degree courses had halved over the previous decade and was continuing to fall, despite the WISE Campaign. She approached the IT Skills Agency with a view to organising a campaign to increase the number of women entering the IT industry.

In April 1987 the IT Skills Agency contracted IT Strategy Services (ITSS) to undertake a study into the feasibility of organising an industry funded campaign. As controlling Director of ITSS, Philip Virgo undertook the study and within a fortnight reported that it was not practical without more substantial support from government as the UK's largest direct and indirect IT employer.

In October 1987 the Department of Trade and Industry agreed to increase their contribution to the study to £20,000 provided that a consortium of at least ten IT employers would put up £30,000 in cash and kind (including staff time). In the event the employers had contributed over £100,000 by the time the study was complete in October 1988. The surplus was used to publish a public version of the report [WIT 89a] and to launch an initial campaign project portfolio while waiting for the response of government.

---

[1] c/o WIT Foundation Ltd, Concept 2000, Farnborough, Hampshire GU14 7LU
[2] The British Computer Society, 13 Mansfield St, London W1M 0BP
[3] Department of Computing, Polytechnic South West, Plymouth

The key finding of the study was that if employers could be provided with ready planned projects, directly relevant to their needs, they would pay for them. They would also provide a limited amount of support towards planning such projects provided that they were not expected to collaborate too closely with their direct rivals in the labour market. However, to knit such exercises into a Campaign would require government participation.

At the launch of the Report, in March 1989, companies who had participated announced a series of projects to demonstrate their commitment. The representatives from the companies were at a senior level. DTI funding towards the Campaign launch and co-ordination was agreed in November 1989 and the "Women into Information Technology Foundation" was created as the legal vehicle for the Campaign with directors representing the main participants.

The first funding was received in January 1990 and the Campaign launched in March 1990. The launch was attended by representatives of over 60 major IT employers, as well as a large number from the world of education and training. A full list of companies participating in WIT can be obtained from the WIT Campaign office.

42.3 Objectives

An "Employer Led" Campaign has to recognise that unless employers have sound commercial reasons for participation they will restrict their involvement to a donation from the "good works" budget. The reasons that employers are beginning to be serious about affirmative action vary. There are simple business reasons:

> "A one per cent reduction in IT staff turnover saves £500,000 off my bottom line and our experience is that women are indeed more loyal if you treat them properly."

There is the mixture of expansion plans and community feeling:

> "We don't have a major turnover problem but we've got major expansions planned, pride ourselves on our community position and don't want to simply raid the small firms in our area."

Such altruism is, however, often mixed with direct self-interest. One major IT employer who had raided the local community in its last expansion had found it so expensive to recruit the requisite number of ready trained staff from a static pool that it cannot afford to repeat the exercise and is looking to the returner market:

> "It's a simple cost equation. If joining the Campaign can attract local trainees of the same quality at under £2,000 a head then it is over 50% cheaper that the graduate milk-round or the fairs."

It's not just the absolute numbers of staff that are the problem, it is the mix of aptitudes:

> "The department's unbalanced. We've got too many technicians and too few "people" people. We have to round out recruitment methods. This gives me an excuse to do the job properly".

There is also a changing attitude to the known lower geographic mobility of women:

> "We've just done a leaver analysis. 40% are going overseas, most to Germany rather than America. We've got to find sources of more loyal staff".

This employer has just calculated that it retains 95% of those who take a break to start a family and has a similarly low loss rate among those, mainly women, recruited locally. However, its loss rate from those recruited on the graduate milk-round, or from other parts of the country, mainly male, is in line with industry averages.

There is the 1992 factor. A number of major employers believe that it will lead to an increased drain of talent for the better after-tax life-styles available on much of the continent for experienced computer staff:

> "We're not taking anyone on at the moment but we expect a major expansion next year. By then the competition for staff, including for women, is going to be really fierce. We've no choice but to position ourselves now as an organisation that takes women's careers seriously."

Then there are those concerned for their own families:

> "I've got two daughters and I know the pressures they are under to go into traditional women's jobs. This gives me an opportunity to help change all that."

Finally there are those aware that the problems are not just on recruitment or retention but with developing the full potential of the women they already have in their existing IT work force:

> "We know they've got the ability but very few of them make it through grade X. We don't want to get tied up with feminism but we can't afford to waste all that talent."

This is an employer driven campaign. It has nothing to do with feminism and everything to do with self-interest. It therefore begins by recognising that we have a major selling job to do.

THE IT INDUSTRY NEEDS WOMEN MORE THAN WOMEN NEED JOBS IN IT.

Even though many employers have not yet recognised the fact they soon will. IT employers need to recruit women far more than most women need a job in IT. Employers therefore have to offer women interesting and worth-while jobs. They have to overcome the image of "sitting at a screen all day programming – a boring job for boring techies who are scared of having to deal with people". That may be a travesty of the reality. But it is the image portrayed by much IT advertising and careers material – all those glossy pictures of people sitting mesmerised at screens.

The mission of the Women into Technology Foundation is to raise the numbers and proportion of women entering and sustaining information technology related careers at all levels. But not at the expense of propagating any messages that hamper employers' ability to recruit the men they also need. In fact experience to date is that a recruitment exercise that is effective in attracting more women will also be effective in broadening the pool of male applicants.

42.4   Means

We need to bring together diverse parts of industry and government, education and training, in co-operation rather than competition and as partners rather than sponsors and clients.

The DTI funding is geared to the support from industry for specific projects and is designed to help recruit and organise project participants and sponsors – rather than to fund projects. By April 1991 we will need to generate at least £1 of project spend to release 9p of DTI contribution to help co-ordinate and publicise the results of those projects. The overall DTI contribution is expected to be around £450,000 over the first three years of what is expected to be a five year campaign. However, the contract allows for additional funding from other government departments and government users are expected to participate directly in the same way as other major IT employers.

All projects are intended to produce practical results. They have objectives and quantified target benefits and will be assessed for cost-effectiveness – to enable others to judge how best to replicate success or learn from failure. The programme of work is co-ordinated by the Council of the WIT Foundation, comprising representatives from major IT employers who have pledged five and six figure sums in support of the campaign, and a Project Steering Committee with observers from outside groups. These are supported by a small campaign office.

Sharing best practice is one of the keys to success and several of the early projects will concern the publication of case studies of best practice from employers who are willing to make freely available affirmative action procedures which have cost a great deal to develop and test. Publicising results is crucial. The WIT kite mark (the KEY) is available for any project that is reputable and meets identified employer requirements, even for projects peculiar to a single employer – provided the results, include the means and costs of achieving those results, are available for publication.

The six main areas targeted so far, together with projects in each area, follow:

42.4.1   SCHOOLS

Mission – to correct and enhance IT related career perceptions amongst girls, teachers and careers advisors, to provide positive IT related education experiences and to help facilitate relevant curriculum enhancements.

Project Areas:

- competitions – schools and employers;

- hands on experience - including with IT employers;

- careers workshops and events;

- enhanced careers materials;

- school-industry link programmes.

The first video competition was organised with the BBC. Over 1200 schools showed initial interest, nearly ten times the number budgeted. The production of the additional competition packs led to a tight timescale for completing videos. The final entry of over 80 videos was very creditable and is understood to be around 50% higher than for any comparable competition. The potential of such innovative competitions for changing attitudes and perceptions and building new industry-education links has been clearly demonstrated [WIT 89b].

42.4.2 RECRUITMENT AND SELECTION METHODS

Mission – to ensure the adoption and use of recruitment and selection methodologies that are in tune with the skills and aptitudes in current and prospective demand.

Project Areas:

- analysis of success of existing methods;

- development of more cost effective methods;

- research into methodologies to detect and remove bias;

- pilot recruitment and selection projects.

The recent EOC report on the Barclays settlement shows the danger of the inappropriate use of aptitude tests introducing bias into previously balanced recruitment programmes. Problems with current tests are being discussed with employers.

42.4.3 CAREER ENHANCEMENT

Mission – to remove the barriers, including psychological barriers, to the career progression of those already working within the IT industry.

Project Areas:

- surveys of career progressions;

- programmes for the advancement of women in participating companies;

- workshops on problems and solutions;

- annual competitions for "Most enlightened WIT employer";

- enquiry routing services on support facilities and advice;

- career development support networks for those in the industry.

The British Computer Society, in conjunction with WIT, have just finished a survey of the Society's female professional members and produced a report entitled *Women and WIT - A Survey of the Female Professional Members of the British Computer Society* [Beech 90].

What sort of IT employers attract women? Are some better than others? What facilities can employers offer to attract more women? Is a science background really necessary for an IT career? These were just some of the questions the survey hoped to answer. Its objectives were twofold:

- to provide employers with information to enable them to attract more women into the IT profession;

- to look at career progression and determine the factors which affect it.

The survey therefore included questions about employer type, qualifications, family size, career breaks, equal opportunities and provision of creches and other facilities.

RESPONSE

Within a month nearly 600 of the 2000 questionnaires sent out had been returned and the final figure was in the order of 750, an amazing and extremely encouraging response rate of 35%. Reassuringly, from a representative point of view, over 80% of the replies came from people aged 45 or under.

EMPLOYERS AND WORKING CONDITIONS

The survey also showed the facilities which should be offered to attract women. These are:

- an equal opportunities policy which works (64%);

- options which assist with family life and complement domestic arrangements - flexible hours (54%), part-time working (50%), and working at home (26%);

- substantial training as part of a career development package.

QUALIFICATIONS AND BACKGROUND

The statistics confirmed that computing is regarded by everyone as a skilled, technical profession. The breakdown of figures showed 80% coming from a science background, 10% from the arts with the remainder not seeing themselves as in either category. For all replies, 50% had degrees, 25% post graduate qualifications and a further 7% HND/HNC. One of the objectives of the WIT campaign is to change this perception of the IT profession and to persuade more people with an Arts background to enter the profession. Encouragingly, the career progression figures show that women with an arts background can do as well as – and in some cases better than – women with a science background.[4]

CAREER BREAKS

The majority of replies indicated a career spanning ten years or more starting in the early twenties. During that time most women would have married and had children. Not being interested in marital status, the questionnaire confined itself to questions on career breaks and family size. Sadly, the results confirmed what was already suspected: with current working conditions and social attitudes a career and family do not mix. The facts are:

- no children, no career break - 46%;
- children without a career break - 24%;
- children with a career break - 30%.

The analysis of salary against age with and without a career break showed quite clearly that having a career break is equivalent to reducing your salary by at least £10,000 per annum.

CAREER PROGRESSION

Despite the small percentage of replies from respondents with an arts background (10%), we felt it would be useful to analyse the replies to discover if educational background made a significant difference to career progression. The results surprised us. With a science qualification, the most likely salary was £16,000 – £20,000 (32%): with an arts background it was £21,000 – £25,000 (30%). Computing/Information Technology is not necessarily a scientific career. There is opportunity and potential for both: what needs to be changed is the image.

42.4.4 NON TECHNICAL RECRUITMENT

Mission – to enhance the recruitment of non-technical graduates into IT related careers.

Project Areas:

- employers/careers advisors conferences;
- experimental training for arts students;
- awareness training for careers advisors;
- targeted careers literature/videos;

---

[4] Note: there are no figures relating career progression for women with an arts background against those, for example, with a qualification in computing.

- business games and simulation exercises.

A workshop with careers advisors was held in January 1990 and identified a number of areas for specific projects. A full report is available [WIT 90]. The major findings were the lack of understanding of what careers in IT and computing offer, of the skills these careers require, and the fact that computer employers were unaware of the poor image they convey to non-technical graduates.

42.4.5 RETURNERS WORKING PARTY

Mission - to foster the provision of returner training on the same scale as first entry training but tailored to the requirement of mature individuals with family and other commitments.

Project Areas:

- employer seminars;

- advice to employers on returner schemes;

- development of new employer sponsored course;

- collaborative recruitment and information programmes for would- be returners;

- employer and employee information services on care and support facilities.

Parts of STC/ICL have done cost-benefit analyses which appear to indicate that flexible home-based workers, working on mainframe system development and support can be up to £8,000 a head less expensive than their office-based equivalents - even allowing for the costs of a sophisticated communications and support structure. They have agreed as part of their contribution to the Campaign, to make available the material developed for their returner and career break schemes.

42.4.6 REGIONAL COMMITTEES

Mission - to facilitate the organisation of local collaborative projects.
Structure:

- employer led;

- linked to Training and Enterprise Councils, education bodies and training establishments.

In February 1991 a national conference is planned to review and publicise the results of the 1990 projects, both local and national. In May 1990 the Nationwide Anglia Building Society hosted the first seminar designed to cover all aspects of the Campaign on behalf of employers in a defined geographic region around Swindon, where there is a skills shortage [WIT 89c]. Delegates from over twenty local employers of

IT staff attended. Many have since followed up their supportive comments by volunteering to participate in one or more of the possible local projects that were discussed.

Usha Seegobin of DECollege, Digital Equipment Co Ltd, addressed the issues of attracting a career entrant. Of particular interest was DEC's experience that former secretaries were often better than technical staff at selling and supporting complex IT systems.

Sue Halbert of ICL addressed the practicality, potential and problems of flexible working. It became clear that much of ICL's success in this area is the result of formal project management and quality assurance procedures on top of well-developed support and training procedures. Faces in the audience went green with envy when she revealed that ICL had never had to advertise for staff for this operation. The flow of unsolicited CV's had so far enabled them to meet their recruitment targets.

Anne Watts, Group Equal Opportunities Director for the Midland Bank plc, then rounded off the speaker sessions with a forceful resume of what was involved in running effective retention and returner programmes. "If we wanted them to work we had to ensure that they actually met the needs of those we most wanted to retain. We also had to keep in touch with them as individuals". She also, however, gave examples of spectacular success using imaginative returner programmes to handle rapidly growing workloads in branches serving Thames Valley boom towns where even the Banks could not keep up with the competing demand for staff.

42.4.7 BENEFITS

What benefits do we expect employers to achieve?

- Enhanced recruitment of women in the IT profession.

- Greatly enhanced recruitment of IT experienced would-be returners.

- Improved staff retention.

- Reduced recruitment costs.

- Competitive edge in future IT Recruitment.

What benefits do we expect employees and prospective employees to achieve? Open, equal and rewarding career opportunities that they can combine with the flexible working arrangements that IT can offer.

What benefits to we expect education and training suppliers to achieve? Enhanced relationships with IT suppliers and employers which help generate the understanding, funding, equipment, materials and other resources they need to meet the increasing demands being placed on them.

The targets are very ambitious. But only an ambitious programme will make the necessary impact on the national skill shortages that are hampering the use of IT to improve the economic prosperity and social welfare of the UK. Over the next three years we envisage a core investment in excess of £4 million in the national programmes triggering a much larger spend by individual employers as they come to appreciate the benefits and by education and training agencies as they respond to the changing demands of employers.

42.5 REFERENCES

[Beech 90] Beech C, *Women and WIT: A Survey of the Female Professional Members of the British Computer Society*, British Computer Society, 1990. Also available from the WIT Campaign Office.

[WIT 89a] *Towards an Open and Equal IT Careers Initiative*, report of the "Women into IT" Campaign Feasibility Study, 1989, available from the WIT Campaign Office.

[WIT 89b] "Schools Projects", from *Women into Information Technology Foundation – First Progress Report*, December 1989.

[WIT 89c] "Success in Swindon", *WIT Newsletter*, p7, October 1989.

[WIT 90] *Information Technology – the new art of communication*, report on Careers Advisory Workshop, Non-technical Recruitment Working Party of WIT, January 1990. Available from Carolyn McQuaker, EXXEL Consultants Ltd, Runnymede Malt House, Runnemede Road, Egham, Surrey TW20 9BO.

43

Networking and the UK Federation of Business and Professional Women

Christine Arrowsmith[1]

43.1 Introduction

The noun NETWORK has 7 different definitions in the *New Collins Dictionary*. They are all derivations of "interconnecting groups or systems". NETWORKING warrants a further three definitions. The one which this article deals with is as follows:

> "Networking is the forming of business connections and contacts through informal social meetings".

A link for the purpose of "networking" has been established between the Women into Computing organisation and the UK Federation of Business and Professional Women.

43.2 Connections and Contacts

Collins dictionary implies that Networking is a recent USA and Canadian concept. This ignores the historical precedent set by the contacts made by the sons of the privileged at public school, the marriageable heiresses at finishing school and the social climber holding an "at-home".

Down the centuries both men and women have tried to gain information, knowledge, priority and power by cultivating social contact. The industrial revolution and the rise of financial and trading activities increased the need for business and social links. As industrialisation and commerce took hold the men "used their contacts" at their clubs to obtain management positions while the women "at home" or on the factory floor "gossiped".

During the decade leading up to the First World War, women made inroads into traditional male preserves. They moved out of the factory and into the office. They entered university and became doctors and lawyers. In many instances they were blazing a trail, there was no one to point out the short-cuts, no role model to copy, no help if they made a mistake.

The First World War accelerated the movement of women into the work place. At the same time they began to realise that not all decisions affecting the running of an

---

[1] c/o The General Secretary, UKFBPW, 23 Ansdell Street, Kensington, London, W8 5BN

organisation were made at the place of work. The "old boys' network" effectively excluded women.

43.3　The Working Women's Network

43.3.1　BACKGROUND

The idea of an organisation for working women, to provide mutual support and to encourage women to achieve their full potential in all walks of life, started in the United States. In 1919 the American Federation of Business & Professional Women's Clubs was founded in Washington, USA.

Eleven years later the International Federation of Business & Professional Women (IFBPW) was formed by the American leaders and a group of European women at a meeting in Geneva. IFBPW was formally founded by five member countries, although representatives from 16 countries were present at the inaugural meeting.

43.3.2　THE UNITED KINGDOM FEDERATION

The original British Business and Professional Women's Organisation was one of the five founder members of IFBPW. It was a collection of trade groups under the leadership of Miss Caroline Haslett, an engineer. Between 1936 and 1938, Miss Gordon Holmes, a successful financier in the City, advocated following the United States example of a club in every town.

With the active help of Zonola Longstreth, an American lawyer, she formed the first three clubs. Westminster members were mainly young students and teachers from a secretarial school in the West End; City of London were executive city women with Gordon Holmes as the president; and Thames members came from many different walks of life with Phyllis Deakin, a journalist with the *Times*, as the club President.

Forty members from these three clubs met in November 1938 to formally approve the formation of the National Federation of Business and Professional Women's Clubs of Great Britain and Northern Ireland.

Despite the difficulty of travelling in the black-out and meetings interrupted by air raids, the work of developing the Federation continued. One new club was formed for each three weeks of war by which time the membership represented over 200 different occupations.

At the first post war meeting of the International Federation, held in Paris in July 1947, the two British organisations agreed to work together. In 1969 the British Federation was dissolved and merged with the National Federation. The organisation for working women took the name it still carries, the United Kingdom Federation of Business and Professional Women (UKFBPW).

43.3.3 AIMS OF THE UKFBPW

The Federation's stated aims are to enable business and professional women to achieve their full potential by:

- encouraging and training women to take an active part in public life and decision making at all levels;

- evaluating changing work patterns and pressing for development in education and training to meet them;

- striving to ensure that the same opportunities and facilities are available to both men and women;

- undertaking studies of problems common to business and professional women in Europe and throughout the world.

43.4 Operation of the Network

43.4.1 STARTING POINT

The Federation operates as a geographical hierarchy. The members at club level are the grass roots. The clubs are grouped into 11 geographical divisions with the National Federation at the top of the country structure. Above this is the International Federation.

The opportunities for making contacts, professionally or socially, exist at all levels in the Federation. These vary from the regular club meetings through to the bi-annual International Congress where delegates and observers from the 40 National Federations and 26 countries with associate clubs meet.

43.4.2 GRASS ROOT CONTACTS

Club or individual membership is open to all working women. Individual membership was introduced for the first time in 1989. It caters for women whose work commitments prevent them from attending a club regularly or who do not have a club near to them. They are attached to the division in which they live and receive information both from the division and the national headquarters in London. They are able to visit any club meeting in any area.

The membership of each club represents a cross section of the local community and a variety of skills and knowledge. Club rules allow a maximum of 25% of non-working women. These can be long standing members who have retired, women taking a career break while caring for children or elderly relatives and students.

Each club is run by the members who arrange a varied program incorporating Federation Business, International Business, local interest and social events. Many clubs organise open seminars on topics of interest to women. Invitations to the club's Annual Dinner or the February International Candle Lighting Ceremony are usually issued to the members of other clubs and organisations in the area and enable members to increase their contacts.

43.4.3 Division and National Contacts

Clubs are grouped into divisions controlled by a committee of members nominated and elected by the clubs. Each division organises two meetings plus a number of seminars and social events each year.

The national committee is also made up of members who have been nominated and elected into the office. National events include the annual three day conference which allows members to debate and decide on policy and activities in line with the organisation's aims.

Each club nominates a delegate to represent the club and its members' interests at Divisional and National meetings. In addition other Club and Individual members are free to attend as observers. Taking part in these events greatly increases the benefits of membership, providing the opportunity to extend a members' network of contacts beyond the confines of her home town.

43.4.4 Specialist Networks

At national level the Federation has recently introduced the concept of "specialist networks". These consist of members with a specialist interest which they wish to pursue. Membership of a Network is open to those who work in the specific field or have a particular interest in the group topic.

To date there are eleven of these Networks covering such topics as Health, Property, Science, Education, Training and Women in Business. The Computer Group was one of the first networks to be formed.

43.5 The Computer Network

43.5.1 Membership

The Computer Network consists of BPW members who:

- work within the data processing departments of UK companies;

- use corporate systems or small business systems as part of their daily work;

- deal in computer hardware or software or sell their expertise in computer-related topics;

- teach IT or office skills;

- have a home computer for word processing and hobby use.

Since the network started it has built up a membership of just over 40 women. Of these approximately half are programmers, analysts or some other IT related professionals. They are employed by such organisations as the FI Group, ICL, local government and other large employers. Five members work freelance as contractors.

There are 8 teachers or college lecturers in the Network. The remainder include a vet, the director of a printing company, a bank official, a lawyer and a methodist minister who uses a word processor for the parish magazine.

43.5.2 BENEFITS OF MEMBERSHIP

The reasons for joining the Computer Network are varied, though all are related to an interest in the use of computers at work, in school or at home. Most members express an interest in sharing information and skills. Some have joined to obtain help from the more experienced professionals.

The teachers are looking for role models from the professionals or information about useful educational software. Business users are looking for impartial guidance. The professional members are interested in training, career structures and even job opportunities.

Meetings are limited due to the wide geographic spread of a small number of members. Since 1989 all of the Networks have been allocated time and accommodation for a meeting as part of the Annual Conference. Networks are seen as a very important part of the Federation's future development.

The Computer group holds a second meeting in London approximately six months after the April Conference. In addition members keep in contact via a group newsletter. The full Federation membership is kept informed of Network activities by the recently introduced quarterly Network News or the bi-monthly BPW News.

43.5.3 BENEFITS TO THE FEDERATION

The main benefit of the specialist groups to the Federation is the availability of a pool of expertise and knowledge. Each network has a single coordinator who reports direct to the network representative on the National Executive Committee.

Frequently the Federation receives requests for comments on topics of national or international importance to women or proposed government legislation. In each case the appropriate network co-ordinator can be contacted and left to organise her group to respond.

The network members can also provide the expertise to research proposed conference motions or to organise seminars and workshops. Members have taken part in local and national career road shows for school girls and women returning to work after a career break.

43.5.4 CONDITIONS OF NETWORK MEMBERSHIP

Any member of the Federation is eligible to join any (or all) of the networks. In general members limit themselves to the network relevant to their own interest. The Computer network has tended to be the exception to this. The increasing use of computers in the work place, education and the home has resulted in a widespread interest in the group's activities. The group has a high profile as the result of contributions to the National Magazine and its involvement with the updating of the HQ computer system. When members decide to join the computer network they are asked to complete a brief questionnaire. This identifies the level of knowledge, reason for joining the group and helps to identify topics which will interest group members. The questionnaire also identifies the professional members who are willing to act as speakers, to visit schools and colleges to talk about their work and act a role models.

43.6 Computer Network Activities

43.6.1 EARLY DAYS

The specialist networks are a new venture for the Federation, but they are proving popular. The idea of a computer network was first advertised in 1985 and formally started in 1986 making it one of the first groups to be formed. The first few months were occupied in identifying the group activities and recruiting members.

43.6.2 FIRST SUCCESS

In 1987 a motion was presented to the Annual Conference requesting the government to fund further research into the health hazards associated with VDU's.

The Computer Network first became involved when all of the motions were circulated to the club members for debate. Three Network members immediately started to investigate if any research was taking place. They established that there was already a government funded research programme in existence. The Federation motion was therefore unnecessary. At the same Conference the Science group became involved in the research and debate over food irradiation. As a result the appropriate specialist groups are now called in to verify motions before they are accepted as Federation policy.

After the conference the Computer Network was asked to write an article for the National Magazine detailing their information about VDU research. This was the first of several contributions that group members have made to the Magazine.

43.6.3 COMPUTER WORKSHOPS

To date the Computer group has held two workshops aimed at members with no knowledge of computers. With the help of external organisations, who provided the equipment, the workshops gave members and their friends an Introduction to Computing.

Each course included a brief tutorial with plenty of hands-on practice. Attendees produced a simple letter, did household budgets with a spreadsheet and had a taste of the complexity of a database. The students were loath to break for the buffet lunch, many carrying their plates back to the keyboard and at the end of the day they had to be "evicted" from the kit.

Since attending the work shop at least one attendee has transferred to work involving office systems and several have bought a basic word processor for home use.

43.6.4 HEAD QUARTERS OFFICE SYSTEMS

Members of the Computer group have also been involved in working with the Head Quarters staff and National Executive to update their office system. Requirements for fast, accurate access to information and the decision to reduce the reliance on outside secretarial services have far outstripped the capabilities of the current system.

Using the IT skills of the group a formal requirement specification is being developed while an information scientist is investigating methods of coding members' career and interests information.

The identification of suitable hardware and software will be the next stage for the Computer Network while the Federation's Financial Network will be occupied with establishing how the system will be funded.

43.6.5 WiC AND WIT

Shortly after "Women into Computing" (WiC) was formed information derived from press reports was circulated in the group newsletter. Confusion between WiC and the "Women into IT Foundation" (WIT) led to members wanting to know if they were one and the same and if not what was the difference.

The organisations were tabled for discussion during the Network meeting held during the Federation Annual Conference in April 1990. The members at the meeting felt that there is a similarity between the aims of WIT, WiC and the Federation. All three organisations are "evaluating changing work patterns and pressing for development in education and training to meet them". Several members at the Network meeting agreed to contact their nearest WIT or WiC branch with a view to keeping BPW members informed of their activities and identifying where they could work together.

Over the years the Federation has cooperated with many organisations in working to achieve its aims. These include the Women's Advisory Council, the Woman's Forum and the British Institute of Management. It was a founder member of the Women's National Commission. Cooperation with WIT and WiC is just an extension of this activity.

Co-operation is still at an early stage. In addition to attendance at the WiC conference at least one member of the UKFBPW Computer Group has acted as a role model for a WiC school girls' seminar.

43.7 Summary

For many women, membership of a specialist organisation related to their career is important. However they should not overlook the importance of social contact. The forming of connections and contacts through informal social meetings is something men do all of the time; why should women be any different?

A much repeated phrase within the Federation is

"I do not know - but I know someone who does".

The opportunity to meet and talk to women of all ages, with a variety of different back grounds, achievements and objectives should not be dismissed lightly. It can prove enlightening, educational and refreshing.

44

Women's Career Paths in Artificial Intelligence

Margaret Bruce[1]
Alison Adam[2]

44.1 Introduction

The area of Artificial Intelligence (AI) really taking off is that of expert systems. Pundits anticipate the rapid growth of expert systems over the next decade, as more and more commercial applications for expert systems are developed. And so, it is likely that there will be good employment prospects for those interested in this area of computing. In comparison with more conventional areas of computing, entrants to AI usually have to have knowledge and/or experience of computing – at least to the level of a conversion MSc. To develop a successful career in AI typically requires an uninterrupted employment history. Such continuous career paths are far more common for men than for women.

This paper considers the factors affecting women's careers in the newer and expanding areas of AI and contrasts the development of AI with that of more conventional computing. Are there particular factors which may affect women's entry and progression into this area of computing? What prospects are there for women? What strategies can employers adopt to recruit women, to retain women and support women's career development?

44.2 What is AI?

Artificial Intelligence (AI) is the branch of computing which is involved with building computer systems which act "intelligently". In other words this means programs which display behaviour which would be described as intelligent in a human being. Such cognitive abilities include the ability to learn, to perceive analogies and similarities, to plan a course of action and so on. Computing algorithms, working out complicated statistical analyses and "number crunching" – in other words what computers have traditionally been good at, and people are not so quick at, are not part of the subject matter of AI. Whereas, cognitive abilities which we take for granted, such

---

[1]Manchester School of Management, UMIST, Manchester M60 1QD
[2]Dept of Computation, UMIST, Manchester M60 1QD

as the language ability of a two year old child, are well beyond "state of the art" AI.

Although we tend to think of AI as being a very new discipline, this is not strictly true. The earliest game playing programs were developed in the 1950s when computing as a discipline was still in its infancy.

Interestingly a study of the early days of AI reveals a macho spirit which permeated the type of intelligence which was modelled in the systems of the time. Young men working in AI in the early days modestly looked to themselves as models of intelligent behaviour. Solomonides and Levidow [Solomonides 85] describe this situation as follows:

> "They were interested in intelligence, and they needed somewhere to start. So they looked around at who the smartest people were, and they were themselves, of course. They were all essentially mathematicians by training, and mathematicians do two things – they prove theorems and play chess. And they said, hey, if it proves a theorem or plays chess, it must be smart. And they found out that, for a number of reasons, this really seemed to miss the point ... The point about people is how they do the easy things, not how they do the hard things."

Artificial intelligence has been hotly debated by philosophers. The main criticism has been the possibility of creating truly artificial intelligence. In his criticism of "strong AI", John Searle[Searle 85] has suggested that it will never be possible to create a computer system which can be said to understand.

It is however, possible to acknowledge the criticisms of AI and indulge in what Searle would term "weak AI". This involved adopting a pragmatic approach to building interesting systems where programs model cognition, but do not claim to model real intelligence. This means that it is possible to work pragmatically without worrying too much about philosophical issues.

The area of AI which recently has taken off commercially is, of course, expert systems. An expert system is a type of knowledge based system where the expertise of a given expert is modelled. The idea is that an expert system performs at or near the level of the human expert, otherwise who would want to use it? We would also expect an expert system not only to provide some kind of decision but to also give us some sort of explanation. After all, if you went along to your doctor with a bad headache and s/he suggested amputating your leg, then you would expect some sort of explanation. Clearly such aims are hard to achieve but expert systems have taken off in recent years. On the one hand, this is due to projects such as the Alvey initiative which created awareness of the potential of AI and establish a pool of skilled researchers across the spectrum of AI and "fifth generation" computing. In AI alone, the number of academics increased from about two dozen to 150 to 200. On the other hand, the industrial world has also woken up to the possibilities inherent in expert systems.

This implies that there has been as expansion in the job market for AI which will continue to grow in the academic world and in industry. However, there is little information about whether women have been able to take up these opportunities and whether or not the factors affecting women's career paths found in other parts of computing and other industries, apply to women working in AI.

The new specialist AI role is that of the knowledge engineer. Knowledge engineers require an equal mix of human and technical skills, perhaps more than any other branch of computing. These individuals must have not only the social skills to communicate with and more importantly acquire the knowledge of domain experts, but also have advanced, up to date technical skills in order to build knowledge based systems.

Computer people rarely have both sets of skills. In particular it is hard to see how that technical whizz-kid, the "hacker", could ever be a good knowledge engineer. Every organisation has its hackers. These are the people who stare into computer screens for long hours of the day and night and seem blissfully unaware of the need to eat or sleep. If they speak to their colleagues at all it is usually in the form of monosyllabic grunts. It comes as no surprise to find that over 95% of hackers are men!

Academic explanations for the scarcity of women in all well paid, high status occupations have concentrated on management and technology, especially the former. The problems encountered by women in management are apparent in their socialisation and education which prepares women for the labour market, thus making it less likely that young women will aspire to management positions. If ambitious to succeed in an unconventional career, women face the strain of continually rediscovering that many men and some women do not expect them to behave is such a way. Technological occupations, like computing, are more masculine than managerial careers and women can come across active discouragement from men in such work. Our concepts of ourselves are influenced by others' reactions to us and so exceptional talent, determination and a supportive environment are needed for success. This is true of computing and especially of AI, where there is kudos to be gained from working in this field.

After looking at approaches to career paths, we make some speculations about how these apply to AI. There is little information to substantiate our claims, as yet.

44.3 Women's Career Paths

There is substantial evidence to show that women, if they have a career or have entered a profession, tend to have different career paths to those of men. Women are more likely to take career breaks and have "phased career" paths with work experience before and after childbirth. In contrast, few men have substantial career breaks and men are more likely to follow a "continuous career" path. Dex [Dex 84] has classified women's career paths as follows:

Domestic career	- no return to work after childbirth
Phased career	- return after all childbirths, usually part-time
Restricted family careers	- early return to work for financial reasons
Unexpected/Unplanned	- discontinuous pattern due to "unexpected" occurrences eg divorce
Continuous career	- the exception rather than the rule

How does Dex's classification relate to careers of men and women in AI? In comparison with other areas of conventional computing, to be effective in the AI field, training and experience in computing is desirable. Recruitment does not take place from a wide range of fields as happens in conventional computing. Also the continuous career path is the most likely route for successful AI professionals. For women, a continuous career path is still the exception rather that the rule.

44.4 Barriers to Getting On

One model of explaining the barriers which women encounter in their endeavours to gaining a career and progressing along a career ladder is that drawn out by Bruce and Lewis [Bruce 90] in relation to the design industry. The "three hurdles" model identifies barriers acting at critical points where women make decisions about their careers. These are "getting qualified", "getting a job" and "getting on in a job". How does this model apply to women in the AI field?

Barriers acting at the first hurdle affecting women's choices, include the presentation of courses as being "technical" and so difficult for women. At the next stage, the stereotyping of jobs can discriminate against women, and finally the ability to get on at work is influenced by women's perception of themselves as being "task" or "career" oriented and so handling themselves in ways to help augment and develop their career.

44.5 Getting Qualifications

The first stage of getting appropriate qualifications raises some interesting issues and points of contrast with more conventional areas of computing. The computing industry recruits from all academic areas and there are conversion courses and in-house training courses available to computing entrants. This is not the case for AI where at least a conversion MSc is needed. More generally, it is clear that women are not choosing the "high technology route". One indication of this is the dramatic decrease in women graduates in computing, a down-turn from 25% in 1979 to 11% in 1989. This is in spite of initiatives (eg Women Into Science and Engineering, WISE) target-

ted at women to encourage them to take up technological jobs and pursue technological careers. At our own university, records show that there is a drop in the percentage of British schoolgirls applying to read computing degrees, certainly in relation
to mature women applications and overseas students. Whilst on degree courses, there
are differences in men and women's attitudes eg women taking computing courses
tend to be much more nervous and lacking in confidence about their programming
skills than their male colleagues, even though they perform at least equally well at
exams. Our analysis of the last five year's degree results from a computing degree
of British university shows the same spread of degree classes amongst women and
men. Sometimes women do better than their male colleagues. Last year, on the same
course, where female representation stood at about 10%, over 40% of the first class
degrees were obtained by women. This suggests that there certainly do not seem to be
any technical reasons why women should not be good knowledge engineers. Being
the only women or in a small minority at college and then at work, can be hard on
a social level and in career terms. Women working in male-dominated environments
cannot relax and be one of the boys; they can be excluded from male networks and
often do not have the same support channels which are open to their male peers. This
is not a trivial comment. It can affect who does and does not get on in career terms.
Are women voting with their feet and not choosing computing because it seems to be
abstract, technical and masculine?

44.6 Getting a Job

The second phase of "getting a job" is another hurdle to go through. It is unlikely that
the first work experience for graduates will be in AI. To pursue a career in AI, it is
important that the candidate gains appropriate work experience which will lead on to
AI, for example with a blue-chip company or a reputable software house. From our
experience, it has been the case that women seem to be more intimidated and lack the
confidence to apply for such jobs. For mature students (of which a high proportion are
women returners) the prospect of job mobility may mean that they turn good offers
down, adversely affecting their career prospects.

Because of the novelty of the technology it is quite hard to uncover the opportunities which are becoming available in AI and to say how men and women fare in
relation to these opportunities. A careers officer at Manchester University Careers
Service suggests that employers still do not explicitly advertise for AI people. This
is because graduate vacancies are usually couched in terms of "graduate trainee",
"analyst/programmer" and so on. Additionally, as AI is still a relatively small area
of employment, potential vacancies are often filled internally within an organisation
where a move into AI could be regarded as a promotion for a "high flyer". However
in the scramble for computing graduates, employers may well begin to offer the carrot
of more glamorous jobs in AI to induce good graduates to join them.

Much of the British experience of knowledge based systems lies in the Alvey programme where IKBS was identified as one of the major enabling technologies and
where many new temporary research jobs were created. One of the explicit aims of

the programme was to train up a new work force in state of the art information technology and in this respect it appears to have been successful. Many of the Alvey projects reported problems, at least in the early stages, in recruiting researchers. But it has always been true that many men regard temporary research jobs as stepping stones to better paid permanent jobs, while for many women researchers their career consists purely of temporary, relatively poorly paid research contracts. Despite the temporary opportunities it created, the Alvey programme has done nothing to change the overall differences in career patterns for men and women working in research.

As the Alvey programme is now over, a major piece of research is required to track down the career paths for former university Alvey researchers. From those we know of, both male and female, some have been recycled into the high education system as lecturers in universities and polytechnics (this is the case for one of the authors), computer officers, researchers on other projects, PhD students and so on. Some have been attracted by the lure of well-paid jobs in more traditional parts of the computer industry, especially as analysts and programmers on short-term contracts; some have indeed moved on to specialist suppliers; some whose contracts have ended are looking for jobs.

Although we have found some women in academic circles it is much harder to find women working as knowledge engineers in industry. In a recent piece of research conducted at UMIST, which included interviews with practically all of the software houses in Britain producing IKBS software, we found only one women knowledge engineer. Not surprisingly, she felt isolated! The lack of women knowledge engineers in industry can clearly act as a deterrent to other women. On the one hand there is the lack of suitable role models. Secondly a male culture can subtly undermine women. Long hours are common in the computing industry. If all the important decisions are made in the pub after 5 pm, then the woman who picks up her child from the nursery at that time has missed out on the real business of the day.

44.7 Getting on in a job

The third hurdle of getting on in a job is related to the second. At the moment, AI is a newer discipline in the computing industry and to work in this field attracts kudos. In one firm we visited, the AI group consisted mainly of "high flyers" and those with ambitions to get on. Perhaps this goes some way to explain why women are not visible in the AI world? Either they are not encouraged to seek a career in AI by those around them or women just do not regard themselves as AI specialists. Women tend to be overly "task-oriented" rather than "career-oriented" so gaining excellent technical skills but without paying due regard to other aspects of work which may be just as, if not more important to getting on in a career. Male networks can act as a barrier because women who are not able to drink or play sports with their male colleagues, may not get to know the politics of their organisations so well.

44.8 Employers' Strategies

An individual's careers path is shaped not only by her/his own desires, skills and expectations but also by what material opportunities and organisational structures allow. The wider demographic debate about projected skills shortages is leading some companies to consider flexible working structures to attract and retain women workers. The company's promotion policies and recruitment practices, their willingness to introduce home-working, job-sharing and nursery provision, may well affect women's careers paths. A continuous career path may become a possibility for an increasing number of women. The computing industry has some experience of this, especially in terms of home-working. It is worth noting that home-working schemes introduced by some employers in the industry, were not made available as a right to all women employees at certain levels, but only to "selected" employees – those who could prove their technical capability and personal suitability through a rigorous selection procedure, (see [Truman 86] for details on career break schemes). The emphasis in the current debate about demographic trends and projected skills shortages is focused on women being required to gain skills to equip them to return to work and yet to still retain responsibility for domestic chores and children. In other words more responsibility falls on women's shoulders [Truman 90]!

Many issues have been raised and speculations made. There is clearly a lack of information about the factors shaping women's career paths especially in the AI field. The fact that only a few women enter this field raises fundamental questions about the gendered nature of computing.

44.9 REFERENCES

[Bruce 90] Bruce M and Lewis J, "Women Designers – Is there a Gender Gap?", *Design Studies*, Vol. 11, No. 2, 1990.

[Dex 84] Dex S, "Women's Work Histories : an analysis of Women and Employment Survey", *Research Paper No. 46*, Department of Employment, 1984.

[Searle 85] Searle J, *Mind, Brains and Machines*, BBC Publications, 1985.

[Solomonides 85] Solomonides T and Levidow L (ed), *Computers as Culture*, Free Association Books, 1985.

[Truman 86] Truman C, *Overcoming the Career Break, A Positive Approach*, The Training Agency, Sheffield, 1986.

[Truman 90] Truman C, "Demographic Changes and 'New Opportunities' for Women : the Case of Employers' Career Break Schemes", *British Sociological Association Annual Conference*, April 1990.

45

Management: Practical Experiences in the UK and Canada

Valeria Edgar-Nevill[1]

45.1 Background

This paper[2] overlaps a number of well-defined research areas, namely:

- Women in Management
- Women in Male Dominated Professions
- Women in Computing/New Technology

In addition, it introduces an element of comparison of career progression opportunities between the UK and Canada. The paper highlights some of the author's experiences as a career-orientated female, working in commercial computing.

There are many books written offering advice to women on how to succeed in management [Koob Cannie 79, Davidson 85]. A lot of the material is equally appropriate to both sexes in terms of understanding the different management styles and the politics of organisational structure. However, the topics of special interest to women are valuable and are now recognised as having the significance to warrant electives within many MBA (Masters of Business Administration) Programs.

It is interesting to note how many of the articles in management journals specifically relating to women, paint a profile of a single or divorced childfree woman. Often this mythical woman resides in a powerful position heading a company of her own making. Her success is due to strong entrepreneurial skills, and her initial motivation due to career frustrations experienced within other organisations [Scase 87].

There is an extensive body of literature illustrating the male dominated nature of many of the professions. In particular, law, medicine and engineering have attracted attention [Spencer 87]. Pursuing the theme of opportunities for career advancement, none of this work can be deemed truly parallel to that found in the computing environment. For considerable numbers in both the legal and medical professions, there are very few steps on the career path. Once established as either a practicing lawyer or general practitioner, senior partnerships or expansion of the client base represents the only form of advancement.

---

[1]Napier Polytechnic, Edinburgh
[2]This paper was presented at the 1988 Conference.

In marked contrast, job titles, functions and types of work abound in information technology. In a structured environment, career advancement with changed responsibilities could occur every two or three years within the first ten years of a successful career in the industry.

A close correspondence between information technology and engineering might be expected, given the similar technician type role of junior appointments. However, strong labelling as a "man's world" leaves women in the engineering profession still very much cast in the role of pioneers. Quoting from [Brown 75]

> "Engineering is probably the toughest profession for a woman to make her way in. The reason for this is that engineering has generally attached to its ranks men who are extremely conservative. They are proving even slower than lawyers or doctors to accept women as their peers or superiors."

Women within computing are indeed fortunate to be involved with such a new industry. We do not have the traditional imagery to combat [Williams 87]. The senior data processing manager with thirty plus years experience and a lot of outdated concepts of a woman's role simply does not exist.

On the subject of women in computing the emphasis has been on how to attract more women into the industry [Crane 86]. This has been approached both through education and government initiatives, raising the awareness of the female population of the employment opportunities which do exist. Conferences such as those of Women into Computing are aimed towards attracting women to the subject and developing computing interest in women.

Through this paper, the career progression within computing will be reviewed objectively. Analysis of differing experiences on both sides of the Atlantic identifies critical issues affecting career development in general and that of women more particularly.

45.2 Career Progression Within Information Technology Line Management

In this part of the discussion, career progression is limited to that of a senior systems analyst or project leader type role. Statistics were collected by Computer Economics (CEL) in 1986 [Shortland 86] which showed clearly that there is a disproportionate number of females in the more junior posts. Table 45.1 illustrates the number of female computing staff working at the various job functions within computing.

Table 45.1 Percentage of staff positions through grades by job group

	Job Management	Males %	Females %
Management	top	98	2
	bottom	98	2
Systems	top	93	7
	bottom	68	32
Programming	top	88	12
	bottom	75	25
Analyst Programming	top	94	6
	bottom	76	24
Technical Support	top	96	4
	bottom	89	11
Operations Support	top	97	3
	bottom	88	12
Operations	top	96	4
	bottom	82	18
Data Control/Job Scheduling	top	57	43
	bottom	22	78
Data Preparation	top	5	95
	bottom	1	99

One of the chief causes identified as inhibiting women reaching their full professional potential has been identified as "career-interrupt" [Sawhill 77]. This can occur when a woman has a child, or when partner relocation is seen to necessitate the termination of the woman's employment. This employment break is particularly significant in a fast changing environment such as computing. However, the successes of companies such as F International have proven beyond doubt that "skill-update" type training programs can be very successful. An approach taken by females in North America was to defer motherhood until career advancement had in some measure distanced them from the superdynamic technical environment.

The major hindrances to early career progress in the UK can be twofold: age discrimination demanding years of experience for senior posts and a clearly defined linear career path being the accepted progression. This involves the acceptance that it is necessary to succeed at one post, and serve time there, before progressing to the next rung on the ladder. Figure 45.1 illustrates the systems development career route generally available to Data Processing staff in the seventies.

Figure 45.1 Conventional Systems Development Career Route

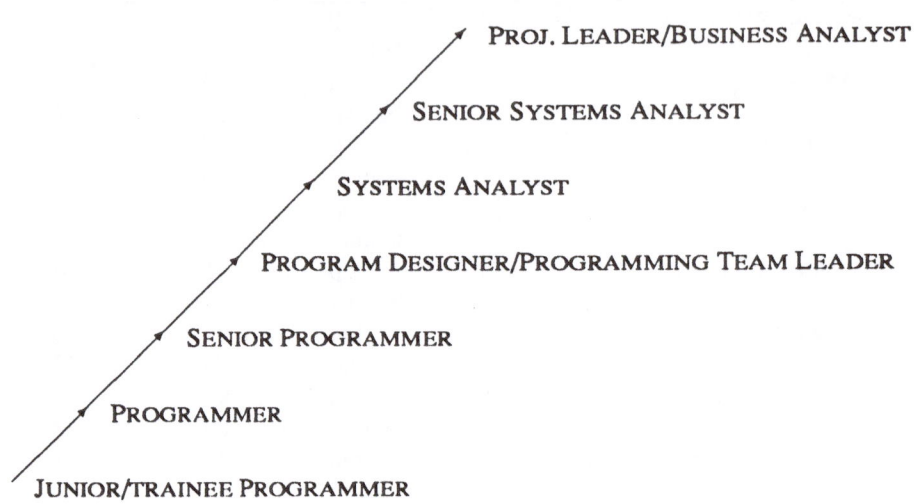

Very many women are as competent in the "technician" role as men but for those who are not suited to the programmer role, promotion from junior posts can prove difficult. [Povall 84] when writing about overcoming barriers to women's advancement in European organisations, describes such linear career paths in terms of "closed systems".

Organisations with many entry points at various levels will have more opportunities for women than "closed" systems. A "closed" organisation has virtually only one entry point – in the least skilled jobs. The extent to which career paths are formalised, the number of career paths and the ease with which people can move from, say, a specialist career path to a more general administrative/managerial path and the number of dead-end jobs, all influence the achievement of equality or opportunity.

The stumbling blocks that exist in the UK may not exist in North America, where staff tend to be placed in a job function well suited to their skills. There are no rules to say that an analyst must be older than a programmer or need be a good technician. Likewise, as a project leader, supervision may include that of many staff with a great deal more experience than one's self. This resource allocation which might be unconventional in the UK is accommodated by allowing flexibility within the salary structures. Staff are given posts which fully utilise their abilities and are paid according to their worth to the company rather than job title.

There are a wide variety of skills required within computing, in addition to those normally associated with its mathematical image. Caroline Blaazer (Head of the Information Technology Department of the Industrial Society) has been reported [Blaazer 88] as verifying my thoughts. She is recorded as emphasising the importance of communication skills, and identifies the project leader role as just as much about effective people management as about technical skills in computing. The advent of fourth generation languages, and the general move towards automation within the systems development environment, favour the non-technical systems specialists.

Shortland's analysis [Shortland 86] of the Computer Economics Statistics discovered that women succeeding to senior posts did so at an earlier age than their male counterparts. A number of factors contribute to these circumstances. Firstly, women's natural nurturing instincts assist them in the team leadership role. A second consideration is their strong motivation to succeed. This may be a race against time to become established in management before a career break, or simply the determined ambition of a dedicated professional. It is only fair to admit a third sexual discriminatory factor. Despite the increasing numbers of women entering computing, they are still very much the minority, and as such it is much easier for them "to be noticed". Of course, this has its disadvantages too, but for the women with career advancement in mind, it does mean a little less effort is required to draw attention to their talents.

In summary, for the highly motivated, career-orientated woman, computing would appear to offer an environment free from many of the prejudices found in the longer established professions. A career break will almost certainly mean retraining but need not limit women's ambition.

45.3 Progressing from Supervisory Line Management towards Middle/Senior Management

Crossing the line between supervision and management demands that an individual be prepared for a series of fundamental changes in the skills required. Hennig and Jardin [Hennig] explain clearly the marked differences between the supervisor and manager roles. Supervision typically involves responsibility for routine, fairly predictable and specific performance by subordinates, in an area of skills with which the supervisor is extremely familiar. Performance goals and objectives are clearly defined and updating on the more technical aspects of the job can be achieved on one's own. More importantly the formal system of relationships required is typically vertical – up the line to one's boss, down the line to subordinates.

In addition management skills include goal-setting, anticipating problems, risk taking and the learning of corporate manners!

In contrast, within management the vertical line of control becomes complicated by a network of lateral relationships with counterparts in other areas, impacting both on the budget and on the productivity of what the manager's department can deliver. There is no formal authority to force a desired result; rather influence, persuasion, favours granted and owed, connections with people who already have influence, and how the manager himself is perceived (winner or loser), all contribute to the outcome of corporate decision-making.

This transition causes problems for all computing specialists, be they male or female. Very often data processing is viewed as a useful adjunct to the primary tasks of the organisation; vital as a supporting role yet distinctly separate from the day to day business operation. Computer specialists tend to act as "behind the scenes" advisors.

They must sell their systems, bargain for resources, but unless they are entrenched in organisational power networks, they have little in the way of favours to exchange. [Kanter], writing on power failure in management circuits, discusses the special case of the staff professional. She noted that specialist ladders often stop short of senior management positions. Systems professionals are frequently hired because of special expertise or a particular background, and management often fails to develop them into a more general organisational resource.

While Shortland's statistical review [Shortland 86] highlighted the scarcity of women in DP management in the UK, the Nicholson and West comparison of UK versus USA statistics for women in management [Nicholson] suggests a brighter picture in North America, where the number of women in management has increased dramatically over the past ten years. The author's practical experience suggests that making the supervisory to management jump is easier in Canada. Perhaps this is principally due to the "Management by Objectives" approach [Tosi 73] adopted by the companies concerned (both in the energy sector).

The career ladder narrows very sharply at this transitional point; project leaders may all appear equal in terms of responsibilities and work allocation, while in fact their promotion prospects may be very different. The opportunities to illustrate ability, and to be known in senior circles, are vital. The MBO approach allows both sexes to be appraised fairly on their performance in terms of deliverables. Traditional evaluation techniques often involve measuring an employee against an ideal or by comparison with the appraiser's own management style. As either alternative will frequently involve evaluation of the women against a male profile, it is discriminatory [Fournies 74].

Once established in the management role the battle is not yet over. As already highlighted, informal communication is a vital part of corporate life. Much has been written around women's exclusion from dining clubs, the golf course, and changing room types of interaction [Spencer 87]. This type of interface is particularly significant in tightly structured organisations. In such companies, the distancing of senior management from the junior/middle managers creates an information gulf which takes the form of a secrecy element with regard to corporate strategy.

Breaking into the political and communication networks is recognised as problematic for both sexes [Lyles] and proves particularly difficult for the woman manager in a traditional establishment orientated environment. However, business management need not be organised so rigidly and the "Open Door" policy [Josefowitz] found in North America is to a woman's advantage. It brings informal communication to the workplace, making it much easier for the perceptive woman to keep in tune both with corporate objectives and the organisation politics. To have contact outside one's own organisation is also vital – here too the American expense account encourages lunch time meetings, and allows women to be included in less formal debate and negotiations. The acceptance of such informal communications enables a woman to keep in touch with the industry as a whole and makes it much easier for her to compete on equal terms with her male counterparts.

Another major aspect of the managerial role is the understanding of the political arena. Women are at an advantage in some ways. They are often good at listening

[Koob Cannie 79]. Men quite enjoy talking to a woman for a change, and as women are generally not viewed in quite the same competitive manner as their male counterparts, they can often be privy to fairly confidential information. However, the shifting balances of power, and dynamic alliances, are initially alien to a woman and require considerable mental adjustment. This difference in the sexes is in part due to conditioning. Activities like team sports are very much part of a man's childhood experience and teach vital managerial skills like group relationships, dealing with winning and losing, the ability to deal with criticism by distancing yourself from it, etc.

In the author's personal experience, transition to the management role and subsequent acquisition of an additional skill set can be made much easier due to a "Mentor". The concept of a "Mentor" is described by Fitt and Newton [Fitt] as the launching and supporting role. To quote from their work:

> "Early in the women's managerial careers, the Mentors – using the status afforded by their high positions in the organisation – strive to give the woman legitimacy in their organisation by conferring an implicit stamp of approval. The executives also try to ensure that the women receive credit for their work so that they can build their reputations."

Reich in his work "The Mentor Connection" [Reich 86] highlights the value for both sexes, in terms of career advancement, of establishing a Mentor connection. The open management style in North America makes the establishment of such ties more achievable. For me, the lessons in understanding the conduct at senior meetings, and in the appreciation of power balances, were both enlightening and vital to survival.

45.4 Conclusions

Information technology affords one of the most equal career opportunities for women. For the technical career-orientated female career progression through line management within computing should prove problem free. The rapid automation of technical roles, and the growth in microcomputing, increasing the number of support and training functions, means that a wide variety of skills are required to fulfil market demand. However, women do have the right (as has any man) to be mediocre [Shirley 88] and for these people in particular, major retraining after a career break may prove daunting.

It is clear that women have the ability to proceed into senior management positions. The current emphasis being placed on the updating and training of British management, will help women indirectly. The advent of the "Free for All" Common Market in 1992 is putting pressure on British business to be both more competitive and more innovative.

It is essential in such a climate that the decision making process devolves. The traditional structure, in which information and instruction flows up and down channels that are also channels of command, is being replaced with a new network of information flows. Any breakdown of the traditional, rigid organisational structures is likely

308

to benefit women. Changes will take time but it is the author's belief that 1992 and the reappraisal it is forcing within British business, will make the management dream more achievable for women.

45.5 REFERENCES

[Blaazer 88] Blaazer C, "The Top Jobs that are just Waiting for the Right Woman", *The Times*, 7 January 1988.

[Brown 75] Brown J M, "A Woman in the World of Engineering", *Transactions on Education*, IEEE, 1975.

[Crane 86] Crane P and Renforth C, "A Study of the Information Technology Industry within Torbay", *Women into Information Technology*, South Devon College of Arts and Technology, Torbay, 1986.

[Davidson 85] Davidson M J, *Reach for the Top - A Woman's Guide to Success in Business and Management*, Platkus, London, 1985.

[Fitt] Fitt L W and Newton D A, "When the Mentor is a Man and the Protegee a Woman", *Harvard Business Review* (Reprint No 81229).

[Fournies 74] Fournies P, "Why Management Appraisal Doesn't Help Develop Managers", *Management Review*, AMA, 1974.

[Hennig] Hennig M and Jardin A, "The Managerial Women", *Pan Business Management*.

[Josefowitz] Josefowitz N, "Management Men and Women: Closed US Open Doors", *Harvard Business Review* (Reprint No 80559).

[Kanter] Kanter R M, "Power Failure in Management Circuits", Harvard Business Review (Reprint No 19403).

[Koob Cannie 79] Koob Cannie J, *The Woman's Guide to Management Success (How to win power in the real organisational world)*, Prentice Hall, 1979.

[Lyles] Lyles M, "Strategies for Helping Women Managers or Anyone", Amacom Periodicals Division, American Management Associations.

[Nicholson] Nicholson N and West M, "Women in Management: Trends in Britain", Referenced in *Women in Management Elective Material*, MBA Program, Cranfield School of Management.

[Povall 84] Povall M, "Overcoming Barriers to Women's Advancement in European organisations", City University Business School, PR 13,1 1984.

[Reich 86] Reich M H, "The Mentor Connection", *personnel*, February 1986.

[Sawhill 77] Sawhill I, "Economic Perspectives on the Family", *Daedalus* (Journal of the American Academy of Arts and Science), Vol 106 No 2, 1977.

[Scase 87] "Women Managers", articles "Room at the Top" and "Destroying the Myths", *Management Today*, March 1987.

[Shirley 88] Shirley S, "A Woman's Right to be Mediocre", *Computing*, April 1988.

[Shortland 86] Shortland S, "Where's the Equality in Data Processing" (On Computer Economic's Survey), *Computer News*, 20 March 1986.

[Spencer 87] Spencer A and Podmore D (eds.), *In a Man's World, Essays on Women in Male Dominated Professions*, Tavistock Publications, London & New York, 1987.

[Tosi 73] Tosi H and Carroll S, "Improving Management by Objectives", *California Management Review*, 1973.

[Williams 87] Williams, "Women: Liberation's", *Director*, October 1987.

46

Grassroot Groups – Experiences in Horticultural Cultivation

Carole Goble[1]
Caroline Moss[2]

46.1 Background

In 1989 we started a WiC group in Greater Manchester (GM-WiC). The first author had tried unsuccessfully to form a group with the help of fellow computing lecturers in higher education, and turned to the Women's Technology Centre hoping for (and getting!) more positive support. Together with Annie Rafferty, manager of the Women's Technology and Enterprise Centre (WOTEC), we founded and still form the cornerstone of the group. At the start we had to be clear in our own minds what we wanted GM-WiC to be like, what its objectives should be and the people we wanted to be part of such a group. We intended the group to have three main aims:

- to produce and disseminate information;

- to be a discussion and support network;

- to raise the awareness of the local people to WiC.

The emphasis was on locality – local information for local people. We were clear that we wanted to be not only a support group for local women, but actually to collect and disseminate information; to *do* something and not just chat amongst ourselves.

To achieve these objectives we envisaged several ways of collecting and spreading information, and heightening awareness:

- producing good and comprehensive local careers information for girls and mature women;

- running workshops, open days and evening classes for local girls and mature women, building on workshops already organised by the authors;

- liaising with schools by giving talks and providing role models;

---

[1] Dept of Computer Science, University of Manchester, Manchester M13 9PL
[2] WOTEC, CCE, Windmill Lane, Denton, Manchester M34 3QS

- liaising with local industry and government, unions and local education authorities for support and raising their awareness;

- creating a contact network of women (and men!) in Manchester.

Although we did not initially consider it, a local WiC newsletter has subsequently proved to be essential for keeping people in contact and spreading the word.

The first meeting was really to set the complexion of the group so some thought was put into the objectives and agenda of the meeting. We wanted it to be a discussion forum and participative. It would be a way of recognising that there are people who are interested in women in computing. We set the objectives to be to:

- brainstorm ideas;

- set obtainable tasks for the group with realistic timescales;

- build a network of contacts;

- decide on the administrative structure of the local group.

We were well prepared with our ideas and tasks, but that did not mean that we intended to dominate the meeting – we wanted active input from the audience but we knew that we would need to get the ball rolling.

Having thought about what we wanted to do, we considered who to invite and how. We decided to mailshot directly over 100 addresses, and intended to advertise in the local press, though we did not get our act together early enough for that. We wanted to capitalise on existing groups and activities so that we could be effective and productive without re-inventing the wheel; this required some preparation to find out which groups existed, and in the end was a little hit and miss. We targeted:

- Greater Manchester residents of the national WiC mailing list;

- Careers advisors of Manchester (which we contacted via the *A-Z Manchester Services* published by Manchester City Council);

- Named contacts in the higher and further education institutions in Greater Manchester;

- The local ITECs;

- Local women computing professionals known to the authors;

- A list of local businesses in the IT industry or users of IT including small and medium sized businesses. This was acquired from the Department of Computer Science's industrial training mailing list. Originally this had been gathered from a number of sources in Manchester's Central Library;

- School contacts that had sent schoolgirls to the Department of Computer Science's WiC workshops in past years;

- Contacts on the Women's Training Network;

- Recruitment agencies, out of the Yellow Pages and computing press;

- Women's groups known to the authors.

We sent each of them general information about WiC, our objectives for a GM-WiC and a form for them to return to inform us whether they would be attending and if not whether they wanted to be kept informed. Where ever possible we tried to send the details to a known, named, sympathetic individual to avoid the "file-in-the-bin" syndrome. We had a good response: about 40 were returned. Many of those sent to industry were returned some time after the first meeting, with complaints that it had taken a long time to filter through their administrative hierarchies.

Our first meeting was held mid-week in September 1989, at a local women's centre in Manchester.

46.2 The Founding Meeting

After giving the background and the past history of WiC, we asked each participant to give a short statement about who they were, why they had come and what they thought a local WiC group could do for them. We led a lengthy brain-storming and discussion session using flip charts. The result was a number of obtainable and measurable goals that were realistic, with named coordinators and attributed timescales. A follow-up meeting was agreed in two months. There are a number of interesting observations.

46.2.1 PARTICIPANTS

Nineteen people came, of which only one was from industry, and she was a direct contact made by the second author. Most were from higher and further education, teachers or careers advisors. The Equal Opportunities Commission (based in Manchester) sent two representatives. Three participants were men, which caused a minor problem as it turned out we were in the "women only" part of the women's centre!

Only eight were actually computing professionals and quite a number had no computing background at all. They were interested in the general issues of women's rights, careers and stereotyping. It turns out that these are the active members of GM-WiC! One or two participants were from the "old school" of feminist discussion groups who were not so concerned with actions as with debate. Clearly we had a wide range of backgrounds and a wide range of expectations which reflected the range of our mailshot.

46.2.2 PASSIVITY

Most of the participants had come to the meeting expecting us to present them with a packaged, no-cost, no-effort solution to their particular area of concern. This was typified by the sentence "I came to see what WiC can do for me". Many problems were aired but actions were thin on the ground.

We made it clear that the people sitting in the room *were* WiC and solutions required positive action by them. The passivity and apathy was difficult to shake, and sometimes we felt as if we were doing a motivational therapy exercise.

46.3 Measurable goals

Such statements as "society is to blame", however true, are unhelpful when formulating realistic actions for a local group. Many practical ideas emerged from the brainstorming session settling on a short-term plan for one year, and a medium-long term strategy for two to five years. The short-term plan has six tasks that will form the basis of the medium term strategy.

It is important to pick on a few practical, measurable tasks that are realistic given people's everyday commitments; the kind of people who get involved with WiC are the kind that get involved in everything! We needed to be able to judge our progress and achievements, so we could not set our sights too high. The tasks were largely based on our original objectives for the group, and reflected the interests, skills and jobs of the attendees. Each task has been assigned to a working party and responsibility allocated to a named individual with a relevant job; in this way it could be legitimately seen as part of their normal job and would be more likely to get done, as well as capitalising on their expertise.

The tasks broadly fit into our three original objectives of information, awareness and support:

1. **An information pack for young women at school or college**
   general information about I.T. careers guidance and lists of I.T. courses in Greater Manchester and intended as a resource for the local schools and careers service. Completion in July 1990 in time for the local WiC schoolgirl workshops.

   coordinator: a school careers advisor;

2. **An information pack for mature women**
   covers the same material as 1, but with emphasis on the woman returner. Due for completion in June 1990 and it is hoped that the local council will take on distribution through libraries for example, and we can acquire sponsorship for production costs.

   coordinators: the manager of the WOTEC and an Adult Education advisor;

3. **Presentation (resource) materials for schools**
   originally intended as a resource pack for talks in schools this has evolved into an in-service pack for teachers, and aimed at the 9-12 year old age group. It is hoped to pilot this in a sympathetic school in the near future.

coordinator: an ex-teacher running a school inner city computer centre for the Manchester City Council;

4. **Presentation (resource) materials for industry**

resource materials for use when giving presentations to industry at professional meetings or seeking sponsorship. We identified a need for fact sheets targeted specifically at industry spelling out why they should employ more women.

coordinator: the hardware manager of an engineering firm;

5. **A Greater Manchester network list**

a resource pool of women from schools, H & FE and industry for talks and workshops, and a list of useful contacts, for example the LEA, EOC etc

coordinator: Caroline Moss (the second author);

6. **A Newsletter**

evolved from meeting minutes to a full newsletter as an essential means for communicating to the passive majority of our supporters, and a way of creating a cohesive sense of identity and spreading information.

coordinator: Carole Goble (the first author).

46.3.1 OBSERVATIONS

The two key roles in the network list and newsletter were taken on by the founders of the group and the majority of working party co-ordinators are *not* IT professionals (only two out seven). One of the coordinators (the school careers advisor) is male.

Stirring up interest in industry and schools proved to be hard work—they did not perceive the lack of women taking IT careers as a problem, or were not even aware that women were not taking up those careers. This is very worrying considering the publicity the issue has attracted in the last 18 months in the trade and national press. For example:

- *working party 2* wrote to a number of employers for case-studies to include in their information pack with a poor response;

- *working party 3* circulated their plans for an in-service pack to a number of IT teachers on relevant LEA committees with a disappointing response;

- *working party 4* was the least successful group, partly because of a lack of interest and support in industry. It has since been decided to leave this task to the local Women into Information Technology committee.

46.3.2 MEDIUM-LONG TERM STRATEGY

We intend to use the short-term tasks, and to expand the workshop programme. The Department of Computer Science at the University of Manchester runs workshops annually for local 14 year old school girls. This programme would be expanded to all higher and further education institutions and extended to include workshops for teachers, primary schools, mature women and careers advisors. We also envisage GM-WiC acting as a discussion forum and facilitator by organising seminars and open meetings.

46.4 GM-WiC's current structure

GM-WiC holds quarterly meetings in the evening at the Manchester Town Hall for free. The meetings are quarterly to give people time to work on their activity and report back. The newsletter is mailed out a month in advance with an agenda. All meetings are open, and includes a report from each working party. A chair is elected at each meeting. There is no membership structure; we have decided to seek sponsorship for each activity on demand and hope to work with the local WIT committee on the issue of funding. The newsletter and mail out is funded through WOTEC and the Dept of Computer Science, University of Manchester.

46.4.1 WiC and WIT

WIT is a DTI and industry sponsored initiative concerned with attracting more women into computing from the industry perspective of needing to fill a skills gap. WIT is beginning to set up local committees around the country, including one in Manchester, which are lead by local industry. Just as the national WiC and WIT bodies have close ties, so it is hoped that the local WIT and GM-WiC will work together to our mutual benefit; GM-WiC members have expertise, resources and positive actions and WIT have industrial contacts who are potential sponsors. GM-WiC has already decided to concentrate on the educational sector where we have most experience and credibility. It is early days.

46.5 Conclusions and Recommendations

From our experiences we can offer some observations and words of advice

- Decide what *you* want a local group to do and direct your mailings to people who will be able to help.

- The activities that your group will undertake is directly related to the people who get involved. If they just want to get together and chat then your group will maybe meet once a month to just chat – forcing activities on an unwilling group is counter-productive.

- Approach people concerned with women's issues and careers rather that just aiming at computing professionals. You will get a much better and more active response.

- Capitalise on initiatives that already exist – COMPACT, local council careers guidance, and other women's groups such as Women in Science and Engineering (WISE), Women's Engineering Board (WEB) or the Federation of Business and Professional Women (BPW).

- Don't expect an active response from local industry – your "doers" will come from women's groups or education. It's best to focus on education and information – concentrate on building links with WIT and professional societies local committees such as the British Computer Society (BCS) and the Institute of Data Processing Managers (IDPM).

- Set specific goals – measurable tasks with deadlines. Make a specific person responsible and try to match their job with the task for best effect.

- You will end up with a small hard-core of committed people, most of whom will be women, and a majority of passive supporters, so a newsletter is essential to keep WiC on their agenda.

And the benefits?

- A mutual support network – you aren't alone!

- Good and helpful contacts – linking together organisations and people and making them aware of one another's initiatives.

- Information that wasn't there before – a sense of doing something.

- Making people aware of the issues of WiC.

Finally, be prepared, have clear and realistic objectives and expect to do most of the work yourselves!

47

Experiences of One Day Workshops for Schoolgirls

**Stephanie Wilson, Carole Goble,
Daphne Tregear**[1]

47.1 Manchester's WiC workshops

Manchester University first ran computing[2] workshops for schoolgirls in 1985. The original motivation was to encourage more women to take up careers in science and, hopefully, to increase the numbers of women studying science subjects at university level.

The intention that year was to run a one day workshop at the end of June, for approximately one hundred 5th form girls. Unexpectedly high demand for places led to two one day workshops instead. The emphasis was (and still is) on "hands on" experience – an attempt to counter negative feelings towards computers, often resulting from experiences at school.

The day was divided into four sessions designed to demonstrate very different aspects of computing: (i) a statistics exercise (ii) building a ripple counter in the electronics laboratory (iii) using Prolog to construct family trees (iv) interactive graphics.

An open discussion concluded the day: the girls were encouraged to tell us what they thought of computers, computing at school, and their attitude to a career in computing.

47.2 Format of workshops

In 1989 we ran our 5th annual Women into Computing workshops. In the years since we started these workshops, the intake of women to the undergraduate courses at Manchester has not improved. Currently, only about 10% of the undergraduates are female, and the figures for the single honours courses are significantly worse.

Over the years we have gained experience in the organisation and running of these events, but we still stick with a format very similar to that of the first workshop. We have considered changing our approach, but cannot come to any consensus of opinion on what might be a feasible alternative. The criteria are (a) we wish to reach as

---

[1] Dept of Computer Science, University of Manchester, Manchester M13 9PL
[2] This paper was presented at the 1989 Conference.

many students as we can cope with, (b) we want to give them some insight into what computing involves, but (c) we are limited in the amount of time that may be devoted to organising and running the workshops.

There has been a change of emphasis. We are no longer concerned with attracting women specifically into careers in science, but with getting across the message that computers are ubiquitous: many different jobs involve using computers and that women *can* do computing. In particular, we wish to destroy the "boys' toys" image of computing and to demystify the subject. This is reflected in the title: the workshops were originally called "Women into Computer Science", now they are titled "Women into Computing".

This year we catered for approximately 400 girls in two workshops on consecutive days at the end of June. We also reduced the target age group to 4th years (mostly 15 year olds). One consequence of this was a much higher demand for places: we had to turn away another 400 girls. It also meant that we had to re-design some of the activities that had run in previous years.

47.2.1 ADVANCE PREPARATION

Logistics dictate that the best time to run our workshops is the end of June (after the end of the academic year but before the school year finishes). Preparations must commence well in advance of this date.

One of the first things to be done is to try and get sponsorship for the events. The cost of running the workshops has escalated over the years. Irrespective of the time and effort put in by members of staff and the machine resources required by the workshops, we require finance to cover correspondence, photocopying, speakers' expenses, refreshments, lunches and the production of folders and their contents.

An initial mailshot is sent to all schools in Greater Manchester and surrounding areas inviting girls of the appropriate age to apply for places at the workshops. We do this before the schools break up for Easter. A subsequent mailshot to the individual students informs those who have been accepted.

Numerous other advance preparations include: organising people to run the activity sessions; getting people to demonstrate on the activities; arranging refreshments, speakers, folders, posters; borrowing equipment etc.

47.2.2 ON THE DAY

We register the students as they arrive and divide them into 5 groups (one for each activity). Each group is denoted by a different colour. All the students are given a folder with a label indicating their name, school, group and login name. The folders contain a timetable for the day, an activity list, a group-activity allocation chart, blank paper, a pen or pencil, a general questionnaire, any sponsor's propaganda, and possibly some careers information.

The day starts with a short introductory session. The speaker explains the problems and the aims of the Women in Computing movement. We describe to the students what they will be doing during the course of the day and we may show a video.

After that, the students take part in each activity on a round robin basis, interspersed with tea-breaks, lunch and speakers. Lunch is a cold buffet in the department. The speakers are usually timetabled around lunch-time, in the hope that the students will talk to them afterwards.

The students are requested to complete a questionnaire on their background at the start of the day. During the workshops they are encouraged to complete another short questionnaire asking them to rate how interesting/boring and easy/difficult they found each of the activities, and for any other comments. This provides input to the running of the workshops. In future we hope to fully evaluate attitude changes to measure the short-term and long-term effectiveness of the day.

47.2.3 ACTIVITIES:

The details and duration of the activities vary from year to year. Last year, 50 minutes was allocated to each session and the students complained they didn't have long enough.

The following description of each activity is the one we hand out to the students.

Activity 1: Graphics

Exploring graphics on SUN workstations. These are powerful computers with high resolution graphics which the department uses for research support and undergraduate and postgraduate teaching.

Activity 2: Programming and software

Exploring the software that runs on computers and makes them useful. The students will look at computer programming and problem-solving, and explore some graphics and artificial intelligence software to see how it works.

Activity 3: Hardware

Exploring the "inner" components which make a computer work. The students can look at the operation of a disk drive, keyboard and monitor along with the integrated circuits (ICs) which perform all the computing functions. Students will be able to build their own electronic circuits to perform some basic functions of a computer.

Activity 4: Electronic communication

Exploring computer networks. The students will use electronic mail and interactive talk to communicate with one another on different computers.

Activity 5: Demonstrations

A room with a variety of machines and software will be available to the students to explore and experiment with at their own pace. Demonstrations include the BBC Domesday machine, desktop publishing, drawing packages, editing speech and music on Macintoshes and a colour paintbox on a SUN.

There is some subtlety involved in ordering the activities. For example, some activities require basic mouse skills and are best placed after activities that involve using drawing packages. This year, the email was very popular because they had just been to the electronics lab where one of the male demonstrators provided the favourite topic of conversation.

47.2.4 FOLLOW-UP

This year we had a post-mortem on the workshops just after the event to determine what had worked well and what hadn't, while it was still fresh in our minds. We decided on several changes for next year.

The short questionnaire filled in by the students was taken into account. On the whole, the responses were gratifyingly enthusiastic about the workshops. The rating of the various sessions indicated that they found the speakers and video boring, and the electronics and programming exercise more difficult than the others. In the remarks section, the most common responses were that they didn't have long enough on the activities, they would like the workshop to run for several days, and that the speakers were, on the whole, terrible. The longer questionnaire was given to psychologists for analysis.

The other form of follow-up which we intend to carry out in future is sending out another questionnaire similar to the long one they fill in on the day. The intention is to see whether the girls' attitudes to computing have changed since coming to the workshop.

47.3 Observations

47.3.1 FINANCE

We are fortunate that our department allocates part of its annual budget to WiC activities, but it is insufficient to cover the cost of workshops on the scale that we presently operate. We have acquired sponsorship in the past, but it is difficult to obtain.

We have made no charge for attending the workshops, but in the future we might be forced to charge a small fee for lunch. There is some speculation that this will encourage those who have accepted places and paid the fee to actually attend on the day.

47.3.2 SELECTION

This year was the first time our workshops were heavily over-subscribed. There were 800 applicants for 300 places. We expanded to take almost 400 students, but were still left with the problem of whom we should select. We took the approach of allowing each school to send up to a maximum of 6 girls. It is far better to decide on how many places should be offered to each school and then guarantee those places.

47.3.3 TEACHERS

The first couple of years the workshops ran, teachers were discouraged from accompanying their pupils. Now we actively encourage them to participate. We hope to increase their understanding of what we are trying to do and to establish contacts in schools who will promote computing and WiC events in the future. Those who do come are asked to join in the activities with the students.

47.3.4 ATTITUDES

The students display great variation in their experience with computers and their keyboard skills. (We stress on the advertising material that no prior experience with computers is necessary). Equally important (perhaps more important) is the variation in their attitudes to something new and their willingness to explore new things. We hope the activities accommodate as much of the range as possible, but there are obviously problems.

47.3.5 DEMONSTRATORS

The attitude of the demonstrators is important. It is tedious to spend two entire days demonstrating the same thing repeatedly. (Each activity requires between 4 and 7 demonstrators at a time). We find it best to ask people to demonstrate for a couple of hours at a time. It is also important that the demonstrators keep calm when the inevitable catastrophes occur.

Many members of staff are involved with helping to demonstrate during the workshops. This increases awareness of the problem amongst male staff.

47.3.6 MEN

We feel it is important to provide the students with role models by staffing the activities predominately with women. The first couple of workshops were staffed entirely by women. This is no longer practical – there just aren't enough women in our department. We now have men helping out with the activities, but the workshops are organised by women, and women occupy the major role on the day.

47.3.7 ENVIRONMENT

The environment has an important effect on the attitude of the students. The undergraduate area in our department (where the workshops are held) is particularly dilapidated. We suspect that this has an adverse effect on the attitude of the girls to computing. It reinforces the view that computing is a male arena.

47.4 Lessons we have learned

47.4.1 THINGS THAT DON'T WORK

- Attempting to contact the schools via the LEAs has not been particularly effective in the past. Some LEAs failed to pass the information on to the schools; in other cases it failed to reach appropriate members of staff in schools. We now have our own lists of schools in the catchment area with a contact name for each.

- Aiming the workshops at 5th formers is a bad idea. They have a high dropout rate because they have already left school by July. Lowering the target age resulted in a much better turnout (the dropout factor in this case was mostly attributable to whole schools failing to arrive).

- Fridays have a higher drop-out than days mid-week possibly because the girls don't have to go to school next day?

- Finishing late, after 4pm, is unpopular. The students tended to disappear. This was partly due to teachers who didn't like finishing after school hours.

- Too many activities lead to cognitive overload – we tried running six shorter activities one year.

- Running the activities for too long or not long enough. There is a delicate balance between the two.

- Activities that involve just watching something haven't worked well (for example, a tour of our Computer Graphics department or chip manufacturing facility). It is much better to arrange activities that involve active participation on the part of the students.

- Tea and lunch breaks shouldn't be too long. The girls get bored and may leave. We are now down to 20 minutes for breaks and 45 minutes for lunch.

- Speakers have been problematic. For several years we have brought in speakers from industry. On occasion we have been let down at the last moment. Often, what they say isn't the message we are trying to get across. They tend to be university educated (maths, computing, physics) and hold fairly high posts in the computing industry. The best were those who related their own experiences as women in computing.

  Careers advisors have also proved disappointing. Getting all the students together for open discussions doesn't work. We wanted them to talk about computing and careers, but most were unwilling to contribute anything in front of so many people.

  Small workshops as part of one of the activities led by female computing professionals promotes a more interactive and informative careers forum.

- We had the idea of using a video as a way of introducing the girls to computing, but it has proved very difficult to find anything appropriate.

- A more specific point is to be careful of too many people trying to do the same thing simultaneously. Our computer systems have collapsed with too many people trying to email each other!

47.4.2 THINGS THAT WORK WELL

- Demonstration rooms with lots of different systems where they can gain "hands-on" experience; for example, Macintoshes, Domesday book, synthesizers. These provoked a lot of interest.

- Inviting people along to demonstrate the use of computers in their work. For example, this year we had some textile designers.

- Providing each student with something they can take home at the end of the day. We hand out folders when they register; each activity supplies additional information.

- Prizes for the best picture resulting from the graphics activity given at the end of the day made the activity popular and also marked end of the workshops.

47.5 Closing remarks

To conclude, we consider that the WiC workshops are valuable and necessary whilst gender bias exists in schools, in the media and in society. The workshops raise the awareness of the participating girls, teachers, schools and demonstrators to the issues of women in computing. However, one day is hardly enough to redress the prejudices encountered in an entire school career: the workshops can only be a beginning and must be actively followed up by schools if the affects are not to fade.

We hope that we can prove to the girls (and teachers) that: computing is interesting; relevant to them in their chosen career whatever that might be; fun; and (most importantly of all) they can do it. We like to think we will succeed.

48

Getting Women into Computing: Strategies for Overcoming Prejudice

Karen Shipp[1]

48.1 Introduction

> When I was a child I was told that only tarts bleach their hair. As I grew older I realised that this was not true, but it still never occurred to me to bleach *my* hair — I just didn't think of it.

This for me is an example of how prejudice operates: things that you don't believe, can still affect you powerfully. I think that prejudice can contribute in a similar way to the low numbers of women in computing – perhaps in the attitudes and actions of people who already work in computing, but also in the decisions of women who do not take up computing as a career or subject of study. It is not possible to grow up in our society without absorbing assumptions about what women should be good at, what is suitable for women, what is feminine. A woman may *think* that women can do anything that men do, yet may not consider going into computing herself because of underlying feelings she has never questioned.

In this paper I am going to discuss the methods used to explore and shift such prejudice at a series of "Women and Computing" workshops run by the Open University.

48.2 The Women and Computing Workshops

These were four one-day workshops, in Reading, Nottingham and Milton Keynes, for women students who were considering whether to do a computing course.[2] The aim was to help them make their decision by providing information, practical experience, and structured discussion sessions. The workshops were loosely linked to two Open University Home Computing courses:

- M205 Fundamentals of Computing

---

[1] Academic Computing Service, The Open University, Milton Keynes

[2] The workshops would not have happened without the vision and commitment of Derek Goldrei, Judy Emms and Dianne Sutton, or the valuable contributions of Hilarie Bateman, Veronica Yuill, Val Looney and Liz Hartnett.

- DT200 An Introduction to Information Technology: Social and Technological Issues.

Practical sessions provided experience of the software used in these courses – an integrated Pascal programming environment in the case of M205, and one of the business packages in DT200.

The workshops were attended by over 70 women, 55 of whom completed a questionnaire at the end of the day. This enabled us to adjust the content of future workshops in the light of their comments.

48.2.1 ATTITUDES AND ETHOS

In planning and revising the workshops several issues came to light.

First of all we were not trying to persuade participants to go into computing. We simply wanted to provide the best environment for them to make an informed decision: one person's realisation that computing was not for them would be as much of an achievement as another's discovery that it was. Every force is met by an equal and opposite force, and putting pressure on students would make it harder for them to make a decision.

Because we wanted to counteract the image of computing as something difficult and mystifying which could only be done by experts, it was important when talking about computing not to behave like computing-expert stereotypes. We didn't want to alienate participants by using jargon, or constantly giving advice and detailed information that emphasised the difference between tutor and student. But at the same time we had to appear professional enough to demonstrate that women can hold their own in computing.

One way of avoiding this "expert" role was to draw on the expertise already in the group, by encouraging participants to answer each other's questions and make the necessary points. Another was to describe our own career paths. This showed that the transition from beginner to professional was possible, and gave participants some realistic role-models.

A feature we constantly encountered was the women's lack of confidence in their ability to handle what was seen as a "technical" subject. So it was important to focus on their own competence and potential and show that they could bring to computing the qualities that they knew were valuable in the other parts of their lives – their ability to organise, their ability to handle people, whatever – rather than making them feel like students who are at the very beginning of something, with no relevant experience and much to learn.

A lack of confidence was apparent in the fact that some students said that they dared attend only because we emphasised that many participants would be complete beginners. It was also apparent in the fact that this emphasis did not deter women of considerable computing experience from attending. Both groups needed encouragement to take the next step into a computing career.

The encouragement and confidence-building were provided as much by the other participants as by the organised activities. Having set up an atmosphere where people could discuss their fears and doubts, it was important to structure the day so that there was space for informal discussion: we had to resist the temptation to pack too much in. This was one of the things we revised in the light of feedback and experience.

All the workshops were run by women. 73% of the women who filled in questionnaires said that this made a difference to them, giving a wide range of reasons:

- "It showed us what women can do and are capable of"

- "... interesting to see women in this field and hear what they had to say"

- "Women understand problems of family, time, and adjusting roles – men can only try"

- "Men leave one feeling inept"

- "I prefer to be able to relax and not mind showing my ignorance. Women are much more sympathetic to difficulties and more eager to impart knowledge"

- "... less intimidating than men"

- "I don't think I would have come otherwise. I would have expected to be outnumbered by whiz-kid men and not been able to keep up. It was much less threatening"

- "... didn't feel talked down to which can happen with men"

- "I think it is easier to say you are stuck"

A potent factor in setting up a positive atmosphere was the lunch. It is easy to under-estimate the importance of such details. Students were surprised to be provided with a fresh and generously prepared meal, and this somehow helped to put across the message that they were valuable people whom the computing world would welcome in, rather than just unimportant students.

48.2.2 STRUCTURE OF THE DAY

The day was made up of three types of activity – information sessions, hands-on computing and structured discussion. But before the first session, an ice-breaker was used to set up a safe but fun atmosphere. Having to say one thing that they were good at, and one that they were bad at, immediately revealed the anxieties people had come along with, as well as a range of supposedly irrelevant skills:

- "I'm no good at Maths"

- "Bad at technical things"

- "Can't think of anything I'm good at"

- "Good at putting on duvet covers"

- "Good at doing three things at once"

- "Good at organising"

We were able to draw some of these revelations into the discussion session that followed and to compare them with the skills that were felt to be necessary in computing.

The purpose of the discussion sessions was to bring to the surface the underlying feelings which people had about computing and about their own ability. The point was simply to bring these to consciousness so that they could be questioned and perhaps changed by the experience of the practical sessions.

The day ended with an opportunity for feedback, both positive and negative. If there were aspects of the day that had left people feeling frustrated, we wanted to hear about it, so that they did not go away with unexpressed negative feelings blotting out other more positive impressions.

48.2.3 INFORMATION SESSIONS

We found at the first workshop that there was enormous anxiety about owning and running a microcomputer – what sort to buy, the hidden costs, and the meaning of technical terms. Because people didn't know the extent of their ignorance, they felt completely impotent and found it impossible to start. They didn't know what to ask, and were reluctant to ask salespeople who might well mislead them or confound them with yet more technical terms. So a question-and-answer session on all of this has become an important part of the workshop. Those with less confidence are encouraged by hearing other people's questions. The assumption that it is all too technical and difficult can be changed by a few jargon-free explanations.

We also gave brief information sessions on the choice of computing courses offered by the Open University, and on our own career paths.

48.2.4 PRACTICAL HANDS-ON WORK

The hands-on sessions were carefully designed to ensure that participants would *succeed*. To shift preconceived ideas about computing, the practical work had to be fun, sociable, creative, understandable and within their ability. It also had to bear some relation to the real world rather than appearing just to be play.

We found that participants worked better in pairs than singly, and that we needed at least one tutor per three machines.

In the first workshop we tried to do too much, giving "taster" sessions on three different packages. Students felt they had not had enough hands-on time by the end of the day. A more integrated approach, using one package in the morning and another in the afternoon, worked better at the other workshops.

The morning session was called "Learn to program in one hour", and used a Pascal programming environment, while the afternoon session used a spreadsheet to do some decision-analysis work.

The morning session was the more demanding, but we felt it was important to tackle immediately what was often perceived as a difficult part of computing. Many participants had used business software before, but most had no experience of programming. Students learnt to use the filer, the editor and the compiler, as well as to understand a little Pascal. At all stages they were given simple but truthful explanations of what was going on, so that they did not feel they were just following instructions.

The exercises had to be simple yet give a sense of achievement. The first example used a fortune-teller program. After running the program, students could edit the text file which held the fortunes, and re-run the program. So within a very short time they were able to run a program which gave the output that *they* had written. As well as involving a little creativity, this set up a good-humoured atmosphere as people had a go on each other's machines.

The second example involved a program to calculate a net monthly salary from a gross annual salary. This was the vehicle for a brief discussion of algorithms, identifiers, variables, sequence, selection and iteration – again all in very simple but truthful terms. This gave the students enough understanding to edit an incomplete version of the program. They could then compile and run it. The session always ran slightly over time, but they all succeeded!

The afternoon session brought together the practical work and the themes of the day by using a spreadsheet for decision analysis – first on the accessible topic of choosing which house to move to, and then to begin to consider the decision they were making about whether to take up computing. As the easier of the two, this practical session left people confident rather than feeling that they had to struggle to succeed.

48.2.5 STRUCTURED DISCUSSION

I want to discuss in some detail the ideas on which this session was based. My intention was to work in a very particular way to bring up doubts and underlying worries and prejudices. The role of the facilitator in such a session has more in common with that of an analyst or psycho-therapist than with that of a teacher. The rationale underlying my approach here is that people change their ideas by speaking and thinking for themselves, rather than by being told. To be able to make such change, a person needs to be listened to, to feel safe, and to be allowed to make mistakes. In Jung's words:

> "We appeal only to the patient's brain if we try to inculcate a truth; but it
> we help him to grow up to this truth in the course of his own development,
> we have reached his heart, and this appeal goes deeper, and acts with
> greater force."

(*Modern Man in Search of a Soul*, 1961, Routledge, first published 1933)

Two vital aspects in leading this sort of discussion are to ask the right questions and to know when *not* to speak. The second of these can be very difficult. When someone says, "You have to be good at Maths to do computing", or "Girls aren't good at Maths", our instinct may be to correct them. It can be very tempting to answer the doubts and misconceptions that people came up with, trying to steer the atmosphere in a positive and encouraging direction, giving information where necessary. But this can inhibit the process of exploration.

Once an unrealistic assumption has been stated, it is brought out into the open where it is accessible to reason. If you immediately say "but that's not true", you are giving the person no time in which to *wonder* whether it is true.

If you jump on such an assumption it will just retreat back into the unconscious, out of the way, unchanged. You are also likely to make the speaker feel she has said something silly, so she will be disinclined to get in touch with or express other views. Other people will also feel unsafe, and say only what they think you will approve of.

It may be that one brave person will state an unreasonable prejudice which others are unknowingly affected by. Hearing it said, and perhaps putting the other point of view themselves, will help them to shift this prejudice. The ideas need to be tossed around, explored, commented on by others in the group, so that people can gradually arrive at the answers themselves, rather than being given the answers.

So the first task is to ask questions which will bring the relevant assumptions to light, and the second is to encourage the group to question these assumptions. It can be useful towards the end of the discussion to draw attention to any connections or contradictions between people's stated skills and experience and the views they have expressed.

One way of getting at feelings which are not necessarily conscious beliefs is to ask questions of the form "What have you heard said about ... ?"

At the Women and Computing workshops we asked students working in pairs to list everything they had ever heard about the sorts of thing that women can do. Then we asked what they had heard about the skills that were needed to work in computing.

This was a fruitful juxtaposition. Several women had already claimed to be bad at maths. Everyone had heard that you needed to be good at maths to do computing. Everyone had heard that girls can't do maths.

Putting it all up on a flip chart, we could see that there were *two* prejudices here influencing us. We didn't believe either of them, but they made a powerful combination.

Having questioned many of society's assumptions about women, and heard from participants with computer experience about the skills that had proved valuable, the picture became less daunting. But it was still easy to see why we could feel that computing was not for women.

Participants were then asked to list all the things that attracted them to computing, and those that repelled them. They would find out how realistic their assumptions were in the practical sessions that followed.

Part of the discussion leader's task is to to make people feel safe enough to explore their prejudices. It is the *authority* of the leader's role which makes this possible: "If she seems to think what I've said is alright, then it must be OK to say it". This authority can be a powerful enabling tool. It is very easy, when trying to find a way of working which is not authoritarian or exploitative, to neglect these more positive aspects of leadership which women – given the way in which their lives are often constructed – can be particularly good at.

48.2.6 FEEDBACK

The success of the Women and Computing workshops was clear. The participants were open-minded, imaginative and thoughtful, and a real pleasure to work with. In their responses to the questionnaire, 95% had found the workshop useful, and 85% were clearer about whether they wanted to do a computing course. Interestingly, 76% felt more likely to do a computing course as a result of the workshop. It was gratifying to find that although the workshops were originally designed with complete beginners in mind, the more experienced participants – including a woman who had spent 12 years as a programmer/analyst before a career break – also found what they were looking for.

48.3 Conclusions

I have discussed the strategies used in four Women and Computing workshops, but I think what was most important was that the workshops happened at all. Being invited to attend such an event showed the women that they were wanted by the computer world, and raised the possibility of their studying a computing course. By deciding to attend the workshop, the participants had already started their decision-making process. The main thing they needed was some space in which to complete the decision. This space, both in terms of time and relief from the pressure of other people's views, can be only too hard to come by for many women.

Our four strategies for giving this space could be listed as:

- Affirmation

- Asking the right questions

- Giving practical experience

- Providing information

But there is a fifth, perhaps the most important of all, which underlies the others: Every force is met with an equal and opposite force, *so don't push.*

48.4 Acknowledgements

I would like to thank Benedict Heal and John Pettit of the Open University for generous help in redrafting this paper, and Bruce Anderson of Essex University for answering the phone at 11:45 PM to give valuable advice on the presentation of these ideas at the workshop itself.

49

Girls into IT at Stockton Sixth Form College, Cleveland

Sue Clark,
Diane Atkins[1]

49.1 Background

The college is situated in Stockton, Cleveland on the North bank of the River Tees. It has 680 students on the roll, who are drawn predominantly from five feeder partner schools (11-16 years) in the area. The Computing Department in the college has established good links with these schools and for two previous years has run one-day computing workshops for 4th year boys and girls. In October 1989, Her Majesty's Inspectorate for Schools asked the Department, "What do you do specifically for girls in the partner schools?".

49.2 March 14th 1990

Twenty 3rd year girls accompanied by women teachers met in the entrance to Stockton Sixth Form College. For many of the girls, it was their first visit inside a sixth form college. They knew the day ahead involved desk top publishing but everything about the day would be unfamiliar – the rooms, the hardware, the software, the teachers, the students, even the dinners. They had sent in some rough sketches of what their group planned to produce but they possibly expected that the fruits of their one day's workshop would be a highly glossy, professional magazine. Their teachers' expectations, however, were that the day's activities were just a starting point. The skills and awareness acquired on the day were to be transferred back to the school and cascaded to others.

The first DTP tutorial session started quietly and with much concentration. This was the atmosphere the girls generated all day. In fact, because the girls listened hard and absorbed what they were told, they made much greater progress in the instructive sessions than we had expected. Although the day gathered momentum as the afternoon deadline approached, the teachers witnessed a no-fuss "busyness"; purposeful and with a community spirit. In the questionnaire at the end of the day, the girls commented that back in the classrooms they can feel intimidated by boys and prefer the quieter,

---

[1] Stockton Sixth Form College, Cleveland

industrious atmosphere. The girls worked well individually but they readily shared their ideas and their newly learnt skills with their group.

To relieve the concentration between the two desk top publishing training sessions, the course members and teachers were taken to see the display of their outline sketches. Each school had chosen its own theme – a friendly timetable for 1st years, a booklet about famous women, a school leaflet to send to a link school in Kenya. A female teacher from the college Art and Design department highlighted aspects of good design in the proposed page layouts. In view of this, many of the pupils modified their ideas.

By mid-morning the girls had gained considerable DTP skills – page layout, frames, headlines, importing text and graphics. Now they were to put their skills into practice with their teachers. The teachers from the five partner schools had attended twilight training; one session in each of the two previous weeks. They were not IT specialists. (The advantage of having non-IT specialists was that these teachers gained new skills.) This was a deliberate policy when approaching their schools back in October 1989. We wanted women teachers who perhaps had little IT experience but who were enthusiastic towards a girls-only day. Their head-teachers had been contacted via a college Vice-Principal and there were no obstacles put forward – almost the contrary. The disadvantage as the girls saw it, was that their group did not have an expert on hand all the time. They had to attempt to solve problems for themselves. How their confidence grew! The girls tried this and that idea, all working with unfamiliar mouse, hardware and software. They lost any inhibitions which might be present in a classroom if boys are dominating the experimentation. Nobody told them that was a stupid thing to try.

A small group of women staff from the college were invited to join the day. They had attended the twilight training because they also had no desk top publishing experience. Their disciplines varied – English, Sociology, Careers and Physics, and they had a range of IT skills. We asked in the questionnaire "Some of the teachers had little experience of DTP and were learning with you. Did you think that this was a good idea?" The replies showed that 75% of the girls were in favour of staff learning alongside pupils. Some said they found it comforting that these teachers made the same mistakes and encountered the same difficulties. One or two though would have liked more expert help on hand when required.

There were three women "experts" from the college. As is so common in computing, many teachers are self-taught with a new software package. Others may regard you as an expert when the reality is far from this. Teachers have to squeeze the learning in between other teaching commitments and it can be months before one feels the expertise. In our case, our expert was an invited visitor from the Cleveland Education Computing Centre. As a Special Educational Needs IT Co-ordinator, this teacher regularly publishes County leaflets using DTP and knew those invaluable hints and tips.

So that the girls had some contact with students, we asked the female A-Level Computing students to help with the day. The college has healthy sized Computing classes but the percentage of female students studying A-Level Computing is only about 20% despite all types of strategies to improve this level. They took the girls to lunch and helped to bring about an informal atmosphere. They themselves gained from the day – using borrowed laser and fax machines and brushing up their DTP skills. One useful task done by the students was to save and print the work as it progressed. On the display boards, the original hand-drawn sketches were replaced by the differing stages of work, so that by the closing session all the schools' work was displayed.

The workshop sessions were punctuated by short talks by two women speakers. These were an architectural assistant and a deputy chief sub-editor from a local newspaper. They described the effects of using technology in their jobs. The reasoning behind these talks was to widen the girls' awareness of technology in industry. Each group sent a fax to industry, to Radio Cleveland and to their schools. One fax that a group sent to a local newspaper editor was published in the write-up of the day.

In order to give the day some status, a photography lecturer from the adjacent technical college took a series of colour and black and white photographs. The day was also recorded on video by a technician. A certificate of attendance was desk top published for each student.

As part of the closing session, the girls completed their questionnaires. What they most enjoyed from the day was learning to use a DTP package, seeing their work in print and talking to the college students. 80% said they wanted to learn more about DTP. 75% found it easier to learn without boys. 0% preferred boys to be present. The Art and Design teacher congratulated the groups on what they had achieved in the hectic day as she summarised and enthused over their displayed work. We thought that the presentation of the certificates would represent a clear ending to the day, yet there were some girls who were eager to continue with their work!

A follow-up meeting of all the teachers involved proved worthwhile to gain more feedback. The aim of the day had been to provide the girls with a positive experience of technology and of the college. The teachers all agreed this was achieved. Clearly the girls had enjoyed the day, had gained in confidence and had their horizons broadened by the experience. Despite the hard work before, during and after the day, it was a worthwhile venture. Would we make any changes? If we had run an extra training session for the teachers back in October 1989, this would have given them a better grounding for their preparation work with the pupils. Making it clear to pupils that a "glitzy" magazine is unlikely to be achieved in a day will prevent disappointment creeping in, if the pupils are very "product orientated". Maybe the examples sent to them were too polished. There were few opportunities for the schools to mix. Restructuring the organisation of the groups, bringing the groups together for the previous twilight session and offering a follow-up session for the girls is being considered for the next time. The hardware and software will move on but repeating the idea is a must. In fact, the date has already been entered into the college diary for Girls into IT 1991.

50

Insight into Attitudes to Computing

P E File,[1] **J Todman**[2],
P I Dugard[1]

At[3] Dundee Institute of Technology we have been running an "Insight into Computing" course for several years. The course is our contribution to Scottish efforts to attract more girls into courses and careers in computing. In the first year all secondary schools in Tayside and Fife were invited to send the names of 2 to 4 girls aged about 15 and the 60 places were allotted on a first-come-first-served basis. Many schools sent extra names in case there were spare places and some schools missed the opportunity by not replying fast enough. Subsequently places have been limited to 2 per school and first options have gone to schools missed out on the previous course. The girls are selected by the schools and usually we are not told how the selection is made. However, there is evidence of keen competition for places and some schools have organised essay competitions for them or used them as rewards for good behaviour. About half of the girls have already studied computing at school. Our aims are to give the girls a very enjoyable encounter with a wide variety of computing experiences and send them back to their schools talking enthusiastically about it to their friends. We provide 6 different laboratories and demonstrations, incorporating plenty of opportunity for successful hands-on experience, and they tour these in groups of 10, spending about 1.5 hours in each on 2 consecutive days. We also invite 4 or 5 women from a variety of computing careers to give short talks to the girls about their education and jobs. At the end of the course, we ask the girls if we should do it again next year and each time we have been asked to make it a week long and residential (many of them make long journeys from quite remote rural areas).

In the first year there was plenty of anecdotal evidence that the girls experienced an initiation into a whole new world – even those who had studied computing already were amazed at the variety of applications they had encountered. Though it seemed probable that participants already felt positively about computers before the course, this informal evidence suggested that their attitudes had been significantly improved by the experience. So in the second year (1987) we decided to use a questionnaire to try to monitor the impact the course was having on the girls' attitudes to computing.

The initial version of the questionnaire had 53 statements about computers pre-

[1] **Dept of Mathematical and Computational Sciences, Dundee Institute of Technology, Dundee DD1 1HG**
[2] **Dept of Psychology, University of Dundee, Dundee DD1 4HN**
[3] This paper was presented at the 1988 Conference.

sented in Likert style format. A Likert scale is a one in which degree of agreement or disagreement with each item is summed to give the total score. We used a scale from 1 (strong disagreement with a positive statement or strong agreement with a negative statement) to 5 (strong agreement with a positive statement or strong disagreement with a negative statement). Examples of the statements included as items are: "computers are fun", "computers are threatening", "there is not a lot you can do with computers". Although these items seem to be getting at different feelings about computers (eg fun, friendliness, usefulness) they all relate to a single, general attitude to computers. Originally the items had been selected to sample seven different aspects of attitudes to computers (ie usefulness, fun, importance, friendliness, aid to learning, reliability, locus of control). Factor analysis of the data suggested that they formed a reasonably coherent single scale. Having decided that what was being measured was a single attitude (which we interpret as a general attitude to computers), we selected those items which best measured this attitude. The refined scale consists of 20 items with 10 which are favourable to computers and 10 which are unfavourable to computers. Details of the questionnaire development and of the data obtained from the 1987 Insight participants are described by Todman and File [Todman 90a].

To ensure that the scale did measure attitudes to computing we used it with 364 third year secondary school pupils who had all had an opportunity to choose to take a computing course. We found that: boys' attitudes were more favourable than girls' and that those who had chosen to do computing courses had more favourable attitudes than those who had chosen not to. Special events such as the Insight courses may encourage or maintain an existing interest in computing, but we need to find ways to foster a more positive attitude among pupils, especially girls, who are not interested or who have already been alienated by bad experiences with computing in school. So we began to explore the idea that girls who are not interested in computing might be put off by the nature of the material used. There is evidence that primary school girls are as interested as boys in using databases to query biographical data about themselves and their peers [Siann 86]. We developed a database package to use with either factual data or personal data about pop record tracks. The personal data here were not biographical data but were data giving personal opinions and descriptions concerning the users of the databases and the record tracks. The factual data consisted of the success of records in UK and US pop record charts which had been extracted from pop record magazines as well as descriptions of the record tracks taken from the personal data users. Pupils were tested in groups of 5. For the factual database, each child used prepared fact sheets to select a measure of success, eg number of weeks in the UK top ten, highest UK chart position, and picked out the tracks and record company which did best on this measure. Finally, they picked out adjectives which had been used by other pupils to describe the tracks. For the personal database, each child selected the tracks which they liked best, selected adjectives which best described themselves and other adjectives which best described the record tracks. Pupils then interrogated their database by selecting queries from a menu. We found that for both boys and girls, attitudes to computers improved following use of the personal but not the factual database. (See Todman and File [Todman 90b] for details of this study).

In 1988 we monitored the effect of the Insight course by administering the attitude questionnaire before and after the event, and we also incorporated an experiment using the personal and factual databases as one of the laboratory sessions in the course.

The mean score on the attitude scale before the course began was 3.76, and afterwards was 4.06 and this difference was significant at the 1% level on a paired t-test (t = 8.43). The initial mean score of 3.76 is similar to the one found for girls who had opted for computing courses in school. (Their mean was 3.74). The final mean score was higher than for boys who had opted for school computing courses. (Their mean was 3.95). So it appears that a sufficiently good experience can (at least temporarily) raise the girls' scores above those for comparable groups of boys.

All the girls used both the personal and the factual database and at the end they were asked which they preferred. Most preferred the personal one (47:9, 4 girls not indicating a preference). These two preference groups showed no difference in mean scores on the attitude scale either before or after the course.

In 1987 only a short form of the questionnaire had been given at the end of the course, using one item from each of the 7 aspects of attitudes to computers. The mean scores for the same 7 items before and after the course were significantly different. (The mean increased by 1.06, t = 3.09). Looking at the 7 items separately, there were positive changes on 6 of them and a small (non-insignificant) negative change on one, but the ones with individually significant changes were those dealing with the aspects: importance, locus of control, and usefulness.

In 1988 the fully developed 20 item questionnaire was used, and taking the items individually 17 showed significant positive change. Of the other 3, "computers are stupid" and "computers are frightening" were exhibiting a ceiling effect – these girls obviously did not find computers stupid or frightening at the start of the course and there was no room for improvement. The other one "computers make things easy to learn" showed a small (non-insignificant) positive change. Other items relating to computers as an aid to learning: "computers are over-rated as a means of teaching people" and "computers make people think more about the topics they are learning" showed significant positive change. The Insight course is quite challenging as well as enjoyable – perhaps the course content is unlikely to make the girls think computing is easy.

There was a feeling among staff on the 1988 Insight course that the girls were more experienced in computing than previous participants. Girls who opt for school computing courses have been shown to have a higher mean score on the attitude scale, so this impression could be checked by looking at the mean scores before the course started for 1988 and comparing with the mean score for 1987 on the 20 items which eventually became the final version of the scale. The results were: for 1987 a mean of 3.71, and for 1988 a mean of 3.76 as already stated above. This difference was not significant, however (t = 0.07). So it seems that the 1988 participants were about the same as the 1987 ones in their attitude to computers at the start of the course.

50.1 Conclusions

The Insight into Computing courses at DIT attract girls who already have positive attitudes to computing, but the courses significantly improve their attitudes, raising their scores higher than those of boys who opt for school computing courses. We do not know how long lasting this effect is. The attitude change is significant in all 7 aspects. Only 3 items of the 20 on the scale do not show significant positive change, and 2 of those are exhibiting a ceiling effect. The other one: "computers make things easy to learn" though positive, was not significantly so. This may reflect the challenging nature of the course.

When these girls were given the choice of using the personal or the factual database, most chose the personal one, but the preference groups did not show significant differences in attitude to computers. Previously these databases have been used with children who had low scores on the attitude scale and, for them, working with the personal database resulted in a larger positive change in attitude than working with the factual one. Further questions could be asked about the effects of working with these databases on the attitudes of children who already hold positive attitudes.

50.2 REFERENCES

[Siann 86] Siann G and Macleod H, "Computers and children of primary school age: issues and questions", *British Journal of Educational Technology*, 17, 133-144, 1986.

[Todman 90a] Todman J B and File P E, "A scale for children's attitudes to computers", *School Psychology International*, vol 11, pp 71-75, 1990.

[Todman 90b] Todman J and File P, *Effects of subjective and objective databases on children's attitude to computers*, manuscript under review, 1990.

51

Action Stations: Let's Organise a Workshop for Schoolgirls!

Helen Watt [1]

51.1 Introduction

This paper describes the various issues which require to be considered by anyone who is planning to run a "Women into Computing" workshop for schoolgirls. The information presented is based on the experience gained from organising one-day workshops held in the Computing Science Department of the University of Glasgow in 1988 and 1989.

The 1988 workshop programme, which was Glasgow's first experience of holding events of this type, was oversubscribed three time within less than a week of invitations being sent to schools. Details of the programme of events for the workshop were presented at the first "Women into Computing" Conference held at the University of Lancaster in July 1988 [Watt 88] and thus will not be covered here. [Watt 88] describes how two one-day workshops were organised for 100 and 200 girls completing their third year at Senior School. Although 300 girls attended in 1988, more than 1500 girls were disappointed.

Therefore in 1989 Glasgow University ran five one-day workshops. Each workshop catered for 200 girls. However, due to the success of the 1988 programme, these 1,000 girls from both public and private schools, represented only 40% of the overall number of 14-15 year old girls who applied to attend in 1989.

The aim of Glasgow University's WiC workshops was to heighten awareness of the opportunities available for women who have skills in computing and information technology. The need for such events is underlined by the fact that the proportion of women applying to enter computing courses in the UK has declined steadily during the last decade. In 1978 more than a quarter of computing students were women compared to only a tenth in the 1988 UK university intake for courses in this discipline.

It is hoped that the organisational issues covered will assist other educational institutions to plan similar events and thus encourage more girls to consider a career in computing as a real option.

---

[1] Computing Science Department, University of Glasgow

51.2 The Organisational Issues

A WiC workshop organiser may use the following subheadings as a comprehensive, but not exhaustive, checklist of the main issues to be considered when planning a schoolgirls workshop programme. Although the issues are presented separately they are inter-related. For example:- staffing, equipment and sponsorship was dependent on the target audience, which in turn will be determined by the workshop's aims and objectives.

51.2.1 AIMS AND OBJECTIVES

The justification for running WiC workshops is taken as axiomatic [Lovegrove 87, Dain 88]. However, before embarking on the process of organising any such event, the organisers must be sure of their institution's specific aims and objectives. Does the organisation wish to increase awareness among schoolgirls regardless of these girls' academic ability? Does it wish to recruit girls to specific courses? If specific recruitment is their aim, within what time scale? etc. Once these have been decided upon, all staff in the department should be circulated with the proposed plans for the event. The workshop will directly or indirectly affect them. Secretarial and technical staff especially need to be made aware of the proposed date.

51.2.2 DURATION OF WORKSHOP

The length of the workshop programme has to be determined. Will the workshop be half-a-day, one day or longer? If the workshop will last for more than one day, will it be residential?

51.2.3 TARGET AUDIENCE

The audience targeted will be dependent on the aims and objectives of the institution. For workshops which do not specify any academic prerequisite it would be an advantage to the institution to contact girls at an early stage of their secondary/senior school when the workshop may influence the girls' future decisions and school curricula can more easily accommodate such an event. If the institution is wishing to recruit more girls to specific courses in the next academic year, then only girls who expect to have obtained the necessary entrance qualifications prior to the start of the next academic year should be targeted. Also the date of the workshop should be prior to the deadline for entrance applications. However, if a longer timescale for entrance has been agreed, then the pool of prospective recruits will be increased if the girls are invited to attend prior to making their curriculum decisions.

51.2.4 SPONSORSHIP

Running a workshop is an expensive business. The cost of photocopying alone can be hundreds of pounds. Therefore it is important to try to raise some sponsorship to help cover the costs. Industry can be approached for assistance in return for an acknowledgement on handouts and in press releases. It is normally best to contact known individuals directly rather than to write to a specific job title within a company. Previous graduates can often be the organiser's first point of contact. A list of graduates and their original destination may be available from the institution's careers office.

51.2.5 EQUIPMENT

Access to computing facilities is a major factor in determining when a workshop can take place and how many schoolgirls can attend. Experiences at Glasgow have shown that the most popular workshop activity is the "hands-on" practical sessions. Therefore it is important to choose a workshop date when facilities are readily available and to give each girl, individually or in pairs, the opportunity to use a computer.

51.2.6 "HAND-ON" PRACTICALS

The content of the practical "hands-on" sessions will depend on the age group and ability of the schoolgirls invited to attend. Exercises need to be designed in a way that each girl can work through them at her own pace and to the best of her ability. Practical sessions should be interesting, enjoyable and challenging. A comprehensive handout needs to be prepared. This handout should help the girls to step through the various tasks to be attempted. Also disks containing the exercises and the required software need to be prepared for each machine.

51.2.7 SPEAKERS/ROLE MODELS

The University of Glasgow workshops programme included a session where girls were able to hear a group of professional women from industry talk about their individual careers, computing interests and the computing environment in which they worked. By inviting women as speakers we hoped not only to provide the schoolgirls with role-models but also to show that a career in computing/IT is a real option. An interesting group of women speakers was arranged by either talking to computing women directly or by telephoning companies which had previously recruited our honours graduates. Women undergraduate and postgraduate students helping in the workshop programme and women lecturing and research staff leading sessions are also excellent role-models.

51.2.8 INFORMATION PACKS

On arrival at the workshop, the girls require to be issued with several pieces of information, eg their timetable for the day, worksheets, handouts etc. Also the girls like to be able to take things home with them. Therefore it is easier to collate these items into a plastic bag or folder ready for issuing to the girls. Information about the university or college, the city or town in which the institution is based, plus a pen and maybe a key-ring or something similar can also be included in the pack. Local banks or building societies will often be happy to provide the small trinkets. These packs need to be made up well in advance of the workshop date. The length of time taken to put the packs together will vary from one day to a week depending on the number of girls who will attend.

51.2.9 CORRESPONDENCE

Invitation letters need to sent to schools, preferably to a named teacher, about two months before the proposed date. Enclosed with the letter, which describes the aims and objectives of the workshop, should be a poster to display on the school notice board and an application form to be returned by a specific date. When the application form has been received, it should be date stamped and an acknowledgement letter should be sent to the school by return of post. This acknowledgement letter need only state that the school's application has been received and is being processed. Telephone enquiries, which should be discouraged whenever possible, should be dealt with by secretarial staff. These staff should not take requests for places over the telephone and should encourage schools to send in their forms. Other enquiries, eg provision for a disabled schoolgirl, should be noted and referred to the workshop organiser. The total number of workshop places requested should be calculated immediately after the closing date for applications. If the workshop is oversubscribed then the number of places allocated per school may be limited to allow representatives from more schools to attend. Because forms were dated on arrival, the workshop places can then be allocated on a first come first served basis. The successful schools can now be sent a letter providing joining instructions, the number of places allocated and a map. The schools which have not been allocated places can be sent a letter apologising for the fact that the workshop was oversubscribed and that they have been placed on a waiting list.

51.2.10 CATERING

Arrangements need to be made for refreshments to be available for workshop partic- ipants and staff at specific times during the programme. It is worthwhile to provide lunch as part of the workshop programme because it gives the girls, teachers, demon- strators and speakers a chance to interact in a less formal manner. The girls can be asked to pay a small registration fee to help defray the cost of providing lunch and re- freshments. At Glasgow University, this registration fee was waived if it would have prevented the girls from a school attending.

51.2.11 STAFFING

Running a Women into Computing workshop is very time consuming. Time is needed prior to the workshop for:

- preparation of exercises, instruction booklets, disks, timetables, invitations, posters, follow-up letters and making information packs;

- obtaining sponsorship and speakers;

- organising rooms, laboratories, equipment and catering;

- setting up and maintaining a database of schools invited;

- allocating workshop places, including replacing cancellations;

- recruitment of demonstrators.

The above will need the involvement of not only the workshop organiser(s) but also lecturing, administrative, secretarial and technical staff.

On the day of the workshop staff are required for registration, leading sessions, tutoring and demonstrating in the laboratories, and overall co-ordination. At a University of Glasgow one-day workshop catering for 200 girls, the number of staff, excluding guest speakers, involved on the one day of the workshop was about 30. Between 16-20 of these were undergraduate and post-graduate students who were employed as demonstrators to help the girls in the laboratories and accompany them to lunch. Whenever possible women members of staff and students were used in order to provide role-models.

The Glasgow workshop programme also catered for teachers accompanying the girls. Teachers attended sessions organised for them by male members of staff. Only the introductory and final sessions were shared with the girls.

51.2.12 PUBLICITY

It is important to attract the attention of newspapers and radio and thus bring the "Women into Computing" workshops to the attention of the general public. Any such attention helps to highlight the message which the WiC workshops are aiming to foster. It is also advantageous when seeking sponsorship for any future events. Attitudes need to be changed, therefore any publicity which makes the general public, and particularly parents, reassess their feelings that computers are "Toys for Boys" can only be constructive. To obtain reasonable coverage, the press need to be notified at least a month in advance of the planned workshop date, in order to get this date in their diaries. The institution's external relations officer should be able to assist the WiC workshop organiser with this task, provided sufficient information is supplied about the planned event and its aims and objectives.

Figure 51.1 Organisational Schedule

At least 6 months before the workshop date ie WD minus ~ 6 mths	Determine institution's aims and objectives Decide on target audience Duration of workshop Availability of equipment Gauge colleagues' support Set workshop date Start to contact sponsors
WD minus ~ 4 mths	Start preparation of exercises Book rooms and laboratories Set up a database of schools to be invited
WD minus ~ 3 mths	Start preparation of instruction booklets Start contacting speakers Notify caterers of date and expected needs
WD minus ~ 2 mths	Send out invitations and posters Check exercises and instructions Start copying instruction booklets Arrange for disks to be copied
WD minus ~ 1 mth	Prepare timetables Allocation of workshop places Send joining instructions to schools Start recruiting demonstrators Start collecting material for information pack Send out first press release
WD minus 2 weeks	Start making up information packs Check on organisational arrangements
WD minus 1 week	Confirm all arrangements Contact press Deal with any last minute hiccups/cancellations Make sure that all staff and demonstrators are prepared
WD minus 1 day	Check that everything is ready and in place
WD	Girls enjoy the experience.

51.2.13 FEEDBACK

It is important to find out whether the workshop has any effect on the girls' attitude towards computing. It is difficult to monitor the long term effects unless a proper study is set up. This would involve accessing attitudes not only "before and after" the workshop of those attending, but also how the girls' initial attitudes compared with those of their peers, and then monitoring the attendees and non-attendees' attitudes over time.

Workshop organisers should at the very least, monitor the change which occurs during the workshop. Attitude changes can be obtained by issuing a questionnaire to be completed by the girls prior to or during the initial session of the workshop programme and then arranging for the girls to complete another questionnaire during the final workshop session. Some questions should be included in both questionnaires for comparison purposes.

51.3 Conclusion

Although organising a Women into Computing workshop for schoolgirls is an elephant task, it can easily be broken down into a set of smaller, more manageable steps. A rough organisational schedule is provided in Figure 51.1. The schedule is only a guideline. Some of the preparation may be left until later than indicated above depending upon the amount of time that workshop organisers have available nearer the workshop date and the amount of support provided by colleagues. However I must emphasise that sponsors should be contacted as early as possible to avoid disappointment. This is because most companies have a limited budget which can be allocated each year to sponsorship.

The importance of running Women into Computing Workshops cannot be overemphasised. It is essential for both the well-being of the computing industry and the British economy that women should take a more active role in the IT industry. More importantly, girls should be encouraged to fulfill their full potential and explore the opportunities which a career in computing/IT may provide. Attending WiC workshops can help girls to overcome some of the prejudices which may be preventing them from considering a career related to computing. WiC workshop organisers will find that such events are not only worthwhile but also rewarding experiences.

51.4 REFERENCES

[Watt 88] Watt H D, "Women into Computing Workshops", in proceedings of *Women into Computing Conference*, 1988.

[Lovegrove 87] Lovegrove G and Hall W, "Where have all the girls gone?", *University Computing*, 9, pp207-210, Blackwell Scientific Publications, 1987.

[Dain 88] Dain J, "Getting women into Computing", *University Computing*, 10:154, Blackwell Scientific Publications, 1988.

52

No Previous Experience Necessary

Sheila Hughes[1]
Ann Maybrey [2]

52.1 Introduction and Overview

The [3] Department of Computer Science at Liverpool University has now run three Women In Computing courses: 7-9 April and 14-16 July 1987, and 22-24 March 1988. Each of the 1987 courses had 100 participants, reducing to 40 for the 1988 course. The numbers were restricted on the most recent course to make the event less unwieldy, and this seems to have been successful. We have found that it is practical to plan in units of a full coachload, implying a maximum of fifty participants per course. In the light of our 1987 experiences, we feel strongly that the post summer examination period is unsuitable for this target audience, particularly because a number of upper sixth participants are accepted. The courses are residential, running from lunch on Tuesday until after lunch on Thursday. In 1987 we charged £25 per person, and in 1988 £28 per person.

The course is intended to encourage young women to consider computing as a career. It is aimed at those in the first year of "A" level study or equivalent, and we have tried to emphasise in all our publicity that it is **not** just aimed at those studying traditional mathematical or scientific subjects. The course includes formal and informal lectures and problem-solving workshops, placing a high priority on the provision of positive role models by the personal involvement of women volunteers from industry, commerce and the academic world.

We hope in this paper to describe briefly the course and the rationale behind its design, and to illustrate how we have begun to change it in response to feedback from students and professionals alike. Some as yet unsolved problems specific to running this kind of course in a city University will be discussed, followed by a brief outline of the more generic problems we perceive as confronting any academic institution holding or planning to hold such courses.

We believe strongly that collaboration and cooperation on many levels among institutions are critical for the future of this kind of "taster" course. We would welcome any comments, feedback and suggestions in response to this paper.

---

[1] Computer Research Group, Royal Insurance (UK) Ltd, New Hall Place, Liverpool 3
[2] Department of Computer Science, University of Liverpool, Liverpool
[3] This paper was presented at the 1988 conference.

52.2 Course Structure

We chose Tuesday to Thursday for the course to take maximum advantage of British Rail's economy fares. The welcome address for the 1987 courses was given by the Vice Chancellor, but he was not available for the 1988 event.

52.2.1 THE FORMAL AND WORKSHOP SESSIONS

The activities on the first afternoon were dictated by the need to prepare the students for the planned workshop sessions. We considered carefully the choice of computer language to be used; our practical criteria were:

1. ready availability of software on sufficient and uniform hardware;

2. an interpreted rather than compiled language to avoid the introduction of unnecessary concepts to the computer-naive, and;

3. support for non-numeric applications.

The third criterion was included and emphasised in order to dispel the myth that computing has to be "about numbers", and thus avoid alienation of the non-scientific part of the audience.

The obvious candidate language to fulfil these criteria was BASIC. However, this was rejected on the grounds that some participants would already be competent BASIC programmers while others would be complete novices. We wanted a workshop where the novice need not feel disadvantaged and inhibited by the obvious existing expertise of her more experienced peers.

In contrast to BASIC, LOGO fulfilled our three practical criteria while also offering a "symbolic processing" approach that we felt would be unfamiliar to all, thus levelling out the expertise differential. LOGO is taught in some schools, but mostly for its turtle graphics capability, which we did not propose to use.

The objectives of the workshops were to help the students to become confident in using the hardware and software, and then to have them discuss the decomposition of a simple familiar problem for solution on the machine. The necessary step-by-step initial guidance was provided in the form of a workbook that led the participants, working in pairs, through simple exercises to reinforce the lecture information. Departmental staff were constantly on hand to act as demonstrators. By the end of Tuesday's practical session, the students were confident with both machine and language.

The second workshop session, on Wednesday, was undertaken in groups of four or five students. Our policy was to allocate the participants to groups where they had not as yet met any of the other student members. This helped to encourage cross-fertilisation of ideas, and had the side-effect of easing social introductions. This was of particular benefit to those who had come as lone representatives of their school. Each group was led by a visiting industrial tutor. These volunteers were women from a variety of computing backgrounds, and were, to a woman, unfamiliar with both the Atari ST and LOGO. However, after a quick seminar, they went gallantly into the fray as "experts in the process of problem-solving". We hoped that they would also act as role models, that the students would find it easier to talk individually about careers and opportunities once the conversational ice had been broken by shared team working. The tutors were also invited to stay to the Course Dinner on Wednesday evening, and in many cases it was clear from the way that students and tutors mingled easily in the social setting that we had to a considerable extent achieved one particular objective.

The workshop problem was to develop a LOGO procedure that could decide which of two candidate names would inherit the throne first. The students were supplied with a collection of data recognisably describing the British royal family. The example chosen does, of course, have an unfortunate anti-female bias in it! Its enormous advantage, however, is that it needs virtually no explanation of the rules governing inheritance, nor of the relationships between the people cited in the data. The workshops were very well received, and are really the focal point of the course.

In the scheduled presentations in the remainder of the course, we attempted to cover several topics. A session on choosing HE/FE courses generated a lot of interest, as did a presentation by a postgraduate student in Computer Science. Our original intention had been to have a current female undergraduate speak, but two factors made this impossible. First, the courses were all held in the University vacation (to allow the use of Halls of Residence etc) so very few undergraduates were still around. Second, there were very few female undergraduates to choose from!

Short presentations from female IT practitioners, illustrating their career history, background and current role, met with a mixed reception. This was disappointing because we felt that this was an important part of demystifying what "a career in computing" really meant.

52.2.2 THE SOCIAL PROGRAMME

The evening events were far more difficult to arrange and control than the formal parts of the course. Liverpool University is a short walk away from the city centre, and the Halls of Residence are about three miles away in a pleasant suburb of South Liverpool. Strange as it may sound, there are no pubs near at hand; and special arrangements are required to open a Hall bar. Most of the course participants were either sixteen or seventeen years old, and for the majority it was the first time they had lived away from home without benefit of the company of family or friends. The age of the students made alcohol consumption by them a particularly thorny problem for us; realistically, the young women were mostly accustomed to going out to pubs at home, and yet we had to acknowledge that for us to sanction this would break the law. On the two 1987 courses, we organised videos and informal chats with university staff and students for the first evening; on both courses over half of the participants insisted on being allowed to go into the city centre for the evening. We noted names and home phone numbers of those going out, and required that they should stay in reasonable sized groups – not less than three – and take taxis to and from the Halls. A curfew of 11 pm was set, and was observed by the vast majority, despite grumbles about not being able to go to nightclubs.

The situation places an enormous responsibility and strain on the members of staff in residence at the Halls. In an attempt to avoid a repetition of this, we decided to take the students to the theatre on the first night of the 1988 course. We did not present this as an option, and there were a few complaints – some would rather have gone into the city centre.

On the second night of each course, we held a Course Dinner in hall, complete with complimentary wine and an after dinner speaker. This was immensely popular with the participants, who in this case felt that they had been treated as adults. However, a minority again wanted to go out after the course dinner, repeating the problems of the previous evening. This was ameliorated in 1988 by offering a pop quiz with prizes; this had been set by an amateur disc jockey from the Computer Science undergraduates (the tutors took part as well!).

Free time on Wednesday afternoon was spent at the Albert Dock, a major redevelopment on the Mersey. It is large and complex, housing the Maritime Museum, fashionable shops, bars and restaurants, boat hire and now notably the Tate Gallery in the North. This visit had been a feature of all three courses, the only modification being an alteration in timing to ensure that the shops were open throughout the visit. We also offered the students the services of a professional guide for a one-hour tour of the Dock, and about one third of the party took this up. The same guide accompanied the students on the coach back to the Hall, taking an indirect route in order to show some of the famous sights of Liverpool.

52.3 Unsolved Problems with the Liverpool Course

The biggest headache of the course is attempting to strike a balance between treating the participants as adults (which is our aim) and accepting responsibility for their welfare while they are with us (which is essential). It seems that this problem is greater in a city university like Liverpool than in a campus-style university such as Warwick or Nottingham. The concern we feel about the students being in the city centre at night, unsupervised, is not a result of being in Liverpool per se; the same situation would arise in the centre of any major city.

The introduction of a theatre visit has improved matters for the first evening, but it is still rather difficult to know what to offer as entertainment after the Course Dinner. A disco has been suggested, but we believe that an all-female disco with soft drinks only may have limited appeal to 17 year olds. The pop quiz idea worked fairly well, but depends on the availability of an altruistic amateur DJ; ours graduated and left in July 1988.

A way to improve the response to the IT professionals' presentations needs to be established. We suspect that the current brief – cover your career history, educational background, current job; and keep it fairly lighthearted and anecdotal – should be altered, perhaps personalised for individuals.

Another thorny problem is that of deciding upon the price charged per participant. This has risen from £25 in 1987 to £28 in 1988. In comparison with similar courses at certain universities, this seems expensive, but against a different selection of universities it is cheap. We are sometimes asked to offer a special non-residential rate for local students, but we have so far refused to do this because we believe that a large part of the benefit of the course arises from being in residence and having a taste of university life. We feel that the fee asked is reasonable, but we have received one or two complaints that it is excessive. We are very aware that overpricing such an event will lead to its becoming exclusive to young women from the more wealthy families. We were pleased to note that many of the past participants have not, in fact, had to bear the cost of the course themselves, but have received bursaries for fees and travel expenses either from their own institution or from the controlling LEA.

Travel can be very expensive, but we hope that participants will make maximum use of economy offers from British Rail or the various bus companies. We take advantage of British Rail's conference travel arrangements, and send each participant a validated application for these special discounts should they choose to use them.

52.4   General Problems and the Need for Collaboration

Many higher education establishments are now running courses with objectives similar to ours. We are delighted to see this, but we foresee problems caused by this very proliferation. The course at Liverpool is very heavily subsidised by contributions from national industry and commerce, as are many other similar ventures. The obvious targets for all appeals for financial support are the same organisations, over and over again. Without some kind of national network, each course will thus be competing for a share of the available resources. Such internecine competition is wasteful; it would seem far more effective to have a national fundraising effort, to be used for all the planned courses. This path forward is fraught with problems, yet to flounder around in our current "everyone for themselves" mode is likely ultimately to prove counterproductive, if not fatal, to our common aim.

Pricing of the courses could also be more effectively done were more information available at some central location. We do not suggest that a rigid pricing code be enforceable; all the courses are different in many respects and this seems a healthy, creative sign. However, it can surely be of help to all involved to be able easily to discover the pricing policies of others in relation to what is being offered. This information is not, by its nature, confidential, yet it is difficult to compile. We propose that some central "register" would benefit the whole community.

While we have no difficulty getting applications for places on the course, we have had great problems in getting publicity out to the right people in many schools. In 1987, we posted two consecutive mailshots to all female-only and co-educational schools and colleges in England and Wales. These were addressed to the head of sixth form. It is perhaps surprising that we did not mailshot the head of computing, but we felt strongly that such a move would in effect be "preaching to the converted"; we were trying to target the young women who had **not** considered computing rather than those who had. As part of the mailshots we also contacted all senior careers officers for the LEA's, requesting them to distribute enclosed posters.

The problem seems to be that in many cases the poster is either lost in the weight of paper deluging schools and colleges, or it is immediately passed to the computer studies teacher, voiding our primary intention. The other consideration about direct mailing is the cost of postage; in 1988 it was this that made us reconsider our publicity policy. In our most recent course we only mailed to LEA offices, asking them to distribute posters along with their regular output to schools in their area. We also experimentally advertised in the VIth Form Casebook, and on TTNS (The Times Network for Schools, a national information network available to any school that wants it).

The arguments for a centralised method of publicising all the courses available are basically those of cost. If the costs were shared between several courses, expenses would be drastically reduced, and more costly but well-aimed methods could be tried, eg Times Educational Supplement advertisements. We also envisage a small booklet to be distributed to VIth form common rooms, for example, containing brief notes on the courses offered nationwide in the coming academic year.

The last two points we wish to raise in a national forum are rather more contentious. First, we have met with something less than enthusiasm from some of our male colleagues in trying to organise the courses. This is unsurprising but it leaves us with no clear policy on the role of male colleagues on these courses. Attitudes have ranged from *what-a-waste-of-time* through *of-course-we-support-you-but-you-won't-want-us-to-get-involved* to a practical *what-chores-can-we-relieve-you-of?* The radical solution of simply excluding male colleagues is exhausting in a department where there are two female and fourteen male academic staff. It is of course a familiar phenomenon for many women that the balancing act required in accepting male involvement can be equally exhausting, though in a rather less practical sense. We recognise that there is no easy solution to this dilemma, but hope that a sharing of experiences with other women will help to ameliorate it.

Finally, and also without any real hope of a solution in the short term, we would like to highlight our own conviction that in designing courses for seventeen-year-olds, we are merely applying a sticking plaster to a well-established wound probably inflicted far earlier in the students' development. Our course only really appeals to those young women who have not already totally accepted the ubiquitous subliminal message that computing is boring/unfeminine/difficult. We accept, of course, that it can be all those things at various times, but then so can housework! We acknowledge the likelihood that courses aimed at much younger girls may be far more important in changing participants' long-term impression of the area; but a university is perhaps not so suited to catering for this much younger audience.

52.5 Summary

The "Women In Computing" course at Liverpool University can, with many others like it, perhaps be dismissed as too little, too late. But the fact remains that for those young women who do choose to spend those three days with us, the effect is very positive. A number of participants told us that they were now prepared to consider a career in computing where they had not previously been thinking of it. We also feel that we have done a little to counteract some of the adverse publicity that the city of

Liverpool attracts from the media, although this was not a primary aim of the course. We have attempted to be egalitarian in our pricing and our workshop strategy, and we believe that our provision of positive role models (at close quarters rather than only as "speakers") is an important factor in the success we have had. Funding and publicity are a growing problem as the number of competing courses increases.

Further details of questionnaires, comments from participants, details of budgets, fundraising and finance can be found in Hughes and Maybrey [Hughes 88].

Acknowledgements

We would like to thank Professor Michael Shave, Head of Department, for his continued support for "Women In Computing" at Liverpool. Our gratitude also goes to Maureen James and Liz Shale for shouldering the paperwork and more; to Sue Flackett at Carte Blanche catering whose brilliant food has, from the very first, been a highlight of the courses; and to all those unsung heroines and heroes of halls, department and elsewhere who have helped, supported and believed in these projects.

52.6 REFERENCES

[Hughes 88] Hughes S and Maybrey A, "No Previous Experience Necessary: Residential Courses at Liverpool", *WiC Conference Proceedings*, 1988.

53

Southampton WiC Workshops

Gillian Lovegrove[1]

53.1 Introduction

There is justification for running Women into Computing workshops[2] for schoolgirls not only to bring to their attention the many job opportunities in Information Technology but also in the hope of increasing the number of women applying for Computer Science or related degrees [Lovegrove 87].

This paper describes the format of two such events which included cooperation and funding by a major technological firm, IBM (UK) Ltd. From the resulting questionnaires it is clear that these workshops at Southampton University were successful but there were useful lessons learned about what the young women from schools themselves expected to find at the workshops, how many attendees there should be, the optimum length of the workshops, and how to structure discussions, demonstrations and visits to industry.

53.1.1 WHICH AGE-GROUP AND HOW LARGE?

There has been a trend to run WiC workshops for the 14 year old age-group, as this is the age before major curriculum choices are made at school. The hope is that, despite pressures from peer group and puberty, young women will take up the option of continuing maths, science or computing, taken up, thereby enabling choices of IT related subjects to be made in the sixth form. An example of an institution running workshops for 14 year olds is Glasgow University [Watt 89] which gives five individual days of workshops to two hundred a day, thus reaching a thousand girls. However it is still not proven that "the bigger the better" is true as far as numbers on workshops are concerned. Edinburgh University have reduced the size of their workshops to about 45 as they had doubts as to the positive impact when the groups were larger [Welch 90].

---

[1] Dept of Electronics and Computer Science, University of Southampton, Southampton SO9 5NH
[2] This paper was written for the 1989 Conference.

53.2 Southampton WiC Workshops

In January 1989, a meeting was held between representatives from IBM UK Ltd, SSTF[3], and members of the University to consider the format of a WiC workshop. It was agreed that this venture should be a modest one, not only because it was the first of its kind at Southampton, but also because of the machine and human resources available. A maximum of 25 girls from 5th and 6th forms, thus aged 16+, would be invited to a two-day workshop, with an overnight stay at a University hall of residence.

IBM UK Ltd has a site at Hursley Park, near Winchester, only 8 miles from the University. They offered to host the group of 25 for lunch and for the last afternoon at Hursley, including talks and smaller group visits to selected centres within Hursley. The contribution of SSTF was to raise sponsorship for the workshop and to manage the major part of the administration.

53.2.1 GIRLS FROM ARTS THROUGH SCIENCE

The workshop was intended for girls from varied backgrounds, and the poster to advertise the workshop indicated that no prior experience with computers was required. In the event, the 25 places were over-subscribed as 110 applications were received, from 24 of the 150 schools mailed to. Thus a decision was made to run a subsequent one-day workshop for any remaining applicants who were willing and able to come. In accordance with the spirit of the workshop, the 25 girls were selected from the 110 using the criteria that the group should include a spread of backgrounds from those who had experience in computer science, those who were mainly scientific in A-levels, through Economics and Management Sciences, to largely Arts-based, and also including some who were not expecting to go to universities. There was one representative from each school and two from one school.

53.3 The Two-day Workshop

53.3.1 FIRST MORNING

The girls were welcomed by the Dean of Engineering, who laid emphasis on the need for women in engineering disciplines, and the role of the workshop as a forum for the exchange of ideas and information. There followed a brief description of how computers were in use today, the components of a typical Computer Science university course and an atypical one (Modern Languages with Computing). Also included in the programme was a talk with slides on the landmarks of computing history, including references to Ada Lovelace and Grace Hopper.

---

[3] SSTF (Southern Science and Technology Forum) exists as a charitable organisation under the umbrella of the Faculty of Engineering and Applied Science at the University of Southampton.

53.3.2 DISCUSSION

After lunch followed a discussion session in which the girls, split up into groups of four or five, went through a series of questions and discussion points. Each group had at least one leader from either the female staff or post-graduates, or from a group of invited guests including one of Southampton's female undergraduates, one of the graduates now working in industry, and a teacher of computer studies from a local sixth form college.

The first set of questions for the girls were general ones concerning the use made of computers at their schools. Apart from being informative, these questions were intended to break the ice. Other scenarios and discussion points were arranged as follows:

- Carol has become very good at computers because her father has one at home. Her uncle has given her some money for her birthday but she decided to spend it on a computer game. She goes into W H Smith's but ends up coming out without the game. What could have happened?

- Sandra wants to get into computing and signs up for an evening course at the youth club. She is told she did not get a place, and finds out later that all the places are filled by boys. Sandra goes to talk to the director of the youth club. How do you think the conversation went?

and discussion points included:

- why do you think women are not entering the sciences and computing in great numbers?

- what would be the single most significant factor that would influence you *to* a career in computing? *against* a career in computing? What would be other factors?

- how can girls ensure that they have a chance to pursue a computing career should they want one?

- how can schools, parents and society help them?

53.3.3 THE VARIATION IN OPINIONS

After 30–45 minutes of discussion, everyone came together again and a spokesperson from each group (in preference a schoolgirl, but with a default of the leader) reported on the main points arising from the discussion. One most interesting observation was the variation between the groups which was quite marked. It is hard to know whether this was a result of the suggestions or dominance of the leader, or the inclinations of the girls, under the influence of one of their own stronger personalities. It was clear that the reasons for being deterred from using computers are complex and varied. There was a general impression that computers are present in the schools today but that teachers can be (not always) unwilling to spend time with interested but non-GCSE students. Sometimes there is a lack of material (suitable or otherwise) to get them started on the machines. There is a lack of motivating software for girls: this was a principle cause for complaint. There was general agreement that the attitude of boys and girls towards working with computers is fundamentally different: boys tend to work alone, competitively, and with less forethought, whereas girls are more likely to work in an organised way in groups, and find greater fulfilment in environments in which there is scope for positive personal and social interaction. This was thought to be a positive aspect as good communication is essential at all levels of life and work.

53.3.4 THREE STREAM SPLIT

After tea on the first day came the first hands-on and demonstration sessions. The girls split up into three groups and visited three separate sessions, each taking about 45 minutes. These were a demonstration of a Mac, a visit to the Image and Video Laboratory, and hands-on session in Smalltalk.

Demonstration of a Mac
In groups of about four, the girls were shown text editing, the spelling checker and MacDraw, and as a result were keen to produce something themselves. They quickly mastered the use of the mouse and menus and produced personalised greetings cars which were then printed.

Visit to the Image and Video Laboratory
One laboratory at Southampton contains both the Vision and Image Processing and also the Interactive Video equipment. After a demonstration of the Image Processing equipment, the girls had their picture taken using a comera, the results coming out on a laserwriter.

Cut, Paste and Create in Smalltalk
It was assumed that the girls were not familiar with the WIMP interface of windows, menus and a mouse. They were given a set of instructions which led them first through selection from text and menus, cutting and pasteing, through to running the demo program which depends largely on turtle graphics. Playing with the demo program increased their confidence with the interface. They were then shown how to add (in true Blue Peter fashion) a new method and menu to create their own demo.

53.3.5 EVENING MEAL AND TALK AT GLEN EYRE HALL OF RESIDENCE

An popular feature of the two-day workshop proved to be the overnight stay at Glen Eyre Hall of Residence. One of the Professors of Computer Science gave the after dinner talk which was informative, entertaining and also containing a strong message as to the worth of women in computing and engineering.

53.3.6 The Main Hands-On Session: Prolog on the Suns

The young women had come to the workshop principally to get to know and have fun with computers, and they indicated through the questionnaires that they would have liked even more hands-on sessions. With 25 on the two-day course and 45 on the one-day course, it was a difficult choice as to which machines and environment to use. The final decision was that Prolog on the Suns would present a novel environment to the majority of the girls, although it meant that on the one-day workshop, there was in some cases one workstation between four people. The questionnaires seemed to indicate that the Prolog Session was indeed a great success, though it was also clear that there was a greater "drop-out of attention" when there were three or four to a workstation.

The girls were given a handout at the beginning of the session and each group of girls had their own login name. The aims of workshop session were to introduce a modern computer language used for AI (Prolog), to type in a simple program and to use an editor (Spy) at the workstation.

53.3.7 Visit To Chilworth: Talk on Parallel Computing

After coffee on the second day, the girls were taken by mini-bus to Chilworth, the Research Park a few miles from the University. Here the Professor of Computation gave a lively talk on the subject of parallel computing, its challenges, complexities and some of the solutions. The talk was well received, though the demonstrations which followed were, for some girls, lacking in impact. Nevertheless this talk was thought to be so vital and entertainingly presented that it was featured as the concluding item on the one-day workshop.

53.3.8 Visit to IBM

From lunchtime onwards on the second day, the girls and invited lecturers were the guests of IBM (UK) Ltd at Hursley Park, near Winchester. IBM had not only organised talks, lunch and tours of various parts of IBM, but also contributed to the general cost of the workshops.

For the girls, the whole of the visit to IBM was substantially better than they had expected. On arrival at IBM everyone was conducted to one of the suites for talks and presentations. The whole atmosphere was relaxed, informal and informative. After an excellent lunch (rated highly), the girls split into six groups and went on two tours each. The choice of tours was predetermined by the workshop organiser on a random basis and included Technical Writing and Publications, CICS Systems Test and Build, Presentation Manager, the Computer Centre, Hardware and Human Factors.

In the closing session at IBM, there was a talk from personnel about the career opportunities and life in general at IBM. Following this, the girls were given a questionnaire composed by the workshop organiser which covered all sections of the two-day workshop.

53.4   The One-day Workshop

The programme for the One-day workshop included a discussion session and hands-on experience with Prolog. There was a talk about IBM and career opportunities by an electronic engineer from IBM and the concluding session was the talk on Parallel Computing.

53.5   Questionnaire Results

The questionnaires completed at the end of the workshops, concentrated on feedback on each of the various activities of the day, often by means of a scale rating from 1 to 5.

The results indicated that both workshops were highly successful in terms of enjoyment. In the light of experience, some of the more theoretical presentations could be shortened and made more fun. The discussion session was fruitful for both workshops. The girls would have liked more hands-on experience, which would require greater organisation and planning as the numbers of attendees increase. It was informally expressed that the girls enjoyed presentations and workshop sessions from men as well as women, with the possible exception of the discussion session.

Questions involving the effectiveness as regards course or career choice were included and showed an appreciable change in attitude. Perhaps the best indication of the success of the workshops is that one attendee, after leaving school to take a higher education course, has now registered for a degree in computing at Coventry Polytechnic. This makes all the effort worthwhile.

IBM appreciated receiving the feedback as regards their own events as well as the workshops as a whole. In this respect, activities and visits where the visitors were able to talk freely to their female hosts, were rated highly, whereas straight "sales" or "careers" talks caused some switch-off in the listeners. A talk by an enthusiastic young man who was working at IBM before going up to a university, created a very good impression. Perhaps the most unexpected positive impact recorded in the questionnaires was that of the unlimited size and quality of the free lunch at IBM!

53.6   Effectiveness: a reassessment of workshop design

The impact of the two-day workshop was greater than that of the one-day. This is largely due to the smaller number of girls, the visit to IBM, and the longer stay including an overnight in a Hall of Residence, which enabled the girls to mix and get to know each other. Increasing the numbers of girls and selecting a lower age-group would bring difficulties in both staffing and equipment resources. At present Southampton has decided to keep to small numbers and older age-group, but also to look into the possibility of making visits to schools in the University catchment area, but outside the immediate vicinity of Southampton. In this way, it is hoped to attract girls to apply to computing courses at Southampton, as well as to consider careers in Information

Technology.

53.7 Acknowledgements and Funding

The workshop activities would not be possible without the support of many members of the Department of Electronics and Computer Science, including the secretarial staff. The undergraduates give freely of their time and enthusiasm. Graduates who work near to Southampton join in our activities and make superb role models. We have had great support from local teachers too.

We are lucky in having SSTF to undertake a substantial amount of the administrative role and also to seek and obtain funding for us. We are especially grateful to them and to IBM at Hursley and British Gas Southern for financial support.

53.8 REFERENCES

[Lovegrove 87] Lovegrove G L and Hall W, "Where Have All the Girls Gone?", *University Computing*, 9, pp207-210, 1987.

[Watt 89] Watt, H *Women into Computing Workshops* , Research Report, January 1989, Department of Computing Science, Glasgow University.

[Welch 90] Welch D and Michaelson G, "The Edinburgh Women in Computing Workshops" in this volume.

54

The Edinburgh Women in Computing Workshops

D Welch[1]
G Michaelson[2]

54.1 Introduction

The[3] Edinburgh Women in Computing group was formed early in 1987 as a group of two representing the Computer Science departments at Edinburgh and Heriot-Watt Universities. As well as broad concern at the declining numbers of women in computing, a major consideration for both departments was the lack of applications from potential women students and therefore the small numbers of women participating on the courses. It was determined that the problem was not just a local one but, nationally, the number of women making applications for computing courses was 9-10% (UCCA figures), slightly lower than our own figures. Several reasons for the continued decrease in women applicants (along with the large increase of male applications) to Computer Science courses have been mooted and it is not the intention of this paper to reiterate these.

Several discussion meetings with psychologists, other computer scientists, careers officers and schoolteachers as well as past and current female students were held during which time the WiC group grew. Following the meetings, it was decided to raise the awareness of computing, particularly with regard to career prospects, by organising and running a workshop on Women in Computing.

At present, the group has representatives from the Edinburgh University Departments of Computer Science, Artificial Intelligence and Psychology, and from the Heriot-Watt University Department of Computer Science. It was felt important that the group transcend institutional and departmental rivalries as the low participation rate of women in computing is a shared social problem, tackled most effectively on a regional basis.[4] Members are predominantly computing officers, research assistants and postgraduate students. The group is mixed though predominantly female. It was

---

[1] **Department of Computer Science, University of Edinburgh, Edinburgh**
[2] **Department of Computer Science, Heriot-Watt University, Edinburgh**
[3] This paper was first presented at the 1989 Conference and has been revised.
[4] Scottish Universities attract mainly Scottish students, with further geographical subdivisions. Thus, Edinburgh and Heriot-Watt attract students mainly from the East of Scotland while Glasgow and Strathclyde attract students mainly from the West.

felt important that, while men should take part in workshop planning and organisation, the workshops should be fronted by and, as far as possible, staffed by women to try to provide positive role models for participants.

The workshops are fully funded by the Edinburgh and Heriot-Watt Computer Science Departments, enabling free participation. Administrative and organisational tasks are shared amongst group members with individuals taking responsibility for particular activities such as writing flyers, stuffing envelopes, schools liaison and arranging workshop session details. Activities are coordinated through regular meetings where decisions are taken by consensus.

54.2   The first and second workshops

The first Women in Computing workshop was held on 16 September 1987. Its aim was to expose schoolgirls who had not decided on their future with certainty to opportunities for women in computing in Scotland. The one day workshop, which concentrated on careers in computing, was open to girls aged 15 and above from all over Scotland. Over 500 applications for places were received which were impossible to accommodate and so numbers from each school were limited. 200 girls attended the event. Throughout the day, presentations were made by recent female Computer Science graduates of the two universities on their jobs, women undergraduates on each of the courses, and invited women guests from industry as well as timetabled practical sessions. The practicals were worksheet-based and use MacPaint, MacDraw and MacWrite as well as a turtle graphics package on the Macintosh, with 2 or 3 participants sharing a computer.

The participants were organised as 3 groups of around 70. Each group attended 3 out of 4 non-practical sessions as well as the practical session.

Overall, the day was a great success with the practical session being extremely popular (see below). We were so encouraged by the success of the event that a replica was organised and run (again being grossly over-subscribed) on 16 March 1988. At the first workshop, the groups were too large for useful interaction so, at the second workshop, for the "Studying Computing in Edinburgh" session each group was further divided into 5 sub-groups of around 14 participants.

Both workshops were free and lunch was provided for all participants.

54.3   The third workshop

Having critically assessed the previous two workshops, it was clear that while they were successful in the general aim of raising awareness of education and careers in computing for young women, they were not addressing the needs of the Computer Science Departments as well as they might. In particular, the workshops did not address directly the question "What is computer science?" and were not attracting enough potential university applicants. Whilst it was agreed that the format of our previous workshops was still important and worthwhile, it was felt that such broad proselytisation was not within the remit or resources of the Departments. It was also felt that having smaller groups at all of the non-practical sessions would enable more active participation.

This in turn placed a lower limit on the number of participants due to problems in finding enough helpers to run an increased number of sub-sessions.

In order to concentrate on potential university applicants (in particular to computer science degrees) it was decided that our target audience should be those girls who had sat or were preparing for Higher Grade examinations[5].

From the analysis of the questionnaires completed after the first two workshops (see below), the most popular event on the programme in each case had been the hands-on experience but this was felt to be too unfocused. It was decided to expand practical work when planning the third workshop and to have more structured sessions based around solving specific problems. To allow more time for practical work it was decided to run the workshop over two days although not to make the course residential. Schools within daily travelling distance of Edinburgh were therefore invited to compete for 50 places, allocating a maximum of 3 per school. As had happened previously, the workshop places were grossly over-subscribed and so trimming mechanisms such as sitting or having already passed H Mathematics were imposed.

The content of the practical work aimed to give the participants a clearer indication of what computer science was. Two practicals were set in which the girls worked together in groups of 3 to 5, guided by an undergraduate or postgraduate student or a member of staff. All participants did both practical exercises, lasting around 2 hours each. One practical involved maze-searching and was written in Pascal: the participants, guided by their group leaders solved specific problems and wrote a few lines of code which served to illustrate backtracking and recursion. The other practical, which was very different in nature, also covered backtracking and recursion by forming a map of Europe by querying a Prolog knowledge base. Although both languages and concepts were new to the schoolgirls, the practical sessions were very well received.

To back up what was learnt about the subject from the practical sessions, the participants attended information sessions about studying (particularly computer science) at university given both by members of staff and undergraduates. Not forgetting career opportunities with a computer science degree, young women with computer science degrees working in industry were invited to address the group and to receive questions after.

The third workshop was held on 13-14 September 1989 and again was highly successful. As before, the workshop was free and lunch was provided on both days. Because of the increased number of small groups and the low number of women in the Departments, more men were involved in helping with the practical sessions than in the first two workshops.

---

[5] The Higher Grade is the standard entry medium to higher education in the Scottish education system. Presentation is one year after O or Standard Grade (approximately equivalent to O Level) and it is common to achieve 5 Higher Grade passes in one sitting. No specific Higher Grade subjects were requested although it is usual to demand a good grade in H Mathematics for entry to Computer Science courses.

54.4   Workshop evaluation

It was felt important to gain feedback from participants on their immediate responses to the workshops both to help with improving and planning subsequent events and to gain a more general profile of young women's attitudes to and experience of computing. Feedback was acquired through questionnaires and these are discussed below.

Results are presented as percentages. The actual numbers of responses in each case differ as some respondents did not answer all questions. Full details of the questionnaires and their analyses are available from the authors.

54.5   Evaluating the first workshop

The first workshop was assessed by a questionnaire assembled in a blind panic shortly before the event. 121 questionnaires were returned and analysed by hand. Responses were broken down by respondent age but the full details are not given here: instead overall responses are totalled.

91.9% of respondents found the workshop "interesting" and 94.6% found it "useful", suggesting that a successful event was held.

Responses to "What was the best part?" (of the workshop) were:

Practicals	41.7%
Careers in computing	12.5%
Undergraduates' presentation	12.5%
Women from industry	10.8%
Postgraduates' presentation	9.1%
Other/no response	13.3%

showing the popularity of the practical work.

An open ended question about how the workshop might be improved elicited a wide range of responses, the most common being to do with the poor quality of sound equipment for speakers and a lack of time for the practical work.

To the ambiguous question "Has the workshop changed your opinion?", 67.7% answered "yes", 11.6% said their opinions had been changed a little, 18.1% said their opinion had not changed and 2.5% did not respond. As shown below, it is wrong to assume that a "yes" response implies a positive change in opinion!

Other questions asked about participants' school computing experience. 59.5% of respondents had studied or were studying computing at school. Surprisingly, 16 and 17 year old girls were more likely to have studied computing than 14 or 15 year olds.

Further questions showed that most girls who studied it found school computing interesting (77.2%) but that a significant minority had encountered difficulties (31.3%), though no overall pattern of problems was apparent.

The questionnaire contained many classic mistakes. In particular, the questions were ambiguous, far too open ended, lacked scales or options for responses, and did not ask about attitudes both before and after the workshop. These deficiencies reduced the value of the questionnaire and made analysis extremely difficult.

54.6 Evaluating the second workshop

For the second workshop, the questionnaire was completely redesigned. Questions were structured more carefully with set responses on a 5 point scale ranging from very positive to very negative. More detailed questions were asked about school and home computer experience, and about individual workshop sessions. Space was left for further comments after each question.

Participants were asked the same four questions about their attitudes to computing before and after the workshop, to try and detect attitude changes. Rather than giving them separate questionnaires, they retained a unitary questionnaire throughout the event so that they could evaluate their final responses in the light of their initial attitudes. This carries its own methodological problems: however, workshops are intended to influence participants and we felt it important that they be aware of that intention.

131 questionnaires were returned and analysed by computer. Once again, responses were analysed by age but only an overall summary is given here.

99.2% thought that the whole day had been worthwhile or extremely worthwhile. Responses to questions about which sessions were best and worst were:

	best	worst
Practical	81.8%	6.5%
Studying computing	6.6%	25.9%
Aspects of computing	5.8%	24.1%
Careers	5.8%	43.5%

once again showing the overall popularity of the practical sessions. However, participants were also asked to rate individual sessions and all the sessions were rated more positively than negatively:

	very positive	positive	neutral	negative	very negative
Practical	69.5%	25.2%	0.8%	2.3%	2.3%
Studying computing	11.4%	69.1%	4.9%	11.4%	3.3%
Aspects of computing	20.5%	54.3%	7.1%	14.2%	3.9%
Careers	14.1%	61.7%	5.5%	17.2%	1.6%

Participants were asked if they would like a job in which computing were a major part, before and after the event. Responses showed that 28.9% were more positive about working with computers after the event and 16.4% were less positive.

Participants were asked if they would like to study computing at university, before and after the event. Responses showed that 33.9% were more positive about studying computing after the workshop and 13.4% were less positive.

Responses to these two questions suggest that the workshop was successful both in encouraging some young women to consider working with or studying computing and in helping a smaller number to decide that computing is definitely not for them.

Participants were asked if computing was just for boys, before and after the event. Responses showed that 93% disagreed strongly with this view before and after the event! None were more positive after the event and 5 (3.9%) were less positive. This question was criticised at the 1989 Glasgow WiC Conference for being somewhat leading. A more neutral question will be asked in 1990.

Participants were asked if computing was mathematical, before and after the event. Responses showed that 20.5% were more positive that computing was mathematical after the event and 21.3% were less positive, suggesting confusion on their and the presenters' parts about the mathematical nature of computing.

Other questions asked about school and home computer use. 68.8% studied computing at school and 70.3% shared homes with computers. Of these, 24.7% did not use the computer, 21.6% used it for writing, 44.3% used it for programming and, contrary to the prevailing stereotype, 69.1% used it for playing games.

54.7 Evaluating the third workshop

For the third workshop, the same questionnaire as for the second was used, with minor changes. There were 41 responses which were analysed by computer. Responses were analysed by age but, again, only an overall summary is given here.

100% of respondents thought that the event was worthwhile or extremely worthwhile.

The best and worst session responses were:

	best	worst
Map exercise	57.9%	6.5%
University life	23.7%	6.5%
Maze exercise	15.8%	54.8%
Careers	2.6%	32.3%

Again, the practical sessions together were very popular, with the map exercise being the most popular session overall. As with the second workshop, the careers session was not very popular overall. Perhaps, for young people about to embark on higher education, it is hard to focus on events which are 3 or 4 years away.

Participants were, again, asked to rate each individual session and, again, all were rated more positively than negatively:

	very positive	positive	neutral	negative	very negative
Map exercise	35.0%	57.5%	0.0%	7.5%	0.0%
University life	61.0%	31.7%	0.0%	4.9%	2.4%
Maze exercise	27.5%	55.0%	0.0%	12.5%	5.0%
Careers	5.1%	82.1%	2.6%	10.3%	0.0%

The university life and careers sessions received higher individual ratings than at the second workshop, suggesting that small groups are a better format for these topics.

While the maze exercise in Pascal received a high individual positive rating, the map exercise in Prolog was seen as better overall. This may suggest that Prolog is a better medium than Pascal for introducing elementary "computer science" ideas.

For the question "Would you like a job in which computing is a major part?", responses showed that 29.3% were more positive after the event and 17.1% were less positive. This is similar to the responses to the second workshop.

For the question "Would you like to study computing at university?", responses showed that 48.8% were more positive after the event and 9.8% were less positive. Comparison with the responses to the second workshop suggests that targeting older girls and having a small group format may be more effective for influencing young women towards studying computing at university.

For the question "Do you think computing is just for boys?", responses showed that 90.2% strongly disagreed before and after the event. After the event, sadly, 2.4%(1) were more positive whereas 4.9%(2) were less positive.

For the question "Do you think computing is mathematical?", responses showed that 19.5% were more positive after the event and 31.7% were less positive. This and the response to the same question at the second workshop suggest that we need to clarify how we present the mathematical nature of computing.

Of the respondents, 61.0% studied computing at school and 56.1% shared homes with computers. Of the latter, 26.1% did not use the computer, 4.3% used it for writing, 39.1% used it for programming and 60.9% used it for playing games. This suggests that many young women are not put off computing by the aggressive and competitive nature of computer games.

54.8 Conclusions

The Edinburgh Women in Computing Group has run both large and small group workshops. As noted above, questionnaire responses suggest that small group format workshops targeted at older girls are more successful for presenting individual topics and in terms of persuading young women to consider studying computing. Certainly, the people who helped run both the second and third workshops thought that the small group format was preferable as it enabled more interaction with and between the participants. This format will be retained for the September 1990 workshop.

Questionnaire responses also suggest that young women are particularly favourable to practical sessions at workshops: these will again be emphasised at the next workshop. Sessions on studying computing and university life are more popular than careers sessions, perhaps because the former topics are more immediately relevant. None the less, a careers session will be retained at the next workshop as it is thought important that studying computing be placed in a broader context.

There seems to be some confusion about the mathematical content of computing, which the workshops fail to clarify. This requires further consideration. However, individual group members have very different ideas about the role of mathematics in computing education. This may make it hard to present a uniform line.

In the long term, the value of Women in Computing activities can only be assessed in terms of increases in the numbers of women studying and seeking careers in computing. Members of the group are monitoring overall application and acceptance rates for courses and intend to try and correlate attendance at workshops with course applications and acceptances. The latter is complicated by the likelihood of participants of Edinburgh workshops applying for courses at other higher education institutions, which might lead to an underestimate of the workshops' impact. It is also impossible to tell what the trends would have been without national WiC activity over the last few years.

This contribution was written on behalf of the Edinburgh Women in Computing Group but any opinions expressed are the authors'. We wish to acknowledge our colleagues', students' and former students' hard work in making the workshops such worthwhile events.

55

Scenes from Europe

Gillian Lovegrove[1]

55.1 Introduction

In April 1990, I was invited to speak at a Special Topic Session on "Gender and Informatics" at the EURIT Conference[2] in Denmark. In this paper I present some of my main impressions and findings inspired by the EURIT Conference, in the hope of sharing ideas and learning lessons. However I would be the first to admit that I have a patchy knowledge, so I have included references and addresses for further research.

In summary, my initial impressions were:

- other nations were equally worried by demographic downturn and plight of women and technology;

- some of them were years ahead in terms of considering the problem;

- some of them were years behind in terms of pro-feminist attitudes;

- they were often better organised as regards adult education (women returners for example);

- we had sometimes made greater progress as regards spreading the word to schoolgirls, but some Scandinavian initiatives are exemplary;

- all governments have no money to spare (this was not a surprise!) but Labour Ministries (or DTIs) are more forthcoming than Education Ministries (DESs);

- the EC has some money if you know where to look for it and whom to ask.

55.2 Background: EURIT Conference

The Special Topic Session in "Gender and Informatics" was chaired by Brita Foged from Aarhus University in Denmark and had two other speakers besides myself – Benthe Stig from Denmark and Barbara Wagner from the Federal Republic of Germany.

---

[1] Dept of Electronics and Computer Science, University of Southampton, Southampton SO9 5NH
[2] European Conference on Technology and Education.

We each spoke for about 20 minutes and then had a lively discussion session with the audience. At the end of the session, the names and addresses of interested participants were collected and this has since grown into an informal European network[3].

55.3 Denmark

Benthe Stig is Danish and has enormous experience, having worked in various jobs, including journalism, and is now in a role in equal opportunities. She is just starting a project in Norway. She has a great deal of experience of the similarities and differences between the women/technology culture in Denmark and Germany particularly, having been awarded a Social Fellowship by the EC to study in the FRG the theme of "Technical Centres for women as a strategy in vocational guidance, vocational training and employment" [Stig 89]. Much of the information in this section originates from her and describes work in Denmark where equal opportunities officers have dealt with questions of gender differences and new technologies.

55.3.1 DENMARK: THE NETWORK GROUP

In 1984 it became compulsory for secondary schools in Denmark to offer computer courses. As in the UK, it was apparent that there would be little in-service training to support the teachers and it was felt important to establish a network for women teachers from primary and secondary schools, vocational schools, technical colleges, commercial schools etc. The network group offered four valuable things to its members:

- it gave an initial introduction to computers in a friendly, non-competitive atmosphere; those in the group who already knew about computers teaching the others;

- it developed awareness of gender inequalities and differences in school in general;

- it supplied the members with curriculum ideas and with materials for staff room discussions on computer teaching;

- it contributed to the personal growth of the members.

One activity was a collaboration between LEGO, the well known construction kit company, and 12 different schools, 2-4 teachers from each school, in which a curriculum was developed which included technology. It was found that at all ages, girls as well as boys liked the technical subjects when they were integrated, as shown in the following example. A small school in a rural area had been working on agriculture as an subject, and then chose to work with technology in agriculture. They visited farms

---

[3] Anyone who wishes to be added to this informal network should contact the author.

and a development centre, interviewed farmers and later built a replica of the technology used in LEGO. They arranged an exhibition, invited the farmers in, and told and showed them what they had learned. They also made a video production of it all. This class decided to continue studying new technologies in a higher grade and established a collaboration with high technology electronic industry in the area. Some of the teachers of the group now instruct other teachers on how to integrate technology into the curriculum.

55.3.2 DENMARK: OPEN COMPUTER WORKSHOPS FOR WOMEN

In 1984 the first computer workshop for women opened in Denmark – at Aarhus [Aben Datastue]. Since then about 20-30 workshops have opened over the country. The Open Computer Workshops are a practical attempt to break down barriers between women and technology, between women and the labour market, and between women and the educational system. Also the Open Computer Workshop is an attempt to develop pedagogic methods in relation to unemployed adult women and new technology.

The main target group is unemployed women over the age of 25 with basic schooling background. The training is free and open for women to walk in from the street and participate without obligations of any kind and without any previous knowledge of computing. The women can attend the workshop for three hours a day, four days a week and for as long a period as they need. Apart from the open walk-in offer, the women can attend courses of shorter or longer periods. The instructors are all women, and an essential factor for the workshop staff is to establish an atmosphere of friendliness and openness, where the women feel secure and respected.

The Open Computer Workshop is an independent institution with a governing board of representatives from local authorities. The activities are financed mainly by public funding: the Employment Office, the municipality and the county authorities. To quote from Benthe:

> "Each (open computer workshop) develops in its own way, and not all of them are exclusively for women. But those that are open to men, do tend to lose some of the values of the computer shops for women. They get influenced by people who have other computer needs and another working style than that of the target group.
>
> Let me summarise what is special about the open computer workshops: the unique walk-in offer; that they combine practical learning with personal development and with a holistic understanding of technology and society; that they have been able to spread their pedagogic conquests to traditionally male systems."

55.4 The Federal Republic of Germany

In Western Germany it is still usual for women to leave their jobs when they marry or at least when they have children. The training initiatives for women in Germany are to a large extent for *Ruckkehrerinnen* – women who after a career break wish to go back to work. As in Britain, there is a social interest in qualifying these women to work with the new technologies, in view of the demographic downturn and skill shortages. The initiatives are primarily aimed at women who are already well educated, but who are now in need of new knowledge, especially word and data processing.

Whereas in Denmark there are equal opportunity advisors at the regional employment services whose *full-time job* is to work for equal opportunities for women and men in the labour market, in Germany all public authorities have *Frauenbeauftragten* – persons who are responsible for women's issues, but with no fixed working hours for this part of their job.

55.4.1 TECHNOLOGY CENTRES AND COURSES FOR ADULT WOMEN

Recently the Ministry of Labour has brought about an evaluation of the impact of computers on the situation of women office staff. One finding was that women now get a wider range of tasks and less straight typing; they feel greater job satisfaction, but they are not better paid; and the men get the new jobs involving the new technology [Mensch 89].

55.4.2 ZENTRUM FUR WEITERBILDUNG

The ZfW (Centre for Further Education) in Frankfurt, run by Barbara Wagner, started as an association of a small group of women and men who were interested and experienced in adult education. The courses for women have become by far the largest part of the activities. The first courses were oriented towards work possibilities for women who were uneducated or whose education was outdated. In 1987, together with a local Frauenbeauftragt, they started offering introductory weekend computer courses, which are now becoming regular weekend and evening courses, introductory as well as advanced.

The ZfW trains women returners as well as unemployed women[4]. They often cooperate with institutions in Frankfurt and surrounding towns on the introductory courses which are then cheap or free of charge.

Present plans are for an education course for women to become skilled industrial mechanics with a further education in systems control, and a technology centre for women offering

---

[4]In Europe generally there appears to be a greater distinction drawn between the term woman returner, who is returning to work after a career break, and the term unemployed woman; in the UK, we tend to use the term woman returner more loosely to include both.

- counselling on further education;

- introductory and advanced training of women and girls;

- workshops for women teaching data processing;

- a meeting place for women working with data processing in industry and administration;

- career guidance to girls.

All courses arranged for women are part-time. Women are not expected to want
full-time jobs. There is no general acceptance of women working full-time.

55.4.3 ACTIVITIES AIMED AT GIRLS/YOUNG WOMEN

"Typisch – Die neuen Madchen" is a four year campaign aimed at motivating girls and
young women for untraditional occupations. The campaign is now in a pilot phase. It
tries to appeal to young women by showing how they can choose untraditional occupations and still remain feminine. Success stories of career women are publicised in
papers, radio and television. Since there is no general acceptance of women choosing
untraditional occupations, they find it important to have the topic debated in public.
At present they also have road shows. They use local bands to attract young people
and then offer them a mixture of entertainment and information.

In Nidersachsen in Germany, the equality activities at present target schoolgirls and
schools. An extensive development and research project "Madchen und neue tech-
nologie" (girls and new technology), included in the programme compulsory computer training in the schools of Nidersachsen. It was decided that computers should
not be taught as a discipline, but as a medium – a tool, and that the use of it should
be developed within the subject area – physics, maths, social studies and German –
rather like our National Curriculum. The programme aimed at developing and testing
curricula and at developing in-service training of teachers.

The evaluation is carried out as qualitative research on girls' approach and access
to new technology. The researchers have had theme-centered group discussions with
boys and girls from classes of the project; they have interviewed the girls one by one;
they made observations during lessons and after certain lessons they let the pupils
have an open debate. During the project they discussed their results with the teachers
involved (14 men 9 women). They realised the dilemma of describing and characterising gender specific approaches and accesses while the course was running, but the
time for developing curricula was so limited that it was thought essential to integrate
the hypothesis of gender specific differences into the project.

The evaluators say that it is not necessarily to the advantage of the boys that they
often have advance knowledge of computers. Sometimes it blocks them by making
them content with only one solution to a problem, whereas girls are creative, using
what they have learned in new ways. In an exercise that was meant to make them
understand the concept of algorithms, the girls who in general had never tried programming, worked well with their own verbal solutions, while the imagination of the

boys was narrowed, exactly because they knew a certain amount about programming and thought in BASIC instead of finding words.

Some classes tried working in boys' and girls' groups. Afterwards the girls would often say they they had dared say more and ask more when there were no boys present, but some were afraid that they would be taught at a lower level, and they wanted to find out if the boys really knew as much as they claimed. The boys did not find the boy's groups had offered any overall advantage to them, and they found it useful for a girl to work together with a boy [Frauenfirschung]. See also [Milner 90] who finds that mixed groups can be advantageous, given the right setting, context and control by the teacher.

These are only a few of the examples of initiatives in the FDR. Further details can be found in [Stig 89].

55.5 The Netherlands

In the Netherlands, there is a Women and Informatics[5] group which wants to increase the level of participation of women in the field of automation, to raise their interest and to help organise them. In a paper describing the activities of the W and I [Women and Informatics], it is stated that often informatics is presented on a very technical level: this scares everyone off very easily, especially women.

W and I want to point out that informatics are not merely a technical matter – that detailed technical knowledge is not necessary to be able to work with computers and control them, and the essential technical knowledge is easy to acquire.

The foundation W and I manages a national centre [6] from where different activities are organised, and an institute for advice, training and courses. The centre and the institute are both situated in Amsterdam. Included in the remit for W and I are:

- **Activities:** information distribution to the public;

- **Collective:** an intermediary function to find women to give speeches and women who can act as tutors in introductory courses;

- **Magazine:** W and I publishes a magazine four times a year: "Magazine for Women and Informatics". It highlights many aspects of informatics and particularly those activities where women participate;

- **Lectures, symposia, conferences etc:** W and I regularly organises lectures on various subjects eg artificial intelligence or systems development; also twice a year a conference or symposium;

- **Management advice:** to companies or education – eg policy of organisation: how do you handle automation? In what way will it affect the organisation?

---

[5]Informatics is the commonly accepted term in Europe for the subject area Computing/Information Systems/Information Technology etc.

[6]Natonal Centre for Woman and Informatics, WG-plein 250, 1054 SE Amsterdam.

How can the employees be involved? How is the training organised? What does career planning mean in this context?

- **Training:** W and I trains groups and teams on request for either introductory or advanced courses;

- **Vocational Training:** W and I developed curricula for vocational training institutes;

- **Educational Study Groups:** six study groups work as part of W and I. They engage themselves with education in informatics on separate levels: elementary and secondary schools, vocational and technical training, university, non-regular informatics training and introductory/orientation courses at school level. The study groups meet on a regular basis. Subjects for discussion are eg development in the education in informatics, or the Government's educational policies and advice in this field. They also work on curricula and develop course and study material;

- **Regional groups:** In several department of Holland, regional groups of W and I are active. The women in these groups exchange information and experiences; they organise meetings about specific themes and generally support each other.

There is a school called the Annie van Dierenschool [7] in Tilburg, the Netherlands, which is the second of an entirely new type of school in the Netherlands for women only and set up by the Women's Union, affiliated to the Federation of Dutch Trade Unions. The most important reason for this initiative was the fact that an increasing number of women want to offer their services (again) on the labour market in order to lead an economically self-supporting life. The percentage of women in the Netherlands **having** a paid job is small, compared with other European countries. The number of women who **want** a paid job (again) is growing fast. Vocational training is hardly accessible to women, with the exception of a few training courses for typically female professions. Schools like the Annie van Dierenschool provide education and courses for women to redress this balance.

55.6 Sweden

The Royal Institute of Technology (KTH) intends to support a project to encourage girls to choose technical education at university level. The concern is to look at the environment for the women students and researchers, and to bring to the teachers an awareness regarding equality questions in the educational system. Another important aspect is to influence the male students to be "equal" engineers with the women students, a necessity in the process of making it possible for men and women to meet in the working life on the same terms.

---

[7] For further information, contact The Annie van Dierenschool, Wilhelminapark 55, 5041 ED TILBURG, The Netherlands.

KTH initiated some girl-oriented activities during 1983. Some of the activities that had a particularly successful outcome include:

- a two-day mini-course about university level engineering studies;

- computer science courses, some at weekends, for girls in the upper level of schools;

- information groups, consisting of female students from engineering colleges and non-traditional study paths in the equivalent of sixth-form colleges, have visited schools for lower age-groups;

- "Think again!" an essay for all girls in the equivalent of sixth forms, sponsored by the Royal Institute of Technology and the magazine Ny Technik. The girls were required to write an essay on the subject of, "If I were an engineer..." – they were required to imagine themselves as engineers and think about how they would change things.

- in-service training days on the subject, "What is technology and how can we get girls interested in engineering study programmes?" have been arranged for study and vocational guidance counsellors and teachers. The need for this type of training is continuous – most of the teachers concerned have not yet been reached by these courses;

- vocational guidance material: the Royal Institute of Technology's regular recruitment pamphlet entitled, "Technology for everyone", contains a special section aimed at encouraging girls to apply to engineering colleges. In another pamphlet, female students say, "Why they chose engineering education and how they like it". There has been a great deal of interest in this brochure.

The main recruitment activities regarding women and technology currently are:

- girls' evenings – girls in sixth forms are invited to get information from women engineers and women engineers-to-be;

- "Carin's Diary" - a new girl's brochure, will be distributed to girls in the secondary schools;

- seminars, debates, information and talks on the wide opportunities in the professions and the suitability for girls – given by the project manager, Christina Sternerup;

- in-service training for study and career counsellors and teachers; where women students and graduate engineers talk about their experience of technical education and having a technical profession;

- education for child-care personel and teachers of young children in the subjects natural science and technology.

Another field of activity that KTH shortly will try, is to introduce a mentor activity – a way to try and bring consciousness to the male graduate engineers-to-be.

55.7 WITEC

WITEC is the COMETT Programme for Women into Technology in the European Community University Enterprise Training Partnership and was established in 1988 as a European network of partners working for the motivation, development and support of women in science, technology and enterprise. The UK branch is based at Sheffield [McShane 90].

55.8 GASAT Conferences

Another source of ideas and information are contained in the proceedings of the Conferences on Gender and Science and Technology (GASAT). GASAT is an association of those concerned with issues arising from interactions between Gender and Science and Technology and has the aim of fostering socially responsible and gender-inclusive science and technology. Their conferences take place annually and the next one will take place in the University of Melbourne, Australia in July 1991 with the theme: "Action for Equity: the Second Decade".

55.9 In conclusion

It is encouraging to find out how many international networks exist, though still confusing to know exactly where to apply for the appropriate support or funding. However all this activity and dissemination of information can only be beneficial. But before we let the thought enter our heads of sitting back and letting someone else do all the work for us, I will quote from Benthe Stig,

> "We need enthusiasts or – as call them in Danish – souls of fire. Without their commitment, their experiments, their wish to spread the message, strategies will not be developed and put into use."

55.10 Acknowledgements

This paper was inspired by Brita Foged, Benthe Stig, Barbara Wagner and their many friends in the Aben Datastue and Cekvina in Denmark. I am also grateful to Ria van Ouwerkerk for information about the scene in the Netherlands and to Dalene McShane for information on WITEC.

55.11 REFERENCES

[Aben Datastue] *Open Computer Workshop: Aarhus, Denmark*, obtainable from Aben Datastue, Aboulevarden 7 st, 8000 Aarhus C, Denmark.

[Frauenfirschung] *ifg Frauenfirschung*, Heft 3/89.

[McShane 90] McShane D, *Women in Technology in the European Community*, in this volume.

[Mensch 89] *Mensch und Computer*, 7, (A special issue on women and computers), 1989.

[Milner 90] *Action Research: Looking at the Beginnings*, in this volume.

[Stig 89] Stig B, *Report of Study in the Federal Republic of Germany*, October 1989.

[WITEC] *The WITEC-UETP*, brochure available from CCVE, University of Sheffield.

[Women and Informatics] *The foundation for women and informatics*, National Centre for Women and Informatics, Amsterdam.

56

Women in Technology in the European Community

Dalene McShane[1]

56.1 Introduction

Women into Technology in the European Community, a University Enterprise Training Partnership (WITEC-UETP) established in 1988, is a European Network of partners working for the motivation, development and support of women in science, technology and enterprise. University-Enterprise Training Partnerships are consortia of
academic institutions, enterprises and other organisations with a direct interest in
training. They are designed to make European industry more profitable by increasing the range of technological skills of their staff, and offer a wide range of services
directly related to training and technology. UETPs are playing an increasingly important role in the preparations for the Single European Market in 1992. WITEC partners
are drawn from all EC and EFTA member states.

  If we are to succeed in widening girls' and women's vocational choices, the issue of inappropriate skills must now be addressed. WITEC seeks to publicise educational programmes in Europe aimed at increasing and diversifying the range of subject
choices available to girls and facilitate the entry of young and adult women into career
paths and jobs in the field of IT, electronics and other technology related industries.

56.2 Women in Europe : some facts and figures

One in three (38%) of Europe's working population is female. In the UK the figure is
even higher at over 40%. Forty-three per cent of married women are members of the
work-force. Eight per cent of women currently work in agriculture, while 21% work
in industry and 71% in the service sector. However, there is wide variation between
different member states, as shown in the following table.

---

[1]Centre for Continuing Vocational Education, University of Sheffield, 65 Wilkinson
Street, Sheffield, S10 2GJ

Table 56.1 : Patterns of employment for women

	Agriculture	Services	Industry
Greece	37.8%	45.6%	11.2%
Netherlands	3.1%	85.7%	16.6%
UK	1.1%	80.8%	18.1%

But how many of these women are at managerial level or above? The answer is very few. Women typically outnumber men in low paid, part-time jobs in the declining areas of the economy, often with little prospect of advancing up the hierarchical system. Of the 36 recognised sectors of activity, 72% of all women workers are in 8 of the lowest paid. For example, in the UK 75.4% of all employees in footwear and clothing are women. Despite legislation on equal pay for equal value, women still earn significantly less that men. Women are also disproportionately affected by unemployment, with 1 unemployed person in 2 being female.

56.3   Education And Training

Most countries have only a small percentage of women in engineering and technological occupations. Technological subjects at the Higher Education level have the lowest proportion of women students compared with any other field of study.

56.3.1   EDUCATION

Educational institutions have an essential role to play in seeking to improve the technological base in the European Community, yet evidence suggests that disproportionately few girls take science and technology options at school.

European boys and girls have the same compulsory education and in theory receive the In the UK, Belgium, France, Ireland, Germany and Luxembourg there are more girls than boys in secondary education. Only after A level or the equivalent, and above the age of 20, do women become the minority. At the age of 24 there are twice as many men as women still in education, with great subject differences between the two groups, as Table 56.2 shows.

It is apparent that all over Europe young men and women still go down very different paths when it comes to preparing for working life. And while women dominate the educational sciences, very few of them will go into teaching technical subjects.

Table 56.2 : Differences in Percentages for Men and Women at Further Education Level

	Men	Women
Physics	85%	15%
Educational Sciences & Teaching	24%	76%
The Arts	51%	49%
Medicine	56%	44%
Business Management & Economics	35%	65%
Architecture & Town Planning	53%	47%
Engineering & Technology	90%	10%

56.3.2 TRAINING

Demand for well trained personnel is increasing throughout Europe. In 1995 there will be 1.2 million fewer 16-19 year olds than in 1989. This dramatic fall in young people entering the labour market mean that women will be an increasingly important source of labour. By the year 2000 it is predicted that 44% of the labour force will be women (Personnel Management, August 1988). Whether or not this poses a problem will depend upon employers' ability to recognise and eliminate explicit and implicit discrimination against women, and to provide for the particular problems facing women returning to work. Much of the necessary training will be difficult for individual companies, particularly small companies, to provide. The European Social Fund and the Equal Opportunities Commission are encouraging women to go into traditional "male" occupations and new technologies. Typical examples of ESF funded projects include training for women in micro-electronics and technical skills, training for women in the building industry and accountancy training. Many member countries have benefited from funding under this scheme, for example, Spain, Portugal and Greece. Unfortunately most of these courses have been too short and too basic to meet the real needs, leading instead to low level jobs in word processing etc. They have also been small scale and very localised.

56.4 WITEC-UETP

The WITEC-UETP was created to try to address some of the training issues. The key points in its development are as follows.

56.4.1 HOW IT ALL BEGAN

In 1987 the Centre for Continuing Vocational Education at the University of Sheffield submitted a proposal to the EC's COMETT arising from ongoing work with the SEFI women's group, part of the European Society for Engineering Education. This group had been working on a programme to encourage girls and women to take up engineering. COMETT appeared to offer a way of achieving their aims by providing funding to create a transnational European network, to facilitate student exchanges and to produce training and distance learning materials specifically targeted to meet women's needs. The intention was to form a Network to bring together parties interested in working with girls and women and to produce courses and materials for use throughout Europe and Scandinavia. At the same time a similar proposal was put forward by the Donna & Sviluppo organisation in Naples. The Commission decided that the best course of action would be to merge the proposals and this was agreed by the two partners in January 1988. Initial funding of 26,000 ECUs (£18,000) was given to establish the European Network. The aim was to establish WITEC contacts in every EC state, each of which would then seek to establish a national network.

At the first full meeting in June 1988 an Executive Committee composed of partners from the UK, Italy, France and Netherlands was established. WITEC was growing fast at this point and already had partners in eight states.

In August 1988 the UETP was successful in its bid for second year funding for the Network and for additional funding to set up a student placements scheme. Fifteen young women were awarded grants of up to £1000 each towards their placement costs. The final reports of the students indicated that the placements had been very successful and a number of companies have asked for further WITEC students to be sent to them in subsequent years.

In September 1989 the 1st Annual WITEC Conference was held on the Isle of Capri, resulting in the establishment of 6 international research projects for which funding is currently being sought. The proceedings of the conference, in Italian and English, are being published in a Dossier which also contains information about projects and work being carried on throughout Europe. Planning is currently underway for the 2nd Conference which will be held in Dublin Castle in May 1991. The conference will once again be workshop based and will centre on the theme of "Enterprise".

In February 1989 WITEC submitted its most ambitious proposal to the EC to date for funds under the COMETT II scheme. Major research and course development proposals have been made and work is currently being undertaken at Sheffield to develop a modular degree course which will feed into WITEC as short courses for women in the field of Risk Management. Other courses proposed are for women returners, training of trainers and managers and professional updating of skills. The student placement scheme is being expanded and it is hoped to have up to 200 placements on offer for periods of 3-12 months.

Due to the rapid expansion and changes in membership, WITEC have recently formalised their management structure as follows:

- Joint Project Directors - CCVE & D & S;

- Executive Committee - 5 National Network Co-ordinators;

- Board of Management - National Network Co-ordinators in all States;

- General Assembly - All Members of National Networks

and 6 Satellite Project Working Groups directed from Italy.

56.4.2 THE NETWORK

The Network is concerned with the need to increase the number of women studying technology, engineering and the management of technological change and taking up careers in these fields across Europe.

A consortium from universities, polytechnics and higher education colleges in partnership with industry and industrial training organisations applied for funding from the European Community COMETT programme to set up a University-Enterprise Training Partnership on Women in Technology. The proposal received the support of the EC and is now in its third successful year of operation. The aim is to involve every EC and EFTA country, with networks being established in each state and the University of Sheffield co-ordinating these at European level.

The initial funding of £15,000 to establish the network was a pump-priming resource and it is expected that the UETP will seek additional funding in resources or cash from industry to progress the project. To date this has been quite successful.

56.5 Aims of WITEC

- To generate a network of universities, enterprises and other organisations committed to increasing the number of girls and women taking up studies, careers and autonomous activities in advanced technological fields across the EC and EFTA states.

- To assist women studying and working in technological fields to surmount barriers which interfere with their entering into the labour market and support their technological career development.

- Tp promote and support research concerning problems in this field and their solutions, and to disseminate the results.

- To publicise problems, strategies and methods already found for dealing with them, especially within the overall COMETT Network.

- To generate action programmes and pilot new initiatives of a general or specific character.

- To encourage women undertaking technological careers to contribute to overcoming reluctance to employing women and at the same time promote information and experience exchanges between universities and enterprises.

- To improve women's language and inter-personal skills.

- To take women with basic maths and scientific knowledge or in lower professional level careers through programmes to the point where they could enter vocational education courses.

- To offer knowledge and skill development in technological fields to women without any previous technological background, via a programme of evaluation of their skills and characteristics and offer tools to facilitate this.

- To contribute to the creation of a favourable learning environment for women.

- To test contents, procedures and communication sources to reach the women the project seeks to address most effectively by collecting and exchanging information on research, statistics, policies and action projects on the theme "Girls and Women in Engineering, Technology, Applied Sciences and Management".

56.6 What WITEC currently does

WITEC has already started to set up a European Database for statistics on European women in scientific and technological studies and careers together with their relative histories, as well as a databank for information on publications, research projects, public and private initiatives and media packages.

A Newsletter is produced to ensure information is spread and to spur on new research and experimental action on connected problems. Other promotional materials like posters, audio-visual materials and literature have also been produced. Contributions are always welcome as we like to give as broad a view as possible and all events are guaranteed to be publicised.

WITEC runs information and consultancy seminars to encourage the formation of strong national networks and it is hoped that international teams will be able to take round trips to present these seminars in several member states from August 1990.

In addition WITEC runs a very successful placement scheme with funding from COMETT. Placements for young female undergraduate and postgraduate students are organised and supported by WITEC industrial project partners sympathetic to women gaining appropriate workplace experience. WITEC is currently in its second year of placements. The aim of the scheme is to offer a period of between 3 and 12 months structured "on the job" training with a company in another member state. Language tuition is provided if necessary. WITEC is constantly seeking additional placements for students and has now joined forces with a number of other UETPs to work in collaboration on placements. Tutor support from the local educational institutions is encouraged to develop links between the placements and the universities.

WITEC is currently seeking funding from the EC for 6 Satellite Research Projects based around work and gender issues; they are described in the following subsections and contributions to these projects are welcome.

56.6.1 FEBE: Women's Training for Advanced Technologies

The aim of this project is to start to plan and to experiment with new systems and new tools for the teaching of advanced technologies for women. These systems and tools have to be able to reach, with respect to needs and relative cognitive styles, the diverse targets of women in the EC.

56.6.2 TETHYS: WHEN A WOMAN CREATES AN ENTERPRISE: IDEAS AND SUPPORT STRUCTURES

WITEC intends to intervene through the provision of advice to help the enterprises run by women. Initially this will be by encouraging and supporting young women and then disseminating their experiences throughout Europe so that mistakes are not repeated.

56.6.3 RHEA: WOMEN & TECHNOLOGY IN EUROPEAN INDUSTRY

This proposal arose from women trying to find and, if it exists, define a gender-separate specificity of the life of a technical working women. The main purpose is to establish connections and promote discussion and comparison between women living common experiences at different levels and in different environments. Then to advice and promote the process of the removal of sexist barriers by the publication and circulation of the research findings to education and enterprises.

56.6.4 DIONE: THE RELATIONSHIP BETWEEN WOMEN AND TECHNOLOGY - AN ALTERNATIVE FRAMEWORK

The aim of this project is to build a Network to determine and evaluate positive action experiences in technological fields in different European situations; to start temporary placements for equal opportunity advisors; to activate co-operation in the consultancy field and to plan and disseminate a multimedia model of a strategic management of technologies that allows improvement of conditions in the level of involvement of women in the sectors of advanced technology.

56.6.5 MIMAS: STEREOTYPES AND EXPECTATIONS IN SCIENTIFIC AND TECHNICAL COURSES

This project investigates the number of women on technical and scientific courses and their scientific imagery with the aim of de-constructing given male stereotypes and examining the pattern of the relationship between the current didactic practices of teachers of technical and scientific disciplines.

56.6.6 IPERIONE: WOMEN & SCIENCE - THE RESULTS OF GENDER RESEARCH

A research and intervention project for the eventual realisation, diffusion and utilisation of a gender conscious education and working programme from the results of scientific and technical research developed from different but related factors.

56.7   How to become involved with WITEC

To become involved with WITEC, individuals or organisations can either join the local WITEC Network or, if no such network exists, join as an International Partner and
establish a local network with financial help from WITEC. The more links we build,
the stronger the Network becomes and the more information that can be exchanged.
   The benefits of membership include the following:

- access to a major network of individuals and organisations across the EC and
  EFTA committed to increasing the numbers of women and girls taking up stud-
  ies and careers in technological fields and to statistics and research from across
  Europe;

- involvement in action programmes and pilot initiatives which are being undertaken to encourage women's ability to engage in the scientific and technological
  areas and in the outcomes of initiatives to promote the awareness of scientific
  and technological trainers to the needs of women;

- invitations to WITEC international events and regional meetings of the UETP;

- first refusal on places at the WITEC Conference.

Membership costs per year are 250 ECUs (£175.00) for full organisational membership or 100 ECUs (£70) for personal membership, but it is also possible for membership to be exchanged for information, services or donations of equipment or materials.

56.8   Further developments

WITEC seeks to address issues through a variety of approaches, ranging from advanced courses of a high degree of complexity to industrial courses where women can
be introduced to be basics. The courses currently being developed consist of multi-
media packages combining materials suitable for both students and their trainers.

56.9   Links with other organisations

We realise that to achieve this task it is necessary to work with other organisations
who share a similar concern and we have made active links with the following:

GASAT - Gender and Science and Technology
SEFI - Working Group on Women in Engineering Education
WES - Women in Engineering Society
WIC - Women into Computing
UNESCO - Working Group on Women in Higher Education

We have also formed collaborative working relationships with many other UETPs in the EC to promote the cause of women.

57

Gender Bias: The East-West Paradox

Lorna Uden[1]

57.1 Introduction

A recent feature article in *The Computer Bulletin* claimed that Singapore, despite the skills shortage in computing, has no problem in attracting women into this field – in fact a higher percentage of women than men are said to be taking up IT courses.

This paper seeks to explore the reasons behind this phenomenon, and to compare the situation in Singapore with that in Britain. It is the author's contention that gender bias and stereotyping is largely a result of mental attitudes. Traditionally the Chinese people have looked upon women as "lesser beings", yet paradoxically the predominantly Chinese nation of Singapore is managing to attract large numbers of women into what the British perceive as a man's world.

One of the reasons may be the high value which the Chinese place upon education; a factor which does not seem to prevail in Britain. This paper explores the differing attitudes in their historical context, and seeks to determine ways in which British attitudes may be changed so that the ratio of women to men entering computing can be improved.

Finally the paper addresses some of the ways of changing the perception of, and attitudes towards, women in all areas of high technology in the 1990's.

A little over a decade ago, computing was a popular field for women, with some 25% of students entering university computing science courses being female. By 1987, the figure for home students had dropped to 10%. Of those women who continued to be attracted to computing courses, the majority were either overseas students or home students from ethnic minority groups such as Indian or Chinese.

The rate of entry of women into professional and technical careers has halved over the past six years. Numbers were falling even before the demographic down-turn. The situation is worse in England and Wales than in Scotland, France and the USA, or even the Far East.

In the UK, women form 21% of programmers, whereas in France it is 39%. Companies here recruit less than 20% of women in their graduate intake, whereas in the USA the figure is over 50%. These statistics show an alarming trend.

What has happened? Why is computing no longer attractive to women? What can be done to halt the downward trend? Women into Computing [WiC 89] was born as a

---

[1] Dept of Computing, Staffordshire Polytechnic, College Road, Stoke on Trent ST4 2DE

response to these questions, and seeks ways of redressing the balance.

According to a recent study by the Information Technology Skills Agency [ITSA], demand for professional IT staff has exceeded supply for the past ten years. This trend is likely to continue, and indeed will be exacerbated by the predicted decline in the number of young people entering the labour market in the 1990's. The computing industry needs to find an additional 100,000 staff over the next five years. The answer to alleviating the problem is to make use of a readily available, but as yet under-utilized resource – women.

Women into Computing, along with other organisations such as WIT, and the Women Returners' Network, have been providing information and help for employers and potential recruits.

Various studies have been conducted to identify the reasons for the downturn in the numbers of women entering computing careers, and several major problems have been identified:

1. it has been shown that in schools, boys tend to physically monopolise computers, and push the girls aside;

2. aptitude tests used by employers tend to be biased towards young males;

3. there is a need for flexible working hours for women, child care facilities in the workplace, and the ability to work from home;

4. there is a great need for role models for girls at school level;

5. universities, polytechnics and colleges must encourage applications for computing courses from mature students, women returners, and those without traditional educational qualifications.

Within the last two years, many of the above recommendations have been taken up by employers and academics in an attempt to alleviate the problem. There has been some success, particularly in the retraining of graduates into professional computing from other disciplines such as arts and languages.

Workshops have been conducted throughout the country to give better career information on the wide variety of jobs available in computing. Despite all this effort, it appears that very little progress is being made. Why should this be so?

Lim Gek Kheng of the Centre for Computer Studies, Singapore, states, "If English girls entered and sustained IT-related careers in the same proportion as American, French or Singaporean girls there would be no current or prospective shortage of trainees" [Lim 90].

Both Britain and Singapore need to develop a pool of highly skilled IT professionals. How is it, then, that Singapore has no problem in attracting women into IT, whereas Britain appears to be failing miserably?

It is in fact paradoxical, considering the traditional role which Chinese women play in society, and the fact that the majority of Singaporeans are Chinese. Coming from a Chinese background, the author was brought up in a culture where the woman is looked upon as a second class citizen! Traditionally women were not expected to seek education or employment, their role being to marry and raise a family.

In 1987, an IT manpower survey in Singapore revealed that females constituted 58% of the applications/analyst programmers in the nation and 52% of systems analyst/designers. More than 50% of the graduates from computer courses in 1980 were female. There is no shortage of girls opting for careers in computing in Singapore. No concerted effort has been made by the government or employers to deliberately draw females into the computing industry. There is, however, a clear sex differential in other areas of study. More males enrol for engineering courses, whereas females tend to choose social sciences, education, arts or accounting courses. The enrolment pattern for computer courses, generally viewed as technically-oriented in Britain, is an exception among the technical courses in Singapore.

There are several possible reasons given for the large proportion of females in the IT industry in Singapore.

Firstly, the government of Singapore has been very active in promoting the use of computers in both the public and private sectors. As part of the economic restructuring of Singapore, a high-level committee on National Computerisation was established in 1980. The Singapore government, in 1985, felt the need to develop an IT oriented economic strategy and the National IT plan was launched with the dual objective of developing a strong export-oriented IT industry and exploiting IT to improve productivity and competitiveness in every economic sector.

Secondly, most Singaporeans feel that IT, as a new growth industry, provides good career prospects and interesting job opportunities. IT professionals are highly paid, and earnings have been pushed up by the high demand for skilled personnel. Both male and female alike are attracted to a highly remunerative career. More girls enrol for computing because boys usually opt for engineering courses - another well paid profession plagued by manpower shortages. It is thought that girls prefer computing to engineering, perhaps because a career in computing would not involve them in getting their hands dirty!

Thirdly, in Singapore both boys and girls are exposed to computers whilst in school; computers are not perceived as toys for the boys only.

Fourthly, women working in the IT industry do not have to take a career break to look after any children they may have. Singaporean women are able to continue working by getting help with their domestic responsibilities. Employers are thus spared the problem of finding replacements for these females.

Lim cited several factors which contribute to the phenomenon of large numbers of women being attracted to careers in computing. There is a combination of economic and social factors; early exposure to computers in schools, the lure of financial rewards, the novelty of a job in computing, and the ability to continue working in spite of family commitments. Last, but not least, is the idea that every individual, whether male or female, is significant in the national development of Singapore, which has emphasised the importance of high technology.

This paper will explore the aforementioned factors which have contributed to Singapore's success story. By taking a deeper look at the underlying principles it may be possible to move closer to finding a method of attracting more women into computing in Britain. Most of the issues raised have already been thoroughly examined before, so is there anything new to be said which may offer a solution? In the author's view, the question of *attitudes* is one which seems to have raised little debate. It is proposed, therefore, to look at attitudes under several different headings.

57.2 Stereotyping

The question of gender differences in attitudes to computers begins at home where the influence of parents plays a crucial role. Traditional patterns of play and primary education have tended to emphasise, and, in some instances, to create learning and behavioural differences between girls and boys. Special efforts are required by parents and teachers to introduce all children to the full range of early learning experiences, and unless this is done boys will continue to gain a head start in their ability to succeed in science and technology. When a child enters school, any sex stereotyping that was begun at home will often be tacitly accepted, and sometimes reinforced.

57.3 Parental attitudes

Parents often encourage their girls to take "soft option" subjects with low academic status. Many girls have been brought up to believe that they have a role to fulfil which is inferior to that of boys. The parents' attitude is clear; girls should not stray into traditional male areas. Parents often have a strong influence on the choice of options that pupils, especially girls, take in school. Perhaps this shows a need for educating parents regarding the current trends in the employment market, and the need for change.

57.4 Teachers' attitudes

There are clear links between gender-specific school subjects and traditional male and female jobs. Teachers' attitudes towards girls are biased, and, generally speaking, boys get more attention than girls. Some teachers actually positively discourage girls from taking traditionally male-dominated subjects, resulting in girls developing a low self-esteem at an early age. It is important that teachers be aware of the influence their attitudes may have on children, and encourage the mixing of boys and girls in all subjects.

57.5 Childrens' attitudes

One of the major differences between the Chinese and the British is that of the relational attitudes children have with their parents, teachers, and society in general. The Chinese have a long history of deference to all who are older (and therefore wiser) than themselves, and respect for one's elders is deeply engrained in the Chinese culture. In Britain, however, respect and discipline seem to have disappeared, almost without trace. Schools here encourage free-thinking and questioning of the *status quo*, which in turn has lead to a breakdown in society. The law of the jungle rules, and only the strongest survive. As the "weaker sex" women are losing out, and this all begins with attitudes instilled during childhood.

57.6 Employers' attitudes

Sex stereotyping is rife in industrial, commercial and government sectors - the women are the data-entry clerks and the men are the managers. Employers in Britain do not appear to believe in the potential of women in technical subjects. Men also appear to be afraid of working with women, particularly if the woman is in a superior position to the man. The traditional male-dominated world expects women to stay at home to look after their children. Male managers are often reluctant to employ women for fear of them taking time off work to care for their families. Employers must be made aware of the potential of women, and perhaps encouraged to act positively towards them. Women should not be discriminated against because of their sex, but accepted solely on their qualifications and the ability to do the job. This contrasts greatly with the attitudes of employers in the Far East. A recent BBC television programme featuring Alan Whicker in Hong Kong brought out the fact that women are respected for the position they hold, and men are quite happy to work for a female boss.

57.7 Women's own attitudes regarding themselves

Often women have a very low level of self esteem, and appear quite content to accept "low-status" jobs with consequentially low salaries. Lack of self confidence manifests itself in a self destructive manner, crushing aspirations and expectations. This is a major area for change.

57.8 Education

Another important factor which has a great influence on the Singapore success story is that of education. The Chinese place a very high value on education and regard a child's education as a form of investment. Singaporeans take great pains to educate their offspring, often to the extent of substantial self-sacrifice. In return children are expected to work hard from an early age, and the taking of five A-levels is considered the norm, rather than the exception. Parents have high expectations of their children in Singapore, and it is the dream of every parent for their children to obtain good jobs and achieve a high status in society. Computing is an area which offers a highly remunerative and high status career, and it is open to both male and female alike.

57.9 Governmental influences

Although the Singaporean government has not actively encouraged women to enter the field of computing, it has been very active in introducing computing to the nation as part of its economic strategy. The traditional respect of the Chinese for government leaders has ensured the success of the plan thus introduced. This may be contrasted with the difficulties the British government has had in introducing its IT policy in 1981.

Conclusions

This study has shown that there can be no gender differences which relate to ability, and the conclusions which can be drawn are that the differences between the two countries are in social and cultural attitudes alone.

Singapore is a fast moving city-state comprising a large proportion of highly motivated young people, eager to "get ahead". Attitudes towards women have changed dramatically in the post colonial days, yet other traditional Chinese values, such as respect for parents and teachers, remain as strong as ever. The work ethic is unchanged. The desire to improve one's lot against all odds is stronger than ever, now that the opportunities are there. The natural acquisitiveness of the Chinese in areas of personal wealth drives these people forward. In many ways Singaporeans are living a hi-tech version of the pioneers and the "Great American Dream", an attitude and spirit which, sadly, Britain seems to have lost. Can we, as women, do anything to regain that spirit? As Winston Churchill once said, "Give us the tools and we'll finish the job!"

57.10 REFERENCES

[Lim 90] Lim Gek Kheng, "WIT: The Singaporean way", *Computer Bulletin*, Vol 2, part 1, Feb 1990.

[WiC 89] *WiC publicity handout*, 1989.

58

Paradox and Practice: Gender in Computing and Engineering in Eastern Europe

Alan Durndell[1]

58.1 Introduction

Over a period when female admissions to university[2] have risen to 44% of the total, with dramatic rises in subjects like Business Management and Accounting, the proportion of female computing admissions has dropped, and is now very similar to the situation in engineering, where the figures have been slowly increasing to approach 10%. In other words, computing and engineering now seem to share a particular technological gender profile. It has quite often been reported in the West that the proportion of female engineers in Eastern Europe has been much higher than that in Western Europe; for instance [Jancar 78] reported that 27% of undergraduate engineers in Bulgaria were female in 1970. The figures often seem to be difficult to get hold of, and are often out-of-date. The contemporary situation in Eastern Europe is therefore of considerable interest with respect to undergraduate technological, engineering and computing education, and this article addresses this question, drawing on a recent visit to Bulgaria, a communist Slav nation which shares many cultural features with Russia.

On being asked what research was being carried out on gender, and to what extent gender was linked to computing and engineering, the initial reaction of researchers in Bulgaria was often blankness. Then they would say that politically the problem was solved as the constitution guaranteed equal rights for males and females. This was not an area that seemed to them particularly important, not a big issue. [Walford 83] observed a very similar reaction on a visit to look at science education and gender in the Soviet Union. The visitors were told that "there is no problem" and had difficulty getting the teachers to understand their interest. In fact it has been an accepted part of government policy in Eastern Europe for many years to, where deemed necessary, produce gender quotas for higher education subjects – see [Jancar 78].

Women form approximately half the workforce in Bulgaria, apparently overwhelmingly in full time occupations. Maternity leave provision was described as good, in-

---

[1]Psychology Department, Glasgow College, Glasgow
[2]This paper was presented at the 1988 Conference.

volving 6 months before birth, 2 years after birth on at least some pay, plus the option of a third year without pay. Paternity leave is possible in place of maternity leave, and a small proportion of males opt for it, especially if the woman's job is better paid than the man's. There appear to be adequate nursery places to cope with the demand, and the government is, if anything, trying to encourage an increase in the birth rate, as the population is relatively stable.

It turned out to be difficult to consider the gender proportions in computing, mainly because the computer revolution had only just begun to hit Bulgaria – for example there were virtually no home computers as yet. However, [Domozetov 86] had studied the introduction of the use of computers in the Savings Bank and amongst scientific workers. He found that in the Savings Bank the routine computer operators were nearly all female, many of whom placed somewhat greater value on their family and children than on their jobs, whilst the managers were virtually all men concerned rather more with their careers. However in fairness many of the men also gave great importance to a happy family life. Amongst the scientific workers, males and females competed for the same jobs. Both men and women in this group considered interesting work a priority, with success at work following for the males and a happy family life following for the females. 31% of the males agreed that "Women can't even deal with simple technical problems" whilst only 3% of women agreed with this statement. A third of the women were worried that family commitments would reduce their chances of gaining qualifications, to which Domozetov argued that specialist "catch up" courses in computer technology should be on offer to cater for re-entering women. However, Domozetov argued that it was believed that the men were better at what he called creative work and programming, whilst the females were more diligent, accurate and persistent and more willing to enter low paid jobs. He also reported that there were very few young women amongst the newish Faculty of Computing staff at the V.I. Lenin Institute. Thus, as far as the information was available, computing appeared to be following, at an early stage, the British pattern of women tending to do the routine operating, and men tending to do the higher status programming.

The position with regard to engineering was entirely different, the situation being so divergent from that in Britain as to be remarkable. Roughly 30-40% of qualified engineers were women, and in Bulgaria the Government was *restricting* the proportion of admissions into engineering degree courses that were female to 50% in order to stop women dominating engineering! The precise details of this policy of restricting the numbers of females was difficult to track down, though in general the policy was widely known about and openly quoted. Attempts to explain how this type of policy might be illegal in Britain and would undoubtedly produce vigorous debate and opposition were countered by some mild amusement and comments about different political systems working in different ways. Nonetheless this can be compared with the situation in Britain where after much effort the proportion of engineering undergraduate admissions that are female has risen to about 10%. This variation appears to completely destroy any biologically oriented theory about gender differences in ability, including spatial ability, and theories of hemispheric differences linked to sex, and conclusively indicates that observed gender differences are culturally and socially produced. It also raises questions about how the engineering situation has come about, and to what extent all gender differences have been eradicated in education in Bulgaria.

Although the discussion from now on concentrates mainly on engineering it can be argued that the factors discussed are relevant to all technologically oriented subjects that attract relatively few females.

58.2 Engineering Losing Status?

The simple conclusion that gender differences in performance and ability are culturally produced was made more problematic when one probed into the background of the situation in Bulgaria. The first difficulty was that it appeared that engineering was losing status in Bulgarian society. Dimitrov, of the Institute of Sociology at Sofia University, said that whilst well over 30% of all students study engineering, the competition to get an engineering degree place had reduced to such an extent that some areas such as mining engineering were unable to attract enough students to fill their places. At the prestigious H.I. of Mechanical and Electrical Engineering in Sofia, the number of candidates per place, which was 15 to 20:1 in the period 1956-1963, had dropped to 3:1 in 1983, 2.1:1 in 1985 and 1.9:1 in 1987. At the same time (1987) the humanities were attracting 10 to 12 applicants per place in subjects like law, sociology, psychology, history and languages. This was of great concern to the engineers, and bore some similarity to the British situation where some engineering courses have had difficulty attracting students.

It was also argued that engineering was of low status because the salaries that could be earned were not particularly good, and it seemed that the prestigious occupations with higher salaries in administration and management were often obtained via study in the humanities or science. Wages for new graduates were apparently controlled, although in general salaries do vary considerably. However, many Bulgarians seemed to think that financial incentives were not large enough – for example in the academic world only the professors, it was claimed, earned more than a bus driver, though the professor had much higher status. It was also said that many engineers became downhearted when brought face to face with the low level of technology available in practice at work, as opposed to the theory that was studied at university, and that the awareness of this situation contributed to engineering's lack of attraction.

This apparent phenomenon of the lowering of the status of engineering raised the question of whether it was partly caused by the entry of large numbers of females into the profession or whether the drop in status preceded the influx of females. The question is unanswerable at present. It is also possible that the lowering in status and the influx of females were unconnected. This seemed somewhat unlikely however, given what has happened in medicine in the Soviet Union, where females dominate in numbers and the status of medicine appears to be low [Lapidus 78].

58.3   Have All Gender Differences Gone?

A second difficulty was that gender differences did occur in higher education in Bulgaria and that they showed some similarities to the British situation. For example, health and medicine were numerically dominated by women, as was the educational area, whilst maths and science (such as physics and chemistry) had majorities of males (cf the comments already made re computing). Whilst in general there appeared to be a greater proportion of female students overall than in Britain, the distribution across subjects was similar with the spectacular exception of engineering.

A third, and major, complicating factor, as indicated above, was that the Government in Bulgaria attempted to regulate (with only some success) the gender proportions of students in particular subjects in higher education, and also to some extent in secondary education. This was attempted by setting different standards for the admission of males and females, and usually seemed to mean setting higher standards for females than for males.

It was very difficult to obtain the detailed figures and gender quotas for different subjects. Most researchers that were contacted did not seem to have considered challenging or arguing about the details of this policy, as gender issues were not a main concern. A particular formula repeatedly appeared in official publications such as the Bulgarian Official Gazette. "The ratio between women and men is 1:1. For some separate professions or specialities and consumers, demanding more men or women, the Ministry of Culture, Science and Education establishes other quotas in the plan for acceptance of new students". This formula obviously avoids giving the interesting details.

The policy of setting higher entrance standards for females in some subjects was justified by the fact that girls on average outperformed boys in the secondary school system, and would otherwise come to dominate the higher education system even more than they do already. Dimitrov called this already existing situation the "Feminisation of the Intelligentsia", and the possible domination of the intellectual professions in Bulgaria by females was seen as a problem by some Bulgarians.

A similar situation appears to exist in the Soviet Union, where for the last few decades females have on average been considerably better educated than males, though the professions that females have subsequently entered still tend to be somewhat poorly paid [Perevedentsev 88].

The third complication led on to two further questions: firstly, why did girls do so well in the secondary educational system, and secondly, why should this have been seen as a problem?

58.4   Why Do Girls Do So Well?

It was argued that girls did better at school because they were more "diligent", they "behaved better" and matured earlier. There was also some anxiety that Bulgarian secondary school teaching in general, and that of engineering in particular, had become more theoretical and less practical, and that this had been to the benefit of the girls.

The views of the group of researchers who visited Soviet schools that was reported on [Walford 83] partially support this. In spite of writing that they had seen only "staged" lessons in "good" schools they commented on the relative lack of experimental work, even in physics and chemistry, and the relatively low quality level of what apparatus there was. However, in terms of gender they observed that boys interacted far more with teachers than girls did in physics and chemistry lessons; that physics textbooks that they saw featured very few illustrations involving people; that when people did appear they were overwhelmingly male, and that many teachers were quite happy to express views that would appear extremely gender stereotyped in Britain (cf [Kelly 85] in Britain).

All children in Bulgaria follow a core curriculum for 7 years, and then at about 14 years of age can choose to specialise to some extent in various Technical Schools, High Schools and Professional High Schools. These might specialise in, for example, languages (where girls would be liable to outnumber boys), maths and science (where boys would be liable to outnumber girls), building/engineering and technical schools and many others such as sports schools, arts schools and schools for gifted children. In some cases after 10 years of schooling further specialisation is possible for 2 years previous to leaving school and applying for university or work. (The 1980 education reform was just working through the system, and it had amongst its aims the creation of a close connection between education, society and science, to be flexible and allow different routes to qualifications, and latterly to introduce microcomputers in schools – see [Raicheva et al 87]). Admission to university was via open competition. An individual's mark came half from the secondary school record of up to 12 subjects, weighted for relevant subjects and composed mainly of subjective assessments by teachers, and half from the appropriate admission exam for the university subject. It was at this stage that girls seemed to do particularly well in outperforming boys. It was argued that the motivation for girls to obtain a degree, any degree, was very strong, and the implication was that some females would realise that it was relatively less difficult to get into engineering, and they would therefore take the easy option and apply to study engineering (why this strategy was not adopted by the relatively weak boys was not made clear).

It was notable how the same educational debates about core curriculum versus specialisation and teachers' assessments versus external exams were going on in Bulgaria and Britain, with the two countries not necessarily moving in the same direction. For example, the Bulgarians were considering moving towards objective exams for school children, whilst in England and Wales the move is towards including teachers' coursework assessments. Similarly the Bulgarians were considering moving towards specialisation, whilst in England and Wales movement is towards a core curriculum. The possibility that it was the core curriculum that had increased girls' chances of good performance in spatial/stereotyped male subjects such as engineering in Bulgaria was confused somewhat by the presence of the specialised secondary schools. Thus, whereas advocates of the core curriculum approach in Britain might argue that girls should maintain maths and science up to about 16 years of age, in Bulgaria they continue to a considerable extent to choose their specialisms at about 14 years. However, along with the stress on technical and science education in general (see [Chivers 87]), this common education might explain the great female interest in engineering.

58.5 Why Is It a Problem That Girls Do Well?

Why should it be a problem that girls do better than boys? The semi-jocular remark was heard that the "boys needed help". There was some feeling that the school marks were too subjective and not reliable, and that the system depended too heavily on lectures and rote learning. Again [Walford 83] also reported that although maths and physics in the Soviet Union were strongly emphasised at school, they were taught in a very traditional and teacher directed manner, with much emphasis on memory work. At the same time Domozetov argued that females had no traditions of achievement in abstract thought and creative insights. The implication was that the educational system was encouraging routine low-level learning which females were good at, though Domozetov did concede that as the whole phenomenon of the "feminisation of the intelligentsia" was only 10–20 years old, females may produce creative insights in the next decade or two. Dimitrov argued that male/female job destinations were different, and quoted a study in 1978 on metal (s)melting engineers where 10% of the women graduates did not work in the discipline, some choosing jobs such as secretaries. (In British terms, it would be remarkable if 90% of graduates in many disciplines actually worked in areas directly relevant to that discipline). Many others turned to education rather than the production process (although it should be recognised that many engineering students are sponsored and have specific jobs to return to). It was also argued that women engineers tended to go for administration and management jobs (rather than production) because of their higher prestige. Finally the example of education was given, where the female domination of teaching was so great, it was claimed, that many boys met very few, if any, male role models when they were at school, and only did so when they did their 2 years national service in the army which was done before going to university (females do not do national service).

58.6 Why So Many Female Engineers?

Returning to engineering, although there was a contradiction between saying that women were poor at producing abstract creative products, yet good at theoretical study at school rather than practical study, nonetheless it could be argued that engineering and schooling in general in Bulgaria had become partly "feminised" by being rather lecture oriented with the practical components that do not appeal to girls being somewhat downplayed. This is reminiscent of the argument in Britain as to whether girls should change to cope with technology, or whether technology should change to attract girls. Some writers (eg [Elliot and Powell 87]) have argued that the entire structure of science and technology is permeated by male oriented values, and that females should be encouraged to challenge and change these values in order to produce a more feminised science oriented towards social benefit. However, this kind of analysis presumably would not present itself as a shift away from the practical to the theoretical, but rather as a fundamental change in the social relations of technological endeavour. If this type of analysis is applied in Bulgaria, the implication might be that it was engineering that had changed by becoming more theoretical and thus also becoming more attractive to girls, rather than the girls that had changed to become more interested in technology. Additionally, the high number of women engineers in Bulgaria could be interpreted in terms of gender stereotypes being eradicated in Bulgaria, and so it would be interesting to see how Bulgarian samples would perform on, for example, the Bem Sex Role Inventory which is an assessment of sex role stereotyping. There appeared to be little research in this area at present, though one study by Randev in Sofia on 15–17 year old children found in general that the differences obtained in the USA were not repeated in Bulgaria. This research suggests that gender stereotypes in Bulgaria might be different from the West. But as pointed out above, differences do still occur between males and females within the Bulgarian educational system.

Returning to the questions posed at the beginning, how can this information be interpreted? Have gender differences been socially eradicated? How has the engineering situation happened? There is no doubt that Bulgarian society officially encourages equality irrespective of sex, and for example, maternity leave and nursery provision appear to be far in advance of the British situation. At the same time gender differences do exist in Higher Education, and whilst males dominate fewer subjects than in Britain, they still do dominate some within a general context of the "feminisation of the intelligentsia". Britain itself could be argued to be moving in the direction of the "feminisation of the intelligentsia", as the proportion of university students who are female is rising and many subject areas such as medicine, psychology, business and financial studies and law now graduate high proportions of female students. However, as females are still in the overall minority in British university admissions (about 44%), this could be a premature conclusion to arrive at. (At least one Polytechnic has recently reported that 52% of its graduates were female however).

The existence of gender differences in higher education in Bulgaria and the complicating factors discussed in this paper indicate that it is not simple to identify the specific factors which have produced the Bulgarian situation vis-à-vis engineering and gender, and therefore extrapolation to other subjects such as computing is difficult. Nevertheless, the dramatic differences between Bulgaria and Britain provide forceful evidence of social and cultural influences. Exactly what these influences are is not absolutely clear. Presumably the perception and place of engineers in the respective societies is part of the overall pattern. To argue that engineering is of declining status as shown by the fall in applicants per place does not of itself explain the attraction of engineering to females in Bulgaria, as the same could be argued in Britain where engineering remains male dominated. The possibility that engineering has become "feminised" by becoming more theoretical and less practical in Bulgaria is interesting, although in Britain engineering is moving away from the "grease and boiler suit" image as well. The core curriculum in Bulgaria, at least up to 14 years, might also be a factor in retaining female contact with engineering related education.

Finally, in Bulgaria one observes a situation where there is something of a reaction against female dominance in undergraduate populations. This fits alongside some uncomfortable overtones coming out of Eastern Europe. In the Soviet Union in particular there is concern at women's "double burden', that is that apart from full time work women also have to look after the home (see [Buckley 86] for some interviews on these matters). Allied to a possible Russian worry about Soviet Central Asian women having far more children that Russian women, there are some indications of pressure on women to increase their childbearing (see [Attwood 88]). In East Germany and the Soviet Union (but not yet in Bulgaria) a special course "The Ethics and Psychology of Family Life" is taught in schools, which Attwood calls an exercise in overt sex role socialisation and pro-family propaganda. In this context, and following all the efforts in many countries this century to make it acceptable for females to study any subject at degree level, it is disturbing to see males being given advantages on admission to university, even if it is in the name of equality.

Acknowledgements

I would like to acknowledge both the help of the British Council in supporting my visit to Bulgaria, and the many Bulgarian academics who exchanged information with me.

58.7 REFERENCES

[Attwood 88] Attwood, L., "Perestroika", *Everywoman*, 35, 12-14, 1988.

[Buckley 86] Buckley, M. (ed.), *Soviet Social Scientists Talking*, London, Macmillan, 1986.

[Chivers 87] Chivers, G., "Information Technology: Girls and Education - a Cross Cultural Review". In Davidson, M.J. & Cooper, C.L. (eds.) *Women and Information Technology*, London, Wiley, 1987.

[Domozetov 86] Domozetov C., "The specificity of the participation of women on the introduction of computer technology in two areas of work". Presented (in German) to the *Internationalen Symposium on Noue Techfologien und Sozialpolitik*, Linowsee bei Rheinsberg, D.D.R., 1986.

[Elliot and Powell 87] Elliot, J. and Powell, C., "Young women and science - do we need more science?", *British Journal of Sociology of Education*, 8, pp 277-286, 1987.

[Jancar 78] Jancar, B.W., *Women under Communism*, Baltimore, John Hopkins Press, 1978.

[Kelly 85] Kelly, A., "The construction of masculine science", *British Journal of Sociology of Education*, 6, pp 133-154, 1985.

[Lapidus 78] Lapidus, G., *Women in Soviet Society*, Los Angeles, University of California Press, 1978.

[Perevedentsev 88] Perevedentsev, V., in the Soviet magazine *Nedelya*, reported in the *Guardian*, 12.2.88.

[Raicheva et al 87] Raicheva, S., Lazarov, D., and Ivasnov, B., "Chemical Education in Bulgaria". Paper presented to Sofia Congress of International Union of Pure and Applied Chemists, 1987.

[Walford 83] Walford, G., "Science education and sexism in the Soviet Union", *The School Sciences Review*, 65, No. 23, pp 213-224, 1983.

59

Women into Computing : some experience from New Zealand

Colin Beardon[1]

59.1 The Environment

This[2] paper describes a large computer science department in a New Zealand university and the attempts that were made to remedy certain biases in the composition of its student body. The environment in New Zealand universities is significantly different from that in the UK. In particular:

- university education is more accessible in New Zealand. Anyone who successfully completes schooling until the age of 17 obtains a certificate that entitles them to study at their local university. In addition, the entry policy for mature students is liberal and it is possible for any member of the public to enrole for courses on a part-time basis. Entrance to university on a full-time basis is accompanied with a right to a grant for up to five years;

- the only strict entitlement is to study at your local university and the level of the grant is barely adequate for home-based students. Perhaps because of this, the majority of students come from the same geographical area as the institution;

- the universities operate a modular degree structure on the US model under which students may take courses from any department, subject to prerequisites. A three year degree normally requires the completion of 22 units and, typically, students take between 8 and 11 units in their majoring subject. This leaves them plenty of scope to try new topics and, as very few subjects have quotas, it is quite easy to change one's majoring subject during the course of a degree.

59.2 The Problems

In 1980 there were about 350 students taking the single first year computer science course and we could perceive three major imbalances.

---

[1] Department of Computing, Brighton Polytechnic, Moulsecoomb, Brighton BN2 4GJ
[2] This paper was presented at the 1988 conference.

- The ratio of male to female students in this course was 2.4 to 1, whereas it was about 1 to 1 in the university as a whole.

- The students were predominantly from the Science and Management Schools, with few from Social Science, Humanities or Education.

- Very few Maaori students took Computer Science (though there were significant numbers from Singapore, Malaysia, Indonesia, Hong Kong and Fiji).

59.3 The Diagnosis

It was believed at the time that there were four major problems with the course.

- Research had shown that, whilst as a general rule the higher the salary the higher the proportion of men in any computing job, gender also played a role. In certain jobs, for example customer education, there was a high proportion of women and relatively high salaries, whereas in other jobs, for example systems programming, there was a high proportion of men yet the salaries were not significantly higher than in, say, programming, where there were equal numbers of men and women.

  In general, this research seemed to show that women were more successful at getting into the more "people-oriented" areas, whereas men were more successful in entering the more "machine-oriented" areas. The course that was being presented was, like most others in computer science, heavily oriented towards the technology itself and the techniques that immediately surround it, without seeing the relationship of the technology to people and their problems as an integral part of the subject.

- The content and presentation of the course was heavily biased towards mathematics and engineering students. This was not only true to the extent that it was a "machine-oriented" course, but even the type of examples chosen and the analogies used to explain concepts seemed to require that you were studying mathematics at university.

  This point was brought home to me by a friend who had worked for IBM and had taught computer science at university and was now looking after his children while his wife went out to work. He did some evening classes in rural areas for our continuing education department, explaining the basic concepts of computing. A classic analogy for how a computer works is that of a clerk sitting at a desk; in fact Turing himself used to explain the computer by analogy with a "stupid clerk". My friend gave an equally valid analogy between a computer and the internal workings of a cow, with its processor (mouth), its registers (first stomach) and its memory (second stomach). Rural people, he maintained, never understood clerks anyway and thought they were all stupid.

I am not saying that we should teach all students using the cow analogy. What I am saying is that education is largely a matter of communication and to do that well, you have to adapt to your audience.

- The course was seen, at that time, as an introduction to computer science, with much stress placed on the word "science". Someone once said that anything that has to put the word "science" in its name probably isn't one. I would argue that computing is largely prescriptive, rather than descriptive, and the attempt to call it a science is an attempt to hide this fact. I certainly believe that whilst there is some need for specialists who do have a mathematical and engineering approach to computing machinery, there is a much greater need for people who understand computing in its human environment. Certainly, in the context of this course, a foundation course in computing seemed much closer to the requirements of most people. By a "foundation course" I mean a course that aims to teach a variety of skills across the spectrum of computer-related studies without necessarily having to present them as a theoretical whole.

- Potential students decide whether or not to take courses in computing largely on the basis of their preconceptions. For example, schools careers advisors and Labour Department officers told young people that being good at mathematics was a prerequisite for doing computer science and that some previous experience of using computers was almost essential. Though this might have been true in the past, we did not want it to be true for the future. Secondly, the fact that there were no female lecturers in the department and only one female tutor (who was leaving) meant there were no role models.

59.4   The Changes

Among the actions that were taken to overcome this perceived bias were:

- the aims, objectives and content of the course were changed to reflect a shift away from mathematics and science and towards more practical computing;

- the attempt was made to teach a foundation course in computing, starting from genuinely no prior knowledge, giving students a variety of experiences, and based around a well-designed and documented practical programme;

- courses were examined for unnecessary bias (eg choice of examples, analogies, etc). From this we developed a "skeleton" syllabus which could be interpreted in various ways for students with specific interests;

- different versions of the same fundamental syllabus were offered for different groups of students (one for mathematics and science students, one for management and accounting students, and one for humanities, education, social science and external students);

- various steps were taken to make the initial introduction to the technology as unthreatening as possible. For example, students were encouraged to work in pairs and to co-operate, particularly in the early stages. A large number of demonstrators were employed during the first six weeks and assessment was not allowed to interfere with the teaching programme;

- efforts were made to encourage external, mature students to take the course, through advertising and sympathetic timetabling of the course (the majority of such students were women);

- we recruited staff from a variety of non-technical backgrounds for teaching at first year. One female lecturer and several female tutors were appointed;

- close contacts were developed with careers advisors in the Labour Department and schools; and an effort was made to not only stress the desirability of a good general education as a background to computing, but also to specifically say that female students were encouraged to study computing.

59.5 The Results

By 1986 nearly 700 students were doing one or both first year computer science courses (that is nearly twice as many as six years previously). Of these, there were approximately equal numbers of men and women. There were also significant numbers of social science and external students and some humanities and education students. There were still very few Maaori students.

There is some evidence, then, that the changes we instituted did lead to greater accessibility to introductory computing courses for people from a wider range of backgrounds. Of course, there were many other changes going on at the same time – the rapid spread of microcomputers, the phenomenal growth of management science, etc – so we cannot claim all the benefit. Yet I know, even if only from some individual cases, that some people who never thought that they could do computing, did take the course and did get a lot out of it.

However, we also experienced some failures and in order to improve we must consider these carefully. The failure to increase the number of Maaori students was, in some sense, predictable as Maaoris have only recently been positively encouraged to attend university and the preference of their elders is that they study subjects like law, economics, politics, etc which they consider directly related to their economic and social recovery. I think this answer is too easy in that, to be honest, we did little to specifically address the enormous gulf that seems to exist between the traditional Maaori culture and the culture that surrounds computer science.

So far, my comments have all referred to our introductory first year courses. The real test, though, is whether any improvement at first year can be sustained. Unfortunately, it could not. Though large numbers of students initially tried to go on to second year computer science courses, there was a significant drop-out of students in the second year. The second year programme was not changed in the same spirit as the first year; on the contrary, it became a focal point for an alternative view of computer science. A "core curriculum" was introduced in which "Theoretical Computer Science" became a compulsory course and technical subjects were stressed. In one year only 40% of students entering the second year completed and passed. In the third (and final) year the ratio of men to women was 4 to 1, and would have been considerably worse had it not been for the significant number of Asian students in roughly equal proportions between the sexes. Counting only home based students, the proportion of men to women in the final year was about 15 to 1.

59.6 Discussion Points

In the light of these experiences it seems to me that there are several interesting topics worth further discussion.

- First, there is a point about the general context in which the population at large sees computing. I would maintain that not only women, but also a large number of men are unhappy about working with computers. Within our Western culture, computers are very closely identified with new management processes (ie deskilling and unemployment), with the military and with technical innovation without real social responsibility. In order to encourage more people into computing we need to make headway with improving that image but, I believe, recently things have been getting worse.

  I have been out of the UK for ten years and during that period something very important has happened. Following the wave of influential reports in the late 1970s, Western economies have come to re-categorise information technology. Pre-1980 it was seen, in economic terms, as part of "process innovation" (ie a new way of producing things). As such, one needed to understand how it affected things that other people did and there was room to debate how good an innovation it was. Since about 1980, information technology has been categorised as "product innovation" (ie IT now generates wealth in its own right). As such, one no longer needs to understand other processes, as a strict division of labour has been introduced between technical and marketing skills.

  The upshot of all this is that the computing workforce is now encouraged to live a blinkered existence because its social and economic concerns are being managed by others.

- Secondly, the relationship of the computer to the work process is a key issue which, I have found, a lot of female students want to discuss yet it is not considered a legitimate part of "computer science" in English-speaking countries. This omission stems, in large part, from the British notion of "professionalism" and its adherence to the traditional right of managers to manage their workforce however they think fit. Any consideration of what end-users need is seen as the thin end of "workers' participation" leading to "workers' control". To avoid this, the needs and opinions of people who actually use systems are deliberately ignored. In other European countries this does not seem to be the case, at least not to the same extent.

- Why is there such a difference in the attitude of men and women towards studying IT in different cultures? Our Western societies are so bad at giving women open encouragement, whereas Asian and Islamic countries do not seem to have this problem (though there are definite class divisions in these societies). In more traditional societies, like the Maaori, there is a definite reticence of both men and women to study computing.

- We know that preconceptions are important, but can we realistically change the preconceptions that careers advisors and others have about computing before we change the nature of computer education? We may wish that more open and accessible courses be taught and we may do our bit towards them, but the institutions are dominated by people of a different persuasion and careers advisors are just reflecting this reality.

59.7 Conclusion

The experience of trying to remedy these imbalances in a mass-teaching environment was valuable because the numbers involved provided a reasonably sized sample to gauge results. The experience tends to support the general belief that the developing trend towards a technical, machine-oriented, "scientific" approach to computing that ignores the human context, deters many people from entering computing. This is not only discriminatory against these people, but will also be detrimental to the future of computing.

Appendix A: Bibliography

[Aben Datastue] *Open Computer Workshop: Aarhus, Denmark*, obtainable from Aben Datastue, Aboulevarden 7 st, 8000 Aarhus C, Denmark.

[Abler 87] Abler R M and Sedlacek W E, "Computer Orientation By Holland Type And Sex", *Career Development Quarterly*, Vol 36(2), 163 169, Dec 1987.

[Adam 90] Adam A and Bruce M, "Do Women Make Better Knowledge Engineers?", *Computing*, 8th February 1990.

[Archer 87] Archer J, "Beyond Sex Differences: Comments on Borrill and Reid", *Bulletin of the British Psychological Society*, 40, pp88-90, 1987.

[Arnfield 88] Arnfield R, "Facing a hard French line on hacking", *The Guardian*, Thurs, 21 April, p25, 1988.

[Arnot 82] Arnot M, "Male Hegemony, Social Class and Women's Education", *Journal of Education*, vol. 164, 1982.

[Ashton Tate 90] The Ashton Tate Partnership, *Target*, Vol 3, no 2, March 1990.

[Askew 88] Askew S and Ross C, *Boy don't cry: Boys and Sexism in Education*, Milton Keynes: OUP, 1988.

[Ball 89] Ball C, *Aim Higher. Widening Access to Higher Education*, I Royal Society for the Encouragement of Arts, Manufacture and Commerce (RSA), London, 1989.

[Bandura 77] Bandura A, *Self-referent thought: a developmental analysis of self efficacy*, National Institute of Mental Health, 1987.

[BBC 85] BBC Educational Broadcasting Services Research Unit, *Microcomputers in Secondary Schools*, (unpublished report), summarised in DES Press Notice 14/85, January, 1985.

[Beech 90] Beech C, *Women and WIT: a Survey of the female members of the British Computer Society*, British Computer Society, 1990.

[Bem 74] Bem S L, "The Management of Psychological Androgyny", *Journal of Counselling and Clinical Psychology*, 42, pp155-162, 1974.

[Bem 81] Bem S L, "Gender Schema Theory: A cognitive account of sex typing", *Psychological Review*, 88, 4, pp354-364, 1981.

[Bem 87] Bem S L, "Masculinity and Femininity Exist Only in the Mind of the Perceiver", In *Masculinity/Femininity: Basic perspectives*, Reinish, Rosenblum and Sanders (eds), N.Y. & Oxford: Oxford University Press, 1 in "The Kinsey Institute Series", 1987.

408

[Bennett 81] Bennett Y and Carter D, "Sidetracked? A look at the Careers Advice Given to Fifth Form Girls", *Equal Opportunities Commission*, Manchester, 1981.

[Bentley 87] Bentley D and Watts M, "Courting the positive virtues", in Kelly A (ed), *Science for Girls*, Milton Keynes: OUP, 1987.

[Berrisford 89] Berrisford S, "Putting Women in Their Workplace", *Computer Weekly*, 12th December, 1989.

[Blaazer 88] Blaazer C, "The Top Jobs that are just Waiting for the Right Woman", *The Times*, 7 January 1988.

[Bleier 88] Bleier R (ed), *Feminist Approaches to Science*, New York: Pergamon, 1988.

[Bourner 87] Bourner T, "Entry Qualifications and Degree Performance: a Report of a Research Project on the Relationship between Entry Qualifications and Degree Performance on CNAA First-degree Courses", *Development Services Publication*, Council for National Academic Awards, London, 10 March 1987.

[Braun 86] Braun C M, Goupil G, Giroux J and Chagnon Y, "Adolescents And Microcomputers: Sex Differences, Proxemics, Task And Stimulus Variables", *Journal Of Psychology*, Vol 120(6), 529 542, Nov 1986.

[Breakwell 86] Breakwell G M, Fife-Schaw C R, Spencer J and Lee T R, "Attitudes to New Technology in Relation to Social Beliefs and Group Memberships", *Current Psychological Research Review*, 5, 1, pp34-47, 1986.

[Brecher 85] Brecher D, *Women's Computer Literacy Handbook*, New York: New American Library, 1985.

[Brown 75] Brown J M, "A Woman in the World of Engineering", *Transactions on Education*, IEEE, 1975.

[Bruce 84] Bruce M, Kirkup G and Thomas C, *Teaching Women Technology Assessment*, Open University, 1984.

[Bruce 90] Bruce M and Lewis J, "Women Designers – Is there a Gender Gap?", *Design Studies*, Vol 11, No 2, 1990.

[Burton 86] Burton L (ed), *Girls into Maths Won't Go*, 1986.

[Bush 82] Bush C, *Taking Hold of Technology*, American Association of University Women, Washington, 1982.

[Butcher 85] Butcher Committee Final Report, *Information Technology Skills Shortages*, DTI, 1985.

[Canter 85] Canter D, Rivers R and Storrs G, "Characterising user navigation through complex database structures", *Journal of Behaviour and Information Technology*, Vol 4 No 2, pp 93-102, 1985.

[Canter 86] Canter D, Powell J, Wishart J and Roderick C, "User navigation in complex database systems", *Journal of Behaviour and Information Technology*, Vol 5 No 3, pp 249-257, 1986.

[Carlsson 90] Carlsson K, *The Percentage of Women on Study Programmes in Technology at Lulea and in the Rest of Sweden, 1980-1989*, Lulea, Sweden: University of Lulea, 1990.

[Carter 90a] Carter R and Kirkup G, "Women into Science and Engineering WISE: Activism and Institutional Change", Contributions *GASAT Conference*, Jönköping, Sweden, 1990.

[Carter 90b] Carter R and Kirkup G, *Women into Science and Engineering (WISE) Report 1990*, Unpublished Report obtainable from authors at Open University, Walton Hall, Milton Keynes.

[Chen 86] Chen M, "Gender Differences In Adolescents' Uses Of And Attitudes Towards Computers", *International Dissertation Abstracts*, Number : 210aac8612723, 1986.

[Chivers 87] Chivers G, Davidson M and Cooper C (eds), *Women and Information Technology*, John Wiley and Sons, Chichester, 1987.

[Chodorow 78] Chodorow N, *The Reproduction of Mothering*, University of California Berkeley Press, California, 1978.

[CLWC] *Working with Computers: The Opportunities for Girls and Women*, Central London Women and Computing.

[Cockburn 85a] Cockburn C, "Technology as a Factor in Occupational Segregation", *EOC Research Bulletin*, 9, Manchester: Equal Opportunities Commission, 1985.

[Cockburn 85b] Cockburn C, *Machinery of Dominance: Women, Men and Technological Know-How*, London: Pluto, 1985.

[Cockburn 87a] Cockburn C, *Two Track Training: Sex Inequalities and the YTS*, London: Macmillan Youth Questions, 1987.

[Cockburn 87b] Cockburn C, "Technological Change: Short Change for Women", *Social Studies Review*, May 1987.

[Collins 85a] Collins H M, *Changing Order, Replication and Induction in Scientific Practice*, Sage, 1985.

[Collins 85b] Collins H M et al, "Where's the Expertise?: Expert Systems as a Medium of Knowledge Transfer" in Merry, M (ed), *Expert Systems 85*, Cambridge University Press, 1985.

[Collins 87a] Collins H M, "Domains in which Expert Systems Could Succeed", *Proceedings of the 3rd International Expert Systems Conference*, Learned Information, 1987.

[Collins 87b] Collins H M, "Expert Systems, Artificial Intelligence and the Behavioural Coordinates of Skill" in Bloomfield B (ed), *The Question of Artificial Intelligence*, Croom Helm, 1987.

[Collis 87] Collis B A, "Sex difference in the association between secondary school students' attitudes toward mathematics and toward computers", *Journal for Research in Mathematics Education*, 18, pp394-402, 1987.

[Cook 85] Cook E P, "Psychological Androgyny", *Pergamon General Psychology Series*, New York: Pergamon Press, 1985.

[Cooper] Cooper J, Hall J and Huff C, *Anxiety as a Consequence of Sex Stereotyped Software*, Princeton: Princeton University, Unpublished manuscript.

[Cowperthwaite 89] Cowperthwaite P, Johnston R, Ryves M (eds), *Access in Action. Breaking down the Barriers*, NIACE/Replan Central Unit, London, October 1989.

[Crane 86] Crane P and Renforth C, "A Study of the Information Technology Industry within Torbay", *Women into Information Technology*, South Devon College of Arts and Technology, Torbay, 1986.

[Croydon 83] *Information Technology in Schools*, EOC/London Borough of Croydon, EOC 1983.

[Croydon 86] *Girls and Information Technology*, Equal Opportunities Commission, Manchester, 1986.

[Cuff 80] Cuff R N, "On Casual Users", *International Journal of Man-Machine Studies*, Vol 14, pp 163-187, 1980.

[Culley 86] Culley L, *Gender Differences and Computing*, Department of Education, University of Loughborough, 1986.

[Culley 88a] Culley L A, "Option choice and careers guidance: Gender and computing in secondary schools", *British Journal of Guidance and Counselling*, 16, pp73-81, 1988.

[Culley 88b] Culley L, "Girls, boys and computers", *Educational studies*, 14, 1, 1988.

[Cusumano 91] Cusumano M, *Japan's Software Factories*, Oxford University Press, (forthcoming in 1991).

[Dain 88] Dain J, "Getting Women into Computing", *University Computing*, 10, pp154-157, 1988.

[Dambrot 85] Dambrot F, Watkins-Malek M, Silling M, Marshall R and Garver J, "Correlates of Sex Differences in Attitudes toward and Involvement with Computers", *Journal of Vocational Behaviour*, 27, pp71-86, 1985.

[Davidson 85] Davidson M J, *Reach for the Top - A Woman's Guide to Success in Business and Management*, Platkus, London, 1985.

[Davidson 88] Davidson M and Cooper C, *Women and Information Technology*, London: Wiley, 1988.

[Deakin 84] Deakin R, *Women and Computing: The Golden Opportunity*, Papermac, Macmillan, 1984.

[Deaux 84] Deaux K, "From Individual to Social Categories: Analysis of a decade's research on gender", *American Psychologist*, 39, pp105-16, 1984.

[Deboer 86] Deboer G E, "Perceived Science Ability As A Factor In The Course Selections Of Men And Women In College", *Journal Of Research In Science Teaching*, Vol 23(4), 343 352, April 1986.

[Deem 84] Deem R (Ed), *Co-education Reconsidered*, Milton Keynes: Open University Press, 1984.

[DES 87] *"Higher Education - Meeting the Challenge*, Department of Education and Science, Cmnd 114, HMSO, W London, March 1987.

[DES 89] *Curriculum Matters - Information Technology 5 to 16*, DES, 1989.

[Dex 84] Dex S, "Women's Work Histories : an analysis of Women and Employment Survey", *Research Paper No. 46*, Department of Employment, 1984.

[Directory] *Directory of Women in Departments of Mathematics, Statistics and Computer Science in Universities and Polytechnics in the United Kingdom*, available from Dr Leone Burton, Head of Mathematics Education, Thames Polytechnic.

[Dreyfus 72] Dreyfus D, *What Computers Can't Do: A Critique of Artificial Intelligence: Applications to Logical Reasoning and Historical Research*, Ellis Horwood, 1972.

[Durndell 87] Durndell A, Macleod H and Siann G, "A survey of attitudes to, knowledge about and experience of computers", *Computers and Education*, 11, pp167-175, 1987.

412

[Durndell 90a] Durndell A, "Why do female students avoid computer studies?", *Research in Science and Technology Education* (in press), 1990.

[Durndell 90b] Durndell A, Siann G and Glissov P, "Gender differences and computing in course choice at entry into Higher Education", *British Educational Research Journal*, 16, pp147-162, 1990.

[Durndell 90c] Durndell A J, "Choice and Image: Gender and Computer Studies in Higher Education", in the *WiC 1990 Proceedings* and in this volume.

[Dutton 85] Dutton W H, Kovaric P and Steinfield C, "Computing in the Home: A research paradigm", *Computers and the Social Sciences*, 1, 1, pp5-18, 1985.

[Eastman 87] Eastman S T and Krendl K, "Computers And Gender: Differential Effects Of Electronic Search On Students' Achievement And Attitudes", *Journal Of Research And Development In Education*, Vol 20(3), 41 48, Sept 1987.

[Eaton 86] Eaton W O and Enns L R, "Sex Differences In Human Motor Activity Level", *Psychological Bulletin*, Vol 100(1), 19 28, Jul 1986.

[Eddowes 83] Eddowes M, *Humble Pi: The Mathematics Education of Girls*. London: Longmans, 1983.

[EEC 89] Commission of the European Communities, *Women in Graphics*, no 30, December 1989.

[EITB 84] Engineering Industry Training Board, *Women in Engineering* occasional Paper No 11, Watford: EITB, 1984.

[Elliott 87] Elliott J and Powell C, "Young woman in science: Do we need more science?", *British Journal of Sociology of Education*, 8, pp277-286, 1987.

[Else 85] Else L, "Wise girls will find the going is tough", *Computing*, 9 May 1985.

[Ennals 85] Ennals R, *Artificial Intelligence: Applications to Logical Reasoning and Historical Research*, Ellis Horwood, 1985.

[EOC 83] EOC/London Borough of Croydon, *Information Technology in Schools: Guidelines for Good Practice for Teachers of IT*, 1983.

[EOC 85a] *Infotech and Gender: an Overview*, EOC, 1985.

[EOC 85b] EOC/London Borough of Croydon (1985) *Girls and Information Technology*, Report of a project in the London Borough of Croydon to evaluate guidelines for good practice in the IT curriculum.

[ESRC 88] ESRC, *Girls and Mathematics: Some Lessons for the Classroom*, 1988, available from ESRC Information Office.

[Evans 87] Evan A and Hall W, "Programming inequality", *Times Education Supplement*, 3718, p4, 1987.

[Everts 90] Everts S, "Social responsibility in technology and feminist visions", in Granstam I (ed), *Contributions GASAT 1990*, Jönköping, Jönköping University, Sweden 1990.

[Faulkner 85] Faulkner W and Arnold E, *Smothered by Invention: Technology in Women's Lives*, London: Pluto, 1985.

[Fennema 87] Fennema and Sherman, "Sex-Related Differences in Mathematics Achievement, Spatial Visualization and Affective Factors", *American Educational Research Journal*, 14, pp51-71, 1987.

[FEU 85] *Changing the Focus: Women and Further Education*, Further Education Unit, London, 1985.

[FEU 88] *Information Technology and the Wasted Resource*, Further Education Unit, London, 1988.

[Fitt] Fitt L W and Newton D A, "When the Mentor is a Man and the Protegee a Woman", *Harvard Business Review* (Reprint No 81229).

[Fleury 89] Fleury B, "Universities caring for the very young: an AUT survey of child care facilities 1989", 4, *AUT Bulletin*, April, 1989.

[Foon 88] Foon A, "The Relationship Between School Type and Adolescent Self Esteem, Attribution Styles, and Affiliation Needs: Implications for Educational Outcome", *British Journal of Educational Psychology*, 58, pp44-54, 1988.

[Fournies 74] Fournies P, "Why Management Appraisal Doesn't Help Develop Managers", *Management Review*, AMA, 1974.

[Frauenfirschung] *ifg Frauenfirschung*, Heft 3/89.

[Gabriel 90] Gabriel C, "Housework", *Computing*, 12th April 1990.

[Gaines 84] Gaines B and Shaw M, *The Art of Computer Conversation*, Prentice/Hall International, 1984.

[Gardner 86] Gardner J R, McEwan A and Curry C A, "A sample survey of attitudes to computer studies, *Computers and Education*, 10, pp293-298, 1986.

[Gerver 85] Gerver E, "Women, Computers And Adult Education", 1 Vol, University Of Strathclyde, Pilley C, *Women And Computing In Scotland*, Report of Conference held by the Joint Working Group on Women And Computers, 14th June 1985.

[Gerver 86] Gerver E, *Humanising Technology: Computers in Community Use and Adult Education*, Plenum Press, 1986.

414

[Girls and Mathematics Research Unit 87] "Girls and Mathematics Research Unit", in *Proceedings of the GSAT Conference 1987* edited by Walkerdine V, University of London, 1987.

[Gold 88] Gold S, "Hackers let off the hook", *The Guardian*, Thursday, 28 April, p27, 1988.

[Gold 89] *The New Hacker's Handbook*, Century Publishing Company, 1989.

[Gramsci 81] Gramsci A, "Selections from the Prison Notebooks", 1981.

[Granstam 86] Granstam I (ed), *Contributions GASAT 1990*, Jönköping, Jönköping University, Sweden 1990.

[Gressard 84] Gressard C and Loyd B H, "An Investigation Of The Effects Of Math Anxiety And Sex On Computer Attitudes", paper presented at *The American Educational Research Association*, New Orleans, 1984.

[Griffin 85] Griffin C, *Typical Girls? Young Women from School to the Labour Market*, London: RKP, 1985.

[Griffiths 85] Griffiths D, "The exclusion of women from Technology", in *Smothered by Invention*, Faulkner W and Arnold E (eds), Pluto Press, 1985.

[Guardian 90] Lancashire Polytechnic Advertisement, *The Education Guardian*, 5th June 1990.

[Hacker 81] Hacker S, "The culture of engineering: Women, workplace and machine", *Women's Studies International Quarterly*, 4 (3), 341-353, 1981.

[Haggis 86] Haggis K, *Computers – Toys for the Boys?*, University of Newcastle, Diploma in Advanced Educational Studies, Special Study 1986.

[Hales 88] Hales M, *Women: The Key to Information Technology*, London Strategic Policy Unit, 1988.

[Harding 81] Harding J, *Sex Differences in Science Examinations*, in Kelly A (ed), *The Missing Half: Girls and Science Education*, Manchester: Manchester University Press, 1981.

[Harding 86] Harding J (ed), *Perspectives on Gender and Science*, London: Falmer, 1986.

[Hartmann 86] Hartmann H, Kraut R E and Tilley L A (eds), *Computer chips and paper clips: Technology and Women's Employment*, Vol 1, Washington, DC: National Academy Press, 1986.

[Harvey 85] Harvey T J and Wilson B, "Gender Differences in Attitudes Towards Microcomputers Shown by Primary and Secondary School Pupils", *British Journal of Educational Technology*, 16, 3, pp183-187, 1985.

[Hennig]   Hennig M and Jardin A, "The Managerial Women", *Pan Business Management*.

[Hess 85]   Hess R D, Miura I T, "Gender Differences In Enrollment In Computer Camps And Classes", Special Issue: "Women, Girls, And Computers", *Sex Roles*, Vol 13(3 4), 193 203, Aug 1985.

[Hofstede 80] Hofstede G, *Culture's consequences: International differences in Work Related Values*, Sage Publications, 1980.

[Hogger 84] Hogger C J, *Introduction to Logic programming*, Chapter VIII.2.1, Academic Press, 1984.

[Hoyles 85] Hoyles C, *Culture and Computers in the Mathematics Classroom*, Institute of Education, University of London, 1985.

[Hoyles 88] Hoyles C, "Girls and Computers", *Bedford Way Papers*, Institute of Education, University of London, 1988.

[Hughes 85a] Hughes M, Macleod H and Potts C, "Using LOGO with infant school children", *Educational Psychology*, 5, 287 301, 1985.

[Hughes 85b] Hughes M, Macleod H, Potts C and Rodgers J, "Are Computers only for boys?", *New Society*, 11 Oct 1985 .

[Hughes 87] Hughes M, Brackenridge A and Macleod H, in Rutkowska J and Crook C, *Computers, Cognition & Development*, John Wiley, 1987.

[Hughes 88] Hughes S and Maybrey A, "No Previous Experience Necessary: Residential Courses at Liverpool", *WiC Conference Proceedings*, 1988.

[Huws 82]   Huws U, *Your Job in the Eighties. A Woman's Guide to New Technology*, Pluto, 1982.

[Huws 86]   Huws U, "The Effect of IT on Women's Lives" in Gill, K S (ed), *Artificial Intelligence for Society*, Wiley, 1986.

[ILEA 85]   *Implementing the ILEA's Anti-Sexist Policy*, ILEA, 1985.

[ILEA 90]   *Tools for the Mind*, ILEA, 1990.

[Irvine 90] Irvine J, "Employer - Education Cooperation", in this volume.

[Josefowitz] Josefowitz N, "Management Men and Women: Closed US Open Doors", *Harvard Business Review* (Reprint No 80559).

[Kanter]   Kanter R M, "Power Failure in Management Circuits", Harvard Business Review (Reprint No 19403).

[Keller 85] Keller E F, *Reflections on Gender and Science*, New Haven and London: Yale University Press, 1985.

[Kelly 84] Kelly A, Whyte J and Smail B, *Girls into Science and Technology – Final Report*, University of Manchester 1984.

[Kelly 85] Kelly A, "The construction of masculine science", *British Journal of Sociology of Education*, 6, pp133-154, 1985.

[Kelly 87] Kelly A, *Science for Girls*, Open University Press, 1987.

[Kelly 88] Kelly A, "Option choice for girls and boys", *Research in Science and Technological Education*, 6, pp5-24, 1988.

[Kiesler 85] Kiesler S, Sproull L and Eccles J, "Poolhalls, chips and war games: women in the culture of computing", *Psychology of Women Quarterly*, 9, 451-462, 1985.

[Kiesler 87] Kiesler S and Sproull L (eds), *Computing and Change on Campus*, Cambridge: Cambridge University Press, 1987.

[Kirkup 89] Kirkup G, "Equal Opportunities and Computing at the Open University", *Open Learning*, 4, 1, 1989.

[Kirkup 86] Kirkup G, *Career-Wise: A Fresh Start in Technology: Women tell their Stories*, Open University, 1986.

[Knuth 68] Knuth D E, *The Art of Computer Programming*, Vol 1, Addison Wesley, 1968.

[Knuth 84] Knuth D E, "Literate Programming", *Computer Journal*, Vol 27, pp97-111, 1984.

[Kolmos 90] Kolmos A, "Women and men in engineering education – different approaches?", in Granstam I, (ed) *Contributions GASAT 1990*, Jönköping, Jönköping University, Sweden 1990.

[Koob Cannie 79] Koob Cannie J, *The Woman's Guide to Management Success (How to win power in the real organisational world)*, Prentice Hall, 1979.

[Lafontaine 86] Lafontaine E and Tredeau L, "The Frequency, Sources, And Correlates Of Sexual Harassment Among Women In Traditional Male Occupations", *Sex Roles*, Vol 15(7 8), 433 442, Oct 1986.

[Lees 86] Lees S, *Losing Out: Sexuality and Adolescent Girls*, Hutchinson, 1986.

[Lepper 85] Lepper M R, "Microcomputers in Education: Motivational and Social issues", *American Psychologist*, 40, pp1-18, 1985.

[Levin 89] Levin T and Gordan C, "Effect of Gender and Computer Experience on Attitudes Toward Computers", *Journal of Educational Computing Research*, 5, 1, pp69-88, 1989.

[Lim 90]   Lim Gek Kheng, "WIT: The Singaporean way", *Computer Bulletin*, Vol 2, part 1, Feb 1990.

[Linden 87]   Linden K, Lebold W and Armstrong P, "Gender differences in computer knowledge, literacy and competency", in Daniels J Z and Kahle J B (eds), *Contributions to the 4th GASAT Conference*, University of Michigan: National Science Foundation, 1987.

[Linn 85a]   Linn M C, "Fostering Equitable Consequences From Computer Learning Environments", *Sex Roles*, Vol 13, Nos 3/4, 229 240, 1985.

[Linn 85b]   Linn M C, "Gender Equity In Computer Learning Environments", *Computers And The Social Sciences*, Vol 1(1), 19 27, Jan-Mar 1985.

[Lloyd 85]   Lloyd A and Newell L, "Women and Computers", in *Smothered by Invention*, Faulkner W and Arnold E (eds), Pluto Press, 1985.

[Lockhead 85]   Lockhead M E, "Women, girls and computers", *Sex Roles*, 13, pp115-122, 1985.

[Lockheed 84]   Lockheed M E and Frakt S B, "Sex Equity: Increasing Girls' Use Of Computers", *Computing Teacher*, 11, 16 18, 1984.

[Lovegrove 87]   Lovegrove G L and Hall W, "Where have all the Girls Gone?", *University Computing*, 9, pp207-210, 1987.

[Loyd 87]   Loyd B H, Loyd D E and Gressard C P, "Gender And Computer Experience As Factors In The Computer Attitudes Of Middle School Students", Special Issue: "Sex Differences In Early Adolescents" of *Journal Of Early Adolescence*, Vol 7(1), 13 19, Sept 1987.

[Lyles]   Lyles M, *Strategies for Helping Women Managers or Anyone*, Amacom Periodicals Division, American Management Associations.

[Macleod 88]   Macleod H A, Siann G and Glissov P, *Cognitive and Motivational Factors in Primary School Computer Use*, Edinburgh: Scottish Education Department, Microelectronics in Education Committee, Project Ref MEC/IRD/19m, 1988.

[Mahony 85]   Mahony P, *Schools for the Boys: Coeducation Reassessed*, Hutchinson, 1985.

[Mandinach 85]   Mandinach E B and Corno L, "Cognitive Engagement Variations Among Students Of Different Ability Level And Sex In A Computer Problem Solving Game", Special Issue: Women, Girls, And Computers, *Sex Roles*, Vol 13(3 4), 241 251, Aug 1985.

[McCrone 88]   McCrone J, "Project Management", *Computing*, May 12th 1988.

[McLeod 84] McLeod H and Hughes M, "Childrens Ideas about Computers", presented to a BPS Conference: *IT, AI and Child Development*, held at the University of Sussex, July 1984.

[McRobbie 78] McRobbie A, "Working class girls and the culture of femininity", in *Centre for Contemporary Cultural Studies, Women Take Issue*, Hutchinson, 1978.

[McShane 90] McShane D, "Women in Technology in the European Community", in this volume.

[Measor 84] Measor L, "Gender and the sciences; pupils' gender-based conceptions of school subjects", in M Hammersley & P Woods (eds) *Life in Schools: the Sociology of Pupil Culture*, Milton Keynes: Open University Press.

[Mensch 89] *Mensch und Computer*, 7, (A special issue on women and computers), 1989.

[Microsyster 87] *Women and Computers in the Office: a conference report*, Microsyster, 1987.

[Milner 90] "Action Research: Primary Schoolgirls and New Technology", in this volume.

[Miura 86] Miura I T, "Understanding Gender Differences In Middle School Computer Interest And Use", Paper Presented At Symposium : *Gender Differences In Computing: Policy Implications*, American Educational Research Assc, 1986.

[Miura 87] Miura I T, "Gender and Socioeconomic Status Differences in Middle-School Computer Interest and Use", *Journal of Early Adolescence*, 7, 2, pp243-254, 1987.

[Morris 89] Morris J, "Women in Computing", *Computer Weekly*, 1989.

[Morris 90] Morris P, Cheng D and Smith H, *Preliminary Report to the B.P.S.: How and why applicants choose to study Psychology at University*, Psychology Department, Lancaster University, 1990.

[Morton 85] Morton P and Jones J H, "Developing professional skills for systems maturity", in *Designing for Systems Maturity*, Pergamon Infotech State of the Art report, 13:7, London: Pergamon, pp43-50, 1985.

[Morton 86a] Morton P, "Tales From the River Bank", *Your Computer*, October 1986.

[Morton 86b] Morton P, "Closing the gender gap", *Educational Computing*, October, 1986.

[Newton 81] Newton P, "Who Say's Girls Can't Be Engineers?", in Kelly A, *The Missing Half*, Vol. 1, Manchester University Press, 1981.

[Newton 82] Newton P and Brocklesby J, *Getting on in Engineering: Becoming a Women Technician* Final Report to the EOC/SSRC Joint Panel, 1982.

[Newton 87] Newton P and Williamson M, "A technology foundation course for women", *International Journal of Science Education*, 9 (3), 367-374, 1987.

[Newton 88] Newton P and Haslam S, "Computing: an Ideal Occupation for Women", *Proceedings of the First National WiC Conference*, University of Lancaster, July 1988.

[NIACE 89] *Adults in Higher Education: A Discussion Paper*, National Institute for Adult Continuing Education (NIACE), Leicester, 1989.

[NICEC 88] *Technological Change and the Work of Women in Industry*, NICEC, Hatfield Polytechnic, 1988.

[Nicholle 90] Nicholle L, "Women Wait for Major Tax Break", *Computer Weekly*, 15th March 1990.

[Nicholson] Nicholson N and West M, "Women in Management: Trends in Britain", Referenced in *Women in Management Elective Material*, MBA Program, Cranfield School of Management.

[O'Leary 74] O'Leary V E, "Some attitudinal barriers to occupational aspirations in women", *Psychological Bulletin*, 81, pp809-826, 1974.

[Ormerod 81] Ormerod M B, "Factors Differentially Affecting The Science Subject Preferences, Chances And Attitudes Of Girls And Boys", in Kelly A, *The Missing Half*, Vol. 1, Manchester University Press, 1981.

[Ormerod 75] Ormerod M B, "Subject Preference and Choice in Co-education and Single-sex Secondary Schools", *British Journal of Educational Psychology*, 45, 3, pp257-267, 1975.

[Pacitti 90] Pacitti I, "School and Industry Links – An Example of Cooperation", in the *WiC 1990 Proceedings* and in this volume.

[Parsons 82] Parsons J E et al, *Socialization of Achievement Attitudes and Belief: Parental Influences*, University of Michigan, 1982.

[Personnel 89] *Personnel Management*, Institute of Personnel Management, August 1989.

[Povall 84] Povall M, "Overcoming Barriers to Women's Advancement in European organisations", City University Business School, PR 13,1 1984.

[Pratt 85] Pratt J, Whyte J, Deem R, Kant, Cruikshank M, *Girl Friendly Schooling*, Methuen, London, 1985.

420

[Raymont 86] Raymont P, "Career Paths: Spotting the Snakes and Ladders", in *Careers in IT* supplement, *Computing*, 4 Sept 1986.

[Reich 86] Reich M H, "The Mentor Connection", *personnel*, February 1986.

[Reisner 81] Reisner P, "Human factors studies of database query languages: a survey and assessment", *Computing Surveys*, 13, pp13-31, 1981.

[Rose 85] Rose H, "Beyond Masculinist Realities: A Feminist Epistemology for the Sciences", in Bleier R (ed), *Feminist Approaches to Science*, Pergamon, 1987.

[Rothschild 83] Rothschild J (ed), *Machina ex dea: feminist perspectives on technology*, New York: Pergamon, 1983.

[Rothschild 88] Rothschild J, *Teaching Technology from a Feminist Perspective*, Oxford: Pergamon, 1988.

[Royal Society 86] Royal Society/Institute of Mathematics and its Applications (1986) *Girls and Mathematics*.

[Sanders 87] Sanders J S, "Closing the Computer Gender Gap in School", *Proceedings of the Fourth GASAT Conference*, University of Michigan, Ann Arbor, Michigan, USA.

[Sawhill 77] Sawhill I, "Economic Perspectives on the Family", *Daedalus* (Journal of the American Academy of Arts and Science), Vol 106 No 2, 1977.

[Scanlon 87] Scanlon E and O'Shea T, *Educational Computing*, Wiley, 1987.

[Scase 87] "Women Managers", articles "Room at the Top" and "Destroying the Myths", *Management Today*, March 1987.

[Scholfield 90] Schofield J, "She's gotta have IT", *The Guardian*, 8/3/90.

[Scott 89] Scott G, "Child Care and Access: Women in Tertiary Education in Scotland", Scottish Institute of Adult and Continuing Education, *Scottish Adult Education Monographs*, 9, 1989.

[Searle 85] Searle J, *Mind, Brains and Machines*, BBC Publications, 1985.

[Sheingold 83] Sheingold K, Kane J H and Endreweit M E, "Microcomputer Use In Schools: Developing A Research Agenda", *Harvard Educational Review*, 53, 412 432, 1983.

[Sheingold 84] Sheingold K, Hawkins J and Char C, "I'm the thinkist: You're the typist", *Journal of Social Issues*, 40, 49-61, 1984.

[Shirley 88] Shirley S, "A Woman's Right to be Mediocre", *Computing*, April 1988.

[Shneiderman 87] Shneiderman B, *Designing The Computer Interface*, Addison-Wesley, pp448, 1987.

[Shortland 86] Shortland S, "Where's the Equality in Data Processing" (On Computer Economic's Survey), *Computer News*, 20 March 1986.

[Shotton 89] Shotton M A, *Computer Addiction? A study of computer dependency*, London: Taylor & Francis, 1989.

[Siann 86] Siann G and Macleod H, "Computers and children of primary school age: issues and questions", *British Journal of Educational Technology*, 17, 133-144, 1986.

[Siann 87] Siann G, "Gender Differences in Computer Use in Children of Primary School Age", in *Proceedings of the GASAT Conference 1987*, University of London, 1987.

[Siann 88a] Siann G, Durndell A, Macleod H and Glissov P, "Stereotyping in relation to the gender gap in participation in computing", *Educational Research*, 30, pp98-103, 1988.

[Siann 88b] Siann G, Glissov P and Macleod H A, "Cognitive and Motivational Factors in Primary School Computer Use", in proceedings of *Women Into Computing: First National Conference*, University of Lancaster, 20-22 July 1988.

[Siann 90] Siann G, Macleod H, Glissov P and Durndell A, "The effect of computer use on gender differences in attitudes to computers", *Computers and Education*, 14, pp183-191, 1990.

[Simmons 81] Simmons G L, *Women in Computing*, Manchester: National Computing Centre, 1981.

[Skills 87] *Skills for the future*, research report, Institute of Information Technology, University of Sheffield, 1987.

[Skirrow 86] Skirrow G, "Positive Action in Scotland", *Women and Computing in Scotland*, Scottish Institute of Adult and Continuing Education, 1986.

[Smail 84] Smail B, *Girl-friendly Science: Avoiding Sex Bias in the Curriculum.*, Longman 1984.

[Smithers 81] Smithers A and Collings J, *Girls Studying Science in the Sixth Form*, in Kelly A (ed), *The Missing Half: Girls and Science Education*, Manchester: Manchester University Press, 1981.

[Smithers 82] Smithers A and Collings J, "Co-education and Science Choice, *British Journal of Educational Studies*, 30, 3, pp313-328, 1982.

[Solomonides 85] Solomonides T and Levidow L (ed), *Computers as Culture*, Free Association Books, 1985.

[Soper 88] Soper P, "Where have all the Women Gone?", *Computer Newsletter*, Jan/Feb, pp7-8, 1988.

[Spavold 89a] Spavold J, "Children and databases: an analysis of data entry and query formulation", *Journal of Computer Assisted Learning*, 1989.

[Spavold 89b] Spavold J, "The child as naive user: a study of database use with young children", *International Journal for Man-Machine Studies*, vol 31, 1989.

[Spear 85] Spear M, Whyte J, Deem R, Kant L, and Cruickshank M, *"Girl Friendly Schooling*, Methuen, 1985.

[Spencer 87] Spencer A and Podmore D (eds.), *In a Man's World, Essays on Women in Male Dominated Professions*, Tavistock Publications, London & New York, 1987.

[Spender 82] Spender D, *Invisible Women: The Schooling Scandal*, Writers and Readers Co-operative, 1982.

[Spender] Spender D and Sarah E (eds), *Learning to Lose: Sexism and Education*, London: Women's Press.

[Sproull 86] Sproull L, Zubrow D and Kiesler S, "Cultural socialisation to computing in college", *Computers in Human Behaviour*, 2, 257-275, 1986.

[Stanworth 81] Stanworth M, "Gender and Schooling: A study of sexual divisions in the classroom", *Explorations in Feminism Series No. 7*, London: Women's Research and Resources Centre, 1981.

[Stig 89] Stig B, *Report of Study in the Federal Republic of Germany*, October 1989.

[Stockdale 87] Stockdale, *Proceedings of the Fourth GASAT Conference*, 1987.

[Straker 85] Straker A, *MEP Primary Project Progress Report No.4*, 1985.

[Swedish Institute 89] Swedish Institute, *Fact sheets on Sweden; Equality between men and women in Sweden*, Stockholm, Sweden: Swedish Institute, 1989.

[THES 90a] *Times Higher Education Supplement*, 18.5.90

[THES 90b] *Times Higher Education Supplement*, "Behind the Bastion", 20.4.90.

[Times 90] The Times, D Broom, *Reformer with a career on the run*, p15, col 6, 28.5.1990.

[Tittle 86] Tittle C K, "Gender Research and Education", *American Psychologist*, 41, 10, pp1161-1168, 1986.

[Todman 90a] Todman J B and File P E, "A scale for children's attitudes to computers", *School Psychology International*, vol 11, pp 71-75, 1990.

[Todman 90b] Todman J and File P, *Effects of subjective and objective databases on children's attitude to computers*, manuscript under review, 1990.

[Tosi 73] Tosi H and Carroll S, "Improving Management by Objectives", *California Management Review*, 1973.

[Truman 86] Truman C, *Overcoming the Career Break, A Positive Approach*, The Training Agency, Sheffield, 1986.

[Truman 90] Truman C, "Demographic Changes and 'New Opportunities' for Women : the Case of Employers' Career Break Schemes", *British Sociological Association Annual Conference*, April 1990.

[Turkle 84a] Turkle S, *The Second Self*, New York: Simon and Schuster, 1984.

[Turkle 84b] Turkle S, "Women and computer programming: a different approach", *Technology Review*, (November-December), 48-50, 1984.

[Turkle 88] Turkle S and Kramerae C, *Technology and Women's Voices*, Routledge and Kegan Paul, London 1988.

[UCCA 89] UCCA, *26th Annual Report 1987/1988*, Cheltenham: UCCA, 1989.

[UDACE 88] *Developing Access, The Discussion Paper*, Unit for the Development of Adult Continuing Education (UDACE), Leicester, April 1988.

[Vasil 87] Vasil L, Hesketh B and Podd J, "Sex Differences in Computing Behaviour among Secondary School Pupils", *New Zealand Journal of Educational Studies*, 22, 2, pp201-214, 1987.

[Virgo 89a] Virgo P, "The Women into IT Campaign", *Information Management Yearbook*, pp74-76, 1989.

[Virgo 89b] Virgo P, "Gender and computing in the 1990's", Paper presented to *SIACE Conference on Bridging the Skills Gap; Women and Education in Scotland*, Strathclyde University, 1989.

[Virgo 90] Virgo P, "The Women into Information Technology (WIT) Campaign", in this volume.

[Voogt 87] Voogt J, "Computer literacy in secondary education: the performance and engagement of girls", *Computer Education*, 11 (4), 305-312, 1987.

[Walden 83] Walden R and Walkerdine V, "Girls and Mathematics: The Early Years", *Bedford Way Papers* No 8, University of London Institute of Education, 1983.

424

[Walden 85]   Walden R and Walkerdine V, "Girls and Mathematics: From Primary to Secondary Schooling", *Bedford Way Paper* No. 24, University of London Institute of Education, 1985.

[Ward 90]   Ward J, "City Poly solves conundrum of how to get women to do computing courses", *Women into IT Newsletter*, March, p12, 1990.

[Watt 88]   Watt H D, "Women into Computing Workshops", in proceedings of *Women into Computing Conference*, 1988.

[Watt 89]   Watt H D, *Women into Computing Workshops* , Research Report, January 1989, Department of Computing Science, Glasgow University.

[Watt 90a]   Watt H D, "Education and Industry Partnerships can change Attitudes", in proceedings of *Women into Computing Conference*, 1990.

[Watt 90b]   Watt H D, "Profile of Glasgow 'WIC' Girls", in the *WiC 1990 Proceedings* and in this volume.

[Welch 90]   Welch D and Michaelson G, "The Edinburgh Women in Computing Workshops" in this volume.

[Whyte 85]   Whyte J, Deem R, Kant L, Cruikshank M, *Girl Friendly Schooling*, Methuen, London, 1988.

[WiC 89]   *WiC publicity handout*, 1989.

[Wilder 85]   WilderG, Mackie D and Cooper J, "Gender and Computers: Two surveys of computer-related Attitudes", *Sex Roles*, 13, 3/4, pp215-228, 1985.

[Williams 87]   Williams, "Women: Liberation's", *Director*, October 1987.

[Wise 87]   Wise G, Robinson-Staveley K and Nelson L, "Report From The Cognitive Motivation Laboratory", *Newsletter Of The Human Information Processing Group At Princeton University*, USA: Princeton University, 3, 1987.

[WIT 89a]   *Towards an Open and Equal IT Careers Initiative*, report of the "Women into IT" Campaign Feasibility Study, 1989.

[WIT 89b]   "Schools Projects", from *Women into Information Technology Foundation – First Progress Report*, December 1989.

[WIT 89c]   "Success in Swindon", *WIT Newsletter*, p7, October 1989.

[WIT 90]   *Information Technology – the new art of communication*, report on Careers Advisory Workshop, Non-technical Recruitment Working Party of WIT, January 1990.

[WITEC]   *The WITEC-UETP*, brochure available from CCVE, University of Sheffield.

[Women and Informatics] "The foundation for women and informatics", National Centre for Women and Informatics, Amsterdam.

[Zimmerman 85] Zimmerman J (ed), *Technological Woman*, Praegar, 1985.

Appendix B: Useful Addresses

British Computer Society, 13 Mansfield St, London W1M 0BP.

British Federation of University Women, Crosby Hall, Cheyne Walk, London SW3 5BA.

The Engineering Council, 10 Maltravers St, London WC2R 3ER.

Engineering Industry Training Board, 54 Clarendon Road, Watford, Herts WD1 1LB.

Equal Opportunities Commission, Overseas House, Quay House, Manchester M3 3HN.

Equal Opportunities Commission, The Training Agency, Moorfoot, Sheffield S1 4PQ.

The Fawcett Society, 46 Harleyford Rd, London SE11 5AY.

Microsyster, Wesley House, 4 Wild Court, London WC2B 5AU.

National Advisory Centre on Careers for Women, 8th Floor, Artillery House, Artillery Row, London SW1P 1RT.

National Women & Computing Network, c/o Microsyster, Wesley House, 4 Wild Court, London WC2B 5AU.

OASIS (Organisation Against Sexism In Software), Sandra Vogel, 3 Alden Court, Stanley Rd, Wimbledon, London SW19 8RD.

Training Access Points (TAPs), Moorfoot, Sheffield S1 4PQ.

United Kingdom Federation of Business and Professional Women, 23 Ansdell St, London W8 5BN.

WES (Women's Engineering Society), c/o Dept of Civil Engineering, Imperial College, Exhibition Road, London SW7 2BY.

WEST (Women into Engineering, Science and Technology), 83 Fordwych Road, London NW2 3TL.

WiC (Women into Computing), c/o Helen Watt, Dept of Computing Science, University of Glasgow, Glasgow.

WIM (Women into Management), 64 Marryat Road, Wimbledon, London SW19 5BN.

WINTECH (Women in Information Technology), 86-100 St Pancras Way, London NW1 9ES.

WISE (Women in Science and Engineering), c/o Engineering Council, 10 Maltravers St, London WC2R 3ER.

WIT (Women into Information Technology), WIT Foundation Office, Concept 2000, Farnborough.

WITEC (Women in Technology in the European Community, c/o CCVE, Sheffield University, 65 Wilkinson St, Sheffield S10 2GJ.

Women Returners' Network, Gloria Walling, Development Officer, 100 Park Village East, London NW1.

Women Returners' Project, David Ellis, System Applied Technology Ltd, 5th Floor, Sheaf House, Sheffield S1 2BP.

Author Index